Lecture Notes in Computer Science

Commenced Publication in 1973
Founding and Former Series Editors:
Gerhard Goos, Juris Hartmanis, and Jan van Leeuwen

Manuel Núñez   Paul Baker
Mercedes G. Merayo (Eds.)

Testing of Software and Communication Systems

21st IFIP WG 6.1 International Conference, TESTCOM 2009
9th International Workshop, FATES 2009
Eindhoven, The Netherlands, November 2-4, 2009
Proceedings

 Springer

Volume Editors

Manuel Núñez
Mercedes G. Merayo
Universidad Complutense de Madrid
Facultad de Informática
28040 Madrid, Spain
E-mail: mn@sip.ucm.es, mgmerayo@fdi.ucm.es

Paul Baker
Motorola's Corporate Software Excellence Team
Basingstoke, Hampshire, RG22 4PD, UK
E-mail: paul.baker@motorola.com

Library of Congress Control Number: 2009936418

CR Subject Classification (1998): D.2.5, D.4.8, I.6, D.2, D.3, F.3, D.2.4

LNCS Sublibrary: SL 5 – Computer Communication Networks
and Telecommunications

ISSN   0302-9743
ISBN-10   3-642-05030-1 Springer Berlin Heidelberg New York
ISBN-13   978-3-642-05030-5 Springer Berlin Heidelberg New York

springer.com

© IFIP International Federation for Information Processing 2009
Printed in Germany

Typesetting: Camera-ready by author, data conversion by Scientific Publishing Services, Chennai, India
Printed on acid-free paper   SPIN: 12772223   06/3180   5 4 3 2 1 0

Preface

This volume contains the proceedings of TESTCOM/FATES 2009, a Joint Conference of the 21st IFIP International Conference on Testing of Communicating Systems (TESTCOM) and the 9th International Workshop on Formal Approaches to Testing of Software (FATES). TESTCOM/FATES 2009 was held in Eindhoven, The Netherlands, during November 2–4, 2009. In this edition, TESTCOM/FATES was part of the first Formal Methods Week (FMweek).

TESTCOM/FATES aims at being a forum for researchers, developers, and testers to review, discuss, and learn about new approaches, concepts, theories, methodologies, tools, and experiences in the field of testing of communicating systems and software. TESTCOM has a long history. Previously it was called International Workshop on Protocol Test Systems (IWPTS) and changed its name later to International Workshop on Testing of Communicating System (IWTCS). The previous events were held in Vancouver, Canada (1988); Berlin, Germany (1989); McLean, USA (1990); Leidschendam, The Netherlands (1991); Montreal, Canada (1992); Pau, France (1993); Tokyo, Japan (1994); Evry, France (1995); Darmstadt, Germany (1996); Cheju Island, Korea (1997); Tomsk, Russia (1998); Budapest, Hungary (1999); Ottawa, Canada (2000); Berlin, Germany (2002); Sophia Antipolis, France (2003); Oxford, UK (2004); Montréal, Canada (2005) and New York, USA (2006). FATES also has its history. The previous workshops were held in Aalborg, Denmark (2001); Brno, Czech Republic (2002); Montréal, Canada (2003); Linz, Austria (2004); Edinburgh, UK (2005) and Seattle, USA (2006). TESTCOM and FATES became a joint conference in 2007: It has been held in Tallinn, Estonia (2007) and Tokyo, Japan (2008).

We received 37 submissions. After a careful reviewing process, the Program Committee accepted 13 papers. Therefore, the acceptance rate of the conference stayed close to 33%. In addition to regular papers, the Program Committee accepted six short papers. The conference program also contained an invited presentation by Wolfgang Grieskamp (Microsoft Research, USA) on "Microsoft's Protocol Documentation Quality Assurance Program."

Several people contributed to the success of TESTCOM/FATES 2009. We are grateful to the Steering Committee, the Program Committee, and the additional reviewers for their work on selecting the papers. We would like to thank Microsoft Research for its financial support and Springer for publishing the proceedings. The selection of papers and compilation of the proceedings was performed through easychair, which strongly facilitated the management of the submissions. Finally, we would like to thank the TESTCOM/FATES 2009 Organization Committee and the FMWeek Coordinators for their help and support.

November 2009

Manuel Núñez
Paul Baker
Mercedes G. Merayo

Organization

Chairs of TESTCOM/FATES 2009

Manuel Núñez (Program Committee Chair)
Paul Baker (Industrial Track Chair)
Mercedes G. Merayo (Organization Chair)

Steering Committee of TESTCOM/FATES

Ana R. Cavalli	Telecom SudParis, France
John Derrick	University of Sheffield, UK (Chair)
Wolfgang Grieskamp	Microsoft Research, USA
Roland Groz	Grenoble Institute of Technology, France
Toru Hasegawa	KDDI R&D Labs., Japan
Alexandre Petrenko	CRIM, Canada
Jan Tretmans	Embedded Systems Institute, The Netherlands
Andreas Ulrich	Siemens AG, Germany
Margus Veanes	Microsoft Research, USA

Program Committee

Paul Baker	Motorola, UK (Industrial Track Chair)
Antonia Bertolino	ISTI-CNR, Italy
Gregor v. Bochmann	University of Ottawa, Canada
Richard Castanet	LABRI, France
Ana R. Cavalli	Telecom SudParis, France
John Derrick	University of Sheffield, UK
Sarolta Dibuz	Ericsson, Hungary
Rachida Dssouli	Concordia University, Canada
Khaled El-Fakih	American University of Sharjah, UAE
Gordon Fraser	T.U. Graz, Austria
Jens Grabowski	University of Göttingen, Germany
Roland Groz	Grenoble Institute of Technology, France
Toru Hasegawa	KDDI R&D Labs., Japan
Rob Hierons	Brunel University, UK
Teruo Higashino	Osaka University, Japan
Dieter Hogrefe	University of Göttingen, Germany
Thierry Jéron	IRISA Rennes, France
Ferhat Khendek	Concordia University, Canada
Myungchul Kim	ICU, Korea

David King	Praxis, UK
Hartmut König	BTU Cottbus, Germany
Victor V. Kuliamin	ISP RAS, Russia
David Lee	Ohio State University, USA
Bruno Legeard	Leirios, France
Giulio Maggiore	Telecom Italia Mobile, Italy
José Carlos Maldonado	University of San Carlos, Brazil
Mercedes G. Merayo	University Complutense of Madrid, Spain
Brian Nielsen	University of Aalborg, Denmark
Manuel Núñez	University Complutense of Madrid, Spain (PC Chair)
Doron Peled	University of Bar-Ilan, Israel
Alexandre Petrenko	CRIM, Canada
Ismael Rodríguez	University Complutense of Madrid, Spain
Ina Schieferdecker	Fraunhofer FOKUS, Germany
Adenilso da Silva Simao	University of San Carlos, Brazil
Kenji Suzuki	University of Electro-Communications, Japan
Jan Tretmans	Embedded Systems Institute, The Netherlands
Andreas Ulrich	Siemens AG, Germany
Hasan Ural	University of Ottawa, Canada
Mark Utting	University of Waikato, New Zealand
M. Ümit Uyar	City University of New York, USA
Margus Veanes	Microsoft Research, USA
César Viho	IRISA Rennes, France
Carsten Weise	RWTH Aachen, Germany
Burkhart Wolff	University of Paris-Sud, France
Nina Yevtushenko	Tomsk State University, Russia
Fatiha Zaïdi	University of Paris-Sud, France
Hong Zhu	Oxford Brookes University, UK

Additional Reviewers

Lydie du Bousquet	José Pablo Escobedo	Fabiano Cutigi Ferrari
Hesham Hallal	Steffen Herbold	Willy Jiménez
Guy Vincent Jourdan	Sungwon Kang	Nicolas Kicillof
Shuhao Li	Ilaria Matteucci	Tomohiko Ogishi
Jiri Srba	Benjamin Zeiss	

Organizing Committee

César Andrés	University Complutense of Madrid, Spain
Alberto de la Encina	University Complutense of Madrid, Spain
Jasen Markovski	T.U. Eindhoven, The Netherlands

Mercedes G. Merayo   University Complutense of Madrid, Spain
                        (Organization Chair)
Carlos Molinero   University Complutense of Madrid, Spain
Luis Llana   University Complutense of Madrid, Spain
                        (Publicity Chair)
Michiel van Osch   T.U. Eindhoven, The Netherlands
                        (Local Organization Chair)
Ismael Rodríguez   University Complutense of Madrid, Spain

Table of Contents

Regular Papers

Short Papers

Testing Real-Time Systems Using TINA

Noureddine Adjir[1], Pierre De Saqui-Sannes[2], and Kamel Mustapha Rahmouni[3]

[1] University of Saida, BP 138 - 20001 Ennasr Saida, Algeria
[2] University of Toulouse ISAE, 31 Avenue Edouard Belin, BP 44032 - 31055, cedex 4 France
[3] University of Oran, BP 1524 - El mnaouar 31000 Oran, Algeria
Adjir_nourd@yahoo.fr, pdss@isae.fr, kamel_rahmouni@yahoo.fr

Abstract. The paper presents a technique for model-based black-box conformance testing of real-time systems using the Time Petri Net Analyzer TINA. Such test suites are derived from a prioritized time Petri net composed of two concurrent sub-nets specifying respectively the expected behaviour of the system under test and its environment.We describe how the toolbox TINA has been extended to support automatic generation of time-optimal test suites. The result is optimal in the sense that the set of test cases in the test suite have the shortest possible accumulated time to be executed. Input/output conformance serves as the notion of implementation correctness, essentially timed trace inclusion taking environment assumptions into account. Test cases selection is based either on using manually formulated test purposes or automatically from various coverage criteria specifying structural criteria of the model to be fulfilled by the test suite. We discuss how test purposes and coverage criterion are specified in the linear temporal logic SE-LTL, derive test sequences, and assign verdicts.

Keywords: Real-time system, Prioritized Time Petri Nets, conformance testing, time optimal test cases.

1 Introduction

Real-Time systems are characterized by their capacity to interact with their surrounding environment and to provide the latter the expected output at the right date i.e. the timely reaction is just as important as the kind of reaction. Testing real-time systems is even more challenging than testing untimed reactive systems, because the tester must consider when to stimulate system, when to expect responses, and how to assign verdicts to the observed timed event sequence. Further, the test cases must be executed in real-time, i.e., the test execution system itself becomes a real-time system.

Model-based testing has been proposed as a technique to automatically verify that a system conforms to its specification. In this technique, test cases are derived from a formal model that specifies the expected behaviour of a system. In this paper, we propose a technique for automatically generating test cases and test suites for embedded real time systems based on Prioritized Time Petri Nets.

We focus on conformance testing i.e. checking by means of execution whether the behaviour of some black-box system, or a system part, called SUT (system under test), conforms to its specification. This is typically done in a controlled environment

M. Núñez et al. (Eds.): TESTCOM/FATES 2009, LNCS 5826, pp. 1–15, 2009.

where the SUT is executed and stimulated with input according to a test specification, and the responses of the SUT are checked to conform to its specification.

An important problem is how to select a very limited set of test cases from the extreme large number (usually infinitely many) of potential ones. So, a very large number of test cases (generally infinitely many) can be generated from even the simplest models. The addition of real-time adds another source of explosion, i.e. when to stimulate the system and expect response. Thus, an automatically generated test suite easily becomes costly to execute. To guide the selection of test cases, a test purpose or coverage criterions are often used. The paper demonstrates how it is possible to generate time-optimal test cases and test suites, i.e. test cases and suites that are guaranteed to take the least possible time to execute. The test cases can either be generated using manually formulated test purposes or automatically from several kinds of coverage criterion—such as transition or place or marking coverage– of the PrTPN model. The coverage approach guarantees that the test suite is derived systematically and that it guarantees a certain level of thoroughness. We describe how the real-time model checker *selt* and the path analysis tool *plan* of the toolbox TINA have been used to support automatic generation of time-optimal test suites for conformance testing i.e. test suites with optimal execution time. Such test suites are derived from a PrTPN composed of two subnets specifying respectively the expected behavior of the SUT and its environment. Especially, the required behaviour of the SUT is specified using a Deterministic Input enabled and Output Urgent PrTPN (DIOU-PrTPN). Time optimal test suites are interesting for several reasons. First, reducing the total execution time of a test suite allows more behaviour to be tested in the (limited) time allocated to testing; this means a more thorough test. Secondly, it is generally desirable that regression testing can be executed as quickly as possible to improve the turn around time between changes. Thirdly, it is essential for product instance testing that a thorough test can be performed without testing becoming the bottleneck, i.e., the test suite must be applied to all products coming of an assembly line. Finally, in the context of testing of real-time systems, we hypothesize that the fastest test case that drives the SUT to some state, also has a high likelihood of detecting errors, because this is a stressful situation for the SUT to handle. To know other advantages on Time optimal test suites, the reader can see [31].

The main contributions of the paper are: Re-implement the toolbox Tina and add functionality to support the composition of PrTPN's, definition of a subclass of PrTPN from which the diagnostic traces of *selt* can be used as test cases; application of time optimal paths analysis algorithms to the context of test case generation; a technique to generate time optimal covering test suites.

The rest of the paper is organized as follows: Section 2 surveys related work. Section 3 presents the LPrTPN model (syntax and semantics). In section4, we present test case generation based on the DIOU-PrTPN model and we describe how to encode test purposes and test criteria. Section 4 concludes the paper.

2 Motivation and Related Works

Among the models proposed for the specification and verification of real-time systems, two are prominent and widely used: Time Petri Nets (TPN) [39] and Timed Automata (TA) [2]. The TA formalism has become a popular and widespread formalism for specifying real-time systems. It has a rich theory and is cited in important research works e.g. fundamentals aspects, model checking, testing…etc. TPN are characterized by their condensed expression power of parallelism and concurrency, and the conciseness of the models. In addition, the efficient analysis methods proposed by [5] have contributed to their wide use. Many other extensions of Petri Nets exist e.g. p-time Petri Nets [29] and timed Petri Nets [43] but none of them has the success of TPN. Much research works compare TPN and TA in terms of expressivity w.r.t. language acceptance and temporal bisimilarity or propose translation from TA to TPN or vice versa e. g. [3], [4], [7], [14], [18] and [37]. It was shown in [14] that bounded TPN are equivalent to TA in terms of language acceptance, but that TA are strictly more expressive in terms of weak timed bisimilarity. Adding priorities to TPN (PrTPN) [7] preserves their expressiveness in terms of language acceptance, but strictly increases their expressiveness in terms of weak timed bisimilarity: it is proven in [7] that priorities strictly extend the expressiveness of TPN, and in particular that Bounded PrTPN can be considered equivalent to TA, in terms of weak timed bisimilarity i.e. that any TA with invariants is weak time bisimilar to some bounded PrTPN, and conversely. The TPN state space abstractions were prior to those of TA and TPN are exponentially more concise than classical TA [14]. In addition, interestingly, and conversely to the constructions proposed for model checking Prioritized TA the constructions required for PrTPNs preserve convexity of state classes; they do not require to compute expensive polyhedra differences [8]. Although, not many papers propose TPN for testing real-time systems e.g. [1] and [38]. So, until this paper, no test tool based on TPN, in particular conformance testing, is available. On the other hand, a lot of works on model based testing is based on TA or their extensions e.g. [15], [16], [17], [21], [24], [26], [28], [31], [32], [33], [34], [35], [36], [40], [41], [42], [45]; and there exist many tools for testing real-time systems based on TA more then ten years e.g. [24], [31], [36], and [40].   •

Many algorithms for generating test suites following test purposes or a given coverage criterion have also been proposed [29,22,18,13], including algorithms producing test suites optimal in the number of test cases, in the total length of the test suite, or in the total time required to execute the test suite. In this paper, we study test suite generation inspired by the analysis technique used in the State-Event LTL model-checker *selt* [8]. The schedules computed by the path analysis tool *plan*, in particular the fastest schedules and the shortest paths, associated to the diagnostic sequences (counterexamples), exhibited by *selt*, will be exploited to compute the optimal-time test suites.

3   Modeling the System and Its Environment

A major development task is to ensure that an embedded system works correctly in its real operating environment and it's only necessary to establish its correctness under the modelled (environment) assumptions (Figure 1(a)); otherwise the environment model can be replaced with a completely unconstrained one that allows all possible interaction sequences. But, due to lack of resources it is not feasible to validate the system for all possible (imaginary) environments. However, the requirements and the assumptions of the environment should be clear and explicit. We assume that the test specification is given as an LPrTPN composed of two subnets: the first models the

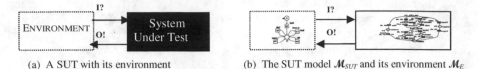

(a) A SUT with its environment   (b) The SUT model $\mathcal{M}_{SUT}$ and its environment $\mathcal{M}_E$

Fig. 1. A SUT with its environment. The SUT model $\mathcal{M}_{SUT}$ and its environment $\mathcal{M}_E$.

expected behaviour of the SUT, noted $\mathcal{M}_{SUT}$, while the second models the behaviour of its environment, and noted $\mathcal{M}_E$ (Figure 1(b)).

3.1 Labeled Prioritized Time Petri Nets

Time Petri Nets (TPN), introduced in [39], are obtained from PN by associating a temporal interval [tmin, tmax] with each transition, specifying firing delays ranges for the transitions. tmin and tmax respectively indicate the earliest and latest firing times of the transition (after the latter was enabled). Suppose that a transition t become enabled for the last one at the time θ, then t can't be fired before θ +tmin and it must be done at the latest at θ +tmax, unless disabled by firing some other transition. Prioritized TPN (PrTPN) extend TPN with a priority relation on the transitions; so a transition is not allowed to fire if some transition with higher priority is firable at the same instant. Such priorities increase the expressive power of TPN. Since we address the testing of reactive systems, we add an alphabet of actions A and a labelling function for transitions. A is partitioned in two separate subsets: input actions A_{in} and output actions A_{out}. Inputs are the stimuli received by the system from the environment. Outputs are the actions sent by this system to its environment. An input (output) is post fixed by ? (!). In addition, we assume the existence of internal actions denoted τ $(\tau \notin A)$. An internal action models the internal events of a system that are not observed by the tester.

Let I^+ be the set of nonempty real intervals with nonnegative rational endpoints. For $i \in I^+$, $\downarrow i$ represent its lower endpoint, and $\uparrow i$ its superior endpoint (if it exists) or ∞. For any $\theta \in R^+, i \div \theta$ denotes the interval $\{x - \theta \mid x \in i \land x \geq \theta\}$.

Syntax. Formally, a Labelled Prioritized Time Petri Net (LPrTPN in short) is a 9-uplet $(P,T,\text{Pre},\text{Post},m_0,I,\prec,A_\tau,L)$ where:

- $(P,T,\text{Pre},\text{Post},m_0)$ is a Petri Net where P is the set of places, T is the set of transitions, $m_0: P \to \mathbb{N}^+$ is the initial marking and Pre, Post $:T \to P \to \mathbb{N}^+$ are the precondition and post-condition functions.
- $I_s: T \to I^+$ is the static interval function which associates a temporal interval $I_s(t) \in I^+$ with every transition in the net. The rational $\downarrow I_s(t)$ and $\uparrow I_s(t)$ are the static earliest firing time and the static latest firing time of t, respectively. In this paper, intervals $[0, \infty[$ are omitted and w in the right end point of an interval denotes ∞.

- $\prec \subseteq T \times T$ is the priority relation, assumed irreflexive, asymmetric and transitive, between transitions. $t_1 \succ t_2$ or $t_2 \prec t_1$ means t_1 has priority over t_2.
- $A_\tau = A_{in} \cup A_{out} \cup \{\tau\}$ is a finite set of actions
- $L : T \rightarrow A_\tau$ is the labelling function that associates to each transition an operation.

A marking is a function $m : P \rightarrow \mathbb{N}^+$. A transition t is enabled at marking m iff $m \geq \mathrm{Pre}(t)$. The set of transitions enabled at m are denoted by $En(m) = \{ t \mid \mathrm{Pre}(t) \leq m \}$.

The predicate specifying when k is newly enabled by the firing of an internal transition t from marking m is defined by:

$$NS_{(t,m)}(k) = k \in En(m - \mathrm{Pre}(t) + \mathrm{Post}(t)) \wedge (k \notin En(m - \mathrm{Pre}(t)) \vee k = t).$$

The predicate specifying when k is newly enabled by the firing of a couple of complementary transitions (t,t') from marking m is defined by:

$$NS_{(t,t',m)}(k) = k \in En(m - (\mathbf{Pre}(t) + \mathbf{Pre}(t')) + \mathbf{Post}(t) + \mathbf{Post}(t')) \wedge (k \notin En(m - (\mathbf{Pre}(t') + \mathbf{Pre}(t'))) \vee k = t \vee k = t')$$

The sets of internal, input and output transitions of the net are defined respectively by: $T_\tau = \{ t \in T / L(t) = \tau \}$, $T_{in} = \{ t \in \overline{T_\tau} / L(t) \in A_{in} \}$ and $T_{out} = \{ t \in \overline{T_\tau} / L(t) \in A_{out} \}$ (with $\overline{T_\tau} = T - T_\tau = T_{in} \cup T_{out}$).

The set of environment model transitions which complement a transition t of the SUT model is noted $CT(t) = \{ t' \in M_E \mid \text{ if } t = a! \text{ (resp. } a?) \text{ then } t' = a? \text{ (resp. } a!) \}$.

A state of an LPrTPN is a pair $e = (m, I)$ in which m is a marking of the net and $I : T \rightarrow \mathbb{I}^+$, a partial function called the interval function, associates exactly a temporal interval in $\mathbb{I}^+$ with every enabled transition $t \in En(m)$. The initial state is $e_0 = (m_0, I_0)$, where I_0 is I_S restricted to the transitions enabled at m_0. The temporal information in states will be seen as firing domains, instead of intervals functions. The initial state $e_0 = (m_0, D_0)$ of the LPrTPN of Figures 2 and 3.a is defined by:

$$m_0 : p_0, q_0 \quad \text{and } D_0 : \quad 0 \leq t_0$$
$$\text{Tidle} \leq t_8$$
$$0 \leq s_0$$

Semantics. The semantic of an LPrTPN $N = (P, T, \mathrm{Pre}, \mathrm{Post}, m_0, Is, \prec, A_\tau, L)$ is the Timed Transition System $E_N = (E, e_0, A_{in}, A_{out}, \rightarrow)$ where E is the set of states (m, I) of the LPrTPN and $e_0 = (m_0, I_0)$ its initial state. $A_{in} = L(T_{in})$ and $A_{out} = L(T_{out})$.

$\longrightarrow \subseteq E \times T \cup \mathbb{R}_{\geq 0} \times E$ is the transition relation between states. It corresponds to two kinds of transitions witch includes discrete transitions (labelled with synchronized or internal actions) and temporal or continuous transitions (labelled by real values).

The continuous (or delay) transitions are the result of time elapsing. We have $(m,I) \xrightarrow{d} (m,I')$ iff $d \in \mathbb{R}_{\geq 0}$ and:

1. $(\forall t \in T)\ \left(t \in En(m) \Rightarrow d \leq\uparrow I(t)\ \right)$
2. $(\forall t \in T)\ \left(t \in En(m) \Rightarrow\ I'(t) = I(t)\ \dot{-}\ d\ \right)$

A continuous transition of size d is possible iff d is not greater then the latest firing time of all enabled transitions. All firing intervals of enabled transitions are shifted synchronously towards the origin as time elapses, and truncated to non negative times.

Discrete transitions are the result of the transitions firing of the net. They may be further partitioned into purely SUT or ENV transitions (hence invisible for the other part) or synchronizing transitions between the SUT and the ENV (hence observable for both parties). Internal transitions are fired individually while synchronizing transitions are fired by complementary actions couples (e.g. a? and a! are complementary synchronization actions). The first component of the couple is a transition of the SUT model, labelled by an input (resp. output) action, and the second component is an environment transition and labelled by an output (resp. input) action.

The discrete internal transitions: we have $(m,I) \xrightarrow{t} (m',I')$ iff $L(t) = \tau$ and :

1. $t \in En(m)$
2. $0 \in I(t)$
3. $(\forall k \in T_\tau)\ \left(k \in En(m) \wedge (k \succ t) \Rightarrow 0 \notin I(k)\right)$
4. $\left(\forall k \in \overline{T_\tau}, \forall k' \in TC(k)\right)\left(k,k' \in En(m) \wedge (k \succ t) \Rightarrow 0 \notin I(k) \wedge 0 \notin I(k')\right)$
5. $m' = m\ -\ \text{Pre}\ (t) + \text{Post}(t)$
6. $(\forall k \in T)\left(m' \geq \text{Pre}(k) \Rightarrow I'(k) = \text{if}\ NS_{(t,m)}(k)\ \text{then}\ I_s(k)\ \text{else}\ I(k)\right)$

An internal transition t may fire from the state (m,I) if it is enabled at m (1), immediately firable (2) and no transition with higher priority satisfies these conditions (3 & 4). In the target state, the transitions that remained enabled while t fired (t excluded) retain their intervals, the others are associated with their static intervals (6).

The discrete synchronizing transition: we have:

$(m,I) \xrightarrow{L(t),L(t')} (m',I')$ iff $t,t' \in \overline{T_\tau}, t' \in TC(t)$ and :

1. $t,t' \in En(m)$
2. $0 \in I(t) \wedge 0 \in I(t')$
3. $(\forall k \in T_\tau)\ \left(k \in En(m) \wedge (k \succ t) \Rightarrow 0 \notin I(k)\right)$
4. $\left(\forall k \in T, \forall k' \in TC(k)\right)\left(k,k' \in En(m) \wedge (k \succ t \vee k' \succ t') \Rightarrow 0 \notin I(k) \wedge 0 \notin I(k')\right)$
5. $m' = m\ -\ \left(\text{Pre}(t) + \text{Pre}(t')\right) + \text{Post}(t) + \text{Post}(t')$
6. $(\forall k \in \overline{T_\tau})\left(m' \geq \text{Pre}(k) \Rightarrow I'(k) = \text{if}\ NS_{(t,t',m)}(k)\ \text{then}\ I_s(k)\ \text{else}\ I(k)\right)$

The complementary transitions t and t' may fire from the state (m, I) if they are enabled (1), immediately firable (2) and neither internal transition (3) nor couple of complementary transitions with higher priority satisfies these conditions (4). In the target state, the transitions that remained enabled while t and t' fired (t and t' excluded) retain their intervals, the others are associated with their static intervals (6).

If the light controller and its environment (Figure 2 and 3) are in their initial state and make a delay of 0.6 time unites ($e_0 \xrightarrow{0.6} e_1$). The new state $e_1 = (m_0, D_1)$ will be:

$$m_0 : p_0, \ q_0 \text{ and } D_1: \ 0 \leq t_0$$
$$\text{Tidle} - 0.6 \leq t_8$$
$$0 \leq s_0$$

The firing of the synchronizing transition (t_0, s_0) from the state e_1 leads to the state e_2 ($e_1 \xrightarrow{touch?, touch!} e_2$). The new state $e_2 = (m_1, D_2)$ will be:

$$m_1 : p_1, \ q_1 \text{ and } D_2: \ 0 \leq t_1 \leq 0$$
$$\text{Treact} \leq s_1 \leq \infty$$
$$0 \leq s_2 \leq \infty$$
$$0 \leq s_3 \leq \infty$$
$$0 \leq s_4 \leq \infty$$

A firing schedule, or a time transitions sequence, is a sequence alternating delay and discrete transitions $d_1\alpha_1 d_2\alpha_2 \cdots d_n\alpha_n$. α_i is a pure transition $(\alpha_i = k \in T_\tau)$ or a synchronizing transition $(\alpha_i = (t, t') | \ t \in \overline{T_\tau} \wedge t' \in TC(t))$ and $\dot{d}_i$ are the relative firing times. A schedule is realisable from the state e if the discrete transitions of the sequence $\sigma = \alpha_1\alpha_2 \cdots \alpha_n$ are successively firable from e at the associated relative firing times $d_1, d_2, \cdots, d_n$. The sequence σ is called its support.

If the pausing time Tidle and the switching time Tsw are respectively equal to 20 and 4 time units then the following time sequence is a realisable schedule $20.(touch?, touch!).0.(bright!, bright?).5.(touch?, touch!).0.(dim!, dim?).4.(touch?, touch!).0.(off!, off?)$

3.2 Tina (TIme Petri Net Analyzer)

Tina is a software environment for editing and analyzing TPN [6]. It includes the tools:

- *nd* (NetDraw) : an editor for graphical or textual description of TPN.
- *tina* : For analysing LPrTPN models, it's necessary to finitely represent the state spaces by grouping some sets of states. *tina* builds the strong state classes graph (SSCG in short), proposed in [8], which preserves states and maximal traces of the state graph, and thus the truth value of all the formulae of the SE-LTL logic.
- *plan* is a path analysis tool. It computes all, or a single, timed firing sequence (schedule) over some given firing transitions sequence. In particular, it computes the fastest schedules and shortest paths. Accordingly, the latter schedules are used for test case generation.

– *selt*: is a model checker for an enriched version of state-event LTL [19], a linear temporal logic supporting both state and transition properties. For the properties found false, *selt* produces a timed counter example. It's called a diagnostic schedule of the property. The realization of this schedule from the initial state satisfies the property.

A diagnostic sequence of a property ϕ is a sequence of discrete transitions (internal and/or complementary transitions). The successive firing of these transitions, from m_0, at the corresponding dates, allows satisfying the property ϕ. A diagnostic trace is a schedule whose support is a diagnostic sequence.

3.3 Deterministic, Input Enabled and Output Urgent LPrTPN

To ensure time optimal testability, the following semantic restrictions turn out to be sufficient. Following similar restrictions as in [31] and [45], we define the notion of deterministic, input enabled and output urgent LPrTPN, DIEOU-LPrTPN, by restricting the underlying timed transition system defined by the LPrTPN as follows: (1) Deterministic: For every semantic state $e = (m,D)$ and an action $\gamma \in A \cup \{\mathbb{R}_{\geq 0}\}$, whenever $e \overset{\gamma}{\to} e'$ and $e \overset{\gamma}{\to} e''$ then $e' = e''$. (2) (Weak) input enabled: whenever $e \overset{d}{\to}$ for some delay $d \in \mathbb{R}_{\geq 0}$ then $\forall a \in A_{in}$, $e \overset{a}{\to}$. (3) Isolated outputs: $\forall \alpha \in A_{out} \cup \{\tau\}$, $\forall \beta \in A_{out} \cup A_{in} \cup \{\tau\}$ whenever $e \overset{\alpha}{\to}$ and $e \overset{\beta}{\to}$ then $\alpha = \beta$. (4) Output urgency: whenever $e \overset{\alpha}{\to}$, $\forall \alpha \in O \cup \{\tau\}$ then $e \overset{d}{\not\to}, d \in \mathbb{R}_{\geq 0}$.

We assume that the tester can take the place of the environment and control the SUT via a distinguished set of observable input and output actions. For the SUT to be testable the LPrTPN modelling it should be controllable in the sense that it should be possible for an environment to drive the model through all of its syntactical parts (transitions and places). We therefore assume that the SUT specification is a DIEOU-LPrTPN, and that the SUT can be modeled by some unknown DIEOU-LPrTPN. The environment model need not be a DIEOU-LPrTPN. These assumptions are commonly referred to as the testing hypothesis.

Figure 2 shows an LPrTPN modelling the behaviour of a simple light-controller (this example is taken from [31]). The user interacts with the controller by touching a touch sensitive pad. The light has three intensity levels: OFF, DIMMED, and BRIGHT. Depending on the timing between successive touches, the controller toggles the light levels. For example, in dimmed state, if a second touch is made quickly (before the switching time $T_{sw} = 4$ time units) after the touch that caused the controller to enter dimmed state (from either off or bright state), the controller increases the level to bright. Conversely, if the second touch happens after the switching time, the controller switches the light off. If the light controller has been in off state for a long time (longer than or equal to $T_{idle} = 20$), it should reactivate upon a touch by going directly to bright level. We leave to the reader to verify for herself that the conditions of DIEOU-LPrTPN are met by the given model.

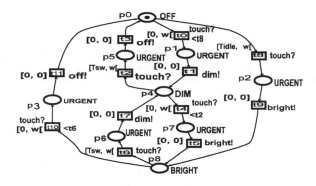

Fig. 2. $\mathcal{M}_{SUT}$: the light controller model

Figure 3 shows two possible environment models for the simple light controller. Figure 3(a) models a user capable of performing any sequence of touch actions. When the constant T_{react} is set to zero he is arbitrarily fast. A more realistic user is only capable of producing touches with a limited rate; this can be modeled setting T_{react} to a non-zero value. Figure 3(b) models a different user able to make two quick successive touches, but which then is required to pause for some time (to avoid cramp), e.g., $T_{pause} = 5$. The LPrTPN shown in Figure 2 and Figure 3 respectively can be composed in parallel on actions $A = \{touch\}$ and $A_{out} = \{off, dim, bright\}$.

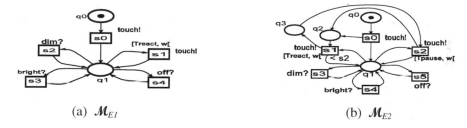

(a) $\mathcal{M}_{EI}$ (b) $\mathcal{M}_{E2}$

Fig. 3. Two light switch controller environment models

The firing of (t_1, s_2) from the state $e_2 = (m_1, D_2)$ leads to the state $e_3 = (m_2, D_3)$ ($e_2 \xrightarrow{dim?, dim!} e_3$):

$m_2 : p_4, q_1$ and $D_2 :$ $Tsw \le t_2 \le \infty$

$0 \le t_4 \le \infty$

$Treact \le s_1 \le \infty$

$0 \le s_2 \le \infty$

$0 \le s_3 \le \infty$

$0 \le s_4 \le \infty$

4 Test Generation

4.1 From Diagnostic Traces to Test Cases

Let $\mathcal{M}$ be the LPrTPN model of the SUT together with its intended environment ENV; and ϕ the property, formulated in SE–LTL, to be verified over $\mathcal{M}$. As SE–LTL evaluate the properties on all possible executions, we consider the formula $\neg\phi$ then we submit it to *selt*. If the response is negative, i.e. all the executions don't satisfy $\neg\phi$, so at least one satisfy its negation ϕ. *selt* provide simultaneously a counter example for $\neg\phi$, i.e. a diagnostic sequence that demonstrates that property ϕ is satisfied. This sequence is submitted to the tool *plan* for computing a schedule, or all the schedules having this sequence as support. This schedule is an alternating sequence of discrete transitions, synchronization (or internal) actions, performed by the system and its environment, and temporal constraints (or transitions firings time-delays) needed to reach the goal (the desirable marking or event).

Once the diagnostic trace is obtained, it's convenient to construct the associated test sequences. For DIEOU-LPrTPN, a test sequence is an alternating of sequence of concrete delay actions and observable actions (without internal actions). From the diagnostic trace above a test sequence, λ, may be obtained simply by projecting the trace to the environment component, $\mathcal{M}_E$, while removing invisible transitions, and summing adjacent delay actions. Finally, a test case to be executed on the real SUT implementation may be obtained from λ by the addition of verdicts. Adding the verdicts depends on the chosen conformity relation between the specification and SUT. In this paper, we require timed trace inclusion, i.e. that the timed traces of the SUT are included in the specification. Thus after any input sequence, the SUT is allowed to produce an output only if the specification also able to produce that output. Similarly, the SUT may delay (staying silent) only if the specification also may delay. The test sequences produced by the technique proposed in this paper are derived from the diagnostic traces, and are thus guaranteed to be included in the specification.

To clarify the construction we may model the test case itself as an LPrTPN $\mathcal{M}_\lambda$ for the test sequence λ. Places in M_λ are labelled using two distinguished labels, **Pass** and **Fail**. The execution of a test case is formalized as a parallel composition of the test case Petri net $\mathcal{M}_\lambda$ and SUT $\mathcal{M}_{SUT}$.

$$\text{SUT } \textit{passes } \mathcal{M}_\lambda \text{ iff } \mathcal{M}_\lambda \| \mathcal{M}_{SUT} \not\Rightarrow \textit{fail}$$

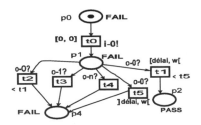

Fig. 4. Test case LPrTPN $\mathcal{M}_\lambda$ for the sequence $\lambda = i_0! \, . \, delai \, . \, o_0 \, ?$

$\mathcal{M}_\lambda$ is constructed such that a complete execution terminates in a **Fail** state (the place FAIL will be marked) if the SUT cannot perform λ and such that it terminates in a **Pass** state (the place PASS will be marked) if the SUT can execute all actions of λ. The construction is illustrated in Figure 4.

4.2 Single Purpose Test Generation

A common approach to the generation of test cases is to first manually formulate a set of informal test purposes and then to formalize these such that the model can be used to generate one or more test cases for each test purpose. Because we use the diagnostic trace facility of the model-checker *selt*, the test purpose must be formulated as a SE-LTL property that can be checked by reachability analysis of the combined model $\mathcal{M}$. The test purpose can be directly transformed into a simple state or event reachability check. Also, the environment model can be replaced by a more restricted one that matches the behaviour of the test purpose only.

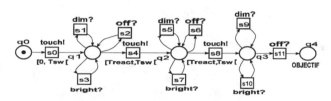

Fig. 5. $\mathcal{M}_{E3}$, test environment for TP2

TP1: check that the light can become bright.
TP2: check that the light switches off after three successive touches.

TP1 can be formulated as a simple SE-LTL property $\phi_1 = \lozenge$ BRIGHT (state property) or $\phi_2 = \lozenge$ *BRIGHT*! (event property) i.e. eventually in some future the place bright of the light controller Petri net will be marked or the event bright! will be executed.

Among all diagnostic sequences exhibited by *selt* that satisfy the property ϕ_1 (or ϕ_2), two sequences are more interesting: the shortest and the fastest sequences. The second is selected as follows: first, we compute the fastest schedule associated for each obtained sequence, and then we keep only the schedule with the smallest accumulated time. Finally, the two schedules associated to the two selected sequences will be transformed to test cases as explained in 4.1. The execution time for each of these test cases is optimal.

For the light controller, the shortest diagnostic trace is $(touch?,touch!)$ $(bright!,bright?)$. It results in the test sequence $20.touch!.0.bright?$. However, the fastest sequence satisfying ϕ_1 is $0.(touch?,touch!).0.(dim!,dim?).0.$ $(touch?,touch!)$. It results in the test sequence $0.touch!.0.dim?.0.touch!.0.bright?$

TP2 can be formalized using the property $\mathcal{M}_{E3} \models \phi_3 = \lozenge$ OBJECTIF with $\mathcal{M}_{E3}$ is the restricted environment model in Figure 5. The fastest test sequence is:
$0.touch!.0.dim?.0.touch!.0.bright?.0.touch!.0.off?$

4.3 Coverage Based Test Generation

A large suite of coverage criteria may be proposed, such as statement, transition, states, and classes, each with its merits and application domain. We explain how to apply some of these to TPN models. In this paper, we use three coverage criteria of the LPrTPN model of the SUT:

Transition Coverage. A test sequence satisfies the transition-coverage criterion if, when executed on the model, it fires every transition of the net. Transition coverage can be formulated by the property $\phi_t = \bigwedge_{i=1}^{n} \Diamond t_i$, where n is the number of transitions of the net. The obtained counter example of the non satisfaction of the property $\neg \phi_t$ ensures transition coverage. Once the diagnostic sequences are obtained, we compute the two schedules: (1) the fastest schedule which has as support the shortest sequence (2) the fastest schedule among all schedules exhibited by *selt*. We transform these schedules in test cases as is indicated in 4.1.

When the environment can touch arbitrarily, the generated fastest transition covering test has the accumulated execution time 28. The solution (there might be more traces with the same fastest execution time) generated by *plan* is:

TC: *0.touch!.0.dim?.0.touch!.0.bright?.0.touch!.0.off?.20.touch!.0.bright?.4.touch!.0.dim?.4. touch!.0.off?*

Place Coverage. A test sequence satisfies the place-coverage criterion if, when executed on the model, it marks every place of the net. Place coverage can be formulated by the property $\phi_P = \bigwedge_{i=1}^{m} \Diamond p_i \geq 1$, where m is the number of places of the net.

Marking Coverage. A test sequence satisfies the marking-coverage criterion if, when executed on the model, it generates all the markings of the net. The test sequences which ensure the marking-coverage are generated by selecting the transition sequence(s), from the SSCG of the model, which generates all the markings of the SUT model. Test cases generation from the diagnostic traces that ensures place coverage and marking coverage are computed as in coverage transition.

4.4 Test Suite Generation

Frequently, for a given test purpose criterion, we cannot obtain a single covering test sequence. This is due to the dead-ends in the model. To solve this problem, we allow for the model (and SUT) to be reset to its initial state and to continue the test after the reset to cover the remaining parts. The generated test will then be interpreted as a test suite consisting of a set of test sequences separated by resets (assumed to be implemented correctly in the SUT).

To introduce resets in the model, we shall allow the user to designate some markings as being reset-able i.e. markings that allows to reach the initial marking m_0. Evidently, performing a reset may take some time T_r that must be taken into account when generating time optimal test sequences. Reset-able markings can be encoded into the model by adding reset transitions leading back to the initial marking. Let m_r the reset-able marking, two reset transitions and a new place q which must be added as:

The transition *reset*! must be added such as their input places are the encoded places (those of m_r) and its output place is the place q. The firing of *reset*! marks the place q.

$$(m_r,-) \overset{reset!}{\to} (q,[T_r,T_r]) \overset{\tau}{\to} (m_0,I_0).$$

4.5 Environment Behaviour

Test sequences generated by the techniques presented above may be non-realizable; they may require the SUT environment to operate infinitely fast. Generally, it is only necessary to establish correctness of SUT under the environment assumptions. Therefore assumptions about the environment can be modelled explicitly and will then be taken into consideration during test sequence generation. We demonstrate how different environment assumptions influence the generated test sequences.

Consider an environment where the user takes at least 2 time units between each touch action, such an environment can be obtained by setting the constant T_{react} to 2 in Figure 3(a). The fastest test sequences become **TP1**: *0.touch!.0.dim?.2.touch!.0.bright?* and **TP2**: *0.touch!.0.dim?.2.touch!.0.bright?.2.touch!.0.off?*

Also re-examine the test suite **TC** generated by transition coverage, and compare with the one of execution time 32 generated when T_{react} equals 2.

TC': *0.touch!.0.dim?.4.touch!.0.off?.20.touch!.0.bright?.4.touch!.0.dim?.2.touch!.0.bright?.2. touch!.0.off?*

When the environment is changed to the pausing user (can perform 2 successive quick touches after which he is required to pause for some time: reaction time 2, pausing time 5), the fastest sequence has execution time 33, and follows a completely different strategy.

TC'': *0.touch!.0.dim?.2.touch!.0.bright?.5.touch!.0.dim?.4.touch!.0.off?.20.touch!.0.bright?.2. touch!.0.off?*

6 Conclusion

In this paper, we have demonstrated that the problem of timed test generation is transformed to a problem of model checking. We have shown that time-optimal test suites, computed from either a single test purpose or coverage criteria can be generated using the Tina toolbox. We have also introduced modifications in the transitions firings algorithms taking into account the reactive character of embedded real-time systems. Unlike the technique based on TA [31], the advantages of using TINA are the following: 1) when computing the SSCG for bounded PrTPN, contrary to the zone graph of TA, no abstraction is required in order to ensure termination; this allows to avoid ad-hoc techniques for enforcing termination of forward analysis; 2) it may help tackling the state explosion problem due to parallel composition of TA.

The DIEOU-PrTPN is quite restrictive, and generalization will benefit many real-time systems.

References

1. Adjir, N., De Saqui-Sanne, P., Rahmouni, M.K.: Génération des séquences de test temporisés à partir des réseaux de Petri temporels à chronomètres. In: NOTERE 2007, Maroc.
2. Alur, R., Dill, D.: A theory of timed automata. Theoretical Computer Science 126(2), 183–235 (1994)

3. Bérard, B., Cassez, F., Haddad, S., Roux, O.H., et Lime, D.: Comparison of the Expressiveness of Timed Automata and Time Petri Nets. In: Pettersson, P., Yi, W. (eds.) FORMATS 2005. LNCS, vol. 3829, pp. 211–225. Springer, Heidelberg (2005)
4. Bérard, B., Cassez, F., Haddad, S., Lime, D., Roux, O.H.: When are timed automata weakly timed bisimilar to time Petri nets? In: Sarukkai, S., Sen, S. (eds.) FSTTCS 2005. LNCS, vol. 3821, pp. 273–284. Springer, Heidelberg (2005)
5. Berthomieu, B., Diaz, M.: Modelling and verification of time dependent systems using time Petri nets. IEEE transactions on software Engineering 17(3) (1991)
6. Berthomieu, B., Ribet, P.O., Vernadat, F.: The tool TINA – Construction of Abstract State Spaces for Petri Nets and Time Petri Nets. Inter. JPR 42(14) (July 2004)
7. Berthomieu, B., Peres, F., Vernadat, F.: Bridging the gap between Timed Automata and Bounded Time Petri Nets. In: Asarin, E., Bouyer, P. (eds.) FORMATS 2006. LNCS, vol. 4202, pp. 82–97. Springer, Heidelberg (2006)
8. Berthomieu, B., Peres, F., Vernadat, F.: Model Checking Bounded Prioritized Time Petri Nets. In: Namjoshi, K.S., Yoneda, T., Higashino, T., Okamura, Y. (eds.) ATVA 2007. LNCS, vol. 4762, pp. 523–532. Springer, Heidelberg (2007)
9. Berthomieu, B., Ribet, P.-O., Vernadat, F.: The tool TINA –construction of abstract state spaces for Petri nets and time Petri nets. IJPR 42(14), 2741–2756 (2004)
10. Berthomieu, B., et Vernadat, F.: State Space Abstractions for Time Petri Nets. In: Handbook of Real-Time and Embedded Systems. CRC Press, Boca Raton (2007)
11. Bouyer, P., Dufourd, C., Fleury, E., Petit, A.: Updatable timed automata. TCS 321(2–3), 291–345 (2004)
12. Bouyer, P.: Forward Analysis of Updatable Timed Automata. FMSD 24(3), 281–320 (2004)
13. Bouyer, P., Chevalier, F.: On conciseness of extensions of timed automata. JALC (2005)
14. Bouyer, P., Serge, H., Reynie, P.A.: Extended Timed Automata and Time Petri Nets. In: ACSD 2006, Turku, Finland, pp. 91–100. IEEE Computer Society Press, Los Alamitos (2006)
15. Braberman, V., Felder, M., Marre, M.: Testing timing behaviour of real-time software. In: Intern. Software Quality Week (1997)
16. Brinksma, E., Tretmans, J.: Testing transition systems: An annotated bibliography. In: Cassez, F., Jard, C., Rozoy, B., Dermot, M. (eds.) MOVEP 2000. LNCS, vol. 2067, p. 187. Springer, Heidelberg (2001)
17. Cardell-Oliver, R.: Conformance test experiments for distributed real-time systems. In: ISSTA 2002. ACM Press, New York (2002)
18. Cassez, F., Roux, O.H.: Structural translation from time Petri nets to timed automata. In: JSS 2006 (2006)
19. Chaki, S., Clarke, E.M., Ouaknine, J., Sharygina, N., Sinha, N.: State/Event-based Software Model Checking. In: Boiten, E.A., Derrick, J., Smith, G.P. (eds.) IFM 2004. LNCS, vol. 2999, pp. 128–147. Springer, Heidelberg (2004)
20. Choffrut, C., Goldwurm, M.: Timed automata with periodic clock constraints. JALC 5(4), 371–404 (2000)
21. Cleaveland, R., Hennessy, M.: Testing Equivalence as a Bisimulation Equivalence. Formal Aspects of Computing 5, 1–20 (1993)
22. David, A., Hakansson, J., Larsen, K.G.: Model checking timed automata with priorities using DBM subtraction. In: Asarin, E., Bouyer, P. (eds.) FORMATS 2006. LNCS, vol. 4202, pp. 128–142. Springer, Heidelberg (2006)
23. Demichelis, F., Zielonka, W.: Controlled timed automata. In: Sangiorgi, D., de Simone, R. (eds.) CONCUR 1998. LNCS, vol. 1466, pp. 455–469. Springer, Heidelberg (1998)
24. de Vries, R., Tretmans, J.: On-the-fly conformance testing using SPIN. STTT 2(4), 382–393 (2000)

25. Diekert, V., Gastin, P., Petit, A.: Removing epsilon-Transitions in Timed Automata. In: Reischuk, R., Morvan, M. (eds.) STACS 1997. LNCS, vol. 1200, pp. 583–594. Springer, Heidelberg (1997)
26. En-Nouaary, A., Dssouli, R., Khendek, F., Elqortobi, A.: Timed test cases generation based on state characterization technique. In: RTSS 1998. IEEE, Los Alamitos (1998)
27. Fersman, E., Pettersson, P., Yi, W.: Timed automata with asynchronous processes: Schedulability and decidability. In: Katoen, J.-P., Stevens, P. (eds.) TACAS 2002. LNCS, vol. 2280, pp. 67–82. Springer, Heidelberg (2002)
28. Fernandez, J.C., Jard, C., Jéron, T., Viho, G.: Using on-the-fly verification techniques for the generation of test suites. In: Alur, R., Henzinger, T.A. (eds.) CAV 1996. LNCS, vol. 1102. Springer, Heidelberg (1996)
29. Khansa, W.: Réseaux de Petri P-temporels: contribution à l'étude des systèmes à événements discrets. université de Savoie, Annecy (1997)
30. Henzinger, T.A.: The theory of hybrid automata. In: Proc. LICS 1996, pp. 278–292. IEEE CSP, Los Alamitos (1996)
31. Hessel, A., Larsen, K.G., Nielsen, B., Pettersson, P., Skou, A.: Time-optimal real-time test case generation using UPPAAL. In: Petrenko, A., Ulrich, A. (eds.) FATES 2003. LNCS, vol. 2931, pp. 114–130. Springer, Heidelberg (2004)
32. Higashino, T., Nakata, A., Taniguchi, K., Cavalli, A.: Generating test cases for a timed I/O automaton model. In: IFIP Int'l Work, Test Comm. System. Kluwer, Dordrecht (1999)
33. Jéron, T., Morel, P.: Test generation derived from model-checking. In: Halbwachs, N., Peled, D.A. (eds.) CAV 1999. LNCS, vol. 1633, pp. 108–121. Springer, Heidelberg (1999)
34. Jéron, T., Rusu, V., Zinovieva, E.: STG: A symbolic test generation tool. In: Katoen, J.-P., Stevens, P. (eds.) TACAS 2002. LNCS, vol. 2280, p. 470. Springer, Heidelberg (2002)
35. Khoumsi, A., Jéron, T., Marchand, H.: Test cases generation for nondeterministic real-time systems. In: Petrenko, A., Ulrich, A. (eds.) FATES 2003. LNCS, vol. 2931, pp. 131–146. Springer, Heidelberg (2004)
36. Krichen, M., Tripakis, S.: An Expressive and Implementable Formal Framework for Testing Real Time Systems. In: Khendek, F., Dssouli, R. (eds.) TestCom 2005. LNCS, vol. 3502, pp. 209–225. Springer, Heidelberg (2005)
37. Lime, D., Roux, O.: State class timed automaton of a time Petri net. In: PNPM 2003, Urbana, USA, pp. 124–133. IEEE computer society, Los Alamitos (2003)
38. Lin, J.C., Ho, I.: Generating Real-Time Software Test Cases by Time Petri Nets. IJCA (EI journal) 22(3), 151–158 (2000)
39. Merlin, P.M., Farber, J.: Recoverability of communication protocols: Implications of a theoretical study. IEEE Trans. Com. 24(9), 1036–1043 (1976)
40. Mikucionis, M., Larsen, K.G., Nielsen, B.: T-UPPAAL: Online Model-based Testing of Real-time Systems. In: 19th IEEE Internat. Conf. ASE, Linz, Austria, pp. 396–397 (2004)
41. Nielsen, B., Skou, A.: Automated test generation from timed automata. In: Margaria, T., Yi, W. (eds.) TACAS 2001. LNCS, vol. 2031, p. 343. Springer, Heidelberg (2001)
42. Peleska, J.: Formal methods for test automation hard real time testing of controllers for the airbus aircraft family. In: IDPT 2002 (2002)
43. Ramchadani, C.: Analysis of asynchronous concurrent systems by timed Petri nets, Cambridge, Mass, MIT, dept Electrical Engineering, Phd thesis (1992)
44. Lin, S.-W., Hsiung, P.-A., Huang, C.-H., Chen, Y.-R.: Model checking prioritized timed automata. In: Peled, D.A., Tsay, Y.-K. (eds.) ATVA 2005. LNCS, vol. 3707, pp. 370–384. Springer, Heidelberg (2005)
45. Springintveld, J., Vaandrager, F., D'Argenio, P.: Testing timed automata. TCS 254 (2001)
46. Tretmans, J.: Testing concurrent systems: A formal approach. In: Baeten, J.C.M., Mauw, S. (eds.) CONCUR 1999. LNCS, vol. 1664, pp. 46–65. Springer, Heidelberg (1999)

A Formal Framework for Service Orchestration Testing Based on Symbolic Transition Systems*

Lina Bentakouk[1], Pascal Poizat[1,2], and Fatiha Zaïdi[1]

[1] LRI; Univ. Paris-Sud, CNRS
[2] Univ. Évry Val d'Essonne
{lina.bentakouk,pascal.poizat,fatiha.zaidi}@lri.fr

Abstract. The pre-eminent role played by software composition, and more particularly service composition, in modern software development, together with the complexity of workflow languages such as WS-BPEL have made composite service testing a topical issue. In this article we contribute to this issue with an automatic testing approach for WS-BPEL orchestrations. Compared to related work, we support WS-BPEL data computations and exchanges, while overcoming the consequential state explosion problem. This is achieved through the use of symbolic transition system models and their symbolic execution. Throughout the article, we illustrate our approach on a realistic medium-size example.

Keywords: Service composition, orchestration, formal testing, test-case generation, WS-BPEL, transition systems, symbolic execution.

1 Introduction

Service composition, and more specifically orchestration, has emerged as a cornerstone to develop added-value distributed applications out of reusable and loosely coupled software pieces. The WS-BPEL language [1], or BPEL for short, has become the de-facto standard for Web service orchestration and is gaining industry-wide acceptance and usage. This makes BPEL orchestration correctness a topical issue, all the more because of BPEL complexity. This has been partly addressed by automatic service composition or adaptation processes [2,3]. Still, these usually assume that services convey semantic annotations, which is, currently, seldom the case. Service orchestrations are therefore developed in a more usual way, *i.e.*, from specifications which are thereafter implemented by service architects. Numerous model-based verification approaches have been proposed for BPEL, *e.g.*, translating BPEL to automata, Petri nets or process algebras [4]. These approaches are especially valuable to check if an orchestration specification is correct. Still, as far as the correctness of an implementation wrt. a specification is concerned, these approaches fall short as, *e.g.*, one may expect service

* This work is supported by the projects "PERvasive Service cOmposition" (PERSO) and "WEB service MOdelling and Validation" (WEBMOV) of the French National Agency for Research.

M. Núñez et al. (Eds.): TESTCOM/FATES 2009, LNCS 5826, pp. 16–32, 2009.

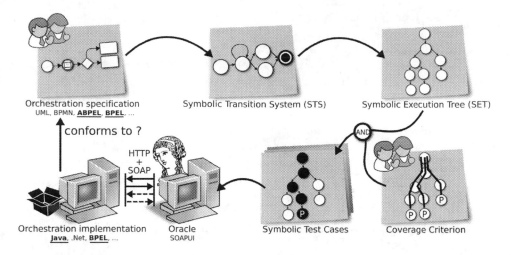

Fig. 1. Overview of the proposed framework

providers to publicise (Abstract) BPEL descriptions of *what* their services do, but not *how* they do it. Here, testing comes as a solution to ensure (i) that some sub-service used in an orchestration really conforms to its publicised behavioural interface, and (ii) that the service orchestration itself conforms to the behavioural interface to be publicised after its deployment.

In this paper, we propose a formal framework for the testing of service orchestrations (Fig. 1). The orchestration specification is first translated into a formal model, namely a Symbolic Transition System (STS) [5]. In a second step, a Symbolic Execution Tree (SET) is computed from this STS. It supports the retrieval of the STS execution semantics, while avoiding the usual state-explosion problem in presence of unbounded data types, as used in full-fledged BPEL. Given a coverage criterion, we generate from the SET a set of execution paths which are finally run by a test oracle against the orchestration implementation.

With reference to related work, our contributions are manifold. A first contribution is the support for the rich XML-based data types available in BPEL. This is achieved first by relying on a symbolic model rather than on the labelled transition systems (LTS) that are usually used –either directly or indirectly from process algebraic or Petri net descriptions– as BPEL models. LTS are known to cause over-approximation or unimplementable test cases (when data are simply abstracted away), and state explosion problems (when message parameters or variables are flattened wrt. their infinite domains). Both are avoided using STS. Symbolic execution [6] also takes part in avoiding state explosion by representing message parameters and variables using symbolic values instead of concrete data. A second contribution is the possibility to take different orchestration specification languages (UML, BPMN, (A)BPEL) into account. This is achieved thanks to the STS model which has already proven to be valuable, *e.g.*, for UML [7], and is here used for BPEL.

Finally, we propose a comprehensive language-to-language model-based testing framework, while most model-based (verification or testing) approaches targeted at orchestration languages either ignore the retrieval of the formal model from the orchestration specification, ignore or over-simplify the rich XML-based data types of services, or do not tackle the execution of test cases against a running service implementation. As a consequence, we have applied our framework to two realistic medium-size case studies, including our extended version, presented herein, of the loan approval service [1].

The remaining of the paper is organised as follows. The following Section introduces our case study. The orchestration and STS models are presented in Section 3. The principles of symbolic execution and the computation of a finite SET from an STS are described in Section 4. Section 5 addresses the retrieval of symbolic test cases from a SET, our online testing algorithm, and tool support. Finally Section 6 discusses related work and we end in Section 7 with conclusions and perspectives.

2   Running Example

In this Section we introduce our xLoan case study. It is an extension of the well-known loan approval example presented in the BPEL standard [1], which usually serves for demonstration purposes in articles on BPEL verification. Our extensions are targeted at demonstrating our support for BPEL important features: complex data types, complex service conversations including message correlation, loops and alarms. Hence, more complex and realistic data types are used, to model user information, loan requests and loan proposals. The specified sub-services respectively deal with loan approval (BankService) and black listing (BlackListingService), with users not being blacklisted asking for low loans ($\leq 10,000$) getting loan proposals without requiring further approval. As-is, these services resemble the ones proposed in [1]. Yet, once a loan is accepted, proposals may be sent to the requester. Further communication then takes place, letting the requester select one proposal or cancel, which is then transmitted to BankService. If the selected offer code is not correct the requester is issued an error message and may try again (select or cancel). Timeouts are also modelled, and the bank is informed about cancelling if the requester does not reply in a given amount of time (2 hours).

There is no official graphical notation neither for orchestration architectures (WSDL interfaces and partner links), nor for the imported data types (XML Schema files) or the service conversation (BPEL <process> definition). For the former ones (Fig. 2) we use the UML notation that we extend with specific stereotypes in order to represent message types, correlations and properties (see Sect. 3 for their semantics). Moreover, XML namespaces are represented with packages. Additionally, there is currently an important research effort on relating the Business Process Modelling Notation (BPMN) with Abstract BPEL or BPEL code [8]. Therefore, concerning the graphical presentation of service conversations, we take inspiration from BPMN, while adding our own annotations

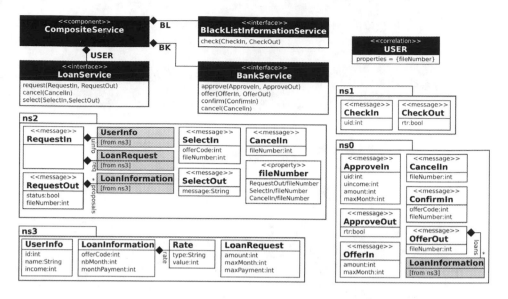

Fig. 2. xLoan Example – Data and Service Architecture

supporting relation with BPEL. Communication activities are represented with the concerned partnerlink (USER for the user of the orchestration, BK or BL for the two sub-services), operation, input/output variables, and, when it applies, information about message correlation.

Figure 3 presents the orchestration specification. The overall process is presented in Figure 3, upper part, while its lower part concerns the (potentially looping) subprocess, GL&S (*Get Loan and Select*), for loan proposal selection.

3   From BPEL to STS

In this Section we present our formal models for services and orchestrations. We also discuss model retrieval from BPEL.

Services may expose information at different interface description levels. The basic level is the *signature level* where a service describes the set of operations it provides. Complex services, including state-full ones, additionally provide a *behavioural description* (conversation) of the way its operations should be called. In this work we focus on these two levels, which are the ones widely accepted and used, with respectively the WSDL and (A)BPEL languages.

Signatures. The *signature* of a service is described using a combination of XML schema (exchanged data structures) and WSDL (operations and messages). We model it as a tuple $\Sigma = (\mathcal{D}, \mathcal{O}, \mathcal{P}, in, out, err, \pi, \downarrow)$.

$\mathcal{D}$ is a set of domains. $dom(x)$ denotes the domain of x. $\mathcal{O}$ is a set of (provided) operations. Operations may be either one-way or two-way. $in, out, err : \mathcal{O} \rightarrow \mathcal{D} \cup \{\bot\}$ denote respectively the input, output, or fault message of an operation ($\bot$ when undefined, *e.g.*, $out(o) = err(o) = \bot$ for any one-way operation o).

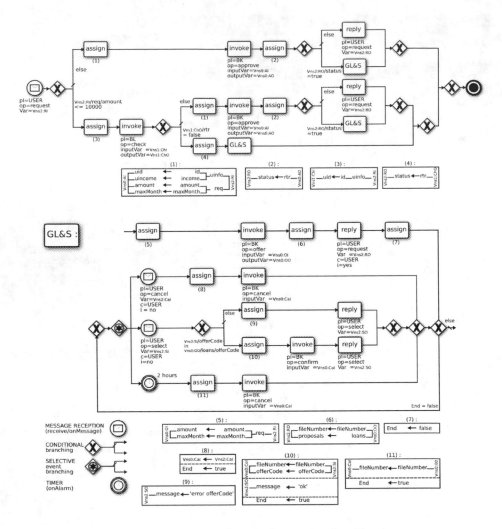

Fig. 3. xLoan Example – Orchestration Specification

$\mathcal{P}$ is a set of property names. Properties, together with property aliases and correlation sets, are important BPEL features that support the definition of sessions and message correlation in between services instances [1]. $\downarrow$ is used to define property aliases for messages: for a message type m, $m \downarrow_p$ denotes the part in m messages that corresponds to property p. Finally, π is used to specify what two-way operations in sub-services are supposed to do: $\pi(o)$, $o \in \mathcal{O}$, is a boolean formula relating o inputs and outputs.

Partnership. An orchestration is built around a partnership, *i.e.*, a set of partner signatures, corresponding to required operations, and a set of signatures for the orchestration itself, corresponding to provided operations. In the sequel we suppose, without loss of generality, that an orchestration has only one of these, named USER. A *partnership* ρ is an ID-indexed set of signatures $\{\Sigma_i\}_{i \in ID}$, where ID is a set of names (USER $\in ID$). Two domains with the same name, including the namespace part, in two signatures correspond to the same thing. More specifically, we suppose they have the same formal semantics.

Events. The semantics of a service conversation depends on message-based communication, which is modelled using *events*. An input event, $pl.o?x$, with $o \in \mathcal{O}(\Sigma_{pl})$ and message variable x such that $dom(x) = in(o)$, corresponds to the reception of the input message of operation o from partner link pl. Accordingly, we define output events $pl.o!x$ ($dom(x) = out(o)$). Service calls may also yield errors (message faults). This is modelled with fault output events, $pl.o!!x$, and fault input events, $pl.o??x$ ($dom(x) = err(o)$). We omit BPEL port types here for simplicity reasons (full event prefixes would be, *e.g.*, $pl.pt.o?x$ for the first example above with input on port type pt). $Ev^?$ (resp. $Ev^!$, $Ev^{??}$, and $Ev^{!!}$) is the set of input events (resp. output events, fault input events, and fault output events). Ex is the set of internal fault events, that correspond to faults possibly raised internally (not in messages) by the orchestration process. We also introduce specific events: τ denotes non-observable internal computations or conditions, χ denotes time passing (time constraints in services are generally soft, hence discrete time is a valid abstraction), and $\sqrt{}$ denotes the termination of a conversation (end of a session). We define $Ev = Ev^? \cup Ev^! \cup Ev^{??} \cup Ev^{!!} \cup Ex \cup \{\tau, \chi, \sqrt{}\}$. We also define hd as $\forall * \in \{?, ??, !, !!\}$, $hd(pl.o * x) = pl.o$, and $hd(e) = e$ for any other e in Ev.

Orchestration. Different models have been proposed to support behavioural service discovery, verification, testing, composition or adaptation [4,9,10,11]. They mainly differ in their formal grounding (Petri nets, transition systems, or process algebra), and the subset of service languages being supported. We base on [12] due to its good coverage of the main BPEL language constructs. Moreover, its process algebraic style for transformation rules enables a concise yet precise and operational model, which is, through extension, amenable to symbolic execution. In this objective, we extend the formalising given in [12] to support a wider subset of BPEL (see below discussion on *BPEL to STS transformation*), including data in computation and messages. As a consequence, our behavioural model grounds on (discrete timed) Symbolic Transition Systems (STS) in place of the discrete timed Labelled Transition Systems (dtLTS) presented in [12].

A *Symbolic Transition System* (STS), is a tuple $(\mathcal{D}, \mathcal{V}, S, s_0, T)$ where $\mathcal{D}$ is a set of domains (as in signatures), $\mathcal{V}$ is a set of variables with domain in $\mathcal{D}$, S is a non empty set of states, $s_0 \in S$ is the initial state, and T is a (potentially nondeterministic) transition relation, $T \subseteq S \times \mathcal{T}_{\mathcal{D}^{\text{Bool}}, \mathcal{V}} \times Ev \times 2^{Act} \times S$, with $\mathcal{T}_{\mathcal{D}^{\text{Bool}}, \mathcal{V}}$ denoting boolean terms, Ev a set of events and Act a set of actions (of the form $v := t$ where $v \in \mathcal{V}$ is a variable and $t \in \mathcal{T}_{\mathcal{D}, \mathcal{V}}$ a term). The transition system is called symbolic as the guards, events, and actions may contain variables. An element (s, g, e, A, s') of T is denoted $s \xrightarrow{[g] \; e \; / \; A} s'$. When there is no guard (*i.e.*, it is true) it is omitted. The same yields for the actions. We impose that variables used in the STS transitions are defined in $\mathcal{V}$. STS have been introduced under different forms (and names) in the literature [5], to associate a behaviour with a specification of data types that is used to evaluate guards, actions and sent values. This role is played here by $\mathcal{D}$ which is a superset of all partners' domains. Consistency of the union is ensured by the above-mentioned restriction on domains sharing names.

An *orchestration* $\mathcal{O}rch$ is a tuple $(\rho, \mathcal{B}, \mathcal{C})$ where ρ is a partnership, $\mathcal{B}$ is an STS, and $\mathcal{C}$ is a set of correlation sets, *i.e.*, a name and a set of associated properties, denoted with *props*. Sometimes a single property is used (*e.g.*, an identifier), but more generally this is a set (*e.g.*, name and surname). A correlation value is a value of a structured domain with items corresponding to the properties. We impose that $\mathcal{B}$ is correct wrt. ρ, *i.e.*, its set of events correspond to partner links and operations defined in ρ, which can be syntactically checked.

BPEL to STS transformation. BPEL is first abstracted away from its concrete syntax using process constructors. The transformation rules are then presented in a process algebraic structural operational semantics way, using one or several rules for each constructor. Due to lack of room, the presentation of the transformation rules is provided in [13]. With reference to the variables used in the BPEL specification, anonymous variables (va_i) are added in $\mathcal{V}(\mathcal{B})$ to follow BPEL communication semantics. Moreover, for each correlation set c in $\mathcal{C}$, we also add two variables, vcs_c (to denote the value of c) and $vcs_c init$ (to check whether c is initialised or not).

We support the main BPEL activities. With reference to [12], we support data (in computation, conditions and message exchange), message correlation, message faults, parallel processing (flows) and the **until** activity. The catch construct of synchronous **invoke** is not directly supported but it can be simulated using a fault handler in a scope around the **invoke**. Links, the **foreach** activity, fault variables in fault handlers, compensations handlers, and termination handlers are future work.

Application. The STS obtained from the example presented in Section 2 is presented in Figure 4 where **tau** (resp. **tick**, **term**) denote τ (resp. χ, $\sqrt{}$). The zoom corresponds to the **while** part. One may notice states 16 (**while** condition test), 17/33 (**pick**), 34 (**onAlarm** timeout), and 18/23 (correlation testing).

4   Symbolic Execution

Symbolic execution [6] (SE) is a program analysis technique that has been originally proposed to overcome the state explosion problem when verifying programs with variables. SE represents values of the variables using symbolic values instead of concrete data [14]. Consequently, SE is able to deal with constraints over symbolic values, and output values are expressed as a function over the symbolic input values. More recently these techniques have been applied to the verification of interacting/reactive systems, including testing [14,15,16].

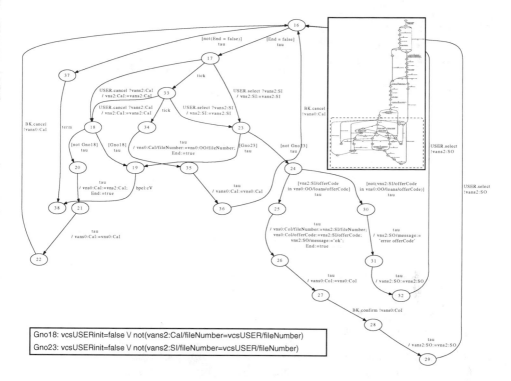

Fig. 4. xLoan Example – Symbolic Transition System

SE-Trees. The SE of a program is represented by a *symbolic execution tree* (SET), where nodes, $\mathcal{N}_{\text{SET}}$, are tuples $\eta_i = (s, \pi, \sigma)$ made up of the program counter, s, the symbolic values of program variables, σ, and a path condition, π. Let $\mathcal{V}_{\text{symb}}$ be a set of (symbolic) variables (representing symbolic values), disjoint from the program variables, $\mathcal{V}$ ($\mathcal{V} \cap \mathcal{V}_{\text{symb}} = \emptyset$). σ is a map $\mathcal{V} \to \mathcal{V}_{\text{symb}}$. The path condition (PC) is a boolean formula with variables in $\mathcal{V}_{\text{symb}}$. The PC accumulates constraints that the symbolic variables must fulfil in order to follow a given path in the program.

Since we apply SE to the STS obtained from orchestrations, the program counter is an STS state, and $\mathcal{V}$ corresponds to the STS variables (either simple, message type, anonymous, or correlation variables from BPEL). The edges of the SET, $\mathcal{E}_{\text{SET}}$, are elements of $\mathcal{N}_{\text{SET}} \times Ev_{\text{symb}} \times \mathcal{N}_{\text{SET}}$ (may be non deterministic), where Ev_{symb} corresponds to the STS events (Ev) with symbolic variables in place of variables.

SET edge computation. The SET is computed in a BFS fashion as follows. The root is $(s_0, true, \sigma_0)$ where s_0 is the STS initial state and σ_0 is the mapping of a fresh variable for each variable of the STS. Each transition $s \xrightarrow{[g] \ e \ / \ A} s'$ then corresponds to an edge $(s, \pi, \sigma) \xrightarrow{e'} (s', \pi', \sigma')$, computed as follows:

1. **guard:** $\pi^G = \pi \wedge g[\sigma(v_i)/v_i]_{v_i \in vars(g)}$ ($\pi^G = \pi$ if there is no guard)

2. **event:** e', $\sigma^E = \begin{cases} pl.o * v_s, & \sigma[v \to v_s] \text{ if } e = pl.o * v, * \in \{?, ??\} \\ pl.o * \sigma(v), & \sigma \quad\quad \text{ if } e = pl.o * v, * \in \{!, !!\} \\ e, & \sigma \quad\quad \text{ otherwise} \end{cases}$

   with $v_s = new^1(\mathcal{V}_{symb}, \sigma)$. If e is a sub-service invocation return ($e = pl.o * v_{out}$, $* \in \{?, ??\} \wedge pl \neq \text{USER}$), we set $\pi^E = \pi(o)[\sigma^E(v_{in})/in, v_s/out]$, where $e = pl.o!v_{in}$ is the label of the (unique) transition before the one we are dealing with, to take into account the operation specification. Else, $\pi^E = \pi^G$.

3. **actions** ($A = \{x_i/path_i := t_i\}_{i \in \{1, \dots, n\}}$):
   $\pi_i^A = \pi_{i-1}^A \wedge (v_{s_{x_i}}/path_i = t_i[\sigma^E(v_j)/v_j]_{v_j \in vars(t_i)})$
   with $\Delta = \{x \in \mathcal{V} \mid (x/path_i := t_i) \in A\}$, $\{v_{s_x}\}_{x \in \Delta} = new^{\#\Delta}(\mathcal{V}_{symb}, \sigma^E)$, $\sigma' = \sigma^E\{[v_{s_x}/x]\}_{x \in \Delta}$, $\pi_0^A = \pi^E$, and $\pi' = \pi_n^A$.

where $vars$ denotes the variables in a term, $new^n(\mathcal{V}_{symb}, \sigma)$ denotes the creation of n new (fresh) symbolic variables wrt. σ, $t[y/x]$ denotes the substitution of x by y in t, and $\sigma[x \to x_s]$ denotes σ where the mapping for x is overloaded by the one from x to x_s. Δ is the set of variables that are modified by the assignments. For each of these, we have a new symbolic variable. We denote by $may(\eta)$, $\eta \in \mathcal{N}_{SET}$, the set $\{e \mid \exists(\eta, e, \eta') \in \mathcal{E}_{SET}\}$.

Feasible paths. Edges with inconsistent path conditions may be cut off while computing the SET. For this, we check when computing a new node η if $\pi(\eta)$ is satisfiable (there exists a valuation of variables in π such that π is true, if not, we cut the edge off). This is known to be an undecidable problem in general. Therefore, if the constraint solver does not yield a solution (or a contradiction) in a given amount of time, we cut the edge off and we issue a warning specifying that the test process is to be incomplete.

Path length criterion. STS may contain loops that would cause SET unboundedness. To solve this issue out, we take into account a path length criterion while computing the SET. Given a constant k, we stop the SET computation at some node whenever this node is at k edges from the SET root. In order to take into account the fact that interactions are the most important part of orchestrations, only non-τ transitions can be counted. Let us note that in some cases this option could suffer from (τ-)livelocks in the STS. Different cutting criteria have been proposed in the literature, e.g., the inclusion criterion in [16], where the SET computation stops at one node when an equivalent node (in terms of program variable valuations validating the path constraint) is on the path to the SET root. Yet, this does not prevent the need to a path length criterion [16].

Application. The SET computed from the Figure 4 STS is presented in Figure 5. There are 10 leaves corresponding to termination (in gray). The zoom presents the path (in black) we use for demonstration in the next Section. Its final node is number 305, and its path condition, π_{305} is also given in the Figure.

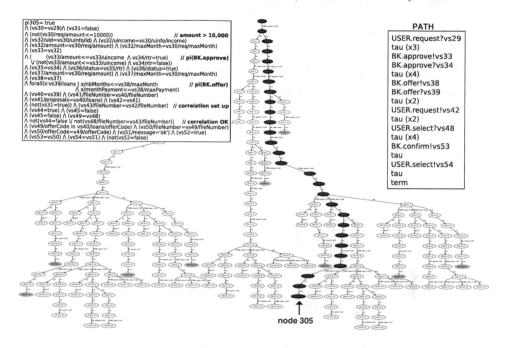

Fig. 5. xLoan Example – Symbolic Execution Tree (k=10, τs not counted)

5   Test Case Realisation and Testing Architecture

In this Section we present the way symbolic test cases are realised and executed on an orchestration implementation. The distinctive features of our approach can be summarised as follows:

- **Functional testing with a SET path coverage criterion:** For the time being, we support two criteria: all paths with length $n \leq k$, and all complete paths (a path ended with $\sqrt{}$) with length $n \leq k$. Paths are constructed in a DFS way.
- **Symbolic input-output trace inclusion:** The conformance relation we use is trace inclusion extended to our symbolic context. It can be related to the conformance relation defined in [15,16] that inspired our work (see *Related Work*). However, we do not require input-enabledness since, for Web services, an exception is returned whenever an unexpected event is received by the service.
- **Online realisation of symbolic test cases:** Test case realisation is performed step by step, by interacting with the Service Under Test (SUT). This is to avoid emitting erroneous verdicts. Take a path $p?x.p!y$, with $\sigma = \{x \rightarrow v_{s_0}, y \rightarrow v_{s_1}\}$ and $\pi = v_{s_0} > 2 \wedge v_{s_1} > v_{s_0}$. Realisation all-at-once would yield a realised path $p?v_{s_0}, p!v_{s_1}$ with, *e.g.*, $\{v_{s_0} \rightarrow 3, v_{s_1} \rightarrow 4\}$. Suppose now we send message p with value 3 to the SUT and that it replies with value 5. We would emit a *Fail* verdict ($5 \neq 4$), while indeed 5 would be a correct reply ($5 > 3$).

Algorithm 1. Online Testing Algorithm

Data: SET + a distinguished path p, $path\ p = n_1 l_1 n_2 l_2 \dots l_{k-1} n_k$;
begin

    $\pi = \pi_k$; $i := 1$; $rtr := Pass$;

    while $i < k$ *and* $rtr = Pass$ **do**

        switch l_i **do**

            case USER.$e?x_s$

                $val := (SOLVE(\pi)[x_s])$;

                try {**send** $(e(val))$; $\pi := \pi \wedge x_s = val$;}

                catch $(e \in Ex)$ { $rtr := Fail$; }

            case USER.$e!x_s$

                start TAC;

                try {**receive** $(e(val))$; $\pi = \pi \wedge (x_s = val)$;

                      if $\neg SOLVE(\pi)$ **then** $rtr := Fail$; }

                catch (timeout_TAC) {$rtr := Fail$;}

                catch (receive e') { **if** $e' \in may(\eta_i)$ **then** $rtr := Inconclusive$;

                                    else $rtr := Fail$;}

            case χ

                wait(1 unit of time);

            otherwise

                skip;

        $i := i + 1$;

    return rtr;

end

- **Branching awareness:** The SUT may send different outputs at some point in its execution due to non-determinism (*e.g.*, due to a flow activity in the implementation). Outputs are non-controllable events from the point of view of the tester. Therefore, a path is realised in the context of its SET (see Alg. 1).

5.1 Online Testing Algorithm

Online testing is presented in Algorithm 1. Its input is the SET with a distinguished symbolic path we want to test. The algorithm then animates the path by interacting, over messages for the USER partnerlink, with the SUT. Accordingly, input (resp. output) events in the path correspond to messages sent (resp. received) by the tester. Generation of data in sent messages and checking of data in received messages is supported using constraint solving over a Path Condition (PC). Initially PC corresponds to the path condition (π) in the last node of the path we test. The treatment of the path edges is then as follows.

- **Input events:** The tester has to generate a message to be sent to the SUT. For this, PC is solved (always succeeds, or the edge would have been cut off in the SET computation). We use the instantiation of the event variable, x_s, to send the message, and to update the PC. If the sent message yields an exception, we return a *Fail* verdict, else we pass to the next edge.

- **Output events:** The treatment of output events corresponds to message reception in the tester. Whenever an emission by the SUT is foreseen, a timer, TAC, is set up. Then three cases may occur. (i). If the timer elapses, we return a *Fail* result. (ii). If we receive the expected message before this, we update the PC with this new information and try to solve it. If it succeeds we continue to the next edge. If it fails we return a *Fail* verdict. If we do not get a result in a given amount of time we return an *Inconclusive* verdict (not in the Algorithm for simplicity). (iii). If we receive an unexpected event, we check in the SET if it is due to the specification non-determinism. If not, we return a *Fail* verdict. If it is the case, we return an *Inconclusive* verdict and the test path needs to be replayed in order to exhibit the behaviour that this test path characterises (for this we assume SUT fairness). Fault output events are supported in the same way.
- **Time passing** (χ)**:** Corresponds to the passing of one unit of time. Accordingly, the tester waits for this time before going to the next event in the path. The unit of time is computed from the specification (one hour in our example). Other events are skipped (see below, *Discussion*, about an alternative for gray-box testing).

5.2   Tool Support and Application

In this part, we end the application to the xLoan example, focusing on the online testing algorithm and on tool support. Our approach is automated by means of prototypes written in Java (BPEL to STS) and in Python (STS to SET) that serve as a proof of concept. As far as constraint solving is concerned, we chose the UML2CSP tool [17], which supports OCL constraint solving over UML class diagrams, that correspond to the constraints we have on XML schema data. Additionally, UML2CSP is able to generate witness object diagrams when the constraints are satisfiable. More precisely, in order to reuse this tool, we proceed as follows:

- we translate XML schema definitions into an UML class diagram, see Figure 2. Additionally, domain limits are set up in UML2CSP according to uniformity hypotheses, *e.g.*, here we have set maxMonth:{12,24,36} and maxPayment: [1000..100000]). This step is done only once.
- to check if some π is satisfiable *before* sending a message, an additional root class (Root) is created wrt. the UML diagram, with as many attributes as symbolic variables in π. The π constraint is translated in OCL. If π is satisfiable, UML2CSP generates an object diagram. From it we get data for the variable of interest to be sent (step $val := (SOLVE(\pi)[x_s])$ in Alg. 1).
- to check if some π is satisfiable *after* receiving a message, we perform as before, but adding an OCL constraint enforcing that the symbolic variable of the reception is equal to the data effectively received (steps $\pi = \pi \wedge (x_s = val)$ and $\neg SOLVE(\pi)$ in Alg. 1).

```
<soapenv:Envelope xsi:...="http:... >
<soapenv:Body>
<ns2:RequestIn>
  <ns3:uInfo>
    <id>1</id>
    <name>Simpson</name>
    <income>10002</income>
  </ns3:uInfo>
  <ns3:req>
    <amount>10001</amount>
    <maxMonth>12</maxMonth>
    <maxPayment>1000</maxPayment>
  </ns3:req>
</ns2:RequestIn>
</soapenv:Body>
</soapenv:Envelope>
```

```
<soapenv:Envelope xsi:...="http:... >
<soapenv:Body>
<ns2:RequestOut>
  <status>true</status>
  <fileNumber>1</fileNumber>
  <ns3:proposals>
    <offerCode>1</offerCode>
    <nbMonths>12</nbMonths>
    <monthPayment>918</monthPayment>
    <ns3:rate>
      <type>fixed</type>
      <value>10</value>
    </ns3:rate>
  </ns3:proposals>
</ns2:RequestOut>
</soapenv:Body>
</soapenv:Envelope>
```

Fig. 6. xLoan Example – a Sent and a Received Message (parts of)

- cutting infeasible paths in the SET computation is a sub-case of satisfaction before message sending (the generated object diagram is discarded).
- strings are treated as integers which represent an index in an enumerated type. This corresponds to a set of specific string constants for the test.

For the time being, interaction with UML2CSP is manual. The automation of this step is under process as part of an Eclipse plug-in we are developing.

Experiments have been applied on an implementation of xLoan which is not isomorphic to its specification as, *e.g.*, the BPEL code relies on additional boolean variables rather than on the workflow structure to decide if the sub-process for loan proposal selection or cancelling is applicable. The implementation size is 246 lines long (186 XML tags). In order to demonstrate our online algorithm, we take one of the 10 complete paths we have in the SET (see Fig. 5). Due to lack of room we focus on the first interaction steps of the path (loan request, loan reply). The first call to UML2CSP with the end path condition, π_{305}, enables one to retrieve values for the RequestIn message (id, name, income, amount, maxMonth, maxPayment), *e.g.*, the part of the path condition relative to the requested amount generates the `Context Root inv PC : not(self.vs30.req.amount<=10000)` OCL constraint, and value 10001 for the request amount. We then generate the message data in Figure 6, left, and send it using SOAPUI[1]. The corresponding received message is in Figure 6, right. We translate this data as an OCL constraint and solving it with UML2CSP we are able to show that it is a correct output. We may then proceed generating data for a correct offer selection (offerCode=1).

5.3   Discussion

We have experimented the application of our framework for functional testing based on structural criteria. We think that it could be used in other contexts. First, one may need to test –at design-time, or at run-time for dynamic service binding– if a SUT may serve as a sub-service, being given a specification of the way one would like to communicate with it. This could be achieved by

---

[1] http://www.soapui.org/

generating a partner service description [18] for this specification, and then apply our technique. Besides, supporting test objectives described as a directed acyclic STS with leaves tagged using $\{Pass, Fail\}$ could be performed using the STS product [19] of this STS with the specification STS prior to SET generation.

Additionally, one could have a gray-box point of view over orchestrations using the information available in the SET. We are experimenting another version of Algorithm 1 where communications with the partners are no longer skipped by the tester which receives invocations of the SUT and replies as if it was the sub-service (generating data respecting the π boolean formula in the sub-service signature specification). For this, we use the same constraint satisfaction approach as presented before.

6   Related Work

The state of practice in service testing has been limited for a long time to the use of tools such as SOAPUI or BPELUnit [20] that release from the burden of the translation into SOAP messages, operation calling and test management. However, test-cases were mainly generated using empirical approaches, often without automation.

In the last years, the software testing community has started to get involved in the service field. As a consequence, several works have tried to bridge the gap between current practice in service testing and state-of-the-art formal and automated software testing. One way to address this issue is to focus on the service signatures, *i.e.*, their WSDL description [21]. This enables to test operations independently. However, WSDL provides neither a semantic information on services nor a behavioural description of them, which is important in presence of composite (orchestration) services.

To the contrary, we chose to focus on this complementary part of orchestrations. This point of view has been adopted by several works, through white-box testing. Approaches based on control-/data-flow coverage criteria are presented in [22,23,24]. Classical testing data-flow criteria are revisited in [22] in order to be suitable to services. A control-flow algorithm is combined in [23] with rewriting graphs to support XPath expressions. The use of BPEL model-checking for white-box test case generation has been proposed in [25,26]. In both cases, test cases are considered as counter-examples and generated, according to several coverage criteria, with the SPIN model-checker. While [25] uses an intermediary model, [26] transforms directly BPEL into Promela. All these white-box approaches assume that the implementation source code is available.

In earlier work [10], we have addressed gray-box testing using translation of BPEL into the IF language and the extension of the IF simulator to generate tests according to a test objective. However, the use of data domain enumeration yields state explosion. To circumvent this problem, we propose in this paper a black-box testing approach using translation into STS and symbolic execution. We took inspiration from previous work on symbolic testing [19,16,15,27]. The works in [19,16], still, did not address components or services. Application to this domain has first been proposed in [15], and later in [27], from a theoretical and generic point a view, without a specification/implementation language in mind. In our work, we propose a comprehensive language-to-language approach with BPEL as target language. Accordingly, compared to the above-mentioned works, we take into account BPEL specific features in test-case derivation.

7   Conclusion and Perspectives

With the development of service reuse through their aggregation in added-value composite services, the testing of orchestrations has become a topical issue. In this paper we have presented a framework for orchestration testing based on symbolic transition systems which, compared to related work, supports the rich XML-based data types used in (Web) services without suffering from state explosion issues. This framework also proposes a comprehensive language-to-language approach, as it deals with both the retrieval of formal models from real service specification languages and with the execution of test cases using the SOAPUI API. Although we tackle BPEL to STS transformation, we advocate that transformations rules can be defined from other languages with workflow features (UML, BPMN) and accordingly provide the software architect with a richer specification environment.

Ongoing work is relative to the re-engineering of our tool prototypes and their integration in a plug-in extension of the Eclipse BPEL Designer, following [28]. A first perspective of our work is to support conformance testing based on test objectives. This would provide a valuable alternative to the path length criterion when dealing with infinite SET. Another perspective is relative to the supported basic XML types, currently only integers and strings. Using String databases, as proposed in [21], in place of simple enumerated values would enhance the tests relevance. Finally, supporting additional parts of BPEL, including compensation/termination handlers and string operators would enable to target a wider range of BPEL specifications.

References

1. OASIS: Web Services Business Process Execution Language (WSBPEL) Version 2.0. Technical report, OASIS (April 2007)
2. Rao, J., Su, X.: A Survey of Automated Web Service Composition Methods. In: Cardoso, J., Sheth, A.P. (eds.) SWSWPC 2004. LNCS, vol. 3387, pp. 43–54. Springer, Heidelberg (2005)
3. Dumas, M., Benatallah, B., Motahari Nezhad, H.R.: Web Service Protocols: Compatibility and Adaptation. IEEE Data Eng. Bull. 31(3), 40–44 (2008)
4. ter Beek, M.H., Bucchiarone, A., Gnesi, S.: Formal Methods for Service Composition. Annals of Mathematics, Computing & Teleinformatics 1(5), 1–10 (2007)
5. Poizat, P., Royer, J.C.: A Formal Architectural Description Language based on Symbolic Transition Systems and Modal Logic. Journal of Universal Computer Science 12(12), 1741–1782 (2006)

6. King, J.C.: Symbolic Execution and Program Testing. Communications of the ACM 19(7), 385–394 (1976)
7. Attiogbé, C., Poizat, P., Salaün, G.: A Formal and Tool-Equipped Approach for the Integration of State Diagrams and Formal Datatypes. IEEE Transactions on Software Engineering 33(3), 157–170 (2007)
8. Ouyang, C., van der Aalst, W., Dumas, M., ter Hofstede, A.: Translating BPMN to BPEL. Technical Report BPM-06-02, BPM Center Report (2006)
9. Bucchiarone, A., Melgratti, H., Severoni, F.: Testing Service Composition. In: Proc. of ASSE (2007)
10. Lallali, M., Zaïdi, F., Cavalli, A., Hwang, I.: Automatic Timed Test Case Generation for Web Services Composition. In: Proc. of ECOWS (2008)
11. Mateescu, R., Poizat, P., Salaün, G.: Adaptation of Service Protocols Using Process Algebra and On the Fly Reduction Techniques. In: Bouguettaya, A., Krueger, I., Margaria, T. (eds.) ICSOC 2008. LNCS, vol. 5364, pp. 84–99. Springer, Heidelberg (2008)
12. Mateescu, R., Rampacek, S.: Formal Modeling and Discrete Time Analysis of BPEL Web Services. In: Advances in Enterprise Engineering I. Lecture Notes in Business Information Processing, vol. 10, pp. 179–193. Springer, Heidelberg (2008)
13. Bentakouk, L., Poizat, P., Zaïdi, F.: A Formal Framework for Service Orchestration Testing Based on Symbolic Transition Systems. Long version, in P. Poizat Webpage
14. Khurshid, S., Pǎsǎreanu, C.S., Visser, W.: Generalized Symbolic Execution for Model Checking and Testing. In: Garavel, H., Hatcliff, J. (eds.) TACAS 2003. LNCS, vol. 2619, pp. 553–568. Springer, Heidelberg (2003)
15. Frantzen, L., Tretmans, J., Willemse, T.A.C.: A Symbolic Framework for Model-Based Testing. In: Havelund, K., Núñez, M., Roşu, G., Wolff, B. (eds.) FATES 2006 and RV 2006. LNCS, vol. 4262, pp. 40–54. Springer, Heidelberg (2006)
16. Gaston, C., Le Gall, P., Rapin, N., Touil, A.: Symbolic Execution Techniques for Test Purpose Definition. In: Uyar, M.Ü., Duale, A.Y., Fecko, M.A. (eds.) TestCom 2006. LNCS, vol. 3964, pp. 1–18. Springer, Heidelberg (2006)
17. Cabot, J., Clarisó, R., Riera, D.: UMLtoCSP: a Tool for the Formal Verification of UML/OCL Models using Constraint Programming. In: Proc. of ASE (2007)
18. Kaschner, K., Lohmann, N.: Automatic Test Case Generation for Interacting Services. In: Feuerlicht, G., Lamersdorf, W. (eds.) ICSOC 2008 Workshops. LNCS, vol. 5472, pp. 66–78. Springer, Heidelberg (2009)
19. Jeannet, B., Jéron, T., Rusu, V., Zinovieva, E.: Symbolic Test Selection based on Approximate Analysis. In: Halbwachs, N., Zuck, L.D. (eds.) TACAS 2005. LNCS, vol. 3440, pp. 349–364. Springer, Heidelberg (2005)
20. Mayer, P.: Design and Implementation of a Framework for Testing BPEL Compositions. PhD thesis, Leibnitz University, Germany (2006)
21. Bartolini, C., Bertolino, A., Marchetti, E., Polini, A.: Towards Automated WSDL-Based Testing of Web Services. In: Bouguettaya, A., Krueger, I., Margaria, T. (eds.) ICSOC 2008. LNCS, vol. 5364, pp. 524–529. Springer, Heidelberg (2008)
22. Bartolini, C., Bertolino, A., Marchetti, E., Parissis, I.: Data Flow-Based Validation of Web Services Compositions: Perspective and Examples. In: de Lemos, R., Di Giandomenico, F., Gacek, C., Muccini, H., Vieira, M. (eds.) Architecting Dependable Systems V. LNCS, vol. 5135, pp. 298–325. Springer, Heidelberg (2008)
23. Mei, L., Chan, W., Tse, T.: Data Flow Testing of Service-Oriented Workflow Applications. In: Proc. of ICSE (2008)
24. Li, Z., Sun, W., Jiang, B., Zhang, X.: BPEL4WS Unit Testing: Framework and Implementation. In: Proc. of ICWS (2005)

25. Zheng, Y., Zhou, J., Krause, P.: An Automatic Test Case Generation Framework for Web Services. Journal of Software 2(3), 64–77 (2007)
26. García-Fanjul, J., Tuya, J., de la Riva, C.: Generating Test Cases Specifications for BPEL Compositions of Web Services Using SPIN. In: Proc. of WS-MaTe (2006)
27. Frantzen, L., Huerta, M., Kiss, Z., Wallet, T.: On-The-Fly Model-Based Testing of Web Services with Jambition. In: Bruni, R., Wolf, K. (eds.) WS-FM 2008. LNCS, vol. 5387, pp. 143–157. Springer, Heidelberg (2009)
28. Foster, H., Uchitel, S., Magee, J., Kramer, J.: WS-Engineer: A Tool for Model-Based Verification of Web Service Compositions and Choreography. In: Proc. of ICSE (2006)

Testing *k*-Safe Petri Nets

Gregor von Bochmann and Guy-Vincent Jourdan

School of Information Technology and Engineering (SITE)
University of Ottawa
800 King Edward Avenue, Ottawa, Ontario, Canada, K1N 6N5
{bochmann,gvj}@site.uottawa.ca

Abstract. Petri nets have been widely studied as tool for specification, modeling and analysis of concurrent systems. However, surprisingly little research has been done for testing systems that are specified with Petri nets. When a formal model is used, variations of Finite State Machines are often used for the automated generation of test cases. In this paper, we study automated conformance testing when the formal specification is given as a *k*-safe Petri net. We provide a general framework to perform these tests, and give a few algorithms for test case generation based on different assumptions. We provide two inefficient, but general algorithms for *k*-safe Petri net conformance testing. We also provide efficient algorithms for testing *k*-safe free-choice Petri nets under specific fault assumptions.

Keywords: Conformance testing, fault model, *k*-safe Petri nets, free-choice Petri nets, automatic test generation.

1 Introduction

Software systems are notoriously incorrect, a problem that only gets worst when dealing with distributed systems. In order to help producing better systems, one common suggestion is to create a formal model of the specification of the system, and then test whether a given implementation *conforms* to the specification, for some suitable definition of conformance. Ideally the tests are automatically generated based on the formal specification. This kind of approach has been mostly researched using Finite State Machines (FSM) as the formal model (see e.g. [1] for a survey). More recently, the same questions have been asked for concurrent systems, for which FSM do not offer a good model. When modeling concurrent systems with FSMs for test generations, *multi-ports* FSM [2,3] and *Partial Order Input/Output Automata* [4] have been used. When modelling concurrent systems in general, a popular formalism among researchers are Petri Nets (see e.g. [5] for a survey). Surprisingly, little has been done in the area of conformance testing of systems specified as Petri Nets, even through Petri Nets have long been used in practice and have for example influenced the design of some UML schema and have been used as a basis for workflow modeling [6]. Other formalisms beside the already mentioned FSMs have been used in the context of testing distributed systems (for example for Labeled Transition Systems [7] or Message Sequence Charts [8]), but in this context Petri Nets have mostly been used

M. Núñez et al. (Eds.): TESTCOM/FATES 2009, LNCS 5826, pp. 33–48, 2009.
© IFIP International Federation for Information Processing 2009

for fault diagnosis (see e.g. [9]). An interesting classification of testing criteria for Petri nets was provided by Zhu and He [10], but without testing algorithms.

In this paper, we investigate the question of automatically testing Petri Nets, to ensure that an implementation of a specification provided as a Petri Net is correct. We focus on *k-safe* Petri Nets, that is, Petri Net for which a place never holds more that k tokens at once, and on free-choice Petri Nets. This modeling paradigm is well suited for certain real-life applications, such as workflows [6] or control flows in networks of processors [11]. When used to model workflows, the traditional *transitions* of Petri Nets are seen as *tasks* of a workflow.

In this context, we provide a precise fault model, capturing what kind of changes could make a candidate implementation not conforming to the specification: some of the specified flow constraints between the tasks may be missing, or some unspecified flow constraints between tasks may be added. We provide a precise framework for the conformance question in Section 2.3. We then provide general testing algorithms for *k-safe* Petri Nets in Section 3. We first show that testing *k-safe* Petri Nets can be reformulated as a special case of state machine testing. This approach makes sense since state machine testing has been extensively studied. Unfortunately, the complexity of the transformation of a Petri Net into an state machines is exponential in the worst case. We then provide a more efficient testing algorithm, which is still exponential in the size of the Petri-Net (in the worst case). In Section 4, we study some particular cases of faults for *k*-safe free-choice Petri Nets, for which a test suite of polynomial length can be proposed. In Section 4.1, we provide an algorithm that generates a test suite that guarantees the detection of any number of missing flow constraints between the tasks in the implementation. Similarly, we discuss in Section 4.3 the testing of implementations with only additional *input flows* between tasks. We show in Section 4.3 that the problem is more difficult for additional *output* flows. We conclude in Section 5. The basic concepts and definitions are introduced in Section 2.

2 Basic Concepts and Assumptions

In this section, we give the definition of Petri Nets and we explain the assumptions that we make about testing environment.

2.1 Petri Nets

Definition 1 (Petri Nets, input/outputs, traces, executable sets, markings). A *Petri Net* is a 4-tuple $N=(P,T,F,M_0)$ where P is a finite set of places, T is a finite set of transitions (or *tasks* in our context), $F \subseteq (P{\times}T){\cup}(T{\times}P)$ is a set of arcs (the *flows* in our context). A marking is a mapping from P to the natural numbers, indicating the number of tokens in each place. We write M_0 for the initial marking of the net.

For a task $t{\in}T$, we note $\bullet t=\{p{\in}P|(p,t){\in}F\}$ the set of *inputs* of t, and $t\bullet=\{p{\in}P|(t,p){\in}F\}$ the set of *outputs* of t. Similarly, for a place $p{\in}P$, we note $\bullet p=\{t{\in}T|(t,p){\in}F\}$ and $p\bullet=\{t{\in}T|(p,t){\in}F\}$.

A task t is enabled for execution if all inputs of t contain at least one token. When a task is executed the marking changes as follows: The number of tokens in all inputs of t decreases by one, and the number of tokens in all outputs of t increases by one. A *trace* of a Petri Net is a sequence of tasks that can be executed starting from the initial marking in the order indicated, without executing any other tasks. An *executable set* of tasks is a multiset of tasks whose task elements can be sequenced into a trace. Clearly, for each trace there is a unique executable set, but several traces may correspond to the same executable set, in which case we say that the traces are *equivalent*. A *marking of a trace t* is the marking obtained after the execution of t from the initial marking. We say that t *marks* P if the place P contains at least one token in the marking of t.

Definition 2 (Petri Net equivalence). Two Petri Nets $PN_1=(P_1,T_1,F_1,M_{10})$ and $PN_2=(P_2,T_2,F_2,M_{20})$ are said to be equivalent if $T_1 =T_2$ and they have the same set of traces.

Definition 3 (Free-choice Petri Nets). A Petri Net $PN=(P,T,F,M_0)$ is *free-choice* if and only if for all places p in P, we have either $| p\bullet| < 2$ or $(\bullet(p\bullet)) = \{p\}$.

Definition 4 (*k*-Safeness). A marking of a Petri Net is *k-safe* if the number of tokens in all places is at most *k*. A Petri Net is *k*-safe if the initial marking is *k*-safe and the marking of all traces is *k*-safe.

Proposition 1. *In a k-safe free-choice Petri Net $PN=(P,T,F,M_0)$, if for some task $t\in T$ and some place $p\in P$ such that $p\in \bullet t$, and $|\bullet t|>1$ there is no trace that marks $(\bullet t)\backslash p$ but not p then removing the input (p,t) from F defines a Petri Net PN' which is equivalent to PN.*

Proof. *Let $PN=(P,T,F,M_0)$ be a k-safe free-choice Petri Net, let $t\in T$ be a task of PN and $p\in P$ a place of PN such that p is in $\bullet t$, $|\bullet t|>1$ and there is no trace of PN that marks $(\bullet t)\backslash p$ but not p. Let PN' be the Petri Net obtained by removing (p,t) from F in PN. We show that PN' is equivalent to PN. Suppose they were not equivalent, that is, PN and PN' do not have the same set of traces. Since we have only removed a constraint from PN, clearly every trace of PN is also a trace of PN', therefore PN' must accept traces that are not accepted by PN. Let Tr be such a trace. Since the only difference between PN and PN' is fewer input flows on t in PN', necessarily t is in Tr. Two situations might occur: either Tr is not a trace of PN because an occurrence of t cannot fire in PN (i.e. $\bullet t$ is not marked at that point in PN), or another task t' can fire in PN' but not in PN. In the former case, because we have only removed (p,t), it mean that $(\bullet t)\backslash p$ is marked but $\bullet t$ is not, a contradiction with the hypothesis. In the latter case, if t' can fire in PN' but not in PN then $\bullet t'$ must be marked in PN' and not in PN. Again, the only difference being t not consuming a token in p in PN', it follows that t' can use that token in PN' but not in PN. In other words, $p\in \bullet t'$, but then $|p\bullet|>1$ and thus $\bullet(p\bullet) = \{p\}$ (PN is free-choice), a contradiction with $|\bullet t|>1$.*

2.2 Assumptions about the Specification, Implementation and Testing Environment

We assume that the specification of the system under test is provided in the form of a *k*-safe Petri Net. Moreover, we assume that there is a well identified initial marking. The goal of our test is to establish the conformance of the implementation to the specification, in the sense of trace equivalence (see Definition 2).

For the system under test, we make the assumption that it can be modeled as a k-safe Petri Net. In addition, we make the following assumptions: the number of reachable markings in the implementation is not larger than in the specification. This assumption corresponds to a similar restriction commonly made for conformance testing in respect to specifications in the form of state machines, where one assumes that the number of states of the implementation is not larger than the number of states of the specification. Without such an assumption, one would not be sure that the implementation is completely tested, since some of the (implementation) states might not have been visited. In the context of state machine testing, methods for weakening this assumptions have been described where it is allowed that the number of states of the implementation may exceed the number of states of the specification by a fixed number; similar considerations may also be considered for Petri nets, however, we do not address this question in this paper.

Regarding the testing environment, we assume that the system under test provides an interface which provides the following functions:

1. At any time, the tester can determine which tasks are enabled[1].
2. The tester can trigger an enabled task at will. Moreover, tasks will only be executed when triggered through the interface.
3. There is a reliable reset, which bring the system under test into what corresponds to the initial marking.

A good example of applications compatible with these assumptions are Workflow Engines. Workflow processes are usually specified by some specification language closely related to Petri Nets. Workflow engines are used to specify (and then enforce) the flow of tasks that are possible or required to perform for a given activity. In that setting, the set of possible tasks is well known, and a given task can be initiated if and only if the set of tasks that directly preceed it are finished. In a computer system, it typically means that at any time, the set of tasks that can be performed are enabled (accessible from the user interface) while the tasks that cannot be performed are not visible. It is thus possible to know what tasks are enabled, and choose one of them to be performed.

2.3 Fault Model

We assume that the difference between the system under test and the reference specification can be explained by certain types of modifications, called faults, as explained below. We do not make the single-fault assumption, thus the difference between the implementation and the specification may be due to several occurrences of these types of faults.

---

[1] We assume that the tester has access to the list of tasks that are enabled from the current marking, an assumption which is compatible with our example of workflow engines. Another option is to obtain such a list by attempting to fire all the tasks from the current marking, resetting the system and driving it to the current marking after each successful firing, This latter option is less efficient, but is still polynomial in the size of the net.

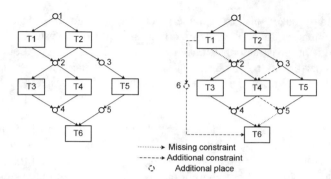

Fig. 1. An example of a Petri Net specification (left) and a Petri Net implementation (right) with several types of faults

1. **Missing output flow:** a task does not produce the expected output, that is, does not put the expected token in a given place. In Figure 1, the specification (left) says that task T1 must produce an output into place 2. However, in the implementation (right), T1 fails do produce this output; this is a missing output flow fault.

2. **Missing input flow:** a task does not require the availability of a token in a given place to fire. In Figure 1, the specification (left) says that task T6 must take an input from place 5. However, in the implementation (right), T6 does not require this input; this is a missing input flow fault.

3. **Additional output flow:** a task produces an output into an existing place, that is, places a token into that place while the specification does not require such output. In Figure 1, the specification (left) says that task T4 does not produce an output into place 5. However, in the implementation (right), T4 produces this output; this is an additional output flow fault.

4. **Additional input flow:** a task requires the availability of a token in a given existing place while the specification does not require such a token. In Figure 1, the specification (left) says that task T4 does not require an input from place 3. However, in the implementation (right), T4 does require this input; this is an additional input fault.

5. **Additional place:** the implementation may contain an additional place which is connected with certain tasks through additional input and output flows. Note: The missing of a place in the implementation can be modeled by the missing of all its input and output flows.

We note that in principle, an implementation may also have missing or additional tasks, as compared with the specification. However, given the first test environment assumption described in Section 2.2, such a fault would be detected easily at the testing interface which displays the enabled tasks in any given state. The situation would be more complex if the tasks of the specification had labels and the observed traces would be sequences of the labels of the executed tasks; however, this situation is outside the scope of this paper.

In the rest of the paper, we are interested only in faults that actually have an impact on the observable behavior of the system, that is, create a non-equivalent Petri Net (in the sense of Definition 2). It may prevent a task to be executed when it should be executable, and/or make a task executable when it should not. It is clear that it is possible to have faults as defined here that create an equivalent system, either because they simply add onto existing constraints, or replace a situation by an equivalent one.

When considering faults of additional output flows, new tokens may "appear" anywhere in the system every time a task is executed. This raises the question of k-safeness of the faulty implementation. One may assume that the faulty implementation is no longer k-safe, and thus a place can now hold more than k tokens. Or one may assume that the implementation is still k-safe despite possible faults. Another approach is to assume that the implementation's places cannot hold more than k tokens and thus additional tokens can "overwrite" others. Finally, and this is our working assumption, one may assume that violation of k-safeness in the system under test will raise an exception that we will catch, thus detecting the presence of a fault.

3 Testing k-Safe Petri Nets: The General Case

3.1 Using the Testing Techniques for Finite State Machines

In this section we consider the use of the testing techniques developed for state machines. We can transform any k-safe Petri Net into a corresponding state machine where each marking of the Petri Net corresponds to a state of the state machine, and each task of the Petri Net corresponds to a subset of the state transitions of the state machine. The state machine can be obtained by the classical marking graph construction method. Unfortunately, the number of markings may be exponentially larger than the size of the original Petri Net.

We note that the state machine obtained by the marking graph construction method is a deterministic labeled transition system (LTS) which is characterized by rendez-vous interactions with its environment. In fact, the triggering of an LTS state transition corresponds to the execution of a task in the Petri net, and according to the first environmental testing assumption (see Section 2.2), this is done in rendezvous with the tester.

Therefore, we may apply here the testing methods that have been developed for LTS. Tan et al. [15] show how the various methods that have been developed for testing FSM with input/output behavior (see for instance [1,13]) can be adapted for testing of LTS, which interact through rendezvous. The paper deals with the general case of non-deterministic LTS and owes much to previous work on testing non-deterministic FSMs [14].

Algorithm 1. State machine testing

1. From the initial marking, enumerate every possible marking that can be reached. Call E this set of markings.
2. Create a finite state machine A having $|E|$ states labeled by the elements of E and a transition between states if and only if in the Petri Net it is possible to go from the marking corresponding to the source state to the marking corresponding to the target state by firing one task. Label the state transition with this task. An example of this transformation is given in Figure 2.

3. Generate test cases for identifying the states in *A* using one of the existing methods for state machines.
4. For each *identified state* of the implementation,

  a.   verify that no task is enabled that should not be enabled (by driving the implementation into that state and listing the tasks that are enabled);
  b.   for each task not checked during state identification, verify that its execution leads to the correct next state.

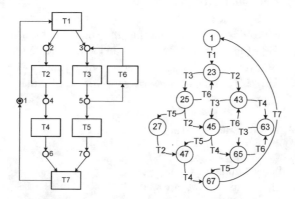

Fig. 2. A simple Petri Net and the corresponding finite state machine

Algorithm 1 will produce an exhaustive verification of the implementation.

Proposition 2. *Under the assumption that the number of markings for the implementation is not larger than for the specification, Algorithm 1 detects every possible combination of faults (in the fault model) resulting in an implementation that is not equivalent to the specification.*

Proof. *If a combination of faults results in a non-equivalent implementation, this means that one of the following cases occurs:*

1. *A given marking of the specification cannot be reached in the implementation. This will be caught by Step 3 We note that the state identification methods for state machines normally assume that the state machine is minimized. We believe that the marking graph of most Petri nets considered here would be minimal. If this is not the case by assumption the number of implementation states does not exceed the number of states of the marking graph of the specification and we can use an extended state machine testing method that allows additional states compared with the minimized specification [13].*
2. *From a given marking, a task that should be enabled is not, or it is enabled but executing it leads to the wrong marking. This will be caught by Step 3 and Step 4(b).*
3. *From a given marking, a task is enabled but shouldn't. This is typically not tested by checking sequences algorithms, but this problem will be detected by Step 5(a)*

of Algorithm 1. Indeed, in our settings, we are able to list all tasks enabled in a given marking. The checking sequence algorithm will give us a means to know how to put the implementation into a state corresponding to a given marking of the specification, thus Step 4 will detect any additional transition.

3.2 Using Techniques Specific to Petri Nets

In the general case, even if we cannot propose a polynomial algorithm, we can still look for a more efficient alternative than Algorithm 1. Indeed, every possible fault is in some senses localized on the net, in that the fault impacts a particular task, not a set of tasks. We still have to deal with the fact that in order to exhibit this fault, we may have to execute any set of tasks, but if we do so, this will indicate one faulty task. The idea is that, instead of testing every possible trace of the system (which is what Algorithm 1 indirectly does), it is enough to try every possible executable set. This is described in Algorithm 2.

Algorithm 2. Optimized generic testing

1.   For all executable sets S
2.   reset the system and execute S ;
3.   verify the status of every tasks of the net .

To illustrate the difference between Algorithm 1 and Algorithm 2, consider the (partial) Petri Net shown Figure 3. The following table shows the traces that will be tested by Algorithm 1, and an example of traces that could be selected by Algorithm 2, regarding this portion of the Petri Net.

To following proposition shows that Algorithm 2 will find every combination of faults:

Proposition 3. *Algorithm 2 detects every possible combination of faults (in the fault model) that results in an implementation that is not equivalent to the specification.*

Proof. *This results from the fact that in the type of Petri Nets we are considering, executing two traces that have the same executable set will necessarily lead to the same marking. In other words, if we execute the same multiset of tasks in any order (that can be executed), starting from the same marking, we always end up with the same marking.*

By definition, an implementation is faulty if and only if there is a trace tr which, when executed, leads to a task T that is in the wrong state (enabled when it shouldn't, or not enabled when it should). If there is such a fault, then there is such a trace, and the algorithm will eventually test an executable set with the same multiset of tasks as that trace. Thus, because the multiset is the same, the same marking will be reached and the same state will be obtained for T. Since the same marking is expected, the same state is expected for T as well, and thus if the state is incorrect for tr, it will also be incorrect for the tested executable set, and the error will be detected.

Algorithm 1	Algorithm 2
T1	*T1*
T1-T2	*T1-T2*
T1-T3	*T1-T3*
T1-T4	*T1-T4*
T1-T2-T3	*T1-T2-T3*
T1-T3-T2	
T1-T2-T4	*T1-T2-T4*
T1-T4-T2	
T1-T3-T4	*T1-T3-T4*
T1-T4-T3	
T1-T2-T3-T4	*T1-T2-T3-T4*
T1-T3-T2-T4	
T1-T2-T4-T3	
T1-T4-T2-T3	
T1-T3-T4-T2	
T1-T4-T3-T2	

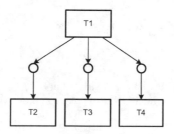

Fig. 3. A simple net (partial) that leads to fewer executions when using Algorithm 2, compared to using Algorithm 1

If violation to *k*-safeness of the implementation is not automatically detected, and additional tokens put into places simply overwrite the existing one, Algorithm 2 does not work, as shown in Figure 4 (with *k*=1), where the additional output from *T2* to *p* does violate the 1-safeness of the implementation, but the resulting error exhibits only if *T2* is executed after *T3*.

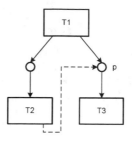

Fig. 4. The additional output fault from T2 to p can be seen only if T2 is executed after T3

4 Testing k-Safe Free-Choice Petri Nets under Assumptions

In this section, we look at some particular cases for which we are able to provide better testing algorithms. We focus our attention on k-safe free-choice Petri nets, on which conflict and synchronization can both occur, but not at the same time. It is a well studied class of Petri nets because it is still quite large, yet more easy to analyze than general Petri nets (see e.g. [11]). In addition to considering free-choice nets, we will also make further assumptions on the possible combination of faults in the implementation.

4.1 Testing for Missing Flow Faults

In some cases, it is possible to have more efficient testing algorithms. One such case is when the only possible faults are of type missing flow, that is, missing input flow or missing output flow. In this case, it is possible to check each input and output flow individually.

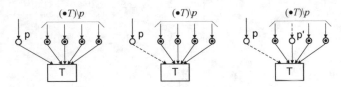

Fig. 5. Missing input flow. When $(\bullet T)\backslash p$ are marked but not p, T is not enabled in the specification (left), but it is enabled in the implementation (center); however, some additional faults may interfere (right).

Intuitively, the principles are the following: for detecting a missing input flow, we note that a task T normally requires all of its inputs to be marked to be enabled. For example, in Figure 5, left, the task T is not enabled because even though places $(\bullet T)\backslash p$ are all marked, place p is not. However, if the input flow from p to T is missing in the implementation (center), then is the same situation, with places $(\bullet T)\backslash p$ marked but place p not marked, T becomes enabled. The testing algorithm will thus, for all tasks T and all places p in $\bullet T$, mark all places in $(\bullet T)\backslash p$ and check if T is enabled. However, as shown in Figure 5 (right), in some case the missing input flow may not be detected; this may happen when at least one place p' in $(\bullet T)\backslash p$ was not successfully marked, because of some other (missing output) faults in the implementation.

The idea for testing for missing output flows is the following: if a task T outputs a token into a place p, and a task T' requires an input from p to be enabled, then marking all the places in $(\bullet T')$ by executing T to mark p (among other tasks) will enable T' (Figure 6, left). If T is missing the output flow towards p, then T' will not be enabled after attempting to mark all the places in $(\bullet T')$ because p will not actually be marked (Figure 6, center). Again, the situation can be complicated by another fault, such as a missing input flow between p and T', in which case T' will be enabled despite the missing output (Figure 6, right).

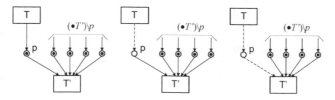

Fig. 6. Missing output flow. Correct situation (left), missing output flow of T (center), and interference by a missing input flow to T'.

The problems of the interference between several faults, as indicated in the right of Figure 5 and Figure 6, will be addressed indirectly by the proof of Proposition 4 which will show that the verification for missing input might fail because of another missing output, and the verification for missing output might fail because of a missing input, but they cannot both fail at the same time.

Formally, the algorithm for testing for missing input flows is the following:

Algorithm 3. Testing for missing input flows

1. For all task T
2.   For all place p in ($\bullet T$)
3.   If there is a trace S that marks ($\bullet T$)\p but not p
4.   Reset the system and execute S
5.   Verify *NOT-ENABLED(T)*

Line 3 is a reachability problem, which is PSPACE-complete for the kind of Petri Nets we are dealing with [12]. This means that the algorithm for determining a test suite for this purpose has a complexity that is PSPACE-complete. However, the length of the obtained test suite is clearly polynomial in respect to the size of the given Petri Net.

As we will see in the proof of Proposition 4, this algorithm is not sufficient on its own, since it can miss some missing input flows, when combined with missing output flows. It must be run in combination with Algorithm 4 which tests for missing output flows:

Algorithm 4. Testing for missing output flows

1. For all task T
2.   For all place p in ($T\bullet$)
3.   For all task T' in ($p\bullet$)
4.   If there is trace S that contains T and marks ($\bullet T'$) with a single token in p
5.   Reset the system and execute S
6.   Verify *ENABLED(T')*

As above, the complexity of the test selection algorithm is PSPACE-complete, however, the obtained test suite is polynomial in respect to the size of the given Petri Net. Proposition 4 shows that executing the tests generated by both algorithms is enough to detect all missing flow faults in the absence of other types of faults. To guarantee the detection of these faults, we must assume that the implementation only contains faults of these types.

Proposition 4. *Executing both Algorithm 3 and Algorithm 4 will detects any faulty implementation that has only missing input and/or output flow faults.*

Proof. *If an implementation is not faulty, then clearly neither algorithm will detect a fault. Assume that there is a task T with a missing input flow from a place p. If there is no trace S that marks ($\bullet T$)\p but not p, then Proposition 1 shows that the input flow is unnecessary and the resulting Petri Net is in fact equivalent to the original one. We therefore assume that there is such a trace S. If after executing S successfully ($\bullet T$)\p is indeed marked, then T will be enabled and the algorithm will detect the missing input constraint. If after executing S T is not enabled, that means that ($\bullet T$)\p is in fact not marked. The problem cannot be another missing input for T, since it would mean fewer constraints on S, not more, and wouldn't prevent T to be enabled. Thus, the only remaining option is that some task T' in $\bullet$(($\bullet T$)\p) did not mark the expected place in ($\bullet T$)\p when executing S, that is, T' has a missing output flow. In conclusion, Algorithm 3 detects missing input flows, except when the task missing the input constraint has another input flow which is not missing but for which the task that was to put the token has a missing output flow.*

Assume now that there is a task T with a missing output flow to a place p. If this output flow is not redundant, then there is a task T' that has p as an input flow and that will consume the token placed there by T. Such a T' will be found by Algorithm 4. Because of the missing output flow, normally T' will not be enabled after executing S and the algorithm will catch the missing flow. However, it is still possible for T' to be enabled, if it is missing the input flow from p, too. In conclusion, Algorithm 4 detects missing output flow, except when the missing output flow is to a place that has an input flow that is missing too.

To conclude this proof, we need to point out that each algorithm works, except in one situation; but the situation that defaults Algorithm 3 is different from the one that defaults Algorithm 4. In the case of Algorithm 4, we need a place that has lost both an input and an output flow, while in the case of Algorithm 3, we need a place that has lost an output flow but must have kept its input flow. Thus, by running both algorithms, we are guaranteed to detect all problems, Algorithm 4 catching the problems missed by Algorithm 3, and vice versa.

4.2   Testing for Additional Input Flow Faults

Testing for additional flow faults is more difficult than testing for missing flow faults because it may involve tasks that are independent of each other according to the specification. Moreover, the consequence of this type of faults can be intermittent, in the sense that an additional output flow fault may be cancelled by an additional input flow fault, leaving only a short window of opportunity (during the execution of the test trace) to detect the fault. In the case of additional input flow faults without other types of faults, we can still propose a polynomial algorithm, but we cannot check for additional output flow faults in polynomial time, even if no other types of faults are present.

An additional input flow fault can have two different effects: it may prevent a task from being executed when it should be executable according to the specification, because the task expects an input that was not specified, or it may prevent some other task from executing because the task with the additional input flow has unexpectedly consumed the token. Figure 7 illustrates the situation: task T has an additional input flow from place p (left). In the case where $\bullet T$ is marked, but p is not (center), T is not enabled, although it should. If p is marked too (right), then T can fire, but then T' cannot anymore, even though it should be enabled.

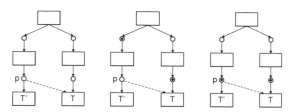

Fig. 7. Additional input flow fault: T has an additional input flow from p (left). This may prevent T from firing (center), or, when T fires, T' becomes disabled (right).

A more general description is illustrated in Figure 8: in order to mark $\bullet T$, some trace is executed (the dashed zone in the Figure). While producing this trace, some other places will also become marked (for example p') while other places are unmarked (for example p). This normal situation is shown on the left. If T has an additional input constraint from p (center), then after executing the same trace, the faulty $\bullet T$ will not be enabled. If T has an additional input constraint from p' (right), then the faulty $\bullet T$ is still marked after generating the trace, so T is enabled, however, if it fires it will disable T'.

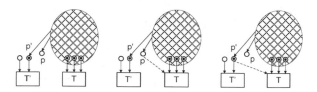

Fig. 8. Additional input flow fault (see explanation above)

Consequently, in order to detect these faults, in the absence of any other type of faults, we use an algorithm that works in two phases: first, a trace is executed that should mark $\bullet T$ and verifies that T is indeed enabled. This shows that either T does not have an additional input constraint, or that the additional input place happens to be marked as well. So the second phase checks that the places that are marked by this trace (and that are not part of $\bullet T$) are not being unmarked by the firing of T. Algorithm 5 gives the details.

Algorithm 5. Testing for additional input flows

1. For all task T
2.   Find a trace S that marks $\bullet T$
3.   Reset the system and execute S
4.   Verify $ENABLED(T)$
5.   For all place p not in $\bullet T$ which is marked by S
6.   If there is a trace S' containing T and another task T' in $p\bullet$ such that
                        p should have a single token when S' is fired
7.   Reset the system and verify that S' can be executed
8.   Else if there is a trace S'' marking $\bullet T$ but not p
9.   Reset the system and execute S''
10.   Verify $ENABLED(T)$

Proposition 5. *Executing Algorithm 5 will detect any faulty implementation that has only additional input flow faults.*

Proof. *If a task T has an additional input from a place p and that fault it not caught at line 4, it necessarily means that p is marked by trace S, and expected to be so because we consider only additional input flow faults. Such a case will be dealt with by lines 5 through 10. If the fault has an impact (i.e. if it leads to a wrong behavior of the implementation), then there must be a task T' in p•and a trace containing both T and T' that is executable according to the specification but not in the implementation. Again, because we consider only additional input flow faults, any trace containing both T and T' and that ends up with no token in p will fail, since when the task consuming the last token in p is executed, the token in p has already been consumed as often as it has been set, that task will not be enabled. Lines 6 and 7 of the algorithm ensure that such a trace will be found and run, therefore a fault with an impact when p is marked will be caught. Finally, the fault might have no impact when p is marked, but if there is another way to enable T without marking p, via some trace S″ then T would not be enabled when S″is executed. Line 9 and 10 of the algorithm address this case.*

4.3 Testing for Additional Output Flow Faults

The fault of an additional output flow to an existing place might enable a task when that task should not be enabled. Detecting this type of faults is more difficult than additional input flows, and we cannot do it in polynomial time even in the absence of other types of fault.

When considering additional output flows, additional tokens may be placed anywhere in the system every time a task is executed. Thus, any trace may now mark any set of places anywhere in the net, so we cannot have any strategy beyond trying everything. This is illustrated in Figure 9, with two additional output flows, one from $T3$ to p and one from $T5$ to p'. Neither $T3$ nor $T5$ are prerequisite to $T11$, so to exhibit the problem requires executing tasks that are unrelated to the problem's location, namely $T3$ and $T5$. Both $T3$ and $T5$ are branching from a choice, and of the 4 possible combinations of choices, there is only one combination that leads to the detection of the problem. For detecting an arbitrary set of additional output flow faults, it is therefore necessary to execute traces for all possible combination of choices.

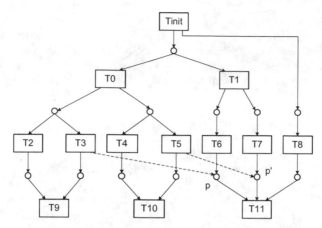

Fig. 9. Additional output flow faults: the additional output flows from *T3* to *p* and from *T5* to *p'* can be detected only if these two tasks are included in the trace

Because of these difficulties, we cannot suggest a polynomial algorithm for these types of faults.

5 Conclusion

In this paper, we look at the question of conformance testing when the model is provided in the form of a k-safe Petri Net. We first provide a general framework for testing whether an implementation conforms to a specification which is given in the form of a k-safe Petri Nets. The types of errors that we consider in this paper include faults of missing or additional flows (inputs to, or outputs from tasks). We provide two general, but inefficient algorithms for testing these faults; they lead in general to test suites of exponential length. The first one is derived from methods originally developed for state machines, while the second one, slightly more efficient but still exponential, is specific to Petri Nets. We then identify special types of faults for which polynomial test suites can be provided when free-choice Petri Nets are considered.

Acknowledgments. This work has been supported in part by grants from the Natural Sciences and Engineering Research Council of Canada.

References

[1] Lee, D., Yannakakis, M.: Principles and methods of testing finite state machines – a survey. Proceedings of the IEEE 84(8), 1089–1123 (1996)

[2] Luo, G., Dssouli, R., Bochmann, G.v., Ventakaram, P., Ghedamsi, A.: Generating synchronizable test sequences based on finite state machines with distributed ports. In: IFIP Sixth International Workshop on Protocol Test Systems, Pau, France, September 1993, pp. 53–68 (1993)

[3] Chen, J., Hierons, R.M., Ural, H.: Resolving observability problems in distributed test architectures. In: Wang, F. (ed.) FORTE 2005. LNCS, vol. 3731, pp. 219–232. Springer, Heidelberg (2005)

[4] von Bochmann, G., Haar, S., Jard, C., Jourdan, G.-V.: Testing Systems Specified as Partial Order Input/Output Automata. In: Suzuki, K., Higashino, T., Ulrich, A., Hasegawa, T. (eds.) TestCom/FATES 2008. LNCS, vol. 5047, pp. 169–183. Springer, Heidelberg (2008)

[5] Murata, T.: Petri nets: Properties, analysis and applications. Proceedings of the IEEE 77(4), 541–580 (1989)

[6] van der Aalst, W., Weijters, T., Maruster, L.: Workflow mining: discovering process models from event logs. IEEE Transactions on Knowledge and Data Engineering 16(9), 1128–1142 (2004)

[7] Bhateja, P., Gastin, P., Mukund, M.: A Fresh Look at Testing for Asynchronous Communication. In: Graf, S., Zhang, W. (eds.) ATVA 2006. LNCS, vol. 4218, pp. 369–383. Springer, Heidelberg (2006)

[8] Bhateja, P., Gastin, P., Mukund, M., Kumar, K.N.: Local Testing of Message Sequence Charts Is Difficult. In: Csuhaj-Varjú, E., Ésik, Z. (eds.) FCT 2007. LNCS, vol. 4639, pp. 76–87. Springer, Heidelberg (2007)

[9] Haar, S.: Law and Partial Order. Nonsequential Behaviour and Probability in Asynchronous Systems. In: Habilitation à diriger les recherches, INRIA (2008),
     http://www.lsv.ens-cachan.fr/~haar/HDR.pdf

[10] Zhu, H., He, X.: A methodology of testing high-level Petri nets. Information and Software Technology 44(8), 473–489 (2002)

[11] Desel, J., Esparza, J.: Free choice Petri nets. Cambridge Tracts In Theoretical Computer Science 40 (1995) ISBN:0-521-46519-2

[12] Cheng, A., Esparza, J., Palsberg, J.: Complexity results for 1-safe nets. Theoretical Computer Science 147(1-2), 117–136 (1995)

[13] Fujiwara, S., Bochmann, G.v., Khendek, F., Amalou, M., Ghedamsi, A.: Test selection based on finite state models. IEEE Transactions on Software Engineering 17(6), 591–603 (1991)

[14] Luo, G., Petrenko, A., Bochmann, G.v.: Selecting test sequences for partially-specified nondeterministic finite state machines. In: Proc. of the International Workshop on Protocol Test Systems (IWPTS 1994), Tokyo, Japan, November, 1994, pp. 95–110 (1994)

[15] Tan, Q.M., Petrenko, A., Bochmann, G.v.: Checking experiments with labeled transition systems for trace equivalence. In: Proc. IFIP 10th Intern. Workshop on Testing of Communication Systems (IWTCS 1997), Cheju Island, Korea (1997)

Implementing MSC Tests with Quiescence Observation

Sergiy Boroday[1], Alexandre Petrenko[1], and Andreas Ulrich[2]

[1] Centre de recherche informatique de Montreal (CRIM), 550 Sherbrooke West,
Suite 100 Montreal, Quebec, Canada
Sergiy.Boroday@crim.ca, Alexandre.Petrenko@crim.ca
[2] Siemens AG, Corporate Technology, CT SE 1, 80200 Munich, Germany
Andreas.Ulrich@siemens.com

Abstract. Given a test scenario as a Message Sequence Chart (MSC), a method for implementing an MSC test in a distributed asynchronous environment is suggested. Appropriate test coordination is achieved using coordinating messages and observed quiescence of a system under test. A formal definition and a classification of faults with respect to the test scenario are introduced. It is shown that the use of quiescence observation improves the fault detection and allows implementing sound tests for a wider class of test scenarios than before.

Keywords: Distributed testing, Message Sequence Charts, sound tests, test implementations, fault detection power.

1 Introduction

With the recent trend towards multi-core processing, multithreading, and system-on-chip development as well as the emergence of Web services and service oriented architecture, asynchronous communication paradigms, concurrency, and distribution become mainstream in software development. This trend poses high strains on the testing process that needs to deal with the concurrent and distributed nature of such systems.

Various proprietary and open-source platforms for distributed testing have emerged in diverse application areas. While quite a variety of programming and scripting languages are used in the testing domain, including TTCN-3, an internationally standardized testing language, a common choice for designing and visualizing tests is the use of Message Sequence Charts (MSC) and derivatives, such as UML2 Sequence Diagrams [5, 6, 9].

Development of supporting tools for distributed testing faces a number of technical challenges. One of them is the fact that test components of the tester have often to be deployed in different environments. However, in our opinion, the major obstacle limiting the success of distributed testing is the lack of a solid theoretical foundation and efficient distributed test generation algorithms and tools.

In this paper, we study the problem of implementing a test derived from a test scenario specification described by an MSC. We focus on a distributed asynchronous environment to run tests, where several independent test components communicate with the system under test (SUT) and between themselves via FIFO channels. The

M. Núñez et al. (Eds.): TESTCOM/FATES 2009, LNCS 5826, pp. 49–65, 2009.

contributions in this paper are twofold. First, a classification of faults that characterize the faulty functional behavior of a distributed system at its external interfaces is proposed. Second, we elaborate a way of observing the SUT quiescence in order to increase the fault detection power of the implemented tests, thus improving previous work in this respect. Based on the suggested classification, the fault detection power of the presented test implementation algorithms is determined.

Section 2 introduces the problem of distributed testing and discusses briefly the related work. Afterwards, the theoretical foundations of the proposed approach, which is based on the poset theory, are laid down in Section 3. In Section 4, the problem of soundness of test implementations is addressed and an algorithm for obtaining a sound test implementation from a given test scenario is elaborated. Section 5 introduces a systematic analysis of distributed system faults resulting in an improved algorithm with a higher and defined degree of fault detection power. Section 6 concludes the paper.

2 The Distributed Testing Problem

Given a distributed system, hereafter called SUT, we assume that a test system is also distributed, executing tests by several cooperating test components, which access different ports/channels of the SUT. All the communications are assumed to be bidirectional, asynchronous and use unbounded FIFO channels. We consider that a test specification is available as an MSC describing the expected order of test and SUT events in a particular test scenario. Thus, test specifications contain no explicit verdicts, which are produced by a designated Master Test Component (MTC). The verdict *pass* should indicate that no error in the SUT has been detected when a given test is executed, namely, that all the expected test events (and only them) have occurred in a correct order. Errors in the SUT manifest themselves as violations of these conditions and should trigger the verdict *fail*. Note that sometimes other verdicts, such as *inconclusive*, are also considered, e.g., within the *ptk* tool [3].

The main challenge in implementing a test specification is to ensure that all the test events are executed in the right order, especially if test components run concurrently and in a distributed way. To address this problem, a proper coordination between test components has to be added to obtain a test implementation. The test engineer can be relieved from solving this task manually by tools that automate the transformation of a test specification into a test implementation with a required coordination. With a proper coordination of test components a test implementation becomes sound, i.e., it avoids false positives (false alarms), when a correct SUT is considered to be faulty by a flawed test implementation; moreover, coordination can improve fault detection, i.e., reduce the number of false negatives. The problem of soundness is important because false positives produced due to ill-conceived coordination can confuse the test engineer and discourage her from further using the test tool. The fault detection power of a test is equally important; although detection of all the possible faults is hardly feasible in distributed testing as shown later. Devising coordination mechanisms in test implementations such that they are sound and have a guaranteed fault detection capability especially when communication delays may mask SUT faults is the main subject of this paper.

Major work on the generation of distributed tests that has been reported previously is given in [1, 2, 3]. The proposed algorithms can deal only with a subclass of distributed test specifications. While the problem of guaranteeing the detection of deviations of the observed behavior from the expected behavior is resolved with the assumption of negligible latency of coordinating messages compared to SUT messages [2], we propose a different solution based on the assumption of the availability of a *null* event (a timeout which suffices for the SUT or test component to send and receive messages over FIFO channels). This event occurrence is interpreted as the observation of the SUT quiescence and is used to resolve races. A designated quiescence observation output was previously used in automata-theoretical testing theories, see, e.g., [15]. An MSC adaptation of the automata based testing approach with quiescence is suggested in the context of centralized testing [17].

The problems of soundness of test implementation and fault detection, formalized in this paper resemble the controllability and observability problems encountered in distributed FSM-based testing [16].

Fault detection in distributed systems is discussed in [7], where the expected behavior is modeled by a partial order input/output automaton which can be viewed as an HMSC. While the work [7] focuses on the generation of several tests to discover faults in implementations of a given transition, we aim to obtain a single test implementation for a test scenario given as an MSC and target the necessary coordination among test components. If several test scenarios are given then we assume that they are mutually output (or verdict) consistent [18].

The work in [10] discusses the synthesis of concurrent state machines from an MSC. The authors consider an MSC scenario description as a closed system (complete MSC). Thus, their contribution is more relevant to the system design process than to the test process. The main difference here is that from the provided scenario a part that represents the test specification (incomplete MSC) has to be extracted before an implementation can be synthesized. It turns out that the test synthesis algorithms are quite different from the algorithms that synthesize the complete, i.e., closed, system. A similar work that considers the behavior model synthesis from scenarios as closed systems can be found in [13].

The authors of [12] present another method to generate tests from UML models using the TGV tool. The obtained tests are represented by input/output transition systems, which can then be transformed into sequence diagrams. In our work, we avoid such an intermediate representation of tests and are more concerned with races and fault detection in the resulting test implementations.

3 A Poset Theoretical Framework for Analyzing Distributed Tests

3.1 Posets

A *binary relation* ρ over a ground set E is a subset of $E \times E$. A transitive closure of ρ is the smallest transitive relation $[\rho]$ over E that contains ρ. A (strict) *partial order* over a set E is an irreflexive transitive and anti-symmetric binary relation over E. A *poset* is a pair of a set E and a partial order over this set.

Two elements e_1 and e_2 of a poset $(E, <)$ are *incomparable* if neither $e_1 < e_2$ nor $e_2 < e_1$. In the context of distributed systems, incomparable elements represent concurrent events. A poset element e_1 *immediately* precedes (follows) another element e_2 if $e_1 < e_2$ ($e_2 < e_1$) and there exists no $e \in P$ such that $e_1 < e < e_2$ ($e_2 < e < e_1$).

A *cover relation* of a partial order is the minimal relation, the transitive closure of which equals the partial order.

A poset $P_1 = (E_1, <_1)$ is called the *restriction* of the poset $P_2 = (E_2, <_2)$ onto E, and denoted $P_2 \downarrow E$, if E_1 is the restriction of E_2 onto E, i.e., $E_1 = E_2 \cap E$ and $<_1$ is the restriction of $<_2$ onto $E_1 \times E_1$, i.e., $<_1 = <_2 \cap E \times E$.

A poset $P_1 = (E, <_1)$ is *finer* than a poset $P_2 = (E, <_2)$ if $<_1 \supseteq <_2$, that is the former partial order contains the latter partial order. In this case, we also say that P_2 is *coarser* than P_1. Note that one poset can be finer or coarser than another poset only if both share the same ground set. A total order that is finer than a given poset is a *linearization* of the given poset. Given a set E, a poset $P_1 = (E_1, <_1)$ is *finer* than a poset $P_2 = (E_2, <_2)$ *on* E if the restriction of P_1 onto E is finer than the restriction of P_2 onto E.

3.2 Messages, Events, and MSCs

An MSC describes message exchange in terms of message send and receive events. Beside these communication events, events not related to the message exchange are sometimes considered too, and are called *local* events.

Given a set of all possible messages, we associate each message m with two distinct events, send of the message $!m$ and the corresponding receive $?m$. Broadcast is not allowed, that is one send event is always matched with exactly one receive event. Thus, send-receive matching is a bijective mapping of sends into receives. This matching is also understood as a send-receive precedence partial order, *match,* where each send precedes the matching receive.

An *MSC* is a collection of pairwise disjoint event posets, called here *local* posets, such that no matching send and receive belong to the same local poset. Each local poset represents the behavior of an MSC instance/liveline. The partial orders of the local posets are referred to as *local* orders.

Thus, the MSC considered in this paper can describe complex concurrent behavior usually visualized with parallel expressions or co-regions, but not branching (alternatives), cycling, or timed behavior.

Here we introduce a designated local event, called *null*. The null event models observation of quiescence, which is usually implemented in practice with a sufficiently long timer. The left-hand part of Fig. 1 shows an MSC, where a timer start and timeout indicate the absence of events at T_1 during 10 time units. With a dotted arrow we show that if time progresses at the same rate for all the instances, the occurrence of a timeout on one instance can have implications on the timing of events on another component.

In this paper, we in fact assume that time does progress at the same rate for all the instances and rely on this assumption in interpreting null events. We represent in MSC timer start and timeout events as a single local null event, as shown in Fig. 1 on the right. The formal meaning of the null event is explained later.

We allow an MSC to be incomplete, namely, some sends or receives do not necessarily have counterparts. In this work, MSCs are used in the context of testing. Thus,

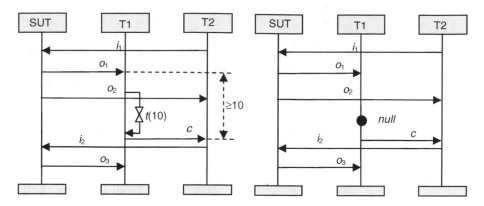

Fig. 1. An MSC with a null event

for simplicity, we assume that in a complete MSC, there is one distinguished instance SUT that represents the behavior of the system under test, while all the other instances represent test components. The messages which neither originate from nor arrive to an SUT are called *coordinating* messages.

3.3 Causal Order, Enforceable Order, and Races of MSCs

We recall the notions of a causal order and a race of an MSC. Let E be a set of all the events of an MSC M. The MSC M is called *consistent* (in asynchronous semantics) if there exists a partial order which is finer than the send-receive precedence partial order *match* on the set E as well as the local orders, and which respects FIFO ordering condition, meaning that if two send events of an instance are ordered in this partial order, then the matching receive events of the same instance are similarly ordered. The coarsest partial order on the set E, which satisfies the above conditions, is called the *causal* order $<_M$, forming with E the *causal* poset of the MSC. If the above partial order does not exist, MSC M is *inconsistent*.

A race occurs between events which are ordered in the MSC, but this order is not enforceable. The *enforceable* partial order of a consistent MSC M is the coarsest partial order which is finer than the send-receive precedence partial order *match* and which respects FIFO ordering condition, ordering of an event and a later send or local (i.e., null) event of the same instance.

Unlike the causal order, the enforceable order describes only the ordering which could be guaranteed in a distributed system [4]. For instance, it is impossible to enforce the order of consecutive receives of the messages sent by different instances, since channel delays are a property of channels and not the receiving instance. Thus, an MSC M contains a *race* when its enforceable partial order differs from the causal order $<_M$, otherwise it is *race-free* [4].

3.4 Causal Order, Enforceable Order, and Races of MSCs with Null Events

Now we consider MSCs which can have designated null events, which do not occur on the SUT instance. Informally, a null event models a delay sufficient for the SUT to become quiescent (stable) and all messages in transit to arrive. As we show later, assuming that all the SUT messages arrive before the null event occurs allows us to build simpler test implementations than before with weaker assumptions. Our assumption implies that while the null event is technically treated as a local event, it affects ordering of events on all the other instances. Consider the example in Fig. 1. The MSC on the right-hand side of Fig. 1 is not race-free since events $?o_2$ and $?c$ are causally ordered and this ordering is not enforceable. This means that if the null event is just a usual local event, which does not satisfy the above assumption, the message o_2 may in fact arrive after c. It may happen when the latency of message o_2 exceeds a delay imposed by the null event, and the latency of the coordinating message is negligible. However, if the delay modeled by the null event at T_1 allows for all SUT messages, including o_2 to arrive, c cannot be sent before the arrival of o_2. As one can see from the diagram on the left-hand side of Fig. 1, the time interval between $!i_1$ and $?c$ is not smaller than the delay represented by the null event, unless time passes with different speed on different components, which is excluded by our assumptions. Therefore, message o_2 must arrive prior to c. Thus a null event on one instance does affect orderings of the events on other instances. This effect is formally defined as follows.

Let $<_\delta$ be the coarsest partial order over the events of an MSC M, called the *null-enforcing* order, such that

- for each send event of a message i to the SUT and each null event e_{null}, such that $!i$ $<_M e_{null}$, it holds for the matching receive event $?i$ that $?i <_\delta e_{null}$;
- for each send event $!o$ of the SUT and each null event e_{null}, if for each $!i$, $!i <_M !o$ implies $!i <_M e_{null}$ then $?o <_\delta e_{null}$;

where $<_M$ is the causal order of the MSC M.

Based on this notion, we formally introduce the causal and enforceable orders, as well as the notions of race and consistency for MSCs with null events.

The causal order of an MSC with null events is defined as for an MSC without them taking additionally into account the ordering imposed by null events. An MSC with null events is called δ-*consistent* if there exists a partial order which is finer than both the causal order $<_M$ and the null-enforcing order $<_\delta$. The coarsest partial order, which satisfies these condition is called the δ-*causal* order and denoted $<_M^\delta$. Along with the set of all the events of the MSC (including null events) it forms the δ-*causal* poset.

For a δ-consistent MSC, the δ-*enforceable* order is the coarsest partial order which is finer than both the enforceable order and null-enforcing order. An MSC with null events has a δ-*race* if its δ-enforceable order differs from the δ-causal order, otherwise the MSC is δ-*race-free*. Note that a race-free MSC is also δ-*race-free*. Indeed, δ-enforceable and δ-causal orders are both transitive closures of the union of the null-enforcing order with the enforceable and causal orders, respectively. Thus in a race-free MSC, not only enforceable and causal, but also δ-enforceable and δ-causal orders coincide.

3.5   Test Scenario, Specification, and Implementation

We consider that the process of test implementation begins when the test designer defines a test scenario, which describes the expected order of message receives and sends by the SUT and test components of a test system. We define a *test scenario* $test_{scen}$ as a complete and consistent MSC, where only one non-empty instance, called the SUT (system under test), communicates with all the other instances, constituting a *test specification* $test_{spec}$ which specifies the behavior of the test components. In other words, the test scenario MSC has neither local events nor communications between test components. In a given test scenario, $(E^{SUT}_{spec}, <^{SUT}_{spec})$ denotes the SUT instance, and $test_{spec} = \{(E^1_{spec}, <^1_{spec}), (E^2_{spec}, <^2_{spec}), ...\}$ is a test specification, where $(E^i_{spec}, <^i_{spec})$ is the specification of the i-th test component. Similarly to the preceding work, we require that each test component specification coincides with the restriction of the casual order of the test scenario onto the event set of this component.

It has to be noted that numerous testing techniques use the notion of test purpose rather than test scenario, e.g., in [1], [8]. We define a *test purpose tp* of a test scenario as a poset of events of test components $E^1_{spec} \cup E^2_{spec} \cup ...$ and the partial order $<_{tp}$ such that one event e_1 immediately precedes another event e_2 in $<_{tp}$ whenever the matching event of e_1 precedes the matching event of e_2 in $<^{SUT}_{spec}$ and either both events belong to the same test component or at least one of them is a send event. Save for consecutive receive events of different test components, the order of which is relaxed in *tp*, the test purpose mirrors $<^{SUT}_{spec}$: two events are ordered in $<_{tp}$ if and only if their matching events are similarly ordered in $<^{SUT}_{spec}$. The order of the receives of different test components is relaxed to reflect the fact that in an asynchronous distributed system, messages consecutively sent by the SUT via different channels could arrive in any order due to variable communication delays. However, other receive events of different test components still can be ordered in the test purpose by transitivity.

Thus, in our framework, a test scenario refers to the behavior of a closed system, while a test purpose refers to that of an open system, which excludes the SUT. Unlike the test specification, the test purpose describes also the order of events that belong to different test components.

It is known [1, 2, 3] that distributed tests may have races, thus in a distributed environment special implementation efforts are needed to enforce a specified order of events. Races are usually resolved by introducing additional coordinating messages. However, here we also rely on null events to construct implementations of the test specifications resolving races related to the SUT. Now we define a test implementation formally.

Let $test_{spec}$ be a test specification. A test *implementation* $test_{imp}$ of $test_{spec}$ is an MSC each instance $(E^i, <^i)$ of which represents a test component T_i such that $(E^i, <^i) \downarrow E^i_{spec} = (E^i_{spec}, <^i_{spec})$. Thus, besides the events of the test specification, the test implementation can have other events which are send and receive events of coordinating messages or null events. We use $<_{imp}^{\delta}$ to denote the δ-causal order of a test implementation. Note that since a test scenario has no null events, the causal order of a test scenario coincides with its δ-causal order.

In the rest of the paper, we suggest two algorithms for constructing test implementations and discuss their fault detection power. While the first suggested algorithm misses some faults, it has a lighter coordination mechanism and thus employs fewer coordinating messages and null events. The second algorithm extends the first one with additional coordination mechanisms in order to detect more faults (up to the maximum possible in our framework).

4 Sound Test Implementations

4.1 Soundness

Soundness is an important property of a test implementation, which, informally, means that the test implementation composes with a correct SUT without deadlocks. Thus, we introduce the following definition of MSC composition.

A (*horizontal*) *composition* $M_1 \cup M_2$ of two MSCs M_1 and M_2 with the disjoint sets of events is an MSC M that contains all the local posets of M_1 and M_2 and only them.

A test implementation $test_{imp}$ of $test_{spec}$ is *sound* with respect to the test scenario $test_{scen}$ if $test_{imp} \cup \{(E^{SUT}_{spec}, <^{SUT}_{spec})\}$ is δ-race-free.

If a δ-race occurs on the SUT, i.e., when certain SUT events are ordered causally but their order is not enforceable, then some messages can be consumed by the SUT in an order inconsistent with $test_{scen}$. If δ-race occurs on the test implementation, the actual order of events on test components could diverge from the expected one even if the SUT is correct.

When a test specification includes concurrent messages to the SUT, its implementation may either obey or eliminate such concurrency. This motivates the following definition. A test implementation $test_{imp}$ is *concurrency preserving* if whenever two SUT receive events, or an SUT receive event and an SUT send event are unordered in $<^{SUT}_{spec}$, the matching events of the test implementation are also unordered in the δ-causal order of the test implementation.

Concurrency preserving test implementations do not order concurrent send events and thus the matching SUT receive events. In other words, they do not exclude any particular linearization of SUT receive events, on which faults may occur. Moreover, such test implementations preserve their soundness during the refinement of test scenarios. We say that a test scenario $test_{scen}'$ is a *refinement* of another test scenario $test_{scen}$ if their instances share the same set of events, $<^{SUT}_{spec}'$ is finer than $<^{SUT}_{spec}$, and whenever an event immediately follows another event in $<^{SUT}_{spec}'$ but not in $<^{SUT}_{spec}$, the former event is a send event. This means that a refinement of a test scenario includes an added dependency of an SUT send event to previously concurrent send or receive events.

Proposition 1. If $test_{scen}'$ is a refinement of $test_{scen}$ then a concurrency preserving test implementation sound with respect to $test_{scen}$ is also sound with respect to $test_{scen}'$.

Hereafter, we consider test implementations which are both concurrency-preserving and sound. Obviously, if in a given test scenario, every SUT receive is ordered in $<^{SUT}_{spec}$ with respect to each other SUT event then each sound test implementation is trivially concurrency preserving. Hereafter, such a test scenario is called *input-sequential*. Most of the previous work is restricted to input-sequential test scenarios. Here, we construct sound test implementations for arbitrary test scenarios; however we claim the highest fault detection power only for test implementations derived from input-sequential test scenarios.

4.2 Generating Sound Test Implementations

To construct a test implementation of a given test specification, it is possible to use the approach proposed in [1] for input-sequential test scenarios. According to this approach, coordinating messages and co-regions are added to the test specification MSC to obtain a test implementation. Concurrency is introduced in the MSC test implementation as a co-region which contains receive events of coordinating and SUT messages. The approach effectively resolves races among these messages. The synchronization ensures that the next message to the SUT is not sent until all the expected messages are received.

The resulting test implementation is not concurrency preserving, since it always sends messages to the SUT sequentially. There are in fact some enhancements of this approach in [2, 3]. They allow concurrent events in the test scenario, but order in fact concurrent SUT receive events prior to the construction of a test implementation. Moreover, races between coordinating messages are resolved due to an additional assumption on negligible latency of coordinating messages and the use of the *inconclusive* verdict.

The work in [1] does not claim that the resulting test implementations are always sound. The reported tool relies more on the test engineer to define synchronization than on a systematic procedure. A more recent technique [2] yields sound test implementations only for a restricted class of test specifications without consecutive SUT receive events. In this case, races, called irresolvable blocking conditions in [14], cannot be resolved. Here, we use the SUT quiescence observation to solve this problem.

Consider the test scenario example with consecutive receive events in Fig. 2. The coordinating message enforces the desired order of send events in the test implementation, however, the race between the two SUT receive events remains, and thus, the test implementation is unsound. Since the test scenario only describes the behavior of the SUT when i_1 arrives before i_2, in the case when i_2 wins the race the SUT behavior is not specified. Assume that there is another scenario where the SUT in response to $?i_2$ followed by $?i_1$ produces $!o_2$ and then $!o_1$. Then the test execution with a correct SUT may proceed as shown in the right part of Fig. 2. This behavior leads to the *fail* verdict since the messages sent by the SUT arrive in the order different from what is expected by T_2. This contradicts the intuition behind soundness. Formally speaking, the composition of $(E^{SUT}_{spec}, <^{SUT}_{spec})$ and the test implementation on the left-hand part of Fig. 2 is not race-free, since, according to the definition of the causal and enforceable orders, the receive events $?i_1$ and $?i_2$ are causally ordered, but this order is not enforceable. To resolve the race it suffices to add a null event (delay) between $?c$ and $!i_2$ in T_1. This delay allows message i_1 to arrive prior to sending message i_2, or, formally, the null event follows $?i_1$ in the null-enforcing order, which contributes both to the enforceable and causal orders, thus resolving the race.

To construct concurrency preserving sound test implementations we extend the approach in [1] using null events as follows. Unlike [2, 3], to obtain concurrency preserving test implementations, concurrent SUT receive events are kept unordered. The idea is that when several messages need to be sent to the SUT concurrently by several test components, all of them have to be notified by a coordinating message by each test component as soon as it receives all the expected concurrent messages from the SUT. The notified test components send messages to the SUT only upon receiving all coordinating messages, which are treated as concurrent events. Thus ordering of

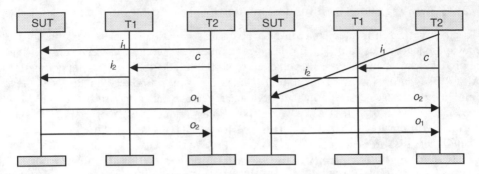

Fig. 2. Unsound test implementation and its possible execution

coordinating messages is avoided. Whenever one send event $!i$ immediately follows a send event of another test component in the test purpose tp, one test component notifies the other with a coordinating message, so the second send event occurs only after the first one. Having received the coordinating message the last test component executes the null event. This delay allows the SUT to receive all the messages just sent. If the send event $!i$ immediately follows several send events and not only one, the null event is executed only after the receive events of all the coordinating messages, preceding $!i$ in the constructed test implementation. The above discussion leads to the following algorithm.

Algorithm 1.
Input: An MSC test scenario $test_{scen}$ with the SUT specification $(E^{SUT}_{spec}, <^{SUT}_{spec})$ and test components specifications $(E^1_{spec}, <^1_{spec}), (E^2_{spec}, <^2_{spec}), \ldots$.
Output: A test implementation $test_{imp}$.

1. The initial relations $R_1, R_2, \ldots$ defining the test components $T_1, T_2, \ldots$ are the cover relations of $<^1_{spec}, <^2_{spec}, \ldots$.
2. $k := 1$.
3. Add coordinating messages c_k as follows:
   For each j and each event e of E^j_{spec}, and each $l, j \neq l$, such that some send $!i, !i \in E^l_{spec}$, immediately follows e in the test purpose tp do
   - $R_l := \{(?c_k, !i)\} \cup R_l$ for each send $!i$ of E^l_{spec}, which immediately follows e in tp;
   - $R_j := \{(e, !c_k)\} \cup R_j$;
   - $k := k + 1$.
4. $m := 1$.
5. Add null events as follows:
   For each test component j and for each send $!i$ of E^j_{spec} which immediately follows a send of another test component in tp do
   - $R_j := R_j \cup (e_{null}^m, !i)$;
   - for each non-null event e such that $(e, !i) \in R_j$, $R_j := R_j \cup (e, e_{null}^m)$;
   - $m := m + 1$.
6. Determine a transitive closure of each R_j, the resulting partial orders define the test components of the test implementation $test_{imp}$.

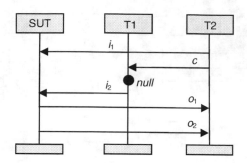

Fig. 3. A sound test implementation composed with the SUT

Proposition 2. The test implementation obtained by Algorithm 1 is sound and concurrency preserving.

The corrected, sound version of the test implementation in Fig. 2 constructed by Algorithm 1 is $\{T_1 = (\{?c, e_{null}, !i_2\}, \{(?c, !i_2), (?c, e_{null}), (e_{null}, !i_2)\}), T_2 = (\{!i_1, !c, ?o_1, ?o_2\}, \{(!i_1, !c), (!i_1, ?o_1), (!i_1, ?o_2), (!c, ?o_1), (!c, ?o_2), (?o_1, ?o_2)\})\}$. The composition of this test implementation with the SUT specification is shown in Fig. 3. Note that the event $!c$ precedes the event $?o_1$ in the causal relation of the composition of the test implementation with a correct SUT.

Concluding this section, we stress that the proposed algorithm for building test implementations ensures soundness, which is different from the related work in [1], and is applicable to a wider class of test specifications allowing consecutive SUT receive events compared to [2].

5 Fault Detection

5.1 Detectable and Undetectable Faults

While soundness is an important characteristic of a test implementation, another essential feature is its ability to detect faults. The behavior of an SUT on a sound test implementation becomes erroneous once it produces a trace of events that cannot be produced by the SUT specification $(E^{SUT}_{spec}, <^{SUT}_{spec})$ of a test scenario. Such observed errors are typically caused by faults within the SUT. Aiming at test implementations that detect as many faults as possible we formally define and classify faults as follows.

An erroneous trace contains an *output* fault if the set of events in the trace does not coincide with the set E^{SUT}_{spec} due to missing or superfluous SUT send events, which are not in E^{SUT}_{spec}. Output faults are detected by any sound test implementation since they always lead to a deadlock. To detect output faults a Master Test Component (MTC) uses a timer to identify deadlock of a test component which has not received an expected message and thus has not informed the MTC about its successful termination. Faults which occur when the SUT executes the expected send events, but in a wrong order, are more difficult to detect, since communication delays may mask such faults. Consider the example in Fig. 4, where message o_2 occurs out-of-order (left-hand: the

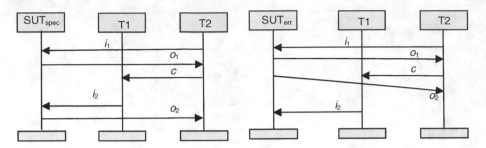

Fig. 4. Premature send event masked by a communication delay

test scenario, right-hand: the erroneous test execution). The premature SUT send event of message o_2 goes undetected with a sufficiently long delay in the channel from the SUT to the second test component.

An SUT trace $t = a_1 \ldots a_n$ over the set E^{SUT}_{spec}, where $n = |E^{SUT}_{spec}|$, has an *order* fault $a_1 \ldots a_k$, $k \le n$, with respect to the test scenario $test_{scen}$, if

- $a_1 \ldots a_{k-1}$ is a prefix of a linearization of $(E^{SUT}_{spec}, <^{SUT}_{spec})$, but $a_1 \ldots a_k$ is not; and
- $a_1 \ldots a_k \downarrow I$ is a prefix of a linearization of $(E^{SUT}_{spec}, <^{SUT}_{spec}) \downarrow I$, where I is the set of receive events in E^{SUT}_{spec}.

The event a_k of the trace is the first premature SUT event, after which a correct ordering of SUT receive events can no longer be guaranteed by a test implementation. The behavior of the SUT may become unspecified afterwards. Considering the type of the premature event in an order fault, we have the following possible violations of the order $<^{SUT}_{spec}$. An SUT send event can permute with another SUT send event or an SUT receive event, while an SUT receive event can only permute with an SUT send event, but not with an SUT receive event. The reasoning behind this is that a sound test implementation enforces the ordering of SUT receive events in $<^{SUT}_{spec}$ by ordering the matching send events accordingly. This observation leads to the following definition of three types of the order faults.

An order fault $a_1 \ldots a_k$ is

- a *swapped send* fault if a_k is a send event that follows another send event in $<^{SUT}_{spec}$;
- a *premature send* fault if a_k is a send event that follows a receive event in $<^{SUT}_{spec}$;
- a *delayed send* fault if a_k is a receive event that follows a send event in $<^{SUT}_{spec}$.

To simplify our discussion, we further assume that a trace contains just a single order fault which involves two events, a send and a receive or two send events. Depending on the number of test components executing the matching send and receive events, the order faults can occur either locally or in a distributed way. A fault is *local* if the SUT exchanges the two messages related to the events in the order fault with the same test component or *distributed* if it does so with two test components.

An order fault cannot always be detected within a trace t by a test implementation $test_{imp}$ if $test_{imp} \cup \{t\}$ has a race, since the race may be resolved in such a way that masks the fault. Recall that the soundness of $test_{imp}$ implies that $test_{imp} \cup \{(E^{SUT}_{spec},$

$<^{SUT}_{spec})\}$ is δ-race-free. Therefore, to guarantee that an order fault is discovered irrespectively of communication delays, we say that a test implementation $test_{imp}$ *detects* an order fault in the trace t if the composition $test_{imp} \cup \{t\}$ is not δ-consistent. Such inconsistency leads to a deadlock in one of the test components, yielding a *fail* verdict (via a timeout in the MTC).

Detection of a swapped send fault depends on its type. A local swapped send fault can directly be detected by the involved test component as an output fault since it receives the SUT messages via a FIFO channel. However, as already discussed above, messages consecutively sent by the SUT via different channels could arrive in any order due to variable communication delays. This implies that distributed swapped send faults cannot be detected at all.

A local delayed send fault involving the events $?i$ and $!o$ such that $!o <^{SUT}_{spec} ?i$ could be detected simply by the test component that restrains sending i until it receives o. To detect a distributed delayed send fault, a coordinating message whose send event follows the SUT receive event $?o$ and whose receive event precedes the SUT receive event $!i$ is additionally required.

A premature send fault is the only fault, whose detection requires null events. The example in Fig. 4 illustrates that an SUT with such a fault composed with a sound test implementation but without null events is a consistent MSC, and thus the fault is not detected. In an input-sequential test scenario, a local premature send fault involving the SUT events $?i$ and $!o$ such that $?i <^{SUT}_{spec} !o$ can be detected if the test component waits for any potential SUT output before actually sending event i. In other words, the test component should observe SUT quiescence by executing a null event immediately prior to the send of message i. Thus, the test component makes sure that message o is sent only in response to message i.

When a premature send fault is distributed, the matching events $!i$ and $?o$ occur in two test components, the test component which receives message o uses a null event and, additionally, coordinating messages to synchronize with other test components including one that sends message i. The coordinating messages ensure that the null event immediately precedes the send of message i. We elaborate an algorithm for implementing tests ensuring the detection of these faults in the next section.

In the case when a test scenario is not input-sequential different concurrent SUT receive events can be involved in a premature send fault. Therefore to determine which particular SUT input triggers the premature SUT send event, one needs to order all the concurrent messages to be sent by the test components. In other words, a premature send fault is not detectable by a single concurrency-preserving test implementation. Construction of several test implementations from a given test scenario is not discussed in this paper, having the goal to build a single test implementation for a given test scenario. Note that considering all potential interleavings of concurrent SUT receive events may lead to the combinatorial explosion.

5.2 Increasing Fault Detection Power of Test Implementations

Test implementations produced by Algorithm 1 clearly detect local swapped send faults. Moreover, they detect delayed send faults. Indeed, if a delayed send fault is local, it is directly observed; if distributed, Step 3 of Algorithm 1 inserts a coordinating message to detect it. We summarize these observations in the following statement.

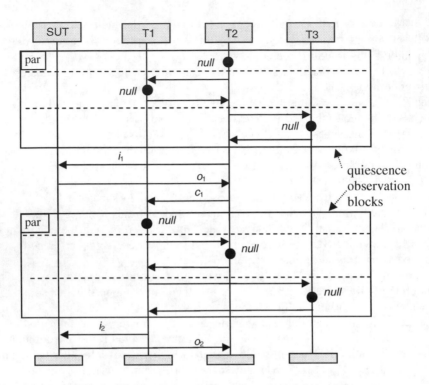

Fig. 5. A straightforward way of observing global quiescence

Proposition 3. A test implementation, generated by Algorithm 1 detects local swapped send and delayed send faults.

The detection of premature send faults cannot be guaranteed using coordinating messages only, but Algorithm 1 can be enhanced by using null events as outlined above. The idea is to check quiescence of the SUT at all test components after all expected SUT messages have been received just before sending a next message to the SUT. Such a quiescence checking ensures that the SUT is in a stable state where no further message can be produced and no message to test components remains in transit. This approach eliminates the possibility of masking an expedited send fault by communication delays. A "global" SUT quiescence should be established using null events accompanied by a proper coordination among test components. A straightforward solution consists in placing null events in all test components prior to sending a message to the SUT. The test component that sends the next message to the SUT, in this case, notifies all partner test components and collects the confirmations that the null events have occurred prior to sending the message, as shown in Fig. 5. This synchronization mechanism allows detection of all the premature send faults when the test scenario is input-sequential.

Such a straightforward approach may result in a high number of coordinating messages and null events, which can slow down test execution. The number of coordinating messages can be reduced if, prior to sending a message to the SUT, only the test components expecting to receive messages from the SUT are notified. Moreover, to reduce the number of null events, we suggest using a null event prior to this notification. In this case, there is no need to use the null events in all the test components. The suggested procedure is summarized as follows.

Algorithm 2.
Input: An MSC test scenario $test_{scen}$ with the SUT specification $(E^{SUT}_{spec}, <^{SUT}_{spec})$ and the test components specifications $(E^1_{spec}, <^1_{spec}), (E^2_{spec}, <^2_{spec}), ...$
Output: A test implementation $test_{imp}$.
1. Apply Algorithm 1.
2. For each send event $!i$ of each test component T,
   ▪ Add a null event prior to $!i$, unless it was already added in Step 3 of Algorithm 1.
   ▪ For each test component T', $T' \neq T$ with receive event(s) of SUT message(s) triggered by the message i, insert two coordinating messages, one sent from T to T' after the null event in T and another one from T' to T before the abovementioned receive event(s) of SUT message(s).

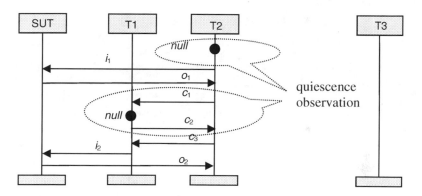

Fig. 6. A test implementation according to Algorithm 2

Compared to the test implementation obtained by Algorithm 1, the test implementation obtained by Algorithm 2 in Fig. 6 has an additional null event, followed by two coordinating messages c_2 and c_3. This allows the detection of the premature send fault due to the reordering of the events $!i_2$ and $?o_2$. The sole purpose of the coordinating message c_3 is to avoid the race between c_2 and o_2. The suggested approach is usually more economical than the straightforward one in the number of null events and coordinating messages (compare the number of null events and coordinating messages in Fig. 5 and 6). However, there is a price to pay. First, in the straightforward approach, a message sent to one test component can arrive concurrently together with the causally independent null event of another test component. In other words, null events can be viewed as a local quiescence observation. Second, the straightforward approach allows for a better diagnosis of faults. Indeed, if a test component of the test specification has no events at all, and an unexpected SUT message is detected, it is impossible to diagnose, which SUT receive event has triggered the unexpected message.

Proposition 4. Given an arbitrary test scenario, the test implementation obtained by Algorithm 2 is sound, concurrency preserving, and detects delayed send and local swapped send faults. Moreover, for an input-sequential test scenario, it also detects premature send faults.

Proposition 5. For an input-sequential test scenario the test implementation returned by Algorithm 2 has the highest fault detection power.

The last proposition holds because the only undetectable type of order faults in Algorithm 2 is a distributed swapped send fault. Table 1 summarizes the fault detection capabilities of both algorithms.

Table 1. Fault detection power of Algorithms 1 and 2

Fault classes		Algorithm 1	Algorithm 2
Output fault		✓	✓
Swapped send fault	local	✓	✓
	distributed	✗*	✗*
Premature send fault	local	✗	✓**
	distributed	✗	✓**
Delayed send fault	local	✓	✓
	distributed	✓	✓

* theoretically undetectable in an asynchronous environment
** for input-sequential test scenarios

6   Conclusions

Based on the analysis of faults in distributed systems, a novel method for distributed testing that involves the use of observable quiescence to implement MSC test specifications is proposed. Unlike the existing methods it does not eliminate concurrency in a test specification and delivers the highest possible fault detection power (according to the suggested classification). The proposed notions of soundness and faults can be also applied to evaluate other test implementations.

A prototype tool implementing the algorithms 1 and 2 is currently in preparation. The tool development concerns representing test implementations in Promela to allow for model checking and simulation as well as mapping the Promela test implementation into various test execution languages. On the theoretical side, we currently consider generalization of the framework to use pomsets in defining test specifications and investigate other algorithms for distributed testing with a known fault detection power. For example, it is known that races can be compensated by input queues [4, 11]. The explicit use of such queues could result in simplified test implementations with a similar fault detection power compared to the algorithms presented here. This area however is subject of further research.

References

1. Grabowski, J., Koch, B., Schmitt, M., Hogrefe, D.: SDL and MSC Based Test Generation for Distributed Test Architectures. In: SDL Forum 1999, pp. 389–404 (1999)
2. Baker, P., Bristow, P., Jervis, C., King, D., Mitchell, B.: Automatic Generation of Conformance Tests from Message Sequence Charts. In: Sherratt, E. (ed.) SAM 2002. LNCS, vol. 2599, pp. 170–198. Springer, Heidelberg (2003)
3. Mitchell, W.: Characterizing Concurrent Tests Based on Message Sequence Chart Requirements. In: Applied Telecommunication Workshop, pp. 135–140 (2001)
4. Holzmann, G., Peled, D., Redberg, M.: Design Tools for Requirement Engineering. Bell Labs Technical J. 2(1), 86–95 (1997)
5. OMG UML Specification, http://www.omg.org/spec/UML/2.1.2/
6. Haugen, Ø.: Comparing UML 2.0 interactions and MSC-2000. In: Amyot, D., Williams, A.W. (eds.) SAM 2004. LNCS, vol. 3319, pp. 69–84. Springer, Heidelberg (2004)
7. von Bochmann, G., Haar, S., Jard, C., Jourdan, G.-V.: Testing Systems Specified as Partial Order Input/Output Automata. In: Suzuki, K., Higashino, T., Ulrich, A., Hasegawa, T. (eds.) TestCom/FATES 2008. LNCS, vol. 5047, pp. 169–183. Springer, Heidelberg (2008)
8. Deussen, P.H., Tobies, S.: Formal Test Purposes and the Validity of Test Cases. In: Peled, D.A., Vardi, M.Y. (eds.) FORTE 2002. LNCS, vol. 2529, pp. 114–129. Springer, Heidelberg (2002)
9. Pickin, S., Jézéquel, J.-M.: Using UML Sequence Diagrams as the Basis for a Formal Test Description Language. In: Boiten, E.A., Derrick, J., Smith, G.P. (eds.) IFM 2004. LNCS, vol. 2999, pp. 481–500. Springer, Heidelberg (2004)
10. Alur, R., Etessami, K., Yannakakis, M.: Inference of Message Sequence Charts. IEEE Trans. on Soft. Eng. 29(7), 623–633 (2003)
11. Mitchell, B.: Resolving Race Conditions in Asynchronous Partial Order Scenarios. IEEE Trans. on Soft. Eng. 31(9), 767–784 (2005)
12. Pickin, S., Jard, C., Jeron, T., Jézéquel, J.-M., Le Traon, Y.: Test Synthesis from UML Models of Distributed Software. IEEE Trans. on Soft. Eng. 33(4), 252–268 (2007)
13. Uchitel, S., Brunet, G., Chechik, M.: Behaviour Model Synthesis from Properties and Scenarios. In: 29th IEEE/ACM International Conf. on Soft. Eng., pp. 34–43 (2007)
14. Baker, P., Bristow, P., King, D., Thomson, R., Burton, S., Bristow, P.: Detecting and Resolving Semantic Pathologies in UML Sequence Diagrams. In: ESEC/SIGSOFT FSE, pp. 50–59 (2005)
15. Tretmans, J.: Test Generation with Inputs, Outputs and Repetitive Quiescence. Software - Concepts and Tools 17(3), 103–120 (1996)
16. Cacciari, L., Rafiq, O.: Controllability and Observability in Distributed Testing. Information and Soft. Technology. 41(11-12), 767–780 (1999)
17. Lund, M.S., Stolen, K.: Deriving Tests from UML. 2.0 Sequence Diagrams with neg and assert. In: 1st International Workshop on Automation of Soft. Testing, pp. 22–28 (2006)
18. Boroday, S., Petrenko, A., Ulrich, A.: Test Suite Consistency Verification. In: 6th IEEE East-West Design & Test Symposium (EWDTS 2008), pp. 235–238 (2008)

Testing Timed Finite State Machines with Guaranteed Fault Coverage

Khaled El-Fakih[1], Nina Yevtushenko[2,*], and Hacene Fouchal[3]

[1] American University of Sharjah, PO Box 26666, UAE
kelfakih@aus.edu
[2] Tomsk State University, 36 Lenin Str., Tomsk, 634050, Russia
ninayevtushenko@yahoo.com
[3] Univ. Antilles Guyane, Guadeloupe, France
Hacene.Fouchal@univ-ag.fr

Abstract. A method is presented for deriving test suites with the guaranteed fault coverage for deterministic possibly partial Timed Finite State Machines (TFSMs). TFSMs have integer boundaries for time guards and the time reset operation at every transition; for TFSM implementations the upper bound on the number of states is known as well as the largest finite boundary and the smallest duration of time guards. We consider two fault models and present corresponding techniques for deriving complete test suites. In the first fault model inputs can be applied at integer time instances while in the second fault model time instances can be rational. The derivation method for integer time instances is extended to the case when the number of states of an implementation under test can be larger than the number of states of the given specification.

1 Introduction

Many conformance test derivation methods are based on a specification given in the form of a Finite State Machine (FSM), such as W [3], [15], partial W (Wp) [6], HIS [12], [13], [16] and the H [4] test derivation methods. For surveys see [2], [9]. In FSM-based testing, one usually assumes that the specification and an Implementation Under Test (IUT) can be modeled as FSMs. An IUT is faulty if it has a behavior different than the behavior of the given specification. Two types of implementation faults are usually considered, namely output faults and transfer faults. Each test derivation method mentioned above provides the following fault coverage guarantee under the assumption that the upper bound on the number of states of an IUT is known: If an FSM IUT with at most m states and a given (reduced) specification FSM has n states, $m \geq n$, a test suite can be derived by the method and the IUT will only pass this test suite if and only if it conforms to the specification, i.e. it does not contain any output nor transfer faults. In many cases, one assumes that $m = n$.

Many systems such as telecommunication systems, plant and traffic controllers and others are written using models with time constraints, and thus, a number of papers

* The second author acknowledges a partial support by the FCP Russian Program, contract 02.514.12.4002.

M. Núñez et al. (Eds.): TESTCOM/FATES 2009, LNCS 5826, pp. 66–80, 2009.

consider test derivation for timed automata and Timed Finite State Machines (TFSMs). Almost all proposed methods are based on deriving from a given timed automaton (or timed FSM) an untimed FSM and then applying FSM-based test derivation methods for the obtained FSM. For example, Springintveld et al. [14] proposed a rigorous strategy for deriving a complete test suite for a timed automaton. The authors show that under the assumption that the specification and an IUT have deterministic behavior and the upper bound on the number of time regions of an IUT is known a complete test suite can be derived using the well known W-method [3]. The main idea behind the approach is to divide time into very small grids such that to assure that each input is applied at some time instance of each time region of each IUT. The same grids are used for all states and inputs. The method proposed in [14] is not practical since it returns test suites with huge length; however, the method has theoretic significance as it demonstrates that there exists an opportunity to derive test suites with the guaranteed fault coverage for timed FSMs without explicit enumeration of all possible implementations. Many papers inherit the idea proposed in [14]; for example the work in [5] extends the method to non-deterministic behaviors. Recently, Merayo et al. [8], [10] proposed a timed possibly non-deterministic FSM model. Time constrains limit a time elapsed when an output has to be produced after an input has been applied to the FSM. When an output is produced the clock variable is reset to zero. The model also takes into account time-outs; if no input is applied at a current state for some time-out period, the (timed) FSM moves from current state to another state using a time-out function. Another timed FSM model is used in [7]. However, [10] and [7] do not consider test derivation, namely, the authors in [8], [10] establish a number of conformance relations and the authors in [7] propose methods for distinguishing timed non-deterministic FSMs. Test derivation for stochastic non-deterministic timed FSMs is considered in [8]. A method has been reported in [18] for generating timed test cases from the model of timed transition systems. For a more detailed review of the above papers and other relevant methods the reader may refer to [5], [8], [14]. We note that many test derivation methods are proposed for timed systems based on simulation relations and thus these methods are not considered in this paper.

In this paper, we consider the TFSM model from [7] and show how a complete test suite can be derived under various test assumptions. We use the same idea as in [14] about the known number of time regions; however, our TFSMs can be partial and thus, time instances when inputs are applied to IUT depend also on the current state of the specification. In other words, different grids are used for different states and inputs. In particular, we consider deterministic possibly partial timed FSMs (TFSMs) where time constraints are used to limit time elapsed at states and we also use one clock variable that is reset at every transition. We consider two fault models and propose corresponding test derivation methods with the guaranteed fault coverage (i.e. methods that derive tests that detect every faulty IUT w.r.t the assumed fault model) More precisely, in the first model, we consider TFSMs with integer boundaries and implementations with the known upper bound on the number of states, known largest finite boundary, and given smallest duration of time guards. In this case timed inputs are applied to an IUT at discrete (integer) time instances. In the second fault model, input time instances can be rational (i.e. continuous). For each considered fault model we propose a complete test derivation technique for the case when the number m of states of an IUT equals the number n of states of the specification TFSM. The technique with integer time instances is adapted to the case when $m > n$. Our methods are based on the HIS method [12], [13], [16] which is an adaptation of the W method for partial, possibly non-reduced FSMs. In particular, we extend the HIS method by defining appropriate fault models and test derivation algorithms for TFSMs.

This paper is organized as follows. Section 2 includes relevant definitions and notations and Section 3 includes test derivation methods for the cases when $m = n$ and $m > n$ for systems with discrete time inputs and a test derivation method for case $m = n$ for systems with continuous time inputs. Section 4 concludes the paper.

2 Preliminaries

In this section, we introduce the notion of a timed Finite State Machine (TFSM) [7] and some other notions and notations used in the paper.

Definition 1. An FSM S is a 5-tuple $(S, I, O, \lambda_S, s_0)$, where S, I, and O are finite sets of states, inputs and outputs, respectively, s_0 is the initial state and $\lambda_S \subseteq S \times I \times O \times S$ is a transition relation.

A timed possibly non-deterministic and partial FSM (TFSM) is an FSM annotated with a *clock*, a time reset operation and time guards associated with transitions. The clock t is a real number that measures the time delay at a state and the time reset operation resets the value of the clock t to zero after the execution of a transition. A time guard g_i describes the time domain when a transition can be executed and is given in the form $\lceil min, max \rceil$, where $\lceil \in \{(, [\}, \rceil \in \{),]\}$ and min and max are non-negative integers such that $min \leq max$. When $min = max$ we consider the interval $[min, min] = \{min\}$. An output delay describes the time domain when an output has to be produced after an input is applied and is also given in the form $\lceil min, max \rceil$ over integer bounds min and max where $min \leq max$. Here we assume that the time reset operation is specified at every transition of a given TFSM.

Definition 2. A timed FSM (TFSM) S often called simply *a machine* throughout the paper, is a 5-tuple $(S, I, O, \lambda_S, s_0)$; the transition relation $\lambda_S \subseteq S \times I \times O \times S \times \Pi \times \aleph$ where Π is the set of time guards and $\aleph$ is the set of output delay intervals over $[0, \infty)$. The behavior of a TFSM S can be described as follows. If $(s, i, o, s', g_i = \lceil min, max \rceil, g_o = \lceil min', max' \rceil) \in S \times I \times O \times S \times \Pi \times \aleph$, we say that TFSM S when being at state s and accepting input i at time t satisfying the time guard $t \in \lceil min, max \rceil$, responds (after the input i has been applied) with output o within the time delay specified in g_o and moves to the state s'. The clock is reset to zero and starts advancing at s'.

A zero output delay, i.e. $g_o = [0, 0]$, indicates that the output is produced instantly at the time when the input is applied. For simplicity, for a transition with $g_o = [0, 0]$ and input guard g_i over $[0, \infty)$, we omit g_o and g_i from the description of the transition. Thus, a transition (s, i, o, s') indicates that being at state s and accepting input i at any time, S responds with output o instantly when i is applied. In this paper, we check only functional equivalence [10] between TFSMs and thus, we do not consider output delays. In other words, in this paper, the transition relation is a 5-tuple, $\lambda_S \subseteq S \times I \times O \times S \times \Pi$.

Given a TFSM $S = (S, I, O, \lambda_S, s_0)$, for every pair $(s, i) \in S \times I$, we use $\Pi_{(s,\,i)}$ to denote the collection of the guards g_i over all transitions $(s, i, o, s', g_i) \in \lambda_S$. If there is no transition $(s, i, o, s', g_i) \in \lambda_S$ then, by definition, $\Pi_{(s,\,i)}$ is the empty set. The notion of $\Pi_{(s,\,i)}$ is very close to the notion of time regions [1]; however, these regions are different for different states and inputs. The latter allows to check transitions with the same input at different states at different time instances.

Given a transition $(s, i, o_1, s', \lceil min, max \rceil) \in \lambda_S$, we refer to $max - min$ as to the *duration* of the time guard of the transition. Moreover, the largest finite boundary, denoted B_S or B, over all guards of all transitions is called the *largest boundary* of the TFSM.

The machine S is (time) *deterministic* if for each two transitions $(s, i, o, s, \lceil min_1, max_1 \rceil)$, $(s, i, o', s', \lceil min_2, max_2 \rceil) \in \lambda_S$, it holds that $\lceil min_1, max_1 \rceil \cap \lceil min_2, max_2 \rceil = \varnothing$; otherwise, the machine S is (time) *non-deterministic*.

The TFSM S is *input enabled* if the underlying FSM is complete, i.e., if for each pair $(s, i) \in S \times I$, λ_S has a transition $(s, i, o, s', \lceil min, max \rceil)$.

The TFSM S is *complete* if the underlying FSM is complete and for each pair $(s, i) \in S \times I$ of TFSM S, the union of time guards over all transitions $(s, i, o, s', \lceil min, max \rceil) \in \lambda_S$ equals to $[0, \infty)$; otherwise, the machine is called *partial*. Given a complete TFSM, the behavior of the TFSM is defined at each state for each input that can be applied at any time instance in $[0, \infty)$. In this paper, we consider only deterministic but possibly partial TFSMs.

Definition 3. Given a TFSM $S = (S, I, O, \lambda_S, s_0)$, a pair (i, t), $i \in I$ and t is a non-negative rational, is a *timed input* that states that an input i is applied at time t.

Definition 4. Given a TFSM S, a sequence over the input (output) alphabet is called an *input* (*output*) sequence. A sequence $(i_1, t_1) \ldots (i_l, t_l)$ of timed inputs is a *timed input* sequence. A timed input sequence $\alpha = (i_1, t_1) \ldots (i_l, t_l)$ is *defined* for TFSM S at state s if the TFSM has a sequence of transitions $(s_j, i_j, o_j, s_{j+1}, g_j)$ such that $s_1 = s$ and for each $j = 1, \ldots, l$, it holds that $t_j \in g_j$. The set of all defined timed sequences at state s is denoted $\Omega_S(s)$ while denoting Ω_S the set of defined timed input sequences at the initial state, for short. The corresponding output sequence $o_1 \ldots o_l$ is denoted as $out_S(s, \alpha)$. As usual, we say that the pair $(\alpha, out_S(s, \alpha))$ *takes* the machine S from state s to state s_{l+1}. A pair "timed_input_sequence_α/output_sequence_ $out_S(s, \alpha)$" is a *timed I/O sequence* or a *timed trace* of S at state s. For a deterministic TFSM, given state s and a timed input sequence $\alpha \in \Omega_S(s)$, s_α is the state in the TFSM reached by the sequence α. We also say that α *takes* the TFSM to state s_α. Given a state s of a deterministic TFSM and a timed input (i, t) defined at s, the (i, t) successor of state s is the state reached by applying (i, t) at state s.

By the above definition, given a defined timed input sequence $\alpha = (i_1, t_1) \ldots (i_l, t_l)$, we assume that the sequence α is applied to the FSM in the following way. The input i_1 is applied at the time instance t_1; for each j, $1 < j \le l$, the input i_j is applied at the time instance t_j while time starts advancing from 0 after the output has been produced to the input i_{j-1}.

Consider TFSM S shown in Fig. 1 shown below with three states named 1 (initial state), 2, and 3, and defined over the input alphabet $\{i_1, i_2\}$ and over the output alphabet

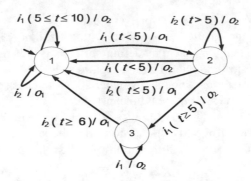

Fig. 1. TFSM S

$\{o_1, o_2, o_3\}$. TFSM S is partial and deterministic. The collection of guards $\Pi_{(1, i1)}$ equals $\{[0,5), [5, 10]\}$, $\Pi_{(1, i2)} = \{ [0, \infty)\}$, $\Pi_{(2, i1)} = \{[0, 5), [5, \infty)\}$, $\Pi_{(2, i2)} = \{ [0, 5], (5, \infty)\}$, $\Pi_{(3, i1)} = \{[0, \infty)\}$, and $\Pi_{(3, i2)} = \{[6, \infty)\}$. The largest finite boundary $B = 10$.

The set of all timed traces of S at state s is denoted $TTr_S(s)$, also denoted TTr_S for short if s is the initial state of S. As usual, the TFSM S is *initially connected* if for each state s, there exists a timed trace that can take the machine from the initial state to state s.

As usual, the behavior of two TFSMs can be compared using their intersection. The intersection of two TFSMs S and P is not defined at state sp for a timed input (i, t) when S and P at states s and p produce disjoint sets of outputs to this timed input.

Definition 5. Given TFSMs S and P, the *intersection* $S \cap P$ is the largest connected submachine of the TFSM $(S \times P, I, O, \lambda_{S \cap P}, s_0 p_0)$ where $(sp, i, o, s'p', \lceil min_1, max_1 \rceil) \in \lambda_{S \cap P}$ if there are transitions $(s, i, o, s', \lceil min_2, max_2 \rceil) \in \lambda_S$ and $(p, i, o, p', \lceil min_3, max_3 \rceil \in \lambda_P$ s.t. $\lceil min_2, max_2 \rceil \cap \lceil min_3, max_3 \rceil \neq \emptyset$ and $\lceil min_1, max_1 \rceil = \lceil min_2, max_2 \rceil \cap \lceil min_3, max_3 \rceil$.

Definition 6. State s of TFSM S and p of TFSM P are *f-distinguishable* [10], denoted $s \underset{f}{\neq} p$, if there exists a timed input sequence $\alpha \in \Omega_S(s) \cap \Omega_P(p)$ such that $out_S(s, \alpha) \neq out_P(p, \alpha)$; the sequence α is said to *f-distinguish* states s and p. If states s and p are not *f*-distinguishable then they are *f-compatible* (*functionally compatible*), denoted $s \underset{f}{\approx} p$. In the same way, *f-distinguishable* states can be introduced for states of a single TFSM. If each two different states of deterministic TFSM S are *f*-distinguishable then S is a *reduced* TFSM. TFSMs S and P are *f-compatible*, denoted $S \underset{f}{\approx} P$, if their initial states are *f*-compatible; otherwise, the machines are *f-distinguishable*, denoted $S \underset{f}{\neq} P$. Timed input sequence α that *f-distinguishes* the initial states of S and P is an *f-distinguishing* sequence of S and P. Given a set W of defined timed input sequences at states s and p, states s and p are *f-compatible* with respect to the set W, written $s \underset{f\ W}{\approx} p$, if s and p are not *f*-distinguishable for every sequence in the set W.

Proposition 1. Given two deterministic TFSMs S and P, the TFSMs S and P are f-distinguishable iff there exists a state (s, p) and an input i such that the behavior of the intersection $S \cap P$ is not defined at state (s, p) for a timed input (i, t) while the behavior of S at state s and the behavior of P at state p are defined under (i, t). In this case, each defined timed input sequence $\alpha.(i, t)$ where α takes the intersection $S \cap P$ to state (s, p), f-distinguishes TFSMs S and P.

Corollary. Given complete TFSMs S and P, if the intersection $S \cap P$ is completely specified then the TFSMs S and P are not f-distinguishable.

A set of timed input sequences $V \subseteq \Omega_S$ is called *a state cover set* of TFSM S if for each state s_i of S, there is an input sequence $\alpha_i \in V$ that takes S to state s_i.

Since the specification TFSM can be partial, the W-method and many of its derivatives cannot be used for deriving test suites with the guaranteed fault coverage. The reason is that, similar to untimed FSMs, a characterization set may not exist for a partial reduced TFSM. The HIS method can be applied when the specification FSM is partial and not reduced. In this paper, we adapt the HIS method for deriving a test suite with the guaranteed fault coverage; correspondingly, we define and use a separating family [17] of state identifiers, also known as a family of harmonized state identifiers [11], [13] for untimed FSMs.

Definition 7. Given state $s_j \in S$ of TFSM S, a set $W_j \subseteq \Omega_S(s_j)$ of timed input sequences is called a *state identifier* of state s_j if for any other state $s_i \in S$ there exists $\gamma \in \Omega_S(s_i) \cap W_j$ that f-distinguishes s_j and s_i, i.e. $out_S(s_i, \gamma) \neq out_S(s_j, \gamma)$. A *separating family* or a family of *harmonized identifiers* is a collection of state identifiers W_j, $s_j \in S$, which satisfy the condition: for any two different states s_j and s_i, there exist $\beta \in W_j$ and $\chi \in W_i$ which have common prefix γ such that $out_S(s_i, \gamma) \neq out_S(s_j, \gamma)$.

In this paper, we consider a Fault Model (FM) $<S, \underset{f}{\approx}, \Im>$, where S is the specification TFSM that is deterministic and reduced, $\underset{f}{\approx}$ is the f-compatibility relation and $\Im$ is the fault domain, i.e., $\Im$ is a finite set of deterministic complete TFSMs with the same input alphabet as the specification TFSM S. A *test suite* (w.r.t. the FM) is a finite set of finite defined timed input sequences of the specification. A test suite is *complete* w.r.t. the FM if for each TFSM $P \in \Im$ s.t. $S \underset{f}{\neq} P$ the test suite has a sequence that f-distinguishes P and S.

Given the FM $<S, \underset{f}{\approx}, \Im>$ where $\Im$ is a finite set of TFSMs, a complete test suite can be derived by explicit enumeration of TFSMs of the set $\Im$ using Proposition 1. However, the set $\Im$ can be huge and for this reason, we would like to develop a test derivation method without the explicit enumeration of the machines in $\Im$. As usual, we impose some restrictions on the specification TFSM and on the fault domain.

3   Deriving Complete Test Suites for Timed FSMs

The main problem when deriving a test suite with the guaranteed fault coverage for the specification TFSM S is that the number of defined timed inputs at each state of S can be infinite. For this reason, for deriving a test suite with the guaranteed fault coverage it is not enough to limit, i.e. have the upper bound, the number of states of an IUT but also it is necessary to limit the number of time regions. Therefore, we limit the finite boundary B_P of transition guards in an IUT. If we assume that each input can be applied only at integer time instances then it is enough to check at each state transitions under all the timed inputs (i, t), $i \in I$, $t \in \{0, ..., B_P + 1\}$. However, the number of such inputs can also be huge and as usual, we further minimize the number of such timed inputs when the low bound on time interval of guards of an IUT is known.

3.1   Separating Family

A separating family for a given reduced TFSM S can be derived in the same way as it is done for untimed FSMs: for every state s_i a of S, consider every other state s_j, $i \neq j$, then derive and add into W_i a timed input sequence γ defined at s_i and s_j, i.e. $\gamma \in \Omega_S(s_i)$ and $\gamma \in \Omega_S(s_j)$, that f-distinguishes the states s_i and s_j. The family of all sets W_i over all states s_i of S is a separating family of TFSM S. A timed input sequence that f-distinguishes two states can be derived using the intersection of the TFSM S with the initial states s_i and s_j, denoted S/s_i and S/s_j (Proposition 1).

As an example, consider the TFSM S shown in Fig. 1 and states 1 and 2 of S. The initial state of the intersection of $S/1$ and $S/2$ is undefined under the timed input $(i_1, 2)$, thus, the sequence $(i_1, 2)$ f-distinguishes states 1 and 2 of S. Thus, we add $(i_1, 2)$ into W_1 and W_2. In this example, the sequence $(i_1, 2)$ also f-distinguishes states 1 and 3. Thus, we add $(i_1, 2)$ into W_1 and W_3. For states 2 and 3, we derive the intersection of $S/1$ and $S/3$ and find that the sequence $(i_1, 3).(i_1, 2)$ of timed inputs f-distinguishes the states. Thus, we add $(i_1, 3).(i_1, 2)$ into W_2 and W_3 and obtain the set $F = \{ W_1, W_2, W_3 \} = \{ \{(i_1, 2), \}, \{(i_1, 2), (i_1, 3).(i_1, 2)\}, \{(i_1, 2), (i_1, 3).(i_1, 2) \} \}$ that is a separating family of TFSM S.

Here we note that two TFSMs can be f-compatible or f-distinguishable depending if a timed input can be applied only at integer time instances. For example, if an input can be applied only at integer time instances, then TFSMs cannot be distinguished with an input that is in the intersection $(a, a + 2)$ and $(a - 1, a + 1)$. In other words, in this case, two deterministic TFSMs S and P are f-distinguishable iff there exist a state (s, p) and an input i such that the behavior of S at state s and the behavior of P at state p are defined under (i, t) and the behavior of the intersection $S \cap P$ is not defined at state (s, p) for the timed input (i, t) where t is an integer. In fact in this case, each defined timed input sequence $\alpha.(i, t)$ where t is an integer, α takes the intersection $S \cap P$ to state (s, p) and inputs of the sequence α are applied at integer time instances, f-distinguishes TFSMs S and P. We further establish a statement (Proposition 2) that takes into account such distinguishability.

3.2   On Test Derivation for Integer Time Instances

Consider a fault model where the guard boundaries of the specification TFSM specification S and of each implementation TFSM P are integers, an implementation

TFSM P has at most n states, where n is the number of states of the specification TFSM S, the upper bound B on the largest finite boundary of an implementation TFSM is known and only timed inputs (i, t) where t is a nonnegative integer can be applied to an IUT.

In this case, each TFSM can be represented as an untimed FSM that for each state s has as defined inputs the finite set of timed inputs (i, t), $i \in \Omega_S(s)$, $t \in \{0, ..., B + 1\}$ intersected with the union of all guards in $\Pi_{(s, i)}$. Then the classical HIS method and its derivatives can be applied to the obtained FSM for deriving a complete test suite w.r.t. to the assumed fault model. However, this test suite will be huge. Similar to [14] it can be shown that it is not enough to apply inputs at finite boundaries of time guards of the specification. Thus, more rigorous analysis is needed to assess the limitations on time guards of an IUT and propose related test suite derivation with the guaranteed fault coverage. These issues will be addressed in the following section.

When interested in TFSMs with up to m states, we use $\mathfrak{I}_m(B, w)$ to denote the finite set of deterministic complete TFSMs with at most m states, which have the same input alphabet as the specification TFSM S, the upper bound B on the largest finite boundary and the minimal duration w of a time guard of an implementation TFSM. When we want to emphasize that inputs can be applied only at integer time instances then we use $\mathfrak{I}^{in}_m(B, w)$ to denote such a set of IUTs.

3.3 Test Derivation for TFSMs with Integer Time Instances When $m = n$

In this subsection, we define a fault model, denoted FM_1, and then present an algorithm that returns a complete test suite w.r.t. this model. Consider the fault model FM_1 = $<S, \underset{f}{\approx}, \mathfrak{I}^{in}_n(B, w)>$, where:

1) The minimal (integer) duration w of a finite time guard of an IUT is known.
2) An implementation TFSM $P \in \mathfrak{I}^{in}_n(B, w)$ is a deterministic complete FSM that has at most n states, where n is the number of states of the specification TFSM S;
3) The upper (integer) bound $B > 0$ on the largest finite boundary of an implementation TFSM is known.
4) Only timed inputs (i, t) where t is a nonnegative integer can be applied to an IUT.

Proposition 2. If only timed inputs (i, t) where t is a nonnegative integer can be applied to TFSM S then guards of the TFSM S can be described in the form $[a, b]$ or in the form $[a, \infty)$ where a and b are integers.

According to Proposition 2, for the example in Fig. 1, we can rewrite $\Pi_{(1, i1)} = \{[0,5), [5, 10]\}$ as $\{[0,4], [5, 10]\}$, $\Pi_{(2, i1)} = \{[0, 5), [5, \infty)\}$ as $\{[0, 4], [5, \infty)\}$, and $\Pi_{(2, i2)} = \{[0, 5], (5, \infty)\}$ as $\{[0, 5], [6, \infty)\}$. We also note that according to Proposition 2, if the specification TFSM has a guard $(a, a + 1)$ then after the transformation this guard is deleted from the transformed TFSM. If the specification TFSM has a guard $(a, a + k)$, $k > 1$, then this guard is transformed to $[a + 1, a + k - 1]$.

Algorithm 1. Deriving a complete test suite w.r.t. the fault model
$$<S, \underset{f}{\approx}, \mathfrak{I}^{in}_n(B,w)>$$

Input: Deterministic, possibly partial, reduced specification TFSM $S = (S, I, O, \lambda_S, s_0)$ in the form of Proposition 2, $|S| = n$, a state cover set V and a separating *family F of S*, upper bound B on the largest finite boundary of an IUT and the smallest duration w of a time guard in a TFSM implementation of S.

Output: A Complete test suite TS with respect to FM_1 = $<S, \underset{f}{\approx}, \mathfrak{I}^{in}_n(B, w)>$

Step 1.

    Append every sequence $\alpha \in V$ with a corresponding state identifier. Denote TS_1 the obtained set. That is for each $\alpha \in V$ which takes S to state s_α, TS_1 has sequences $\alpha.W_\alpha$, where $W_\alpha \in F$ is a state identifier of state s_α;

    If $w = 0$ or $w = 1$ then assign integer $u = 1$;

    Else assign integer $u = w - 1$;

Step 2.

    For every pair $(s, i) \in S \times I$ such that there exists a transition under i at state s:

        For each subset $g = [a, b] \in \Pi_{(s, i)}$ do:

            Derive a set $T_g = g \cap \{a, a + 1 \cdot u, \dots, a + (k-1) \cdot u, b\}$, $a + (k-1) \cdot u < b$ and $a + k \cdot u \geq b$;

        Endfor

        For each subset $g = [a, \infty) \in \Pi_{(s, i)}$ do:

            Derive a set $T_g = g \cap \{a, a + 1 \cdot u, \dots, a + (k-1) \cdot u, B\}$, $a + (k-1) \cdot u < B$ and $a + k \cdot u \geq B$;

        Endfor

        Denote $T_{(s, i)}$ the union of obtained sets of time instances T_g;

    Endfor

Step 3. For every sequence $\alpha \in V$ that takes the specification FSM to state s_α and for each input i such that there exists a transition under i at state s_α:

        Append α with timed input $(i, t).W_k$ for every $t \in T_{(s_\alpha, i)}$ where W_k is a state identifier in F of the (i, t)-successor s_k of state s_α. Denote TS_2 the obtained set.

    Endfor

Step 4. Return $TS := TS_1 \cup TS_2$ □

Example: As an application example for Algorithm 1, consider TFSM S shown in Fig. 1. The set $V = \{\varepsilon, (i_1, 2), (i_1, 2).(i_1, 6)\}$ is state cover set of S. We recall that the set of state identifiers of states 1, 2, and 3 are $W_1 = \{(i_1, 2)\}$, $W_2 = \{(i_1, 2), (i_1, 3).(i_1, 2)\}$, and $W_3 = \{(i_1, 2), (i_1, 3).(i_1, 2)\}$, respectively. The set $F = \{W_1, W_2, W_3\}$ is separating family of S. Assume that an IUT P of S has up to 3 states (as $n = 3$), length of each time interval w of S and P is at least 4, highest bound B of IUT equals and $u = w - 1 = 3$.

We apply Step-1 and obtain the sequences $TS_1 = \varepsilon.W_1 + (i_1, 2).W_2 + (i_1, 6).W_3 = \varepsilon.(i_1, 2) + (i_1, 2).(i_1, 2) + (i_1, 2).(i_1, 3)(i_1, 2) + (i_1, 6).(i_1, 2) + (i_1, 6).(i_1, 3)(i_1, 2)$. Then in Step-2, we consider the collection of guards of S, $\Pi_{(1, i1)} = \{[0, 4], [5, 10]\}$, $\Pi_{(1, i2)} = \{[0, \infty)\}$, $\Pi_{(2, i1)} = \{[0, 4], [5, \infty)\}$, $\Pi_{(2, i2)} = \{[0, 5], [6, \infty)\}$, $\Pi_{(3, i1)} = \{[0, \infty)\}$, and $\Pi_{(3, i2)} = \{[6, \infty)\}$. For the pair $(1, i_1)$, we have $\Pi_{(1, i1)} = \{[0, 4], [5, 10]\}$ and correspondingly the set of time instances $T_{[0,4]} = \{0, 3, 4\}$ and $T_{[5,10]} = \{5, 8, 10\}$. Thus, $T_{(1, i1)} = \{0, 3, 4, 5, 8, 10\}$. For the pair $(1, i_2)$, the collection $\Pi_{(1, i2)} = \{[0, \infty)\}$ and consequently $T_{(1, i2)} = \{0, 3, 6, 9, 12\}$. For the pair $(2, i_1)$, $\Pi_{(2, i1)} = \{[0, 4], [5, \infty)\}$, and consequently, $T_{(2, i1)} = \{0, 3, 4, 5, 8, 11\}$. For $(2, i_2)$, $\Pi_{(2, i2)}$ $\{[0, 5], [6, \infty)\}$ and $T_{(2, i2)} = \{0, 3, 5, 6, 9, 12\}$ and for $(3, i_1)$, $\Pi_{(3, i1)} = \{[0, \infty)\}$ and $T_{(3, i1)} = \{0, 3, 6, 9, 12\}$, and finally for the pair $(3, i_1)$, $\Pi_{(3, i2)} = \{[6, \infty)\}$ and $T_{(3, i2)} = \{6, 9, 12\}$.

Then at Step-3, consider $\alpha = \varepsilon \in V$ and $T_{(S\alpha, i1)} = T_{(1, i1)} = \{0, 3, 4, 5, 8, 10\}$. For instance $t = 0 \in T_{(1, i1)}$, the sequence $\varepsilon.(0, i_1)$ reaches state 2, thus form and add into TS_2 the sequences $\varepsilon.(i_1, 0).W_2$. Similarly consider every other instance $t \in T_{(1, i1)}$ and add into TS_2 the sequences $\varepsilon.(i_1, 3).W_2$; $\varepsilon.(i_1, 4).W_2$; $\varepsilon.(i_1, 5).W_1$; $\varepsilon.(i_1, 8).W_1$; $\varepsilon.(i_1, 10).W_1$. Then, consider $T_{(1, i2)} = \{0, 3, 6, 9, 12\}$ and add into TS_2 the sequences $\varepsilon.(i_2, 0).W_1$; $\varepsilon.(i_2, 3).W_1$; $\varepsilon.(i_2, 3).W_1$; $\varepsilon.(i_2, 9).W_1$; $\varepsilon.(i_2, 12).W_1$. For $\alpha = (i_1, 2) \in V$, $T_{(S\alpha, i1)} = T_{(2, i1)} = \{0, 3, 4, 5, 8, 11\}$. Consider every $t \in T_{(2, i1)}$ form and add into TS_2 the sequences $(i_1, 2).(i_1, 0).W_1$; $(i_1, 2).(i_1, 3).W_1$; $(i_1, 2).(i_1, 4).W_1$; $(i_1, 2).(i_1, 5).W_3$; $(i_1, 2).(i_1, 8).W_3$; $(i_1, 2).(i_1, 11).W_3$. Then consider $T_{(S\alpha, i2)} = T_{(2, i2)} = \{0, 3, 5, 6, 9\ 12\}$ and add into TS_2 the sequences $(i_1, 2).(i_2, 0).W_1$; $(i_1, 2).(i_2, 3).W_1$; $(i_1, 2).(i_2, 5).W_1$; $(i_1, 2).(i_2, 6).W_3$; $(i_1, 2).(i_2, 9).W_3$; $(i_1, 2).(i_2, 12).W_3$. Finally, for $\alpha = (i_1, 2) (i_1, 6) \in V$, form and add into TS_2 corresponding sequences and return $TS_1 \cup TS_2$.

Proposition 3. Given the fault model $<S, \underset{f}{\approx}, \mathfrak{I}^{in}_n(B, w)>$, Algorithm 1 returns a test suite TS that is complete with respect to this fault model.

Proof. Let $P = (P, I, O, \lambda_P, p_0) \in \mathfrak{I}^{in}_n(B, w)$ be an implementation TFSM that has the expected output response to each input sequence of the set TS_1. In this case, TFSM has exactly n states and moreover, we can establish the one-to-one correspondence h between states of S and P. $h(s) = p$ iff $s_j \underset{f\, W_j}{\approx} p_j$.

Suppose now that output responses of S and P at states s and $h(s)$ to some defined timed input $(i, t) \in \Omega_S(s)$ are different or the (i, t)-successor of state $h(s)$ does not equal $h(s')$ where s' is the (i, t)-successor of state $h(s)$ then the implementation TFSM does not have the expected output response to each input sequence of the set TS_2.

Let $w = 0$ or $w = 1$. In this case, for every input and state, each boundary of S and P is in the form $[a, a]$, $[a, a+1]$, $[B, B]$, or $[B, B+1]$, respectively, each timed input (i, t), t is an integer and $t = a$, $\{a, a+1\}$, B, $\{B, B+1\}$, such that the specification behavior is defined at state s for the timed input (i, t) is applied to an IUT at state $h(s)$. Thus, if the IUT has the expected behavior for all sequences of the set TS then the IUT is f-compatible with the specification.

Assume now that $w > 1$, i.e., $u = w - 1$. It is sufficient to show that for each non-empty intersection that contains at least one integer t of two guards $[a, b] \in \Pi_{(s, i)}$ and $[a_1, b_1] \in \Pi_{(h(s), i)}$ it holds that the intersection of $[a_1, b_1]$ and the set $T_{(s, i)}$ is not empty.

Consider guards $[a, b] \in \Pi_{(s, i)}$, $b - a \geq w$, and $[a_1, b_1] \in \Pi_{(h(s), i)}$, $b_1 - a_1 \geq w$, s.t. the intersection g of $[a_1, b_1]$ and the $T_{(s, i)}$ has at least one integer. A number of cases are possible.

1) $[a_1, b_1] \subset [a, b]$ then since $b_1 - a_1 \geq w$ and $u = w - 1$, there exists l s.t. $a + lu \in [a_1, b_1]$. In this case $a + lu \in T_{(s, i)}$ and thus, $a \in [a_1, b_1] \cap T_{(s, i)}$.

2) $[a_1, b_1] \not\subset [a, b]$ and $a \in [a_1, b_1]$. In this case, $a \in T_{(s, i)}$ and thus, $a \in [a_1, b_1] \cap T_{(s, i)}$.

3) $[a_1, b_1] \not\subset [a, b]$ and $a \notin [a_1, b_1]$, i.e., $b \in [a_1, b_1]$ and thus, $b \in T_{(s, i)}$.

In the same way, we can prove that for each non-empty intersection of the guards $[a, b] \in \Pi_{(s, i)}$ and $[a_1, \infty) \in \Pi_{(h(s), i)}$, $[a, \infty) \in \Pi_{(s, i)}$ and $[a_1, b_1] \in \Pi_{(h(s), i)}$, $[a, \infty) \in \Pi_{(s, i)}$ and $[a_1, \infty) \in \Pi_{(h(s), i)}$ it holds that the intersection of $[a_1, b_1]$ (or correspondingly of $[a_1, \infty)$) and $T_{(s, i)}$ is not empty.   □

3.4   Test Derivation for TFSMs with Integer Instances When $m > n$

As other FSM-based test derivation methods with the guaranteed fault coverage, the method presented in this paper can be adapted for the case when the number m of states of an IUT can be larger than the number n of states of the specification FSM, i.e. $m > n$. In this case, the fault domain of the fault model contains all TFSM implementations up to m states, i.e. $\Im_m(B, w)$. In this paper we show how Algorithm 1 can be adapted for deriving a complete test suite for the fault model $<S, \underset{f}{\approx}, \Im^{in}{}_m(B, w)>$.

In this case we derive not only a state cover V but the set V^{m-n+1} in order to cover each timed transition of an IUT and then as usual append sequences of the set V^{m-n+1} with corresponding state identifiers.

Algorithm 2. Deriving a complete test suite w.r.t. the fault model
$$<S, \underset{f}{\approx}, \Im^{in}{}_m(B,w)>$$

Input: Deterministic, possibly partial, reduced specification TFSM $S = (S, I, O, \lambda_S, s_0)$, $|S| = n$, a state cover set V and a separating *family F of S*, upper bound B on the largest finite boundary of an IUT, integer $m \geq n$, and the smallest duration w of a time guard in a TFSM implementation of S.

Output: A Complete test suite TS with respect to FM_2 = $<S, \underset{f}{\approx}, \Im^{in}{}_m(B, w)>$

Step 1. TS: = $\emptyset$;.
   If $w = 0$ or $w = 1$ then assign $u = 1$;
   Else assign $u = w - 1$;

Step 2.
   For every pair $(s, i) \in S \times I$ such that there exists a transition under i at state s:
      For each subset $g = [a, b] \in \Pi_{(s, i)}$ do:
         Derive a set $T_g = g \cap \{a, a + 1 \cdot u, ..., a + (k-1) \cdot u, b\}$, $a + (k-1) \cdot u < b$ and $a + k \cdot u \geq b$;
      Endfor

For each subset $g = [a, \infty) \in \Pi_{(s, i)}$ do:
 Derive a set $T_g = g \cap \{a, a + 1 \cdot u, ..., a + (k-1) \cdot u, B\}$, $a + (k-1) \cdot u < B$
 and $a + k \cdot u \geq B$;
Endfor
Endfor

Step 3. Assign $l: = 1$ and $V^l: = V$
 While $l \leq m - n + 1$
  For every sequence $\alpha \in V^l$ that takes the specification FSM to state
  s_α and each timed input (i, t) that is defined at state s_α:
   Include into V^{l+1} a sequence $\alpha(i, t)$ for every $t \in T_{(s_\alpha, i)}$;
  Endfor
 Increment l by 1;
 Endwhile

Step 4.

For every $\alpha \in V^1 \cup V^2 ... \cup V^{m-n+1}$
 Append α with a corresponding state identifier. That is for α where
 α takes S to state s_α, add to TS the sequences $\alpha.W_\alpha$, where $W_\alpha \in F$
 is a state identifier of state s_α;
Endfor
Return TS.   □

Similar to the statement of Proposition 3 we can prove the following statement.

Proposition 4. Given the fault model $<S, \underset{f}{\approx}, \mathfrak{I}^{in}_m(B, w)>$ the above described algorithm returns a test suite TS that is complete with respect to $<S, \underset{f}{\approx}, \mathfrak{I}^{in}_m(B, w)>$.

3.5 Test Derivation for TFSM with Rational Time Instances

Here we use the same fault model FM_1 defined above, in addition, we assume that time instances t of timed inputs (i, t) can be applied to an IUT at rational rather than only at integer time instances. In this case, we cannot transform TFSMs according to Proposition 2 and as the following example shows, it is not enough to apply inputs at integer time instances. Suppose that the specification TFSM has a guard (a, b), $b > a + 1$ for input i while the implementation TFSM has a guard $(a - 1, a + 1)$ for this input. The intersection of these guards is $(a - 1, a + 1)$ and in order to check the behavior of the implementation TFSM at a defined time instance we should apply a timed input (i, t), $t \in (a, a + 1)$, i.e. t is a rational. Correspondingly such rational time instances have to be considered in Step 2 of Algorithm 1.

Algorithm 3. Deriving a complete test suite w.r.t. FM_1 when time instances are rational

Input: Deterministic complete reduced specification TFSM $S = (S, I, O, \lambda_S, s_0)$, a state cover set V and a separating *family F of S*, upper (integer) bound B on the largest boundary of an implementation under test, and the minimal (integer) duration of w of a time guard in a TFSM implementation of S.

Output: A Complete test suite TS with respect to $<S, \underset{f}{\approx}, \Im_n(B, w)>$

Step 1. Append every sequence $\alpha \in V$ with a corresponding state identifier. Denote TS_1 the obtained set. That is for each $\alpha \in V$, let s_α be the state reached by α, TS_1 has sequences $\alpha.W_\alpha$, $W_\alpha \in F$;

If $w = 0$ or $w = 1$ assign $u := 1$;

Else $u := w\text{-}1$;

Select Δ, $0 < \Delta < 1$;

Step 2.

For every pair $(s, i) \in S \times I$ such that there exists a transition under i at state s:

For each subset $g = \lceil a, b \rceil \in \Pi_{(s, i)}$ do:

Derive a set $T_g = g \cap \{a, a + \Delta, a + 1 \cdot u, a + 1 \cdot u + \Delta, ..., a + (k\text{-}1) \cdot u, a + (k\text{-}1) \cdot u + \Delta, b, b - \Delta\}$, $a + (k\text{-}1) \cdot u < b$ and $a + k \cdot u \geq b$;

Endfor

For each subset $g = \lceil a, \infty) \in \Pi_{(s, i)}$ do:

Derive a set $T = g \cap_{\!\!2} \{a, a + \Delta, a + 1 \cdot u, a + 1 \cdot u + \Delta, ..., a + (k\text{-}1) \cdot u, a + (k\text{-}1) \cdot u + \Delta, B, B + \Delta\}$, $a + (k\text{-}1) \cdot u < B$ and $a + k \cdot u \geq B$;

Endfor

Denote $T_{(s, i)}$ the union of obtained sets of time instances T_g;

Endfor

Step 3. For every sequence $\alpha \in V$ that takes the specification FSM to state s_α and for each input i such that there exists a transition under i at state s_α:

Append α with timed input $(i, t).W_k$ for every $t \in T_{(s_\alpha, i)}$ where W_k is a state identifier in F of the (i, t)-successor s_k of state s_α. Denote TS_2 the obtained set.

Endfor

Step 4. Return $TS := TS_1 \cup TS_2$ □

Proposition 5. Given the fault model $<S, \underset{f}{\approx}, \Im_n(B, w) >$, Algorithm 3 returns a test suite TS that is complete with respect to this fault model.

Proof. Let FM $= <S, \underset{f}{\approx}, \Im_n(B, w)>$ and $P = (P, I, O, \lambda_P, p_0) \in \Im_n(B, w)$ be an implementation TFSM that has the expected output response to each input sequence of the set TS_1. In this case, TFSM has exactly n states and moreover, we can establish the one-to-one correspondence h between states of S and P. $h(s) = p$ iff $s_j \underset{f \, W_j}{\approx} p_j$.

Suppose now that output responses of S and P at states s and $h(s)$ to some defined timed input $(i, t) \in \Omega_S(s)$ are different or the (i, t)-successor of state $h(s)$ is not equal $h(s')$ where s' is the (i, t)-successor of state $h(s)$ then the implementation TFSM does not have the expected output response to each input sequence of the set TS_2. Similar to the proof of Proposition 3, it is sufficient to show that for each non-empty intersection that contains at least one integer t, of two guards $\lceil a, b \rceil \in \Pi_{(s, i)}$ and $\lceil a_1, b_1 \rceil \in \Pi_{(h(s), i)}$ it holds that the intersection of $\lceil a_1, b_1 \rceil$ and $T_{(s, i)}$ is not empty.

Let $w = 0$. Consider a guard $\lceil a_1, b_1 \rceil$ of an IUT s.t. $g \cap \lceil a_1, b_1 \rceil \neq \emptyset$. If the guard $\lceil a_1, b_1 \rceil$ has at least one integer then $\{0, \Delta, 1, 1 + \Delta, ..., B, B + \Delta\} \cap \lceil a_1, b_1 \rceil \neq \emptyset$. Here we note that since $\lceil a_1, b_1 \rceil$ can be $[a_1]$ for each $a_1 \in \{0, 1, ..., B\}$, we have to include all these integers into the set intersected with $\lceil a_1, b_1 \rceil$. If $\lceil a_1, b_1 \rceil = (a_1, b_1)$ and $b_1 - a_1 = 1$ then there are no integers inside (a_1, b_1). In this case, we have to apply an input at the time instance $(a_1 + \Delta)$, $a_1 \in \{0, 1, ..., B\}$.

Let $w = 1$. Consider a guard $\lceil a_1, b_1 \rceil$ of an IUT s.t. $g \cap \lceil a_1, b_1 \rceil \neq \emptyset$. If the guard $\lceil a_1, b_1 \rceil$ has at least one integer $t \leq B$ then since $b_1 - a_1 \geq 1$, it holds that $\{0, \Delta, 1, 1 + \Delta, ..., B, B + \Delta\} \cap \lceil a_1, b_1 \rceil \neq \emptyset$.

Let $w > 1$ and $g \in \Pi_{(s, i)}$, i.e., $u = w - 1$. Consider a guard $\lceil a_1, b_1 \rceil$ of an IUT s.t. $g \cap \lceil a_1, b_1 \rceil \neq \emptyset$.

Consider guards $\lceil a, b \rceil \in \Pi_{(s, i)}$, $b - a \geq w$, and $\lceil a_1, b_1 \rceil \in \Pi_{(h(s), i)}$, $b_1 - a_1 \geq w$. Similar to the proof of Statement 3, a number of cases are possible.

1) $\lceil a_1, b_1 \rceil \subset \lceil a, b \rceil$ then since $b_1 - a_1 \geq w$ and $u = w - 1 > 0$, there exists $t \in [a_1, b_1]$
   s.t. $t = a + lu$. If $a_1 = a + lu$ and $\lceil a_1, b_1 \rceil = (a_1, b_1]$ then $a_1 + lu + \Delta \in T_{(s, i)}$.
2) $\lceil a_1, b_1 \rceil \not\subset \lceil a, b \rceil$ and $a \in \lceil a_1, b_1 \rceil$. If $\lceil a, b \rceil = [a, b]$ then $a \in T_{(s, i)}$ and thus, $a \in$
   $\lceil a_1, b_1 \rceil \cap T_{(s, i)}$. If $\lceil a, b \rceil = (a, b]$ then $(a + \Delta) \in T_{(s, i)}$.
3) $\lceil a_1, b_1 \rceil \not\subset [a, b]$ and $a \notin \lceil a_1, b_1 \rceil$, then $b \in \lceil a_1, b_1 \rceil$. If $\lceil a, b \rceil = \lceil a, b]$ then $b \in T_{(s, i)}$
   and thus, $b \in \lceil a_1, b_1 \rceil \cap T_{(s, i)}$. If $\lceil a, b \rceil = \lceil a, b)$ then $(b - \Delta) \in T_{(s, i)}$.

In the same way, we prove that for each non-empty intersection of the guards $\lceil a, b \rceil \in \Pi_{(s, i)}$ and $\lceil a_1, \infty) \in \Pi_{(h(s), i)}$, $\lceil a, \infty) \in \Pi_{(s, i)}$ and $\lceil a_1, b_1 \rceil \in \Pi_{(h(s), i)}$, $\lceil a, \infty) \in \Pi_{(s, i)}$ and $\lceil a_1, \infty) \in \Pi_{(h(s), i)}$ it holds that the intersection of $\lceil a_1, b_1 \rceil$ (or correspondingly of $\lceil a_1, \infty)$) and $T_{(s, i)}$ is not empty. □

4 Conclusion and Future Work

Two fault models and corresponding test derivation methods are presented for deriving tests with the guaranteed fault coverage from a deterministic possibly partial specification Timed Finite State Machine (TFSM). In the first model (timed) inputs can be applied at integer (or discrete) time instances and in the second at rational (or continuous) time instances. The test derivation method with integer time instances is extended to the case when an implementation under test can have more states that the given specification.

The considered TFSM model assumes a reset operation is employed at every transition. We think that the methods presented in the paper can be adapted to consider timed FSMs where there is no reset at every transition. Another possible extension of the proposed work is to adapt test derivation with the guaranteed fault coverage for non-deterministic TFSMs.

References

1. Alur, R., Dill, D.L.: A Theory of Timed automata. Theoretical Computer Science 126(2), 183–235 (1994)
2. Bochmann, G.v., Petrenko, A.: Protocol Testing: Review of Methods and Relevance for Software Testing. In: International Symposium on Software Testing and Analysis, Seattle, pp. 109–123 (1994)
3. Chow, T.S.: Test Design Modeled by Finite-state Machines. IEEE TSE 4(3), 178–187 (1978)
4. Dorofeeva, R., El-Fakih, K., Yevtushenko, N.: An Improved Conformance Testing Method. In: Wang, F. (ed.) FORTE 2005. LNCS, vol. 3731, pp. 204–218. Springer, Heidelberg (2005)
5. En-Nouaary, A., Dssouli, R., Khendek, F.: Timed Wp-Method: Testing Real-Time Systems. IEEE TSE 28(11), 1023–1038 (2002)
6. Fujiwara, S., Bochmann, G.v., Khendek, F., Amalou, M., Ghedamsi, A.: Test Selection Based on Finite State Models. IEEE Trans. SE 17(6), 591–603 (1991)
7. Gromov, M., El-Fakih, K., Shabaldina, N., Yevtushenko, N.: Distinguishing Nondeterministic Timed Finite State Machines. In: 11th Formal Methods for Open Object-Based Distributed Systems and 29th Formal Techniques for Networked and Distributed Systems, FMOODS/FORTE. LNCS, vol. 5522, pp. 137–151. Springer, Heidelberg (2009)
8. [HMN09] Hierons, R.M., Merayo, M.G., Nunez: Testing from a Stochastic Timed System with a Fault Model. Journal of Logic and Algebraic Programming 72(8), 98–115 (2009)
9. Lee, D., Yannakakis, M.: Principles and Methods of Testing Finite State Machines-A Survey. Proc. of the IEEE 84(8), 1090–1123 (1996)
10. Merayo, M.G., Nunez, M., Rodriguez, I.: Formal Testing from Timed Finite State Machines. Computer Networks 52(2), 432–460 (2008)
11. Petrenko, A.: Checking Experiments with Protocol Machines. In: Proc. 4th Int. Workshop on Protocol Test Systems (IWPTS), pp. 83–94 (1991)
12. Petrenko, A., Yevtushenko, N.: Testing from Partial Deterministic FSM Specifications. IEEE Trans. Computers 54(9), 1154–1165 (2005)
13. Petrenko, A., Yevtushenko, N., Lebedev, A., Das, A.: Nondeterministic State Machines in Protocol Conformance Testing. In: Proc. of the IFIP 6th IWPTS, France, pp. 363–378 (1993)
14. Springintveld, J., Vaandrager, F., D'Argenio, P.: Testing Timed Automata. Theoretical Computer Science 254(1-2), 225–257 (2001)
15. Vasilevskii, M.P.: Failure Diagnosis of Automata. translated from Kibernetika 4, 98–108 (1973)
16. Yevtushenko, N., Petrenko, A.: Test derivation method for an arbitrary deterministic automaton. In: Automatic Control and Computer Science, vol. 5. Allerton Press Inc., USA (1990)
17. Yannakakis, M., Lee, D.: Testing Finite State Machines: Fault Detection. Journal of Computer and System Sciences 50, 209–227 (1995)
18. Cardell-Oliver, R., Glover, T.: A Practical and Complete Algorithm for Testing Real-Time Systems. Formal Techniques for Real-Time Fault Tolerant Systems (1998)

Applying Testability Transformations to Achieve Structural Coverage of Erlang Programs

Qiang Guo, John Derrick, and Neil Walkinshaw

Department of Computer Science,
The University of Sheffield,
Regent Court, 211 Portobello, S1 4DP, UK
{Q.Guo,J.Derrick,N.Walkinshaw}@dcs.shef.ac.uk

Abstract. This paper studies the structural testing of Erlang applications. A program transformation is proposed that represents the program under test as a binary tree. The challenge of achieving structural coverage can thus be interpreted as a tree-search procedure. We have developed a testing-technique that takes advantage of this tree-structure, which we demonstrate with respect to a small case study of an Erlang telephony system.

Keywords: Erlang, Testing, Transformation, FBT, Structural Coverage.

1 Introduction

Erlang [1] was, along with its Open Telecoms Platform (OTP), originally developed by Ericsson for the rapid development of network applications. However, its usage has now spread beyond that domain to a number of sectors. Erlang has been designed to provide a paradigm for the development of distributed soft real-time systems, where multiple processes can be spread across many nodes in a network.

With its OTP libraries, complex Erlang applications can be rapidly developed and deployed across a large variety of hardware platforms, and this has caused it to become increasingly popular, not only within large telecoms companies such as Ericsson, but also with a variety of SMEs in different areas. It is increasingly used to develop applications that are business-critical, for example, its use in Ericsson's AXD-301 switch that provides British Telecom's internet backbone.

The ability to rigorously test Erlang applications is vital. In recognition of this, there has recently been a concerted drive to develop more automated testing tools, which complement the rapid Erlang development cycle. Tools such as QuickCheck [2] are being eagerly adopted within the community.

So far, the main thrust of the Erlang testing effort has been directed towards functional testing. Structural code-coverage has not been considered. This is however an important problem, and is often a requirement if the system under test is to be certified for a range of safety standards (e.g. the US Federal Aviation Authority software standards [13]). Achieving code coverage is a well-established challenge; the tester has to find a suitable set of test inputs that

M. Núñez et al. (Eds.): TESTCOM/FATES 2009, LNCS 5826, pp. 81–96, 2009.

will exercise every branch for every predicate in the program. Finding a suitable (and reasonably sized) set of inputs is often problematic, and a number of techniques such as symbolic execution [7], evolutionary search algorithms [9] and testability-transformations [6] have been proposed to address it.

This paper presents a technique that leverages certain features of the Erlang language to enable complete structural test coverage. The approach is inspired by Harman et al.'s notion of testability transformations [6]. We have developed a transformation that transforms an Erlang program into a binary tree. Each node in the tree corresponds to either a true or a false evaluation of a predicate in the original program. Predicates that may be hidden within functions in the original program are made explicit. Identifying a suitable test set to achieve structural coverage is thus reduced to a search over the binary tree.

To facilitate the debugging process, a simple debugging framework is presented. The framework takes advantage of the tree structure of the transformed program. This enables the developer to control and observe the execution of a program by directly manipulating the internal variable and parameter values.

The paper is structured as follows. Section 2 provides a background to Erlang and the structural testing problem. Section 3 introduces our program transformation. Section 4 shows how tests can be generated to cover the transformed program. Section 5 contains a case study with respect to a small telecommunications system, and section 6 contains conclusions and future work.

2   Background

This section provides a brief introduction to Erlang.

2.1   Erlang

Erlang is a concurrent functional language with specific support for the development of distributed,fault-tolerant systems with soft real-time requirements [1]. It was designed from the start to support a concurrency-oriented programming paradigm and large distributed implementations that this supports.

The Open Telecom Platform (OTP) is a set of Erlang libraries for building large fault-tolerant distributed applications. Extensive libraries for common network-applications and protocols are included, and there is a collection of source code and trace-analysis tools that provide a base for debugging and profiling tasks. It also provides a set of common and reusable *behaviours*, which encapsulate common behavioural patterns for processes, where the library module implements the generic behaviour, and the developer is left to add those aspects of behaviour that are specific to their system.

With the OTP, Erlang applications can be rapidly developed and deployed across a large variety of hardware platforms, and this has caused it to become increasingly popular, not only within large telecoms companies such as Ericsson, but also with a variety of SMEs in different areas such as Yahoo! Delicious, and the Facebook chat system.

However, verification and validation of Erlang systems is to-date a largely ad-hoc, manual process. Consequently there is an inherent danger that important functionality remains untested and undocumented. Thus along with its recent growth in popularity, there has been a concerted drive to develop more auto-mated and systematic techniques.

2.2 Structural Testing of Erlang Implementations

In structural testing, the goal is to achieve some level of coverage of the source code. Branch coverage, where the aim is to cover every branch from every decision point in the source code, is one of the most popular measures. The challenge of generating a suitable test set is two-fold: (1) to identify a suitable set of test inputs that will reach every branch, and (2) to ensure that this set of tests is sufficiently small so that can be executed in a reasonable amount of time.

An Erlang program consists of a set of modules, each of which defines a number of functions. Functions that are accessible from other modules need to be explicitly declared by the *export* command. A function named *f_name* in the module *module* and with arity N is denoted as *module:f_name/N*. An Erlang function f_i is coded as a sequence of executional units $f_i = \langle cp_{i(1)}, ..., cp_{i(n)} \rangle$, each of which defines a set of statements. An example is demonstrated in Figure 1.

From the structural-testing perspective, the aim is to identify a set of test-inputs that will collectively ensure that every branch in *client:idle* is executed at least once. Along with the input parameters, it is also necessary for the tester to control the values that are returned by *gen_server*. In this case, we would need to ensure that the variable *P1* is at some point assigned to one of the four predicate conditions (e.g. {*error,invalid_mobile*}), as well as an aribitrary value that corresponds to none of them.

```
-module(client).                                  :    {error,already_connected}→
-export([idle/2]).                                :        action:show(already_connected),
idle(AT,{MB,RS,CSs})→                             :        {next_state,connected,
    P1 = gen_server:                              :            {MB,RS,CSs},?T};
        call(hd(CSs),{request,AT,MB}),:           {error,busy}→
    case P1 of                                    :        action:show(sever_busy),
        {error,invalid_mobile}→                   :        idle(AT,{MB,RS,
            action:show(invalid_mobile),      :            lists:append(tl(CSs),hd(CSs))}});
            {next_state,idle,{MB,RS,CSs}};::      _Other→
        {ok,connected,_CalledFS, RS}→    :            action:show(action_invalid),
            action:show(mobile_connected),:           {next_state,idle,{MB,RS,CSs}}
            {next_state,connected,            :    end.
                {MB,RS,CSs},?T};              :
```

Fig. 1. An Erlang Example

The simplest strategy is to construct a separate test set for each branch. For each unit $cp_{i(k)}$ a test set is designed and applied to f_i. The I/O behavior observed from $\langle cp_{i(1)}, ..., cp_{i(k)} \rangle$ is used to evaluate $cp_{i(k)}$. When the test of $cp_{i(k)}$ is complete, the process continues to the next unit. The process continues until all units have been tested.

Such a test strategy could give rise to two disadvantages. First, this approach can be wasteful; testing $cp_{i(k)}$ requires the execution of all preceding units, $\{cp_{i(1)}, ..., cp_{i(k-1)}\}$, regardless of whether $cp_{i(l)}$, $l < l < k$, has already been tested. Secondly, identifying a suitable combination of inputs can be very challenging. The execution of $cp_{i(k)}$ is heavily dependent by the results of executing $\langle cp_{i(1)}, ..., cp_{i(k-1)} \rangle$ as the parameters for $cp_{i(k)}$ may be affected by previous results.

From this small example, it is possible to identify the input requirements by hand, simply from inspecting the predicate conditions. However, this approach becomes intractable when the software increases in scale and complexity. Given a conventional Erlang system with multiple modules, where certain branches can only be reached by complex combinations of conditions, an automated approach is required.

3   Transforming an Erlang Program into Binary Format

This paper proposes a program transformation that converts an Erlang function into a tree-structure. The transformed function retains the functional behavior, but makes the predicates that control its behavior explicit. This has two benefits that address the problem mentioned above. The tree-shaped structure makes it possible to identify an efficient test-set. Making the predicates explicit makes it possible to automatically identify the set of inputs that are required to reach every unit in a function. The rest of this section will introduce the program transformation.

3.1   Notations

To formalize the description, we introduce the following notations. Let $cp_{i(k)}|_{cond(k)}$ denote that the unit $cp_{i(k)} \in f_i$ is executed under the condition of $cond(k)$. If $cond(k) = true$, $cp_{i(k)}$ is activated for execution; otherwise a dummy operation[1] is performed. Let $cp_{i(l)} << cp_{i(m)}$ denote that $cp_{i(m)}$ is executed after $cp_{i(l)}$. The function f_i can be expressed as $f_i = cp_{i(1)}|_{cond(i(1))}$ $<< ... << cp_{i(n)}|_{cond(i(n))}$, $cp_{i(l)}|_{cond(i(l))} << cp_{i(m)}|_{false} << cp_{i(n)}|_{cond(i(n))} \equiv$ $cp_{i(l)}|_{cond(i(l))} << cp_{i(n)}|_{cond(i(n))}, \forall (l < m < n)$. If $cp_{i(l)} \in f_i$ is an unconditional unit, $cond(i(l))$ is automatically set to $true$; otherwise, the value of $cond(i(l))$ is determined by the pattern evaluation. For example, the function $idle$ shown in Figure 1 is expressed as:

---

[1] A dummy operation is a function that maps the inputs to the outputs without changing the values of the inputs.

$func =$

$P1 = gen\_server : call(hd(CSs), \{request, AT, MB\})|_{true} <<$

$(action : show(invalid\_mobile)|_{true} <<$

$\{next\_state, idle, \{MB, RS, CSs\}\})|_{cond(matches(P1,\{error,invalid\_mobile\}))} <<$

$(action : show(mobile\_connected)|_{true} <<$

$\{next\_state, connected, \{MB, RS, CSs\}, ?T\})|_{cond(not(matches(P1,}$

$\quad\quad _{\{error,invalid\_mobile\})) \land matches(P1,\{ok,connected,\_CalledFS,RS\}))} <<$

$\quad\quad << ... <<$

$(action : show(action\_invalid)|_{true<<}$

$\{next\_state, idle, \{MB, RS, CSs\}\})|_{cond(not(matches(P1,\{error,invalid\_mobile\})))}$

$\quad\quad _{\land ... \land not(matches(P1,\{error,busy\})) \land matches(P1,\_Other))}$

where the function *matches* evaluates whether *P1* matches *PV*, $PV \in \{\{error, invalid\_mobile\}, \{ok, connected, \_CalledFS, RS\}, \{error, already\_connected\}, \{error, busy\}, \_Other\}$.

The above expressions show how each unit $cp_{i(k)} \in f_i$ can be represented by a generic pattern, $cp_{i(k)}|_{cond(i(k))}$. If $cond(i(k))$ is *true*, $cp_{i(k)}$ is executed; otherwise, $cp_{i(k+1)}|_{cond(i(k+1))}$ is evaluated.

3.2   Function Transformation

The transformation we introduce here decomposes a single large function f_i into a set of atomic functions $f'_{i(k)}$. Each function f_i is transformed into a set of ordered calls to atomic functions $f'_{i(1)} << ... << f'_{i(n)}$ where n is the number of executional units of f_i. The benefit of this is that the guards on the execution of these atomic functions are made explicit, and it becomes easier to control their execution, or even influence their execution for the purpose of debugging (this is demonstrated in the following sections).

The unit $cp_{i(k)} \in f_i$ is transformed into a called function defined as:

$$f'_{i(k)}(true, Args) \rightarrow cp_{i(k)};$$
$$f'_{i(k)}(false, Args) \rightarrow f'_{i(k+1)}(cond(i(k+1)), Args).$$

The function $f'_{i(k)}$ is guarded by a *switch* that can only be set to *true* or *false*. If *switch* is *true* $(cond(i(k)) = true)$, the functional executions defined in $cp_{i(k)}$ are performed; otherwise, the function $f'_{i(k+1)}$ is invoked where $cp_{i(k+1)}|_{cond(i(k+1))}$ is evaluated.

When $f'_{i(k)}$ is invoked, if $f'_{i(k)}$ is derived from a unconditional unit $cp_{i(k)}$, *switch* is automatically set to *true*; otherwise, the pattern match evaluation function *patterns_match* is applied to decide the value of *switch*. Definition of the function *patterns_match* is discussed in the subsection 3.3. According to the pattern under evaluation, the function *patterns_match* returns *true* or *false*. If $cp_{ik} \in f_i$ defines a list of variables RV_k, when $cp_{im} \in f_i, m > k$, is transformed to $f'_{i(m)}$, RV_k is configured as an argument of $f'_{i(m)}$.

idle(AT,{MB,RS,CSs})→
  idle_st_1(true,
    [AT,MB,RS,CSs,do_not_care]).

idle_st_1(true,[AT,MB,RS,CSs,_P1])→
  P1 = gen_server:call(hd(CSs),
              {request,AT,MB}),
  idle_case1(pattern_match([P1],[{error,
    invalid_mobile}]),[AT,MB,RS,CSs,P1]);
idle_st_1(false,[AT,MB,RS,CSs,P1])→
  idle_case1(pattern_match([P1],[{error,
    invalid_mobile}]),[AT,MB,RS,CSs,P1]).

idle_case1(true,[AT,MB,RS,CSs,P1])→
  action:show(invalid_mobile),
  {next_state,idle,{MB,RS,CSs}};
idle_case1(false,[AT,MB,RS,CSs,P1])→
  idle_case2(pattern_match([P1],
    [{ok,connected,do_not_care,sys_var}]),
      [AT,MB,RS,CSs,P1]).

idle_case2(true,[AT,MB,RS,CSs,P1])→
  action:show(mobile_connected),

{next_state,connected,{MB,RS,CSs},?T};
idle_case2(false,[AT,MB,RS,CSs,P1])→
  idle_case3(pattern_match([P1],[{error,
    already_connected}]),
      [AT,MB,RS,CSs,P1]).

idle_case3(true,[AT,MB,RS,CSs,P1])→
  action:show(already_connected),
  {next_state,connected,{MB,RS,CSs},?T};
idle_case3(false,[AT,MB,RS,CSs,P1])→
  idle_case4(pattern_match([P1],
    [{error,busy}]),[AT,MB,RS,CSs,P1]).

idle_case4(true,[AT,MB,RS,CSs,P1])→
  action:show(sever_busy),
  {next_state,idle,{MB,RS,CSs}};
idle_case4(false,[AT,MB,RS,CSs,P1])→
  idle_case5(pattern_match([P1],
    [do_not_care]),[AT,MB,RS,CSs,P1]).

idle_case5(true,[AT,MB,RS,CSs,P1])→
  action:show(action_invalid),
  {next_state,idle,{MB,RS,CSs}}

Fig. 2. Transformed Erlang program

Thus, the defined rules transform the original function f_i into a set of calls to functions $\{f'_{i(1)}, ..., f'_{i(n)}\}$ where n is the number of units defined in f_i. Each function $f'_{i(k)}$ is coded by generic pattern with a *true* branch and a *false* branch being defined. The *true* branch performs the functional executions defined in $cp_{ik} \in f_i$, while, the *false* branch invokes the function $f'_{i(k+1)}$ where $cond(i(k+1))$ is evaluated. Such a transformation is called Binary Transformation (BT). The *true* branch of a called function is called Functional Execution Branch (FEB) and the *false* branch is called Pattern Evaluation Branch (PEB). By applying the defined rules, the function *idle* shown in Figure 1 is transformed as shown in Figure 2.

The defined rules only transform the structure of P into P'. The functionalities implemented in P are preserved in P'. The functions in P' are of simpler structures. The predicates that guard the execution of those functions are explicitly defined. Compared to P, P' is well structured and easier to test.

Proposition 1. *Given an Erlang program P and its BT P', P' is functionally equivalent to P.*

Proof. Given an Erlang program P and its BT transformation P', it is sufficient to prove P' is functionally equivalent to P, if for $f_i \in P$, $i = 1, ..., m$, the following conditions hold: (1) each unit $cp_l \in f_i$ has a unique called function $f'_{i(l)}$ in P'; (2) the functional behavior (input/output) of $f'_{i(l)}$ is identical to that of cp_l and (3) the called order of the FEB of f_i' is defined by the order of the executions of cp_i, namely, $(cp_{i(m)}|_{cond(i(m))=true} << cp_{i(n)}|_{cond(i(n))=true}) \rightarrow (f_{i(m)}'(true, Args) << f_{i(m+1)}'(false, Args) << ... << f_{i(n-1)}'(false, Args) << f_{i(n)}'(true, Args)), \forall(n > m)$.

The proof for the first condition is obvious as the transformation rules define that the relation between a unit and its called counterpart is a one-to-one mapping, that is, for each unit $cp_{i(l)} \in f_i$, there is only one called replacement $f_{i(l)}'$ in P'.

The transformation rules define that (1) the functional executions defined in $cp_{i(l)}$ are performed in the FEB of $f_{i(l)}'$; (2) if $cp_{i(g)} \in f_i$, $g < i$, returns a value to the variable $RV_{i(g)}$, $RV_{i(g)}$ is defined as an input of $f_{i(l)}'$, and (3) the name of $RV_{i(g)}$ is unique (module name plus function name plus variable name). These rules guarantee that the function $f_{i(l)}'$ and the unit $cp_{i(l)}$ receive the same input set and perform the same functional executions. Thus, $f_{i(l)}'$ and $cp_{i(l)}$ have the same functional behavior.

The third condition can be obtained by contradiction. Let $cp_{i(m)}|_{cond(i(m))=true} << cp_{i(n)}|_{cond(i(n))=true}$ be true. This implies that $cond(i(k)) = false$, $m < l < n$, as $cp_{i(m)}|_{cond(i(m))=true} << cp_{i(n)}|_{cond(i(n))=true} \equiv cp_{i(m)}|_{cond(i(m))=true} << cp_{i(l)}|_{cond(i(l))=false} << cp_{i(n)}|_{cond(i(n))=true}$, $\forall(m < k < n)$. Suppose in the transformation counterpart, there exists a called function $f_{i(l)}'$, $m < l < n$, such that $f_{i(l)}'(true, Args)$ is activated. According to the transformation rules, the PEB of the function $f_{i(l-1)}'$ must have invoked the function $f_{i(l)(cond(i(l)),Args)}'$ with $cond(i(l))$ being evaluated to $true$. This, however, contradicts to the fact that $cond(i(l))$ is $false$. Thus, $(cp_{i(m)}|_{cond(i(m))=true} << cp_{i(n)}|_{cond(i(n))=true}) \rightarrow (f_{i(m)}'(true, Args) << f_{i(m+1)}'(false, Args) << ... << f_{i(n-1)}'(false, Args) << f_{i(n)}'(true, Args)), \forall(n > m)$. $\qquad\square$

3.3   Pattern Match Transformation

Erlang makes extensive use of pattern matching in its function definitions. This work transforms the pattern matching clauses into a binary format. To do so, the technique [4] proposed to eliminate overlapping between patterns are applied. Specifically, pattern match clauses in a function are replaced by a series of called functions, each of which is guarded by the *pattern_match* function.

A data type called the Structure Splitting Tree (SST) [4] is defined and applied for pattern evaluation, and its use guarantees the pattern match clauses being represented in binary formats.

3.4   Functional Binary Tree

After P is transformed into P', it is easily to see that all functions in P' are represented with a generic pattern as shown in Figure 3. The pattern is a binary tree with one entry and two exits. The entry is identified with a function name

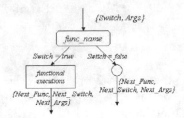

Fig. 3. Generic pattern of the called function

func_name that takes a list of arguments *Args* as input. Both exits define a tuple {*Next_Func, Next_Switch, Next_Args*} where *Next_Func* states the function next to be called; *Next_Switch* defines the guard for *Next_Func*, and *Next_Args* consists of the arguments for *Next_Func*. *Switch* is applied to guard the selection of the *true* and the *false* branches. The *true* branch defines both the functional executions and the function to be called next, while the *false* branch only states the next called function. Such a binary tree is defined as a Functional Binary Tree (FBT).

If all called functions in P' are represented with their FBTs, a Complete Functional Binary Tree (CFBT) can be derived where the nodes that define no *Next_Func* constitute the terminals. For example, Figure 4 demonstrates the CFBT of the program shown in Figure 2.

4   Structural Testing from Transformation

This section discusses the test generation for structural coverage from the program transformation.

4.1   Test Generation

As discussed in the Section 3, a program P can be transformed into its BT P'. Proposition 1 proves that P' is functionally equivalent to P. This suggests that, instead of testing P directly, one can test P' and use the test results to evaluate the correctness of P. Any errors detected in P' imply that the implementation of P is faulty. The structure of P' is a binary format and the predicates for controlling the execution of a node are explicitly specified. Deriving data to test an execution branch in P' should not be a difficult task. Compared to P, P' is easier to achieve structural coverage.

This section discusses the derivation of tests for P'. As P' can be represented by a CFBT, it is easy to see that a test set whose elements traverse and test all nodes in the CFBT will test P', and the test achieves complete structural coverage. Thus, the generation of a test set for P' is achieved by the construction of data that traverse every node in the $CFBT_{P'}$ and test the corresponding

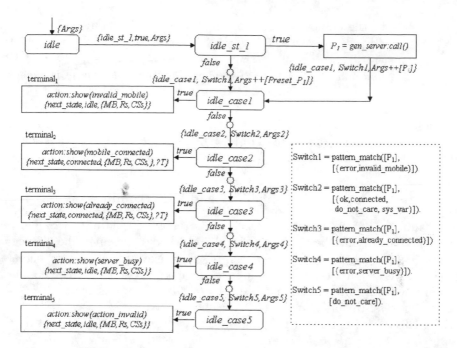

Fig. 4. Complete Functional Binary Tree derived from the program shown in Figure 2

function at least once. As a CFBT is a binary tree, standard techniques for the search of nodes in a tree such as a breadth-first search algorithm [3] or a depth-first search algorithm [3] can be applied.

As an example, a test for the CFBT shown in Figure 4 is defined by constructing a set of data TS whose elements traverse and test each node in the graph at least once. To do so, each terminal $terminal_i \in \{terminal_1, ..., terminal_5\}$ needs to be tested by $ts_i \subseteq TS$ at least once. Let ts_3 test $terminal_3$. The test ts_3 is constructed by examining the path between the root node (the entry of the function $idle$) and the terminal $terminal_3$. The path between $terminal_3$ and $idle$ is $\langle terminal_3, idle\_case3(true), idle\_case2(false), idle\_case1(false), idle\_st\_1, idle \rangle$. The function $idle\_st\_1$ can pass P_1 to its successor. The value of P_1 can be either computed from the execution $gen\_server : call()$ or preset. The subsection 4.2 discusses the technique on deriving partial testing by presetting the inputs for the functions under evaluation.

Thus, in the test, P_1 should receive $\{error, already\_connected\}$ (either received from the gen_server:call() or preset). When the test is applied, the IUT must produce the message $already\_connected$.

Proposition 2. *Given a program P and its binary transformed P' represented by the complete functional binary tree $CFBT_{P'}$, if a test set TS achieves complete structural coverage of P', the elements in TS must traverse all nodes in $CFBT_{P'}$ and test the corresponding functions at least once and vice versa.*

Proof. Let n be the number of functions in P' and N_i be the node that stands for the function $f'_i \in P'$ in the $CFBT_{P'}$. Suppose a test set TS has achieved complete structural coverage of P', there must exist a subset $ts_i \subseteq TS$ such that ts_i tests the function $f'_i \in P'$, which implies that the function f'_i is executed by ts_i at least once. This is equivalent to that ts_i traverses the node N_i in the $CFBT_{P'}$ at least once. Similarly, if a set of data ts_i traverses the node N_i in $CFBT_{P'}$, it should execute and test the function defined in N_i once. The union of all such sets of data constitutes a test set TS, $TS = ts_1 \cup ... \cup ts_n$, that achieves complete structural coverage for P'. □

4.2 Improving Test Controllability and Observability

Once faults are detected, tests need to be constructed to isolate these faults. The process of identifying the locations of faults is called *debugging*. The debugging process defines a number of tests, each of which executes a set of designated functions whose outputs should exhibit the properties defined by the design. A test in the debugging process is called a *partial test*. By observing the results of all partial tests, the faults are expected to be isolated.

The effectiveness of the debugging process is primitively determined by two factors - the *test controllability* and the *test observability*. The *test controllability* determines whether it is always possible to derive a partial test, while the *test observability* determines whether it is always possible to observe the outputs when the test is executed.

This work shows that, by applying the program transformation, the test controllability and the observability are improved. As discussed in the section 3, in the transformation program P', all functions are represented by the BFTs. If $f'_i \in P'$ is further modified into the format as shown in Figure 5, the function under test is then assigned with two running modes, the *normal* mode and the *debugging* mode. In the debugging mode, a debugging framework is associated. The debugging framework is used to track the values of the variables under evaluation, or bypass the functional execution of f'_i by presetting its *switch* to *false*.

For example, in Figure 5, if f'_i is previously set to the debugging mode, the results of all internal computations RS_1, ..., RS_i will be posted to the debugging framework for comparison. Before f'_{i+1} is called, the values of the inputs $Switch, Arg_1, ..., Arg_k$ will be sent to the debugging framework. The debugging framework returns a tuple $\{NextMode, DSwitch, [DArg_1, ..., DArg_k]\}$ where $NextMode$ specifies the running mode of f'_{i+1}; $DArg_1,...,DArg_k]$ consists of the inputs for f'_{i+1} with $DArg_l$, $1 \leq l \leq k$, being preset; $DSwith$ saves the value of *switch*. If $DSwith$ is set to *false*, the evaluation of f'_{i+1} is bypassed and the testing moves on to f'_{i+2}.

Thus, the configuration of the debugging process can be modelled as shown in Figure 6. Each function f'_i either takes input values computed from f'_{i-1} or preset by the debugging framework. The functional executions of f'_i can be controlled by presetting the value for *switch*. If *switch* is preset to *false*, the functional

f'_i(Switch,$[Arg_1,...,Arg_k]$,Mode)$\rightarrow$
   RS_1 = functional_execution_1($[Arg_1,...,Arg_k]$),
    ...
   RS_n = functional_execution_n($[Arg_1,...,Arg_k]$),
   case Mode of
      normal$\rightarrow$ nothing;
      debugging$\rightarrow$ RS={func$_i$,[{'RS$_1$',RS$_1$},...,{'RS$_n$',RS$_n$}]},
               debug_panel:setting(RS)
   end,
   Switch = pattern_match($[Arg_1,...,Arg_k]$,[pattern defined for f'_{i+1}]),
   {NextMode,DSwitch,$[DArg_1,DArg_k]$} =
      debug_panel:setting(func$_{i+1}$,[{'Switch',Switch},{'Arg_1',Arg_1},...,{'Arg_k',Arg_k}])
   f'_{i+1}(DSwitch,$[DArg_1,...,DArg_k]$,NextMode).

Fig. 5. The generic debugging pattern of a function

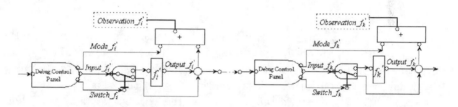

Fig. 6. Debugging framework

execution of f'_i is bypassed; otherwise, f'_i will be functionally evaluated. When f'_i is running on the debugging mode, all computational results performed within the function can be externally observed.

By using the debugging framework to control the values of the inputs for a function under test, the test controllability is improved and, by opening the observation windows in the debugging framework, tracking the changes of the variables under evaluation is possible, which helps to improve the test observability.

5   A Case Study

A case study is used to evaluate the proposed model. The case study simulates a telecommunication system.

5.1   System Infrastructure

The telecoms uses a client-server structure, and comprises of a database server (DBS) that maintains all client's data and a number of functional servers to process clients' requests. An FS has a capacity that defines the maximum number of mobiles to be connected.

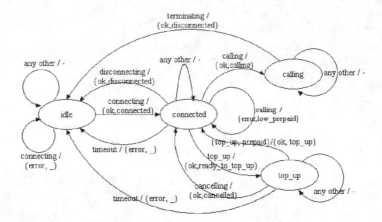

Fig. 7. Client behaviour modelled as an FSM

A client can communicate with any FSs and perform some functional operations such as *calling* and *top-up*. Each client has an account maintained in the DBS, and in order to make a phone call, a client needs to top-up enough money in its account. Before performing any functional operations, a client needs to connect to an FS. A client can only be connected to one FS, and if a client has connected to an FS and tries to connect to another FS, the request will be denied.

The behavior of a client (mobile) is modelled as a finite state machine (FSM), and the initial design is shown in Figure 7. There are four states: *idle*, *connected*, *calling* and *top_up*, where initially, the system is set to the *idle* state.

The FSM defines the behavior of a number of operations: *connecting*, *disconnecting*, *calling*, *terminating*, *top_up* and *cancelling*. Before performing any operations, a client FSM needs to connect to an FS through sending the *connecting* request.

A client FSM has a timing restriction applicable when in states *connected* or *top_up*. Specifically, when the FSM is directed to the state *connected* or *top_up*, a timer will be instantiated which enables the timing process. If, within the predefined time period, no action is performed by the client, a *timeout* event will be generated and sent to the FS. By receiving *timeout* event, the FS cuts off the connection and releases the resource from its user list. The FSM is then reset to the state *idle*.

5.2   Erlang Implementation

Erlang is used to implement the telecoms system, making use of the OTP design patterns as is common practice. The FS is implemented using the Erlang/OTP *gen_server* module. A generic server is implemented by providing a *callback module* where (*callback*) functions are defined specifying the concrete actions of the server such as server state handling and response to messages.

The client behavior is realized using the OTP *gen_fsm* module. In accordance with the design, four state functions are defined: *idle, connected, calling* and *top_up*. The state function *idle* shown in Figure 1 initiates a *connecting* request to an FS.

The state function *connected* evaluates the requests for the consequent actions. For example, if *calling* is requested, the function will call the FS to check if the client has saved enough money to make a call. The reply {*ok,calling*} enables the client's calling request, which moves the FSM to the state *calling*.

```
connected(timeout,{M,SVR,SVRList})→              display(client,calling),
  gen_server:call(SVR,{request,timeout,M}),       {next_state,calling,
  display(M,timeout),                                 {M,SVR,SVRList}};
  {next_state,idle,{M,nil,SVRList}};              {error,low_prepaid}→
connected([Act,_SVR],{M,SVR,SVRList})→             display(low_prepaid),
  case Act==terminating of                         {next_state,connected,
    true →                                             {M,SVR,SVRList},20000};
      display(action,invalid),                    {ok,ready_to_top_up}→
      {next_state,connected,                        display(ready_to_top_up),
          {M,SVR,SVRList},20000};                   {next_state,top_up,
    false →                                             {M,SVR,SVRList},20000};
      F=gen_server:call(SVR,{request,Act,M}):      _Other →
      case F of                                      display(action,invalid),
        {ok,disconnected}→                           {next_state,connected,
          display(disconnected),                         {M,SVR,SVRList},20000}
          {next_state,idle,                      end
              {M,SVR,SVRList}};                 end.
        {ok,calling}→
```

The state function *calling* enables the calling process and when the FSM is in the state *calling*, only the *terminating* action can stop the process. This prevents the calling from being disrupted by any unintended actions.

```
calling([Act,_SVR],{M,SVR,SVRList})→                 {M,nil,SVRList}};
  case Act of                                   false →
    terminating →                                 display(server,invalid),
      gen_server:call(SVR,{request,Act,M}),       {next_state,calling,
      display(call,terminating),                      {M,SVR,SVRList}}
      {next_state,idle,                        end.
```

When being in the state *connected*, the client can ask to top up its account by sending the *top_up* request to the FS. If {*ok,ready_to_top_up*} is replied, the top up process is enabled, and the FSM moves to the state *top_up*. An action will trigger the state function *top_up* to either start the transaction by {*top_up, Prepaid*} operation (*Prepaid* is the amount of money the client is about to transfer), or cancel the process by sending the *cancelling* request.

```
top_up(timeout,{MB,RS,CSs})→          :          {MB,RS,CSs},20000};
  gen_server:call(RS,{request,timeout,MB}),:  {ok,cancelled} →
  action:show(timeout),               :          action:show(top_up_cancelled),
  {next_state,idle,{MB,nil,CSs}};      :          {next_state,connected,
top_up(AT,{MB,RS,CSs})→               :              {MB,RS,CSs},20000};
  P₃=gen_server:call(RS,{request,AT,MB}) :  _Other →
  case P₃ of                          :          action:show(action_invalid),
    {ok,top_up} →                     :          {next_state,top_up,
      action:show(top_up_completes),   :              {MB,RS,CSs},20000}
      {next_state,connected,           : end.
```

When the FSM moves to the state *connected* and *top_up*, a timer is initiated. The timer is set to 20,000ms. If within the time period, no action is performed, a *timeout* event will be generated and sent to the FS. The FSM is reset to the state *idle*. A function *command* is defined to simulate the receiving of external actions. It calls *gen_server:send_event* to triggers the state functions.

5.3   Test Design

The implementation is tested by applying the proposed testing scheme. The programs of the FS and the client are transformed into the BT formats. The corresponding CFBTs are constructed for test generation. The BT programs are further modified into the debugging mode as discussed in the subsection 4.2. For example, the function *idle_st_1* shown in Figure 2 is modified to the debugging mode:

```
idle_st_1(true,[AT,MB,RS,CSs,_P₁],Mode)→
  P₁ = gen_server:call(hd(CSs),{request,AT,MB}),
  case Mode of
    debugging→ debug_panel:posting({{idle_st_1,true},[{'P₁',P₁}]});
    running→ nothing
  end,
  {NextMode,DSwitch,DAT,DMB,DRS,DCSs,DP₁} =
      debug_panel:setting({idle_case1, [{'Mode',debugging},
          {'Switch',pattern_match([P₁],[{error,invalid_mobile}])},
          {'AT',AT},{'MB',MB},{'RS',RS},{'CSs',CSs},{'P₁',P₁}]}),
  idle_case1(DSwitch,[DAT,DMB,DRS,DCSs,DP₁],NextMode);
idle_st_1(false,[AT,MB,RS,CSs,_P₁],Mode)→
  {NextMode,DSwitch,DAT,DMB,DRS,DCSs,DP₁} =
      debug_panel:setting({idle_case1, [{'Mode',debugging},
          {'Switch',pattern_match([P₁],[{error,invalid_mobile}])},
          {'AT',AT},{'MB',MB},{'RS',RS},{'CSs',CSs},{'P₁',P₁}]}),
  idle_case1(DSwitch,[DAT,DMB,DRS,DCSs,DP₁],NextMode).
```

To derive a partial test to check a particular system property, one needs to identify the set of designated functions from the CFBT and preset the inputs for each function by using the debugging framework. For example, to test "*A client is the state idle and sends the connecting request to the FS svr_1. When {ok,connected,_CalledFS,svr_1} is replied, the connection is set up*". The set of functions is identified from the CFBT (Figure 4) as [*idle_st_1, idle_case1, idle_case2*]. The settings for the the corresponding functions are: [{*idle_st_1*, [ ]}, {*idle_case1*, [{*'Switch',false*}, {*idle_case2*, [{*'P₁'*, {*ok, connected, _CalledFS, svr_1*}}]}]}]. The debugging framework presets P_1 to {*ok, connected, _CalledFS, svr_1*} and bypasses the functional executions of *idle_case1*. For each function, the default running mode is *debugging*. The function *idle_st_1* will post the result of P_1 to the debugging framework for comparison before the executions are completed.

After the inputs being applied, the program should produce the message *mobile_connected*; otherwise, the implementation on such a property is faulty.

6 Conclusions and Future Work

Erlang is becoming an increasingly popular language, because it provides a sophisticated platform for the rapid development of concurrent and distributed applications. These often play a business-critical role, which makes testing a crucial component of the Erlang development process. So far, the majority of testing techniques and tools that have been developed for Erlang have focussed on functional testing. Tools such as QuickCheck [2] have become popular because they can rapidly test the system during development.

So far there has been no established technique for the structural testing of Erlang programs. Achieving targets such as branch-coverage has always depended on the ability of a developer to manually identify the necessary sets of test inputs. This paper has presented a technique to automate this process by applying a testability transformation [6].

The basic technique transforms an Erlang IUT into a functionally equivalent counterpart where each atomic function is represented by a binary format called the Functional Binary Tree. These functions are then aggregated into a complete tree (the Complete Functional Binary Tree). An important attribute of the tree is that every predicate that is required to reach any part of the tree is made explicit. The set of tests required to exercise the entire program simply correspond to those tests that are required to explore the entire tree.

A debugging framework is presented to facilitate the observation and manipulation of internal program variables as it is executed. As a function is executed, it provides the ability to track variable values. The execution of specific functions can be bypassed, and the input parameters to functions can be altered via the framework. This is particularly valuable for homing in on faulty areas in the source code.

A small telecoms case study has been presented to illustrate and evaluate the proposed model. By applying the proposed testing scheme, the components in the implementation were transformed into binary formats and then modified into the debugging mode. The CFBT was then constructed to derive the tests.

There still remains much to be done. Future work will apply the techniques here to larger industrial examples. When deriving a partial test to check a particular system property, the proposed model manually checks the CFBT to identify the set of functions. This on occasion can be very time consuming, and it is of interests if one can express the system properties with a formal language such as temporal logic [8], and use the formal expression as a guide to automatically identify the set of functions. This, however, remains a topic for the future work.

Acknowledgements

This work was funded by the FP7 project *ProTest*, number 215868: www.protest-project.eu. We're grateful to its academic and industrial members for input to this work and suggestions to improve the process.

References

1. Armstrong, J., Virding, R., Wikström, C., Williams, M.: Concurrent Programming in Erlang, 2nd edn. Prentice-Hall, Englewood Cliffs (1996)
2. Arts, T., Hughes, J., Johansson, J., Wiger, U.: Testing Telecoms Software with Quviq Quickcheck. In: Feeley, M., Trinder, P.W. (eds.) Proceedings of the 2006 ACM SIGPLAN Workshop on Erlang (Erlang 2006), pp. 2–10. ACM Press, New York (2006)
3. Bang-Jensen, J., Gutin, G.: Digraphs: Theory Algorithms and Applications. Springer, London (2001)
4. Guo, Q., Derrick, J.: Eliminating overlapping of pattern matching when verifying Erlang programs in μCRL. In: 12th International Erlang User Conference (EUC 2006), Stockholm, Sweden (2006)
5. Guo, Q., Derrick, J., Hoch, C.: Verifying Erlang Telecommunication Systems with the Process Algebra μCRL. In: Suzuki, K., Higashino, T., Yasumoto, K., El-Fakih, K. (eds.) FORTE 2008. LNCS, vol. 5048, pp. 201–217. Springer, Heidelberg (2008)
6. Harman, M., Hu, L., Hierons, R., Wegener, J., Sthamer, H., Baresel, A.: Testability Transformation. IEEE Transactions on Software Engineering 30(1), 3–16 (2004)
7. King, J.: Symbolic Execution and Program Testing. Communications of the ACM 19(7) (1976)
8. Kröger, F.: Temporal logic of programs. Springer, New York (1987)
9. McMinn, P.: Search-based software test data generation: a survey. Softw. Test, Verif. Reliab. 14(2), 105–156 (2004)
10. Mottu, J.-M., Baudry, B., Traon, Y.: Model Transformation Testing: Oracle Issue. In: Frantzen, L., Merayo, M., Múñez, M. (eds.) 28th International Conference on Software Testing, Verificaiton and Validation Workshop (ICSTW 2008), Washington, DC, USA, pp. 105–112. IEEE Computer Society Press, Los Alamitos (2008)
11. Naslavsky, L., Ziv, H., Richardson, D.J.: Using Model Transformation to Support Model-based Test Coverage Measurement. In: AST 2008: Proceedings of the 3rd international workshop on Automation of software test, pp. 1–6. ACM, New York (2008)
12. Sun, C.-A.: A Transformation-Based Approach to Generating Scenario-Oriented Test Cases from UML Activity Diagrams for Concurrent Applications. In: 32nd Annual IEEE International Computer Software and Applications Conference, pp. 160–167. IEEE Computer Society Press, Los Alamitos (2008)
13. US Department of Transportation, Federal Aviation Administration. Software Approval Guidelines (2003) 8110.49
14. Voas, J., Miller, K.: Software Testability: The New Verification. IEEE Software 12(3), 17–28 (1995)
15. Zhu, H., Hall, P.A.V., May, J.H.R.: Software Unit Test Coverage and Adequacy. ACM Computing Surveys 29(4), 366–427 (1997)

Interaction Coverage Meets Path Coverage
by SMT Constraint Solving

Wolfgang Grieskamp[1], Xiao Qu[2], Xiangjun Wei[1],
Nicolas Kicillof[1], and Myra B. Cohen[2]

[1] Microsoft Corporation
[2] University of Nebraska, Lincoln, USA

Abstract. We present a novel approach for generating interaction combinations based on SMT constraint resolution. Our approach can generate maximal interaction coverage in the presence of general constraints as supported by the underlying solver. It supports *seeding* with general predicates, which allows us to combine it with path exploration such that both interaction and path coverage goals can be met. Our approach is motivated by the application to behavioral model-based testing in the Spec Explorer tool, where parameter combinations must be generated such that all path conditions of a model action have at least one combination which enables the path. It is applied in a large-scale project for model-based quality assurance of interoperability documentation at Microsoft.

1 Introduction

Combinatorial interaction testing (CIT) generates test cases that contain a specified set of combinations of parameter values for testing. The most common type of CIT for testing is pair-wise CIT where all 2-way combinations of parameter values are tested together in at least one test case [3]. CIT serves to reduce the full Cartesian product space of a set of parameters, which may be extremely large in real-world applications.

In a model-based testing tool in the style of Spec Explorer [10], CIT can play a role for generating parameter combinations for actions of the system-under-test. In these approaches, a labeled transition system or finite state machine is constructed from a set of guarded state update rules, where each model rule is associated with a parameterized action. The model rule is executed using symbolic path exploration, seeding parameter assignments for testing which cover all paths of the model. However, the implementation may have black-box behavior which is over-abstracted in the model, creating the need for generating more parameter combinations than needed for covering the model. This gap can be closed by combining path exploration with CIT. Thereby, the challenge is to come up with a CIT generator which aims at fulfilling the interaction coverage goal *and* the path coverage goal.

In this paper, we present a novel CIT algorithm which addresses this challenge. Our solution is integrated into the Spec Explorer model-based testing tool [10,11,13] version 2, and is driven by application requirements in protocol testing for Microsoft's interoperability program [12]. In protocol testing, actions represent messages sent via the network, which often have many different parameters. The implementation is naturally black-box, and not all its behavior is revealed in the model, therefore creating the

M. Núñez et al. (Eds.): TESTCOM/FATES 2009, LNCS 5826, pp. 97–112, 2009.

need to use different parameter combinations in tests beyond those that can be derived from the behavioral model.

The solution we have developed differs significantly from existing ones. Leveraging the performance and feature set of an SMT solver, we have devised an algorithm which generates interaction combinations solely based on constraint resolution and model enumeration as provided by the constraint engine. In this work we use the SMBT solver Z3 [9]. While other SMT solvers may also suffice we have not experimented with this. The algorithm works in reverse to existing algorithms (e.g. [8]): instead of constructing combinations bottom-up, it enumerates combinations using the solver in a top-down fashion, starting with the largest partitions of interactions. While this approach requires some heuristics to overcome scalability issues, the investigation of which is still preliminary, we have clearly identified the core of a novel algorithm, which will guarantee the maximum interaction coverage obtainable, while also satisfying general constraints and path coverage seeding. In our initial benchmarks, this algorithm performs comparatively well, and it is also used already on a daily basis for interoperability testing.

2 Motivation

In order to motivate the work we begin with an example. Suppose we have a highly abstracted file server. The file server provides two operations: write content to a file and read content from a file. **Write** takes several parameters. Its effect depends on the current state of the file system on the server. **Read** extracts the current file content. Part of the modeling and testing problem is to predict which content to expect after one or more write operations have happened.

A problem like this can be modeled in Spec Explorer using one of its supported notations, C#. The model is given in Fig. 1. It defines a global state variable `fileSys` which models the current state of the server as a mapping from file names to file contents. It next defines two actions and their state transition rules as C# methods. In `Write(doOverride, doAppend, name, content)`, the `doOverride` parameter indicates whether an existing file is allowed to be overridden. The `doAppend` parameter specifies whether content should be appended to an existing file. The remaining parameters describe the file name and content to write. `Read(fileName)` delivers the content of the file in the current state, as predicted by the model. We have used the `Contracts.Requires` statement as an enabling condition for this action, which excludes attempts to read files with unknown names.

For the general approach on how such models are executed and explored by Spec Explorer, we refer readers to the other publications about this technology ([10,11,13,14]). For this exposition it should suffice to know that model exploration yields a transition system where each state represents the model state (in this case the file server content). Transitions are drawn from source to target states for all methods which carry the `[Action]` attribute *if* there exists a set of parameters such that the enabling condition is true in the source state. The target state then results from updates performed in the method.

Fig. 2(a) shows the expected result of exploring this model (as constructed and rendered by Spec Explorer) with our approach to CIT, given the following settings (provided in a configuration file):

```
static MapContainer<string,string> fileSys;

enum ErrorCode { Ok, FileExists }

static ErrorCode Write(
  bool doOverride, bool doAppend, string fileName, string content)
{
  if (fileSys.ContainsKey(fileName))
    if (!doOverride) return ErrorCode.FileExists;
    else if (doAppend) fileSys[fileName] = fileSys[fileName] + content;
    else fileSys[fileName] = content;
  else
    fileSys[fileName] = content;
  return ErrorCode.Ok;
}

[Action]
static string Read(string fileName)
{
  Contracts.Requires(fileSys.ContainsKey(fileName));
  return fileSys[fileName];
}
```

Fig. 1. The File Server Model

1. In the initial state, the server's file system contains one file named "f1", the content of which is "a";
2. The domain of values for the file name parameter of Write has been fixed to the set {"f1","f2"};
3. The domain of values for the file content parameter of Write has been fixed to the singleton set {"c"};
4. The three parameters doOverride, doAppend, and fileName are declared to be in pairwise interaction;
5. The allowed sequences of actions have been sliced to be just one Write followed by one Read using Spec Explorer's approach to model extraction and slicing (see e.g. [11])

Fig. 2(a) shows that five parameter combinations have been generated. In contrast, Fig. 2(b) shows only four combinations. The four combinations are in fact sufficient to cover all 2-way interactions of three parameters with the 2-ranked domains. However, as the model exploration graph shows, these four combinations do not cover all possible paths of the Write method: a combination is missing which covers the case where content is appended to an existing file. The reason is that the condition of this path actually represents a 3-way interaction: for to be path to be covered, a certain combination for the three parameters doOverride, doAppend, and fileName must be chosen, which will only by luck be generated when selecting 2-way interactions. On the other hand, having declared the problem as a full 3-way interaction in the first place, would have generated 8 combinations. As can be seen, this difference in the size of the solution set can easily explode when generalizing this observation to real-world samples.

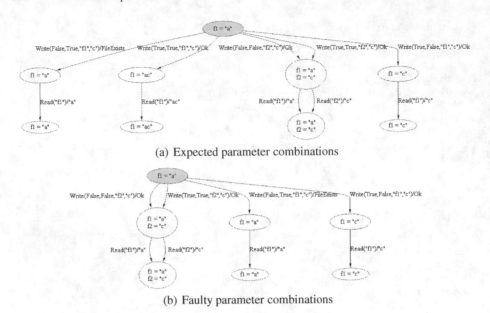

(a) Expected parameter combinations

(b) Faulty parameter combinations

Fig. 2. Exploration Result of File Server Model

Path Exploration and Seeding. Spec Explorer (the newest version 2 – also called Spec Explorer for Visual Studio, [10]) performs model exploration by symbolic execution of the model code. In order to integrate CIT, we have established a suitable separation of concerns, which allows us to formulate the CIT problem independent from the model exploration problem.

Spec Explorer's model exploration is based on forward symbolic execution of a model rule, using the exploring runtime (XRT, [14]). Initially, all parameters are set to symbolic values. When execution proceeds and hits a branching point which depends on a symbolic value, Spec Explorer forks execution and continues with two paths, one assuming the branch condition to be true, and the other one assuming it to be false. It thereby effectively spawns a tree, where the leafs represent the final path condition as a conjunction of all branch conditions taken in that path, depending on the symbolic parameters. Loops are dealt with by pruning them according to code coverage and bounds.

For our example in Fig. 1, the path conditions of the **Write** operation are annotated in the code in Fig 3. Here, we assume execution in a state where the file system contains a single mapping of name "f1" to content "a"; in other states, the conditions may be different.

In order to generate combinations for parameters such that path conditions are respected, we not only need to provide the combination algorithm with interaction goals, but also to *seed* it with the set of path conditions, such that the generated combinations satisfy each path condition at least once. Seeding has been introduced in other CIT algorithms [2,3,8], but concrete values as seeds are not sufficient for our purpose, we also need to be able to seed with general constraints.

```
if (fileSys.ContainsKey(fileName))
  if (!doOverride)
    return ErrorCode.FileExists;   ⤳ fileName  =  "f1"  ∧  ¬  doOverride
  else if (doAppend)
    fileSys[fileName] = fileSys[fileName] + content;
         ⤳ fileName  =  "f1"  ∧  doOverride  ∧  doAppend
  else
    fileSys[fileName] = content;
         ⤳ fileName  =  "f1"  ∧  doOverride  ∧  ¬  doAppend
else
  fileSys[fileName] = content;   ⤳ fileName  ≠  "f1"
return ErrorCode.Ok;
```

Fig. 3. Annotated Path Conditions of `Write`

Requirements for the CIT Algorithm. From the observations above, the abstraction of the CIT algorithm in the context of the exploration problem is designed to take the following inputs:

1. A set of *interactions*, expressed as relations between parameters. The algorithm should generate the smallest set of value combinations it can find that includes the Cartesian product of each interaction relation (of variable strength).
2. A *constraint*: every solution the algorithm generates should satisfy the constraint. The constraint describes the possible overall solution set for the parameters, by giving for example ranges for individual parameters.
3. A set of *seeds* represented as predicates. There should be at least one solution satisfying each seed, provided it is consistent with the constraint.

Having such an algorithm, we can integrate well with the exploration. Assuming the user has defined the interaction relation, a general constraint that must be satisfied, and seeds, the overall exploration method including CIT is as follows.

1. Compute the symbolic transitions and path conditions of each action method in the current state (by symbolic execution, concolic execution, or any other method).
2. Enrich user supplied seeds by a seed for each path condition.
3. Compute the combinations from the user supplied interactions, enriched seeds, and constraint.
4. For every symbolic transition, instantiate it (including the target state it reaches) for each generated solution which satisfies the path condition.

This approach has worked well for integration of CIT into the Spec Explorer tool. We will not formalize the actual integration but focus on the CIT algorithm we have implemented to fit the procedure outlined above.

3 Solution

In this section, we formalize the CIT problem as a constraint problem, and derive the algorithm based on the constraint resolution engine Z3. In general CIT generation is an NP hard problem; algorithms use heuristics to minimize the size of solutions [3].

Background. Let X be a given set of variables (symbols), V a set of primitive values, OP a set of primitive operations, and T a set of terms, as defined below:

$$
\begin{array}{lll}
x \in X & & \textit{variables} \\
v \in V & ::= \text{true} \mid \text{false} \mid 0 \mid 1 \mid \ldots & \textit{values} \\
op \in OP & ::= \wedge|\vee| \neg \ |=|<| + | - | \ldots & \textit{operations} \\
f \in F & & \textit{fields} \\
t \in T & ::= x & \textit{variable} \\
& \mid \ v & \textit{value} \\
& \mid \ op(t_1, \ldots, t_n) & \textit{operation} \\
& \mid \ [f_1 \Rightarrow t_1, \ldots, f_n \Rightarrow t_n] & \textit{tuple} \\
& \mid \ t.f & \textit{selection}
\end{array}
$$

Primitive values, V, and operations, OP, support at least Booleans and integers, but other types (like floats, strings) may be supported as well without additional conceptual complications. Note that terms can be used to denote values as well as constraints, which we consider to be Boolean terms. Henceforth we will call a Boolean term a constraint. Tuples are used to represent structured values and have named fields $f \in F$. It holds that $[\ldots, f \Rightarrow v, \ldots].f \equiv v$. We assume terms are well typed (for example, only Boolean terms are combined with logical operators $\wedge$, $\vee$) but omit the details of the type system here for the sake of readability.

The subset of terms which only consists of primitive values or tuple values is given as follows:

$$
T_V \subseteq T ::= v \mid [f_1 \Rightarrow v_1, \ldots, f_n \Rightarrow v_n]
$$

Given a value assignment $\sigma \in X \to T_V$, the evaluation of terms is described by the function $\text{eval}_\sigma \in T \to T_V$ which maps every term into a value term. We omit the obvious definition. This function is defined as the usual homomorphism over the structure of terms, substituting variables with their assignment in σ, computing the result of applying primitive operations $op(v_1, \ldots, v_n)$ to values in dependency of the semantics of the operation, and reducing tuple field selections. We omit the obvious definition.

Given a set of variables $Y \subseteq X$, and a constraint c which is closed under Y (all variables it contains are in Y), the *models* of Y for c are the value assignments under which the following constraint is true:

$$
\mathsf{M}(Y, c) = \{\sigma \in Y \to T_V \mid \text{eval}_\sigma c = \text{true}\}
$$

We next define projections over model sets w.r.t. a given set of terms. Given $Y \subseteq X$ a set of variables, $M \subseteq Y \to T_V$ a set of models for it, and $S \subseteq T$ a set of terms closed under Y, we write $M \uparrow S$ to denote the evaluations of those terms under each model in M.

$$
M \uparrow S = \{\text{eval}_\sigma \lhd S \mid \sigma \in M\}
$$

In the above notation, $f \lhd S$ denotes the domain restriction of a function to the set S $(f \lhd S = \{(x, y) \in f \mid x \in S\})$.

With help of projection we can easily describe the exhaustive Cartesian combination of values for a set of terms as extracted from a model set. For example, if $Y = \{x, y\}$, $c = 0 \leq x \leq 1 \wedge 0 \leq y \leq 1$, and $S = \{x + 1, y + 1\}$, then $\mathsf{M}(Y, c) \uparrow S = \{\{x+1 \mapsto 1, y+1 \mapsto 1\}, \{x+1 \mapsto 1, y+1 \mapsto 2\}, \{x+1 \mapsto 2, y+1 \mapsto 1\}, \{x+1 \mapsto 2, y+1 \mapsto 2\}\}$.

CIT Problem. Having defined the notions of terms, constraints, and models, we can now define CIT with generalized seeds.

A CIT problem with seeds (in the remaining of this paper, CIT problem for short) is a tuple $\Pi = (P, I, S, c)$, where $P \subseteq X$ is a set of variables, $I \subseteq \mathbb{P}T$ is a set of sets of terms, called the interaction relation, $S \in \mathbb{P}T$ is a set of constraints, the seeds, and $c \in T$ a general constraint. All terms (constraints) appearing in interactions, seeds, and the general constraint are closed under P, i.e. do not contain other variables than P.

An interaction $i \in I$ describes a set of terms which are declared to be in mutual interaction. For example, if we have parameters x, y, z, and they should be in pairwise interaction, we will have $I = \{\{x, y\}, \{y, z\}, \{z, x\}\}$. Note that we do no restrict interactions to be just built from variables: they can be arbitrary terms. If the problem is to express pairwise interaction between the fields of tuple x with three fields a, b, c, we will have $P = \{x\}$ and $I = \{\{x.a, x.b\}, \{x.b, x.c\}, \{x.c, x.a\}\}$. And if the problem is to express pairwise interactions between the three first bits of a number x representing a bit mask, we will have $P = \{x\}$ and $I = \{\{x\&1 \neq 0, x\&2 \neq 0\}, \{x\&2 \neq 0, x\&4 \neq 0\}, \{x\&4 \neq 0, x\&1 \neq 0\}\}$.

A CIT algorithm $Alg(\Pi)$, with $\Pi = (P, I, S, c)$, produces a set of models for P. While a unique model set for the interaction combination problem does not exist in general, we can characterize the requirements for $Alg(\Pi)$ as follows:

- All models satisfy the constraint c and the disjunction of the seeds in S:

$$Alg(\Pi) \subseteq \mathsf{M}(P, c \wedge \vee S) \tag{1}$$

- For every seed $s \in S$, if there exists a model which satisfies $c \wedge s$, then at least one such model must be contained in the solution set:

$$\mathsf{M}(P, c \wedge s) \neq \varnothing \Rightarrow Alg(\Pi) \cap \mathsf{M}(P, c \wedge s) \neq \varnothing \tag{2}$$

- For every interaction $i = \{t_1, \ldots, t_n\} \in I$, the models for the t_i should be exhaustively combined:

$$\mathsf{M}(P, c \wedge \vee S) \uparrow i = Alg(\Pi) \uparrow i \tag{3}$$

Solver. Our implementation uses the SMT solver Z3 [9], based on the satisfiability-modulo-theory method. The constraints produced by Spec Explorer's path exploration include encodings of the full .NET type system with numerous basic types and object references, as well as special types for modeling as symbolic recursive free data types and collections. While these domains can be in principle passed on to other solvers supporting a sufficiently expressive formalism, Z3 provides a match for our application as it is particularly targeted to solving such domains efficiently.

Assume the solver works on terms as have been described before, where constraints are represented as Boolean terms. The abstraction of the solver we use in this paper provides one single entry point: given a constraint c over variables $Y \subseteq X$, solve(c) delivers either the constant fail, indicating that it did not found a solution for the variables in c, or a model $\sigma \in Y \to T_V$ which gives evidence that the constraint can be evaluated to true with the given variable assignment.

In order to have a solver exposing such an API enumerate all solutions for a term t under a constraint c, a loop as the one below is typically used:

given c, t
while $\sigma = \mathsf{solve}(c) \neq \mathsf{fail}$
    output $\mathsf{eval}_\sigma(t)$; $c := c \wedge \neg\, (t = \mathsf{eval}_\sigma t)$

Z3 is efficient at enumerating solutions this way. For a constraint of small to medium size, which is common for our relatively localized problem of generating parameter combinations, Z3 can enumerate thousands of solutions in a matter of seconds. While the solver is based on heuristics in order to deal with problems which are generally exponential, in current applications we rarely encountered situations where those failed.

Algorithm. The algorithm we developed appears to be straightforward in comparison to other algorithms for generation of interaction combinations. It is based on the idea that the solver can be leveraged during enumeration to not only exclude complete solutions previously seen (as we have shown above), but also partial ones which represent combinations for interactions.

Suppose $\Pi = (P, I, S, c)$ a CIT problem. We construct *partitions* of interactions from the power set $\mathbb{P}I$ and process them with decreasing cardinality (please note that the notion of partition used here is not the same as in set theory, but just means a subset of $\mathbb{P}I$ – we borrow the definition from other CIT work). For each of the partitions, we enumerate the solutions and exclude the full solution as well as each individual interaction combination in that solution. We continue until partitions have cardinality one. This process ensures that we first attempt to put as many interactions as possible into one solution.

As an example, let $I = \{i_1, i_2, i_3\}$. We first generate solutions for partition $\{i_1, i_2, i_3\}$, trying to fit as many interactions as we can. We continue then with partitions $\{i_1, i_2\}$, $\{i_2, i_3\}$, and $\{i_1, i_3\}$. If we have not yet covered all interactions, we will try $\{i_1\}$, $\{i_2\}$ and $\{i_3\}$, which will finally ensure that we have reached the maximum possible coverage. To exclude solutions repeating interaction on the same partition level, we add an exclusion constraint for each of the interactions of the given partition. Let $part = \{\{x, y\}, \{y, z\}\}$, and $\sigma = \{x \mapsto 1, y \mapsto 2, z \mapsto 3\}$. Then the exclusion constraint for the entire solution and for the partition will be

$$\neg\, (x = 1 \wedge y = 2 \wedge z = 3) \wedge$$
$$\neg\, (x = 1 \wedge y = 2) \wedge \neg\, (y = 2 \wedge z = 3)$$

In order to deal with seeds, we inject their processing into the processing of each partition. Maintaining a set of seeds which have not yet been covered, we try on each partition first to cover any of the seeds, before allowing generation of solutions for seeds which are already covered. If any seeds remain at the end that have not been covered with any partition, we will generate a solution for them. (This is possible since we may stop iterating partitions early, when all interactions have been covered.)

Of course, the full power set of I, which stands for all partitions, may be huge ($2^{\#I}$). However, we can use the solver to check whether enumeration of solutions for one partition has closed some interactions, i.e. fully covered them. Every subsequently processed

```
# Input and Variables
given Π = (P, I, S, c)
var φ := c ∧ (∨ S)
var coverage ∈ I → ℙ(T → T_V) := {i ↦ ∅ | i ∈ I}
var open ∈ ℙ I := I
var seeds ∈ ℙ S := S
# The algorithm
proc Algo
      # process partitions
      for card := #I downto 1
            var parts := {part ∈ ℙ open | #part = card)
            while parts ≠ ∅
                  let part = choose(parts); parts := parts \ {part}
                  if SolvePartition(part)
                        parts := {part ∈ parts | part ⊆ open}
                  else
                        parts := prune(parts, part)
      # process uncovered seeds
      foreach s ∈ seeds
            Solve(s)
# Generate solutions for one partition
proc SolvePartition(part)
      var progress := false
      # attempt to cover seeds in this partition
      foreach s ∈ seeds
            if Solve(ExcludeCovered(part) ∧ s)
                  seeds := seeds \ {s}; progress := true
      # enumerate all remaining solutions of this partition
      while Solve(ExcludeCovered(part))
            progress := true
      return progress
# Generate solution for a given constraint
proc Solve(τ)
      if σ = solve(φ ∧ τ) ≠ fail
            output σ # output solution
            φ := φ ∧ Exclude(σ)
            foreach i ∈ open
                  coverage(i) := coverage(i) ∪ (σ ↑ i)
                  if solve(φ ∧ ExcludeCovered({i}) = fail)
                        # no more solutions, close interaction
                        open := open \ {i}
            return true
      else return false
# Construct exclusion constraint for interactions
proc ExcludeCovered(interactions)
      return ∧ {Exclude(f) | i ∈ interactions, f ∈ coverage(i)}
# Construct exclusion constraint for term assignment
proc Exclude(assignment)
      return ¬ ∧ {t = t' | (t, t') ∈ assignment}
```

Fig. 4. Algorithm

partition containing a closed interaction can be then skipped. This drastically reduces the number of partitions that actually require solution enumeration for the average case.

Nevertheless, the situation can arise where the algorithm reaches a "plateau": that happens if for a given partition, no solution at all is found. The algorithm may search for a long time (and virtually not terminate) to find partitions that would contribute to the solution set and eventually close interactions. In this case, a heuristic to prune some of the partitions of higher cardinality is applied. As partitions of cardinality one are never pruned, the heuristic only affects the size of the solution set, by potentially producing more solutions than required, but never its correctness.

The algorithm is given in pseudo-code in Fig. 4. It is based on two primitives that represent heuristics, over which it is parameterized: choose selects the next partition to process from a set of partitions of equal cardinality, and prune prunes the set of partitions of equal cardinality in case a plateau is reached.

The primitive choose($parts$) chooses which partition to process next from the set of partitions $parts$. A good choice may influence efficiency, and decrease the chance of running into a plateau. In our current implementation of the algorithm, this has not been exploited, and the choice is arbitrary.

The primitive prune($parts$, $part$) represents the heuristic to prune partitions in case the algorithm has reached a plateau. Currently, we have implemented a very simple heuristic, which will just skip the entire cardinality level:

$$\text{prune}(parts, part) = \varnothing$$

A deep investigation of heuristics has not been conducted yet for our approach, leaving space for improvement. However, even with the most simple heuristics as currently implemented, the algorithm performs well in comparative benchmarks and in everyday applications.

Illustration. We illustrate the algorithm based on a small example. This simulation in particular shows how partition enumeration works. Suppose the CIT problem $\Pi = (P, I, S, c)$ where:

$$P = \{a, b, c\}$$
$$I = \{i_1, i_2\} \textbf{ where } i_1 = \{a, b\}, i_2 = \{b, c\}$$
$$S = \{s_1, s_2\} \textbf{ where } s_1 = (a = b = c), s_2 = (\neg\, s_1)$$
$$c = a \in [0..1] \wedge b \in [0..1] \wedge c \in [0..2]$$

The constraint c defines the range of the parameters. Note that $x \in [l..u]$ is just a shortcut for $x \geq l \wedge x \leq u$. The constraint can be more general than simple value ranges. However, for the CIT algorithm to terminate, the number of possible solutions to the parameters under the constraint and seed disjunction must be bounded. These are the steps perform by the algorithm for that input:

1. Initialize $\phi := c \wedge \vee S$ (i.e. $\phi = c$ as $\vee S = $ true).
2. Solve partitions of cardinality 2. There is only one such partition. This leads to the call *SolvePartition*($\{i_1, i_2\}$), which is processed as follows:
    (a) Call *Solve*(*ExcludeCovered*($\{i_1, i_2\}$) $\wedge$ s_2). As there is no coverage at this point, this amounts to *Solve*(s_2). The solution the solver produces is $(0, 0, 1)$,

and henceforth ϕ will be updated to $\phi := \phi \wedge \neg (a = 0 \wedge b = 0 \wedge c = 1)$. Moreover, interaction solutions $\{a \mapsto 0, b \mapsto 0\}$ and $\{b \mapsto 0, c \mapsto 1\}$ are added to $coverage(i_1)$ and $coverage(i_2)$, resp.

(b) Remove the seed s_2 from the $seeds$ set.

(c) Call $Solve(ExcludeCovered(\{i_1, i_2\}) \wedge s_1)$. This amounts to the call $Solve(\neg (a == 0 \wedge b == 0) \wedge \neg (b == 0 \wedge c == 1) \wedge s_1)$. The only solution the solver can produce is $(1, 1, 1)$. Hence, $\phi := \phi \wedge \neg (a = 1 \wedge b = 1 \wedge c = 1)$, and interaction solutions $\{a \mapsto 1, b \mapsto 1\}$ and $\{b \mapsto 1, c \mapsto 1\}$ will be added to $coverage$.

(d) Remove the seed s_1 from the $seeds$ set which becomes empty at this point.

(e) From now on, additional solutions will be generated without involvement of seeds. The solutions are $(1, 0, 0)$ and $(0, 1, 2)$. At the end of this step, we have:

$$coverage(\{a, b\}) = \{(0, 0), (1, 1), (1, 0), (0, 1)\}$$
$$coverage(\{b, c\}) = \{(0, 1), (1, 1), (0, 0), (1, 2)\}$$

This closes interaction $i_1 = \{a, b\}$, which will be removed from the $open$ set; yet, i_2 is still open.

3. The algorithm now goes to partition cardinality level 1. While there exists two partitions at this level, namely $\{\{i_1\}\}$ and $\{\{i_2\}\}$, since i_1 is not longer open, only one call $SolvePartition(\{i_2\})$ will be processed. As there are no seeds open at this point, the algorithm will try to produce as many solutions as it can using $Solve(ExcludeCovered(\{i_2\}))$. In the first iteration, the exclusion expands to $Solve(\neg (b = 0 \wedge c = 1) \wedge \neg (b = 1 \wedge c = 1) \wedge \neg (b = 0 \wedge c = 0) \wedge \neg (b = 1 \wedge c = 2))$. The algorithm produces subsequent solutions $(0, 0, 2)$ and $(0, 1, 0)$. This adds the missing coverage for $i_2 = \{b, c\}$, while necessarily repeating some of the already covered combinations for i_1.

Implementation. The implementation of our CIT solution follows the conceptual approach as shown in Fig. 4. However, there are a few notable differences which result from efficiency considerations. Instead of constructing the exclusion constraints from scratch over and over again, they are incrementally built. Moreover, Z3's capability to maintain nested contexts and assert constraints in these contexts is exploited to avoid passing the exclusion constraint as a whole wherever this is possible. Instead, in the loop where models are generated, exclusions are added in each iteration to the current active Z3 context. This allows the solver to maintain internal caches and analysis results for the accumulated constraint, and is key to efficiency. In addition, calls to the solver are avoided when possible, e.g. for the closure check, which only needs to be performed on those interactions which have new solutions, and only at the end of each partition processing.

4   Benchmarks

In order to measure the efficiency of the CIT algorithm, we have compared it with other available tools. Such a comparison is not completely adequate, as our approach is more expressive by enabling general constraints and seeds, but useful anyway to assess the cost of the generalization. The results are shown in Table 1.

Table 1. Benchmark Results (number of solutions/execution time)

GROUP 1 Fixed Strength with or without "Excludes" [6]

NO	Problem definition	mAETG_SAT	SA_SAT	PICT	TestCover	Our
1	CA(3, 5^4)	143	127	151	NA	147
2	CA(2, 6^3)	37	36	39	36	38
3	CA(2,3^3) Excludes: {(5,6), (4,6), (0,7), (2,3), (2,8), (1,5,8)}	10	10	10	10	10
4	CA(3, 6^4) Excludes: {(4,20),(15,19),(8,20),(7,14)}	241	251	250	NA	244
5	t=2 SPIN simulator without constraints	25/0.4s	16/25.6s	23/1s	NA	40/3s
6	t=2 SPIN simulator with constraints	24/1.5s	19/694.3s	26/1s	NA	43/4s

GROUP 2 Variable Strength: Disjoint Interaction Sets (average of ten runs) [4]

NO	Problem definition	mAETG_SAT	SA_SAT	PICT	TestCover	Our
7	CA(2,$4^3 5^3 6^2$) 3-way(V_0, V_1, V_2, V_3, V_4)	NA	101	NA	NA	176/1.4s
8	CA(2,$4^3 5^3 6^2$) 3-way(V_0, V_1, V_2); 3-way(V_3, V_4, V_5)	NA	125	NA	NA	142/0.8s
9	CA(2,$4^3 5^3 6^2$) 3-way(V_0, V_1, V_2)	NA	180	NA	NA	187/0.8s
10	CA(2,$3^9 2^2$) 3-way(V_0, V_1, V_2); 3-way(V_3, V_4, V_5); 3-way(V_6, V_7, V_8)	NA	27	NA	NA	50/0.7s
11	CA(2,3^{15},{CA(3,3^4), CA(3,3^5),CA(3,3^6)}) 3-way(V_0, V_1, V_2, V_3); 3-way(V_4, V_5, V_6, V_7, V_8); 3-way($V_9, V_{10}, V_{11}, V_{12}, V_{13}, V_{14}$)	NA	34.8	NA	NA	120/4s

Many tools [3,4,5,17] are available to generate t-wise CIT samples, where t is fixed between all parameter interactions, and is usually equal to 2 or 3. Some of these are also able to handle certain types of constraints expressed as "exclusions": specific value combinations that must not occur in the sample. We use the benchmarks proposed by Cohen et al. [6] as the first group, since they are in this category and are based on real CIT problems for configurable software. We compare our results with the published results from 4 tools [6]: mAETG_SAT, a greedy algorithm; SA_SAT, a simulated annealing meta-heuristic algorithm; and two commercial tools, PICT and TestCover [8,20].

The first column of Table 1 defines the problem for each benchmark. We use a notation similar to that of [4,6] to make the comparison easier. CA($t,v_i^{x_i}$) means there are x_i parameters, each with v_i values, and t is the testing (or interaction) strength. All parameters will be combined with the same interaction strength. Values for each parameter are written as unique continuous integers starting from 0, across all parameters. For instance, if the first parameter has 3 values, then these are assigned 0, 1, 2, while the next parameter values start at 4. CA(2,$4^3 5^3 6^2$) stands for a pairwise CIT sample between 8 parameters: the first 3 parameters contain 4 values each, the second 3 parameters contain 5 values each, and the last 2 parameters contain 6 values each. In this example, the total number of unique values is 39 labeled from 0 to 38. "Excludes" sets contain combinations of values that must be excluded.

The first group can be divided into 2 subgroups. The first subgroup (case 1 to 4) is composed of benchmarks containing a small number of parameters – no more than 5–, while the other is composed of real subjects (like the "spin simulator" – case 5 and 6) that contain between 20 and 60 parameters. The definitions can be found in [6].

Since the problems in the former subgroup are small, execution time is not provided in [6]. We compare these by measuring the number of solutions only: the smaller the solution size, the less effort testing will require. From this viewpoint, our approach works well by generating solutions within the middle of the range of other tools. For the larger sized problems, as in the latter subgroup, both size and time are used to measure the results. In this subgroup (5 and 6), we find that our approach takes less than 5 seconds to run, but generates more solutions than the other tools. Note that when disabling our preliminary pruning heuristic the size of the solution set becomes comparable to the best in the group; however, this can cause our algorithm to hang for some cases (not the given benchmarks).

In the second group, we provide additional subsets of parameters that are to be combined at higher strengths of testing. We use the notation (V_i) to represent the parameter indexed from left to right that is contained within the higher strength subset. For example, in case 9, in addition to pairwise interactions between each pair of variables, a 3-way interaction among variables V_0, V_1 and V_2 is also required. The data in this group is from Cohen et al. [4] (average of ten runs) where variable strength is restricted to disjoint sets.[1]

For the second group, only the SA algorithm is available for comparison. We use the benchmarks that were created to measure it [4]. In case 7 through 9, where there are a small number of parameters – less than 10– our approach sometimes generates a solution comparable in size to that of SA, in less than 1 second. However, some of our solutions (case 1) are considerably larger. As the number of input parameters increases to 15 (case 11), although our approach still can find solutions within 5 seconds, the size of the generated solutions increases to nearly 4 times that of the solutions produced by SA.

In summary, our approach is able to generate small sized solutions competitive with other tools for small problems, containing less than 10 parameters, as in cases 1, 2, 3 and 4. Our absolute run-times, although sometimes greater than those of other tools, never exceed a minute across all runs and most finish within 10 seconds. In the context of the application to Spec Explorer, this additional time is marginal compared to other processes, such as symbolic exploration in general.

As the number of parameters increases, our approach generates solutions larger than those of some other tools. In these cases, the failure point is the pruning heuristic failed, since in previous benchmarks where pruning was not yet applied, timing and solution size were very competitive. However, pruning is required, as we discovered when testing the algorithm against other samples, and finding a better heuristic than the current one needs further investigation.

---

[1] PICT may be able to handle this, but its public version is not.

5   Related Work

There has been a large body of work on generating test suites and configuration samples using CIT [1,3,15,22,18]. Applications of CIT include functional input testing, [3], configuration sampling [22], regression testing [18] and more recently event sequence testing [23]. In most of this work the focus has been to construct a CIT sample using a model that has a single interaction strength across all parameters of the problem. Two primary algorithm types have been used for CIT sample generation – greedy methods [3,8,17] and meta-heuristic search [4,5]. Other techniques use direct or recursive mathematical constructions (see [15] for a survey). The focus of much of this work has been on minimizing the CIT sample size.

There has been limited work on constructing and applying variable strength CIT [3,4,8,22]. The work of both D. Cohen et al. [3] and Czerwonka [8] models hierarchies of parameters represented as varying strengths into their greedy construction algorithms. In both [4,22] a restricted type of variable strength CIT is generated and empirically evaluated. The solution is limited to a subset of cases where interactions are partitioned into disjoint sets for stronger testing and a base CIT sample is maintained over the whole set of parameters. Our work goes further, by making interaction sets the primary focus of our construction – they drive the generation and there is no restriction on the relationships between interaction sets.

Inter-parameter dependencies (or constraints) have been the subject of several recent papers. They were first studied by D. Cohen et al. in [3]. The primary method for resolving constraints in that work is to remodel interaction definitions. Work by Cohen et al. [6,7] introduces the use of Boolean SAT solvers to ensure that samples generated by heuristic search and greedy algorithms cover all required interactions while satisfying constraints. In this work all constraints are translated into "exclude" constraints and generalized seeds are not provided. Recent work by Calvagna et al. [2] provide a way to consider temporal constraints for execution sequences. Hnich et al [16] use a SAT solver to generate CIT samples, but do not incorporate any type of inter-parameter constraints. Their work is limited to generating pair-wise CIT samples with a small number of values.

The work that most closely resembles ours is that of Calvagna et al. [1,2] who have developed an algorithm to generate CIT samples using the SAL model checker, which relies on an SMT solver. In this work the authors use a formal specification to derive the interaction model and enumerate the required test predicates, which are then encoded as negations to iteratively generate counter examples for each t-set. Heuristics determine predicate search order and a reduction step is included to remove duplicate test cases. As in our work, the approach uses only constraint resolution and they allow generalized seeds. A primary difference, however, is that they generate only a single fixed strength CIT sample that does not include isolates. In addition, our algorithm is direct – we do not have a reduction step, but rather avoid duplicates through the dynamic addition/deletion of constraints. Finally, they have integrated CIT into their model based testing tool, but our work explicitly uses the state machine path conditions to define varying sets of interactions and is therefore more tightly coupled with the behavioral model.

6   Conclusion

We have presented an integration of combinatorial interaction testing into path exploration as applied for the behavioral model-based testing tool Spec Explorer. The approach we have shown can be also well integrated with tools which do path exploration
on program code, like PEX or CUTE [19,21].

The requirements derived from this application have led to a novel CIT algorithm
heavily dependent on constraints as inputs. In particular, generalized seeds, represented
as constraints, need to be considered by the algorithm. This naturally led to an approach
based entirely on constraint resolution, powered by the constraint engine Z3 [9]. The
algorithm can process arbitrary constraints on the solution set, seeds as constraints,
and interactions of variable strength. It also supports generalized isolation of solution
tuples by a predicate, which we have not shown in this paper due to space restrictions.
(Isolation helps exclude certain solutions from counting for interaction coverage, as
they may hit error situations in the system under test or other special behavior that
overrides the effect from other combinations in the path.)

Our design is simple and comprehensible, and the performance of our implementation is comparatively fast. The size of the generated solution set is not always as good
(small) as it could be, which we relate to a poor heuristic in plateau pruning requiring
further investigation.

Our approach has been motivated by a real-world application of model-based testing
in a large scale industry project [12]. Since put in place, it is being increasingly used on
an every-day basis by test suite developers for documentation interoperability testing of
network protocols.

Acknowledgments. Keith Stobie provided requirements and has been one of the driving
forces to make CIT part of Spec Explorer. Yiming Cao and the Spec Explorer development and testing team gave many feedback and implemented some of this work.
Special thanks go to Nikolaj Bjørner and Leonardo de Moura for their work on Z3
and their prompt and continuous support when developing this application of their tool.
This work was supported in part by the National Science Foundation through award
CCF-0747009.

References

1. Calvagna, A., Gargantini, A.: A logic-based approach to combinatorial testing with constraints. In: Beckert, B., Hähnle, R. (eds.) TAP 2008. LNCS, vol. 4966, pp. 66–83. Springer,
   Heidelberg (2008)
2. Calvagna, A., Gargantini, A.: Using SRI SAL model checker for combinatorial tests generation in the presence of temporal constraints. In: Workshop on Automated Formal Methods
   (AFM), pp. 1–10 (2008)
3. Cohen, D.M., Dalal, S.R., Fredman, M.L., Patton, G.C.: The AETG system: an approach to
   testing based on combinatorial design. IEEE Transactions on Software Engineering 23(7),
   437–444 (1997)
4. Cohen, M.B., Colbourn, C.J., Collofello, J.S., Gibbons, P.B., Mugridge, W.B.: Variable
   strength interaction testing of components. In: Proceedings of the International Computer
   Software and Applications Conference, pp. 413–418 (2003)

5. Cohen, M.B., Colbourn, C.J., Gibbons, P.B., Mugridge, W.B.: Constructing test suites for interaction testing. In: Proceedings of the International Conference on Software Engineering (ICSE), May 2003, pp. 38–48 (2003)
6. Cohen, M.B., Dwyer, M.B., Shi, J.: Interaction testing of highly-configurable systems in the presence of constraints. In: International Symposium on Software Testing and Analysis, July 2007, pp. 129–139 (2007)
7. Cohen, M.B., Dwyer, M.B., Shi, J.: Constructing interaction test suites for highly-configurable systems in the presence of constraints: A greedy approach. IEEE Transactions on Software Engineering 34(5), 633–650 (2008)
8. Czerwonka, J.: Pairwise testing in real world. In: Pacific Northwest Software Quality Conference, October 2006, pp. 419–430 (2006)
9. de Moura, L., Bjørner, N.S.: Z3: An Efficient SMT Solver. In: Ramakrishnan, C.R., Rehof, J. (eds.) TACAS 2008. LNCS, vol. 4963, pp. 337–340. Springer, Heidelberg (2008)
10. Grieskamp, W.: Multi-paradigmatic Model-Based Testing. In: Havelund, K., Núñez, M., Roşu, G., Wolff, B. (eds.) FATES 2006 and RV 2006. LNCS, vol. 4262, pp. 1–19. Springer, Heidelberg (2006)
11. Grieskamp, W., Kicillof, N.: A schema language for coordinating construction and composition of partial behavior descriptions. In: Whittle, J., Geiger, L., Meisinger, M. (eds.) SCESM, pp. 59–66. ACM, New York (2006)
12. Grieskamp, W., Kicillof, N., MacDonald, D., Nandan, A., Stobie, K., Wurden, F.L.: Model-Based Quality Assurance of Windows Protocol Documentation. In: ICST, pp. 502–506. IEEE Computer Society, Los Alamitos (2008)
13. Grieskamp, W., Kicillof, N., Tillmann, N.: Action Machines: a Framework for Encoding and Composing Partial Behaviors. International Journal of Software Engineering and Knowledge Engineering 16(5), 705–726 (2006)
14. Grieskamp, W., Tillmann, N., Schulte, W.: XRT – Exploring Runtime for.NET: Architecture and Applications. Electr. Notes Theor. Comput. Sci. 144(3), 3–26 (2006)
15. Hartman, A., Raskin, L.: Problems and algorithms for covering arrays. Discrete Math. 284, 149–156 (2004)
16. Hnich, B., Prestwich, S., Selensky, E., Smith, B.M.: Constraint models for the covering test problem. Constraints 11, 199–219 (2006)
17. Lei, Y., Kacker, R., Kuhn, D.R., Okun, V., Lawrence, J.: IPOG: A general strategy for t-way software testing. In: IEEE International Conference on the Engineering of Computer-Based Systems, pp. 549–556 (2007)
18. Qu, X., Cohen, M.B., Rothermel, G.: Configuration-aware regression testing: An empirical study of sampling and prioritization. In: International Symposium on Software Testing and Analysis, July 2008, pp. 75–85 (2008)
19. Sen, K., Marinov, D., Agha, G.: CUTE: a concolic unit testing engine for C. In: Wermelinger, M., Gal, H. (eds.) ESEC/SIGSOFT FSE, pp. 263–272. ACM, New York (2005)
20. Sherwood, G.: Testcover.com (2006), http://testcover.com/pub/constex.php
21. Tillmann, N., de Halleux, J.: Pex–White Box Test Generation for .NET. In: Beckert, B., Hähnle, R. (eds.) TAP 2008. LNCS, vol. 4966, pp. 134–153. Springer, Heidelberg (2008)
22. Yilmaz, C., Cohen, M.B., Porter, A.: Covering arrays for efficient fault characterization in complex configuration spaces. IEEE Transactions on Software Engineering 31(1), 20–34 (2006)
23. Yuan, X., Cohen, M., Memon, A.M.: Covering array sampling of input event sequences for automated GUI testing. In: ASE 2007: Proceedings of the 22nd IEEE international conference on Automated software engineering, pp. 405–408 (2007)

Automatic Testing of Access Control for Security Properties*

Hervé Marchand, Jérémy Dubreil, and Thierry Jéron

INRIA, centre Rennes - Bretagne Atlantique
first.last@irisa.fr

Abstract. In this work, we investigate the combination of controller synthesis and test generation techniques for the testing of open, partially observable systems with respect to security policies. We consider two kinds of properties: integrity properties and confidentiality properties. We assume that the behavior of the system is modeled by a labeled transition system and assume the existence of a black-box implementation. We first outline a method allowing to automatically compute an ideal access control ensuring these two kinds of properties. Then, we show how to derive testers that test the conformance of the implementation with respect to its specification, the correctness of the real access control that has been composed with the implementation in order to ensure a security property, and the security property itself.

1 Introduction

There has been an increasing interest in research about computer security in the past decades. Indeed, the emergence of web services and the improvements of the possibilities of mobile and embedded systems allow lots of new and interesting features. But some of these services such as on-line payment, medical information storage or e-voting systems may deal with some critical information. In the meantime, having more applications and devices for accessing these services also increases the possibilities for such information to flow or to be erased/corrupted. To avoid security breaches, using automatic tools based on formal methods for security analysis can be beneficial. In this context, there has been a growing interest in verification [4,13], active testing of security properties [8] or passive testing (supervision) [14]. In order to specify such automatic analysis methods, security properties are generally classified into three different categories [3]: *availability* (actions allowed by the security policy are always available), *integrity* (something illegal cannot be performed) and *confidentiality* (secret information cannot be inferred) [5]. We focus here on particular classes of confidentiality and integrity properties.

In this paper, we assume that the system can be modeled by a finite transition system labeled over an alphabet Σ. The communication interface between the system and a user (possibly an attacker) is given by a subalphabet $\Sigma_a \subseteq \Sigma$.

---

* This work was partially supported by the Politess RNRT project.

M. Núñez et al. (Eds.): TESTCOM/FATES 2009, LNCS 5826, pp. 113–128, 2009.

The integrity properties we are considering are properties that can be expressed
by means of regular sets of execution trajectories in Σ^*. To describe the confidentiality properties, we adopt the formalism of [5]: the confidential information
is the membership of trajectories to a secret given by a regular language, and
the secret is said to be *opaque* whenever the attacker, partially observing the
system, cannot infer that the current trajectory belongs to the secret. Note that
the definition of opacity is general enough to model other notions of information
flow like trace-based non-interference and anonymity (see [5]). Notice also that
secrecy [1] can be handled as a particular case of opacity and thus our framework
applies to secrecy as well.

In order to avoid security breaches (information flow or integrity violation),
a possible solution consists in coupling the system with a monitor, in charge
of detecting when confidential information has leaked (resp. integrity has been
violated) or will leak (resp. will be violated). Assuming that monitors observe
only a subset Σ_m of the actions of the system, necessary and sufficient conditions
for the existence of monitors were obtained in [11]. In [9], we went one step
further and provided techniques allowing to compute the least restrictive access
control allowing to restrict the behavior of the system in order to avoid the
violation of the properties. In this work, we assumed that the controller observes
only a subset Σ_m of Σ, including all controllable actions, and in the case of
confidentiality, we also requested the two alphabets Σ_m and Σ_a, the alphabet of
the attacker, to be comparable.

In this paper, we investigate the problem of testing whether an implementation conforms to a security policy. We consider an implementation $\mathcal{I}$ of the system, a specification S and an implementation $\mathcal{I}_{AC}$ (composed with $\mathcal{I}$) in charge
of ensuring the required security policy. To validate this implementation $\mathcal{I} \times \mathcal{I}_{AC}$
(having Σ_a as communication interface with the users), we adapt the classical
conformance testing method by deriving testers that test both the security properties and the conformance of the implementation (as in [7] for observable safety
properties[1]) to its specification, and also test the implemented access controls
$\mathcal{I}_{AC}$. Our testing process is as follows: Step 1 concerns the automatic synthesis
from S of a formal model C of an access control with respect to the security
properties; Step 2 is a test generation algorithm that takes the specification, a
security property and its corresponding access control, and produces a test case
for checking the security property on the implementation and the implemented
access control; finally, Step 3 is standard conformance test execution, which may
detect the following inconsistencies:

– violation of the access control by the controlled implementation;
– violation of the security policy by the controlled implementation;
– violation of conformance of the implementation w.r.t. its specification

To generate the testers, we first adopt the attacker's point of view (i.e. the test
execution is performed via the interface Σ_a) and then the administrator's point
of view (whose communication interface may differ from Σ_a and Σ_m).

---

[1] In [7], the safety properties are only concerned with the observable behavior of the
system and not with its internal behavior, as it is the case in this paper.

The structure of the document is as follows: In section 2, we define the mathematical terminology and notions used throughout the paper. In Section 3, we formalize the notions of confidentiality and integrity and outline the verification of these properties. Section 4 describes how to compute an access control that prevents the violation of an information flow or an integrity property. Finally, Section 5 is devoted to the presentation of our testing methodology.

2   Models and Notations

Let Σ be a finite alphabet of actions. A *string* is a finite-length sequence of actions in Σ and ε denotes the empty string. Given a string s. The set of all strings formed by actions in Σ is denoted by Σ^*. Any subset of Σ^* is called a *language* over Σ. Let L be a language over Σ. L is said to be *extension-closed* when $L.\Sigma^* = L$. The *prefix-closure* of L is defined as $\overline{L} = \{s \in \Sigma^* \mid \exists t \in \Sigma^* \text{ s.t. } st \in L\}$. A language L is said *prefix-closed* whenever $L = \overline{L}$.

We assume that the behaviors of systems are modeled by Labeled Transitions Systems (LTS for short). The formal definition of an LTS is as follows:

Definition 1 (LTS). *An LTS is a 4-tuple $S = (Q_S, \Sigma, \rightarrow_S, q_S^0)$ where Q_S is a finite set of states, Σ is the alphabet of actions, $q_S^0 \in Q_S$ is the initial state, and $\rightarrow_S \subseteq Q_S \times \Sigma \times Q_S$ is the partial transition relation.*

Notations. we consider a given LTS $S = (Q_S, \Sigma, \rightarrow_S, q_S^0)$.

- We write $q \xrightarrow{a}_S q'$ for $(q, a, q') \in \rightarrow_S$ and $q \xrightarrow{a}_S$ for $\exists q' \in Q_S, q \xrightarrow{a}_S q'$. We extend $\rightarrow_S$ to arbitrary sequences by setting: $q \xrightarrow{\varepsilon}_S q$ for every state q, and $q \xrightarrow{s\sigma}_S q'$ whenever $q \xrightarrow{s}_S q''$ and $q'' \xrightarrow{\sigma}_S q'$, for some $q'' \in Q_S$.
- Given $\Sigma' \subseteq \Sigma$, S is said to be Σ'-*complete* whenever $\forall q \in Q_S, \forall a \in \Sigma', q \xrightarrow{a}_S$.
- We set for any language $L \subseteq \Sigma^*$ and any set of states $X \subseteq Q_S$,

$$\Delta_S(X, L) \triangleq \{q \in Q_S \mid \exists s \in L, \exists q' \in X, \ q' \xrightarrow{s}_S q\}.$$

  A set of states $X \subseteq Q_S$ is said to be *stable* if $\Delta_S(X, \Sigma^*) \subseteq X$.

- $L(S) = \{l \in \Sigma^*, q_S^0 \xrightarrow{l}_S\}$ denotes the set of trajectories of the system S. Given a set of marked states $F_S \subseteq Q_S$, the *marked language* is defined as $L_{F_S}(S) = \{l \in \Sigma^* \mid \exists q \in F_S, q_S^0 \xrightarrow{l}_S q\}$, i.e. the set of trajectories that may end in F_S.

We now define the parallel composition of two LTSs.

Definition 2 (Parallel composition). *Let $S^i = (Q^i, \Sigma^i, \rightarrow_{S^i}, q_{S^i}^0)$, $i = 1, 2$ be two LTSs. The parallel composition between S^1 and S^2 is an LTS $S^1 \times S^2 = (Q^1 \times Q^2, \Sigma^1 \cup \Sigma^2, \rightarrow_{S^1 \times S^2}, (q_{S^1}^0, q_{S^2}^0))$, where $\rightarrow_{S^1 \times S^2}$ is the smallest relation in $(Q^1 \times Q^2) \times (\Sigma^1 \cup \Sigma^2) \times (Q^1 \times Q^2)$ satisfying*

$$(q_1, q_2) \xrightarrow{\sigma}_{S^1 \times S^2} \begin{cases} (q_1', q_2') & \text{if } \sigma \in \Sigma^1 \cap \Sigma^2 \ \wedge \ q_1 \xrightarrow{\sigma}_{S^1} q_1' \ \wedge \ q_2 \xrightarrow{a}_{S^2} q_2' \\ (q_1', q_2) & \text{if } \sigma \in \Sigma^1 \setminus \Sigma^2 \ \wedge \ q_1 \xrightarrow{\sigma}_{S^1} q_1' \\ (q_1, q_2') & \text{if } \sigma \in \Sigma^2 \setminus \Sigma^1 \ \wedge \ q_2 \xrightarrow{\sigma}_{S^2} q_2' \end{cases}$$

Clearly, if $\Sigma^1 = \Sigma^2$, $L(S^1 \times S^2) = L(S^1) \cap L(S^2)$ and for sets of marked states $F_i \subseteq Q^i$, $i = 1, 2$, we have $L_{F_1 \times F_2}(S^1 \times S^2) = L_{F_1}(S^1) \cap L_{F_2}(S^2)$. If for $i = 1, 2$ the set F_i is stable in S^i, $F_1 \times F_2$ is stable in $S^1 \times S^2$.

Definition 3 (Completion). *Given an LTS* $S = (Q, \Sigma, \to, q^0)$, *a fresh state* q_{new} *and a subalphabet* $\Sigma' \subseteq \Sigma$, *the* (Σ', q_{new})-*completion of* S *is an LTS* $Comp_{\Sigma'}^{q_{new}}(S) = (Q \cup \{q_{new}\}, \Sigma, \to', q^0)$, *where*

$$\to' = \to \cup \{q \xrightarrow{a} q_{new} \mid q \in Q \cup \{q_{new}\}, a \in \Sigma' \text{ s.t. } \neg(q \xrightarrow{a})\}$$

Observable Behavior. The interface between a user and the system is specified by a subalphabet of actions Σ_a. The behavior that is visible by a user, is then defined by its *projection*. denoted by Π_{Σ_a} from Σ^* to Σ_a^* that erases in a sequence of Σ^* all actions not in Σ_a. Formally,

$$\Pi_{\Sigma_a} : \Sigma^* \to \Sigma_a^*$$
$$\varepsilon \mapsto \varepsilon$$
$$s\sigma \mapsto \begin{cases} \Pi_{\Sigma_a}(s)\sigma & \text{if } \sigma \in \Sigma_a \\ \Pi_{\Sigma_a}(s) & \text{otherwise} \end{cases}$$

This definition extends to any language $K \subseteq \Sigma^*$: $\Pi_{\Sigma_a}(K) = \{\mu \in \Sigma_a^* \mid \exists s \in K, \ \mu = \Pi_{\Sigma_a}(s)\}$. In particular, given an LTS S over Σ and a set of observable actions $\Sigma_a \subseteq \Sigma$, the set of *observed traces* of S is $T_{\Sigma_a}(S) = \Pi_{\Sigma_a}(L(S))$. Conversely, given $K \subseteq \Sigma_a^*$, the *inverse projection* of K is $\Pi_{\Sigma_a}^{-1}(K) = \{s \in \Sigma^* \mid \Pi_{\Sigma_a}(s) \in K\}$. Given an observation trace μ of S, we define $[\![\mu]\!]_{\Sigma_a}$ as the set of trajectories of S *compatible* with μ. These are trajectories of S having trace μ. Formally:

$$[\![\mu]\!]_{\Sigma_a} \overset{\Delta}{=} \Pi_{\Sigma_a}^{-1}(\mu) \cap L(S)$$

An LTS S is said to be *deterministic* if for all $q \in Q_S$, for all $a \in \Sigma$, $q \xrightarrow{a}_s q'$ and $q \xrightarrow{a}_s q''$ implies $q' = q''$. In the sequel, we will need to build, a deterministic LTS $Det_{\Sigma_a}(S)$ over the alphabet Σ_a preserving the set of traces of a (non-deterministic) LTS S, i.e. $L(Det_{\Sigma_a}(S)) = T_{\Sigma_a}(S)$.

Definition 4 (Determinization). *Let* $S = (Q_S, \Sigma, \to_s, q_S^0)$ *be an LTS and* $\Sigma_a \subseteq \Sigma$ *the subalphabet of observable actions. The determinization of* S *with respect to* Σ_a *is the LTS* $Det_{\Sigma_a}(S) = (\mathcal{X}, \Sigma_a, \to_d, X^0)$ *where* $\mathcal{X} = 2^{Q_S}$ *(the set of subsets of* Q_S *called macro-states),* $X^0 = \Delta_s(\{q_S^0\}, [\![\epsilon]\!]_{\Sigma_a})$ *and* $\to_d$ *defined by the set* $\{(X, a, \Delta_s(X, [\![a]\!]_{\Sigma_a})) \mid X \in \mathcal{X} \text{ and } a \in \Sigma_a\}$.

With the above definition, $\Delta_{Det_{\Sigma_a}(S)}(X^0, \mu)$ consists of states reached from q_S^0 by trajectories in $[\![\mu]\!]_{\Sigma_a}$ in S.

3   Security Properties

In this section, we formalize two kinds of security properties, namely confidentiality (something secret cannot be revealed to an attacker) and integrity (an attacker cannot make the system evolve into some bad configurations). We also outline the verification of these properties on the specification of the system S.

3.1 Integrity Property

We consider integrity properties that can be expressed as safety properties on the trajectories of the system. As usual we model their negation by an observer.

Definition 5 (Integrity). *The negation of an integrity property ψ is given by the marked language of a complete deterministic LTS $\bar{\psi} = (Q_{\bar{\psi}}, \Sigma, \rightarrow_\psi, q_{\bar{\psi}}^0)$, with a stable set of accepting states $F_{\bar{\psi}}$. We denote $L_{\bar{\psi}} = L_{F_{\bar{\psi}}}(\bar{\psi})$.* ◇

Intuitively, the trajectories of S that belong to $L_{\bar{\psi}}$ are sequences that violate the integrity property. Note that the set of states $F_{\bar{\psi}}$ is stable, because, once the integrity property is violated, it is forever. The verification is as follows:

Definition 6. *Given a system S and an integrity property ψ, ψ is satisfied (noted $S \models \psi$) whenever $L_{F_{\bar{\psi}}}(\bar{\psi}) \cap L(S) = \emptyset$.*

If ψ is not satisfied by the system, the unique supremal sublanguage of $L(S)$ that satisfies ψ is regular and given by $L(S) \setminus L_{\bar{\psi}}$.

3.2 Confidentiality Property

Consider an LTS S over Σ and $\Sigma_a \subseteq \Sigma$. The alphabet Σ_a defines the interface allowing a user to interact with S. We formalize a secret φ as follows:

Definition 7 (Secret). *A secret φ is defined by the marked language of a complete and deterministic LTS, $\varphi = (Q_\varphi, \Sigma, \rightarrow_\varphi, q_\varphi^0)$ with a set of accepting states $F_\varphi \subseteq Q_\varphi$. We denote $L_\varphi = L_{F_\varphi}(\varphi)$.* ◇

The language L_φ represents the confidential information on the execution of S. Now a user is considered as an attacker ($\mathcal{A}$) willing to catch this confidential information. It is armed for this with full information on the structure of S but only partial observation upon its behavior, namely the observed traces in Σ_a^*. This leads to the definition of opacity adapted from [5] for secret predicates given as regular languages.

Definition 8 (Opacity). *Given a system S, a secret φ is said to be opaque w.r.t. $L(S)$ and the interface Σ_a if for all $s \in L(S)$, $[\![\Pi_{\Sigma_a}(s)]\!]_{\Sigma_a} \not\subseteq L_\varphi$* ◇

Intuitively, a secret is opaque whenever every secret sequence s of the system is observationally equivalent to at least one non secret sequence s'. Equivalently, L_φ is opaque w.r.t. $L(S)$ and Σ_a if and only if for all $\mu \in T_{\Sigma_a}(S)$, $[\![\mu]\!]_{\Sigma_a} \not\subseteq L_\varphi$.

Example 1. Let S be the LTS of Figure 1 with $\Sigma = \{h, p, a, b\}$, $\Sigma_a = \{a, b\}$. The secret, that should not be revealed is the occurrence of the (unobservable) action h (namely, $L_\varphi = \Sigma^* h \Sigma^*$). L_φ is not opaque w.r.t. S and Σ as the sole compatible sequence with the trace b is $h.b \in L_\varphi$. □

The definition of opacity extends to a family of languages $\mathcal{L} = \{L_1, L_2, \cdots, L_k\}$: the secret $\mathcal{L}$ is *opaque* with respect to S and Σ_a if for all $L \in \mathcal{L}$, for all $s \in L(S)$,

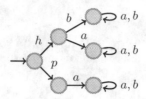

Fig. 1. An example of interference

$[\![\Pi_{\Sigma_a}(s)]\!]_{\Sigma_a}) \nsubseteq L$. Thus within our framework, it is also possible to express other confidentiality properties. For example, [1] introduced the notion of *secrecy* of a language L_φ. Intuitively, L_φ is *secret* w.r.t. S and Σ_a whenever after any observation μ, the attacker neither knows that the current execution is in L_φ nor in $L(S) \setminus L_\varphi$. Secrecy can thus be handled considering the opacity w.r.t. to the family $\{L_\varphi, L(S) \setminus L_\varphi\}$. This notion is suitable when the secret concerns the value of some variables.

Remark 1. All the results presented in this paper for opacity with a single secret can be extended to a family of secrets and thus to secrecy.

The following proposition gives a necessary and sufficient condition for opacity.

Proposition 1. *Given a system* $S = (Q_s, \Sigma, \rightarrow_s, q_s^0)$*, a secret* $\varphi = (Q_\varphi, \Sigma, \rightarrow_\varphi, q_\varphi^0)$ *equipped with* $F_\varphi \subseteq Q_\varphi$*, and an interface* $\Sigma_a \subseteq \Sigma$*,* φ *is opaque w.r.t.* S *and* Σ_a *if and only if* $L_F(Det_{\Sigma_a}(S \times \varphi)) = \emptyset$*, with* $F = 2^{Q_S \times F_\varphi}$*.*

It is easy to see that $L_F(Det_{\Sigma_a}(S \times \varphi))$ is the set of observations traces μ such that all trajectories in S compatible with μ fall into $L_{F_\varphi}(\varphi)$, i.e. the set of observations for which the attacker $\mathcal{A}$ knows that the current execution reveals φ. Hence, checking the opacity of φ consists in checking that this language is empty. This can be done by checking that F is not reachable in $Det_{\Sigma_a}(S \times \varphi)$.

Remark 2. Let S_1 and S_2 be two LTSs acting upon Σ, a secret φ such that $L_\varphi \subseteq \Sigma^*$ and an interface Σ_a. If φ is opaque w.r.t. $L(S_1)$ and $L(S_2)$, then it is opaque w.r.t. $L(S_1) \cup L(S_2)$, but not necessarily w.r.t. $L(S_1) \cap L(S_2)$. Given three LTSs S_1, S_2 and S_3 acting upon Σ such that $L(S_1) \subseteq L(S_2) \subseteq L(S_3)$, φ may be opaque w.r.t. $L(S_2)$ but not opaque w.r.t. $L(S_1)$ or $L(S_3)$.

When φ is not opaque w.r.t. $L(S)$ and Σ_a, it may be still possible to restrict the behavior of S so that L_φ becomes opaque. This is the aim of the next proposition.

Proposition 2 ([2]). *Given a system* S *and a secret* φ*, the supremal prefix-closed sub-language* $L' \subseteq L(S)$*, s.t* φ *is opaque w.r.t.* L' *is regular and given by*

$$\text{Op}^\uparrow(L(S), L_\varphi, \Sigma_a) = L(S) \setminus ((L(S) \setminus \Pi_{\Sigma_a}^{-1}(\Pi_{\Sigma_a}(L(S) \setminus L_\varphi))).\Sigma^*) \qquad (1)$$

Intuitively, the language $\Pi_{\Sigma_a}^{-1}(\Pi_{\Sigma_a}(L(S) \setminus L_\varphi))$ is the set of "safe" trajectories that do not reveal L_φ, whereas any trajectory in its complement $L(S) \setminus \Pi_{\Sigma_a}^{-1}(\Pi_{\Sigma_a}(L(S) \setminus L_\varphi))$ reveals L_φ (as well as any extension with a sequence in Σ^*, because, once L_φ has been revealed, this holds forever). Complementing again gives the supremal language $\mathrm{OP}^\uparrow(L(S), L_\varphi, \Sigma_a)$.

4   Automatic Synthesis of an Access Control

In this section, we propose to enforce opacity or integrity by supervisory control which consists in restricting the system behavior by pairing it with an access control. For implementability reasons, conditions on the admissible restrictions of $L(S)$ have to be put (controllability and normality). We assume that the interface of the controller is $\Sigma_m \subseteq \Sigma$. We will explicit the conditions under which the most permissive opacity (resp. integrity) control can be computed. The next section introduces a few notions of supervisory control theory.

4.1   Supervisory Control Theory Overview

Given a prefix-closed behavior $K \subseteq L(S) \subseteq \Sigma^*$ expected from the system S, the goal of supervisory control is to enforce this behavior on S by pairing this system with a monitor (also called controller) modeled by an LTS $C = (Q_C, \Sigma_m, \to_C, q_C^0)$ that observes a subset Σ_m of the actions in Σ and controls a subset Σ_c of the actions in Σ, i.e. enables or disables each instance of these controllable actions. $\Sigma \setminus \Sigma_c$ is the set of uncontrollable actions. $\Sigma \setminus \Sigma_m$ is the set of unobservable actions. We now recall some basic concepts of supervisory control theory [6].

Definition 9 (Controllability and Normality). *A prefix-closed language $K \subseteq L(S)$ is*

- *controllable w.r.t. $L(S)$ and Σ_c if $K.(\Sigma \setminus \Sigma_c) \cap L(S) \subseteq K$.*
- *Normal w.r.t. $L(S)$, Σ_m if $K = \Pi_{\Sigma_m}^{-1}(\Pi_{\Sigma_m}(K)) \cap L(S)$,*

Controllability means that no uncontrollable action needs to be disabled to exactly confine the system $L(S)$ to K. Normality means that K can be exactly recovered from its projection and from S. Under the assumption $\Sigma_c \subseteq \Sigma_m$, there exists a supremal controllable and normal prefix-closed sub-language $K^\uparrow$ of K corresponding to the largest language included in K that can be enforced by control and this language is regular. If not empty, there exists a controller C, said *maximal* such that $L(C \times S) = K^\uparrow$. Example 2 in Section 4.2 illustrates the computation of this controller ([6] for a more complete review of the control theory of discrete event systems).

4.2   Access Control Synthesis

In the sequel, we assume that an attacker has full knowledge of the structure of S, that he knows the controller's interface Σ_m and is able to perform all the computations made by the administrator to compute the controller. In particular, the attacker knows that the controller is maximal and since there is only one

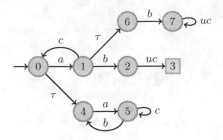

Fig. 2. $S \times \bar{\psi}$

optimal controller, the structure of the controller can be deduced by the attacker. In the rest of the paper, it is always assumed that $\Sigma_c \subseteq \Sigma_m$ (the controllable actions are observed by the controller). Next, we outline the methodologies allowing to compute access controls for ensuring a confidentiality property and then for ensuring an integrity property.

Ensuring an Integrity property. Given a system S and an integrity property ψ, modeled by the negation of a safety property $\bar{\psi}$, the aim is to compute (when it exists) the maximal controller $C = (Q_C, \Sigma_m, \to_C, q_C^0)$ such that $C \times S \models \psi$. For such a property, the solution can be simply obtained using the control theory presented in the previous section by computing the greatest controllable and observable sublanguage of $L(S) \setminus L_{\bar{\psi}}$. The following example illustrates the computation of this controller.

Example 2. Figure 2 describes the product $S \times \bar{\psi}$ in which the state 3 is marked. Hence, a sequence that reaches the state 3 is violating ψ. We assume that $\Sigma_m = \{a, b, c, uc\}$ and that $\Sigma_c = \{a, b, c\}$. The controller decisions are performed according to the observed behavior of the system (depicted in Figure 3(a)). If the controller observes a sequence in $a.(c.a)^*.b.uc$, then he knows that the system is either in state 3 or 7. Thus, in order to avoid the state $\boxed{3,7}$, the controller needs to disable the event b (uc being uncontrollable). The obtained LTS (only

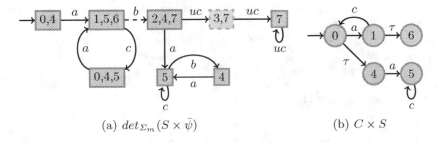

(a) $det_{\Sigma_m}(S \times \bar{\psi})$ (b) $C \times S$

Fig. 3. Ensuring an integrity property by control

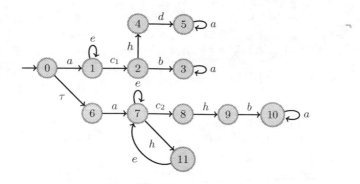

Fig. 4. Control of non-opacity (I)

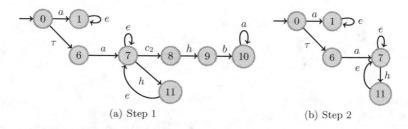

(a) Step 1   (b) Step 2

Fig. 5. Control of non-opacity (II)

keeping the accessible part) is the maximal controller such that $C \times S \models \psi$. The behavior of the controlled system is given in Figure 3(b). ◇

Ensuring a confidentiality property. Given a system S and a secret φ, our purpose is to decide whether there exists a maximally permissive controllable and observable access control $C = (Q_C, \Sigma, \rightarrow_C, q_C^0)$ such that φ is opaque w.r.t. $L(S \times C)$ and then to compute this controller C. We first illustrate the approach through an example.

Example 3. The system to be controlled is given in Figure 4. We assume that $\Sigma_a = \{a, b, d, e\}$, $\Sigma_m = \{a, c_1, c_2, b, d, e\}$, and $\Sigma_c = \{b, c_1, c_2, e\}$. The secret is given by the language $L_\varphi = \Sigma^*.h.\Sigma^*$. When observing d, the attacker knows that h occurred and the secret is revealed (in state 5). By control, action c_1 is disabled, thus avoiding the uncontrollable sequence $h.d$ to be triggered, and the LTS depicted in Figure 5(a) is obtained.

However, doing so, the secret is now revealed to the attacker who knows the control law after the observation of the action b, which leads to disable the action c_2, giving the LTS of Figure 5(b). The secret is now opaque with respect to this LTS, which is the maximal sub-LTS of the system with this property. ◇

We now give sufficient conditions under which such a maximal access control exists. For details, please refer to [9,10].

Theorem 1. *[9,10] Let S be a system and φ a secret. Under the assumption $\Sigma_c \subseteq \Sigma_m$, there exists a maximal access control C such that φ is opaque w.r.t. $L(S \times C)$ and Σ_a whenever*

- *φ is opaque w.r.t. $L(S) \cap \Sigma_{uc}^*$ and Σ_a,*
- *(1) $\Sigma_m \subseteq \Sigma_a$, or (2) $\Sigma_a \subseteq \Sigma_m$.*

Assumption (1) means that the attacker's observation is better than the controller's one. In this case the controlled system can be obtained by computing $\mathrm{OP}^\uparrow(S, \varphi, \Sigma_a)$ and the supremal controllable and observable sub-language of this language. Assumption (2) means that all actions of the attacker are observable by the controller, but only a subset is controllable. One can imagine a firewall for Internet services where the controller can filter out the requests sent by the attacker to the system, whereas the outputs of the system cannot be disabled by the controller. In this case, a novel algorithm has been introduced to compute the controller (details can be found in [9,10]).

5 Automatic Test Generation for Security Policies

In this section, we propose to test whether an implementation of the system behaves as expected with respect to its specification model, and with respect to the security properties and the access control computed in the preceding section. We adapt the conformance testing framework whose aim is to establish whether a black-box implementation conforms to its specification model.

We consider an implementation $\mathcal{I}$ of the system[2], a specification model S and a security property (either a confidentiality property for which the secret is given by φ or an integrity property ψ). We assume that an access control C with interface Σ_m has been computed for S in order to ensure one of these security properties at the specification level, and that an implementation of this access control $\mathcal{I}_{AC}$ has been connected to $\mathcal{I}$ (we thus have $L(\mathcal{I} \times \mathcal{I}_{AC}) \subseteq L(\mathcal{I})$) with the same interface.

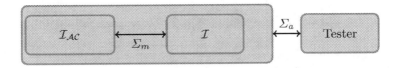

Fig. 6. Tester Architecture

We consider the test architecture depicted in Fig. 6, in particular the tester is considered as an attacker with interface Σ_a, and we make explicit the difference between inputs and outputs of the system by partitioning the set of observable actions as $\Sigma_a = \Sigma_? \cup \Sigma_!$, where $\Sigma_?$ are inputs and $\Sigma_!$ are outputs.

---

[2] As usual we consider that the implementation behaves like a model.

The aim of the test campaign is then to check that the implemented access control $\mathcal{I}_{AC}$ reduces the behavior of $\mathcal{I}$ such that the security property is ensured. Hence, test execution is expected to detect the following inconsistencies:

- invalidation of the access control specification C by the controlled implementation,
- violation of the security property by the controlled implementation,
- violation of conformance between the implementation $\mathcal{I}$ and its specification S. The chosen conformance relation is $\leq_{io}$, a version of IOCO [15] in which quiescence is not taken into account. $\leq_{io}$ is formally defined by:

$$\mathcal{I} \leq_{io} S \triangleq T_{\Sigma_a}(S).\Sigma_! \cap T_{\Sigma_a}(\mathcal{I}) \subseteq T_{\Sigma_a}(S) \tag{2}$$

Intuitively, after any trace of the specification and implementation, all outputs of the implementation must be specified.

We propose a test generation algorithm, which takes a specification S and a security property φ (or ψ) and its corresponding synthesized access control C, and produces a test case that, when executed on an implementation, attempts to push the implementation first into invalidating the implemented access control and second into violating the security property.

It is worthwhile noting that the properties on which the tests will be based do not only concern the observable behavior, but also the internal behavior. Thus assumptions are needed that bind the internal behavior of the implementation to the one of the specification. Hence, in the sequel, we shall assume that:

Assumption 1: $\mathcal{I} \leq_{io} S \Rightarrow L(\mathcal{I}) = L(S)$

This assumption means that the behavior of the implementation corresponds to the one of the specification as far as the test campaign does not reveal any non conformance. Even though relatively restrictive, this assumption is necessary if one wants to test the implemented access control. Indeed, if $L(\mathcal{I})$ differs from $L(S)$, then the access control plugged on $\mathcal{I}$ would be different from the one on S. Remember (Remark 2) that opacity is not preserved by inclusion. Thus, if we assume that, for example, $L(\mathcal{I}) \subseteq L(S)$, then there could exist in $\mathcal{I}$ some information flows not present in S and reciprocally, which entails a different mechanism to enforce opacity.

Remark 3. If the aim of the test campaign was to discover whether an information flow exists (and if we were not interested in testing the access control itself), then Assumption 1 could be relaxed and become:

Assumption 2: $\forall \mu \in T_{\Sigma_a}(\mathcal{I}) \cap T_{\Sigma_a}(S), \Pi_{\Sigma_a}^{-1}(\mu) \cap L(\mathcal{I}) \subseteq L(S)$

This assumption means that whenever an observation trace of the implementation is accepted by the specification, then all the sequences of the implementation compatible with this observation are also sequences of the specification. In particular, it entails that, if the secret is revealed in S after a trace μ, then it would be surely revealed in the implementation.   ◇

In the sequel we shall assume that assumption 1 holds.

5.1   Computation of the Canonical Tester

In the following sections we focus on the automatic test generation for confidentiality properties (the methodology for integrity properties would be similar). We first build a *Canonical Tester* which is the most general tester that can detect the inconsistencies described above. In the following section we will then describe how to select some test cases from this canonical tester.

As previously mentioned, we want to test the confidentiality property as well as the access control that has been plugged with the implementation in order to ensure confidentiality. The tester will thus be derived from the specification $S = (Q_\text{s}, \Sigma, \to_\text{s}, q_\text{s}^0)$, the secret $\varphi = (Q_\varphi, \Sigma, \to_\varphi, q_\varphi^0)$ equipped with F_φ, and the system controlled by the access control computed previously $S_C = S \times C = (Q_\text{sc}, \Sigma, \to_\text{sc}, q_\text{sc}^0)$. S_C specifies a safety property, the largest observable and controllable safety property included in $L(S)$ which guaranties that the secret φ is not leaked. $Comp_\Sigma^{V_{AC}}(S_C)$ equipped with the marked state V_{AC} is then an observer recognizing the negation of this property. Let us first consider the following LTS:

$$S_\varphi^C = (Q_\varphi^C, \Sigma, \to_\varphi^C, q_{0_\varphi}^C) = S \times \varphi \times Comp_\Sigma^{V_{AC}}(S_C)$$

S_φ^C can be equipped with the two following sets of marked states

- $F = Q_S \times F_\varphi \times (Q_\text{c} \cup \{V_{AC}\})$;
- $F_{AC} = Q_S \times Q_\varphi \times \{V_{AC}\}$.

Let us describe some properties of S_φ^C. As both φ and $Comp_\Sigma^{V_{AC}}(S_C)$ are complete, we get $L(S_\varphi^C) = L(S)$. Moreover, $L_F(S_\varphi^C) = L(S) \cap L_\varphi \subseteq L_\varphi$ whereas $(L(S_\varphi^C) \setminus L_F(S_\varphi^C)) \cap L_\varphi = \emptyset$ and $L_{F_{AC}}(S_\varphi^C) \cap L(S_C) = \emptyset$. The role of F is to recognize trajectories of S satisfying the secret, while the role of F_{AC} is to recognize trajectories of S that violate the access control.

Example 4. Back to Example 3, the LTS S_φ^C is represented in Figure 7 with the rules that the square states belong to F_{AC} whereas the dashed square states belong to F.   ◇

A canonical tester for testing the conformance with respect to S is usually defined by $Test(S) = Comp_{\Sigma_!}^{Fail}(Det_{\Sigma_a}(S))$ [7]. As our aim is also to test the access control and confidentiality, the canonical tester is here built from S_φ^C as follows:

$$Test(S, \varphi) = (X, \Sigma_a, \to_t, X_o) = Comp_{\Sigma_!}^{Fail}(Det_{\Sigma_a}(S_\varphi^C))$$

$Test(S, \varphi)$ can be seen as a refinement of $Test(S)$. In fact, besides the detection of the non conformance of the implementation, $Test(S, \varphi)$ can also be used to detect the information flow induced by the secret φ as well as an incorrect implementation of the access control. But due to the test architecture, in particular the fact that the tester partially observes the system through Σ_a, the tester's verdicts are not given to trajectories but to observation traces, thus identifying all trajectories with the same observation.

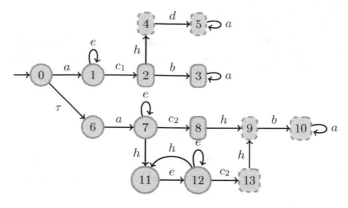

Fig. 7. S_φ^C

For an observation $\mu \in \mathcal{T}(\mathcal{I} \times \mathcal{I}_{AC}) \cap L(Test(S, \varphi))$, the following verdicts are attached to $Test(S, \varphi)$:

$$\mathcal{O}_{Test(S,\varphi)}(\mu) = \begin{cases} NotConf & \text{if } \Delta_{Test(S,\varphi)}(X_0, \mu) = \{Fail\} \\ Leak & \text{if } \Delta_{Test(S,\varphi)}(X_0, \mu) \subseteq F \\ Violate_{AC} & \text{if } \Delta_{Test(S,\varphi)}(X_0, \mu) \subseteq F_{AC} \wedge \Delta_{Test(S,\varphi)}(X_0, \mu) \not\subseteq F \end{cases}$$

The interpretation of the verdicts is as follows:

- If $\mathcal{O}_{Test(S,\varphi)}(\mu) = NotConf$, then by definition of $Comp_{\Sigma_!}^{Fail}(Det_{\Sigma_a}(S_\varphi^C))$, $\exists \mu' \in \Sigma^*, a \in \Sigma_!, \mu = \mu'.a$ with $\mu' \in L(Det_{\Sigma_a}(S_\varphi^C)) = \mathcal{T}_{\Sigma_a}(S_\varphi^C) = \mathcal{T}_{\Sigma_a}(S)$, which entails that $\mu \in \mathcal{T}_{\Sigma_a}(S).\Sigma_!$, and $\mu \in \mathcal{T}_{\Sigma_a}(\mathcal{I} \times \mathcal{I}_{AC}) \subseteq \mathcal{T}_{\Sigma_a}(\mathcal{I})$, but $\mu \notin L(Det_{\Sigma_a}(S_\varphi^C)) = \mathcal{T}_{\Sigma_a}(S)$. Thus by definition of $\leq_{io}$, $\neg(\mathcal{I} \leq_{io} S)$ and the test campaign can be stopped.
- If $\mathcal{O}_{Test(S,\varphi)}(\mu) = Leak$, it means that $[\![\mu]\!]_a \subseteq L_F(S_\varphi^C)$ thus $[\![\mu]\!]_a \subseteq L_\varphi$, which entails that there is an information flow and the access control is not well implemented.
- If $\mathcal{O}_{Test(S,\varphi)}(\mu) = Violate_{AC}$, it means that $[\![\mu]\!]_{\Sigma_a} \subseteq L_{F_{AC}}(S_\varphi^C)$. But as $L_{F_{AC}}(S_\varphi^C) \cap L(S_C) = \emptyset$, we get $[\![\mu]\!]_{\Sigma_a} \cap L(S_C) = \emptyset$.

  Now, as $[\![\mu]\!]_{\Sigma_a} \not\subseteq L_{F_{AC}}(S_\varphi^C)$, there exists $s \in [\![\mu]\!]_{\Sigma_a} \setminus L_\varphi$. This implies that the access control is not well implemented, but the secret is not revealed so far.

Example 5. Back to example 4, The tester $Test(S, \varphi)$ is given by the LTS of Figure 8. We here assume that $\Sigma_a = \{a, b, d, e\}$ with $\Sigma_! = \{b, e\}$ and $\Sigma_? = \{a, d\}$. The verdict $Violate_{AC}$ is emitted if the state $\boxed{3,10}$ is reached, meaning that the access control is not well implemented. If the sequence a.d is observed, the secret is revealed and the tester emits the verdict Leak (the state $\boxed{5}$ belongs to F). The verdict $Fail$ is emitted whenever the Fail state is reached (the output "e" should not be observed when the tester is either in state $\boxed{0,6}$ or $\boxed{3,10}$). ◇

Remark 4. **Test from an administrator point of view.** *If the test campaign is performed via the interface $\Sigma'_m = \Sigma'_! \cup \Sigma'_?$ of an administrator $\mathcal{M}$ and does*

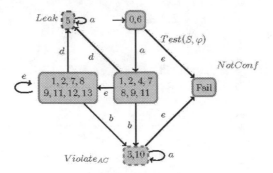

Fig. 8. $Test(S, \varphi)$

not use the interface of the users, we need to adapt the computation of the tester in order to take into account the difference of observations [11].

The main difference concerns the computation of the verdict $Leak$. Indeed, the secret φ is revealed to the attacker by an execution $s \in L(S)$ if and only if $\Pi_a(s) \in L_F(Det_{\Sigma_a}(S \times \varphi))$. In other words, we are interested in testing the property: "The secret φ has been revealed to the attacker", which corresponds to the extension-closed language: $\Pi_a^{-1}(L_F(Det_{\Sigma_a}(S \times \varphi))) \cdot \Sigma^*$. This language can be recognized by an LTS Ω, equipped with a set of final states F_Ω such that:

$$\mathcal{L}_{F_\Omega}(\Omega) = \Pi_a^{-1}(L_F(Det_{\Sigma_a}(S \times \varphi))) \cdot \Sigma^* \qquad (3)$$

Further, the computation of the tester $Tester_{\mathcal{M}}$ can simply be done by replacing φ by Ω in the test generation algorithm that we just described.   ◇.

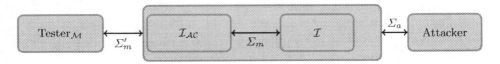

Fig. 9. Tester Architecture (II)

5.2   Test Selection

This operation is useful to target the test cases with respect to some particular behavior of the systems under test. For example, if we want to discover information flow, this operation consists in suppressing from $Test(S, \varphi)$ the subgraphs that cannot lead to some accepting set of states (e.g. F^3). In that case, the main goal of testing is to check the violation of the opacity property after a trace of the specification and, if an implementation leads a tester (extracted from the specification) into a subgraph that cannot lead to $Leak$, the current test experiment will never be able to achieve this goal and it could be interesting to stop the test campaign. It that particular case, a new verdict $Inconclusive$ is emitted.

---

[3] The selection can be performed with any combination of accepting states, depending on what the test campaign is focused on.

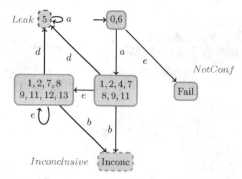

Fig. 10. The new tester $Test(S, \varphi)$

There are two situations, depending on whether the subgraph (from which $Leak$ is unreachable) was entered through an input or an output:

- the subgraph has been entered by an *input*. In this case, the transition labeled by that input (together with the whole subgraph) are removed. Intuitively, the tester has control over this action, thus, it may decide not to stimulate the implementation with such input if it is sure that this will never lead to a $Leak$ verdict.
- the subgraph has been entered by an *output* (that does not directly lead to $Fail$). In this case, only the transition labeled by that action is kept (the rest of the graph is removed). The destination of the transition is set to a new state called $Inconc$, which means that no $Leak$ verdict can be given any more (but the conformance was not violated). Hence, for completeness, in this situation the verdict $Inconclusive$ is emitted, i.e.

$$\forall \mu \in \mathcal{T}_{\Sigma_a}(\mathcal{I} \times \mathcal{I}_{AC}) \cap L(Test(S, \varphi)),$$

$$\mathcal{O}_{Test(S,\varphi)}(\mu) = Inconclusive \text{ if } \Delta_{Test(S,\varphi)}(X_0, \mu) \subseteq \{Inconc\}.$$

Example 6. Applying this operation to the tester $Test(S, \varphi)$ of Figure 8 leads to the LTS depicted in Figure 10. After the reception of a "a" from the implementation, if the tester observes the output "b", then the tester knows that the secret cannot be revealed anymore, and the test campaign can be stopped.

6   Conclusion

In this work, we have been interested in the automatic test generation for security properties on partially observed systems by using the controller synthesis methodology to drive the test. Adopting a model-based approach, we assumed the existence of a specification of the system modeled by a finite transition system as well as the existence of a black-box implementation. We focused on two kinds of properties: integrity (safety property) and confidentiality (opacity property). The first step of our method consists in automatically computing access controls ensuring these two kinds of properties on the specification. We then show how to derive testers that not only test the conformance of the implementation with respect to its specification, but also the security property itself as well as the correctness of the implemented access control composed with the implementation in order to ensure the security policy.

An interesting extension of this work would be to consider more expressive models mixing control and data. For these infinite models, the problem is that the computations of the controller and the tester rely on approximate analyses. This leads to investigate control and test techniques for security properties using the abstract interpretation theory. It would also be important to define the exact knowledge of the attacker in a case where computing the set of all behaviors may be impossible, as tackled by [12] for non-interference. Another issue would be to relax the hypothesis (1) linking internal behaviors of the implementation and the specification, while preserving the soundness of verdicts.

References

1. Alur, R., Černý, P., Zdancewic, S.: Preserving secrecy under refinement. In: Bugliesi, M., Preneel, B., Sassone, V., Wegener, I. (eds.) ICALP 2006. LNCS, vol. 4052, pp. 107–118. Springer, Heidelberg (2006)
2. Badouel, E., Bednarczyk, M., Borzyszkowski, A., Caillaud, B., Darondeau, P.: Concurrent secrets. Discrete Event Dynamic Systems 17, 425–446 (2007)
3. Bishop, M.: Introduction to computer security. Addison-Wesley Professional, Reading (2004)
4. Blanchet, B., Abadi, M., Fournet, C.: Automated Verification of Selected Equivalences for Security Protocols. In: 20th IEEE Symposium on Logic in Computer Science (LICS 2005), Chicago, IL, June 2005, pp. 331–340 (2005)
5. Bryans, J.W., Koutny, M., Mazaré, L., Ryan, P.: Opacity generalised to transition systems. International Journal of Information Security 7(6), 421–435 (2008)
6. Cassandras, C., Lafortune, S.: Introduction to Discrete Event Systems. Kluwer Academic Publishers, Dordrecht (1999)
7. Constant, C., Jéron, T., Marchand, H., Rusu, V.: Integrating formal verification and conformance testing for reactive systems. IEEE Transactions on Software Engineering 33(8), 558–574 (2007)
8. Darmaillacq, V., Fernandez, J.-C., Groz, R., Mounier, L., Richier, J.-L.: Test generation for network security rules. In: Uyar, M.Ü., Duale, A.Y., Fecko, M.A. (eds.) TestCom 2006. LNCS, vol. 3964, pp. 341–356. Springer, Heidelberg (2006)
9. Dubreil, J., Darondeau, Ph., Marchand, H.: Opacity enforcing control synthesis. In: Workshop on Discrete Event Systems, WODES 2008, Gothenburg, Sweden (2008)
10. Dubreil, J., Darondeau, Ph., Marchand, H.: Supervisory control for opacity. Technical Report 1921, IRISA (February 2009)
11. Dubreil, J., Jéron, T., Marchand, H.: Monitoring information flow by diagnosis techniques. In: European Control Conference, ECC (August 2009)
12. Giacobazzi, R., Mastroeni, I.: Abstract non-interference: parameterizing non-interference by abstract interpretation. In: POPL 2004: Proceedings of the 31st ACM SIGPLAN-SIGACT symposium on Principles of programming languages, pp. 186–197. ACM, New York (2004)
13. Lowe, G.: Towards a completeness result for model checking of security protocols. Journal of Computer Security 7(2-3), 89–146 (1999)
14. Schneider, F.B.: Enforceable security policies. ACM Trans. Inf. Syst. Secur. 3(1), 30–50 (2000)
15. Tretmans, J.: Testing concurrent systems: A formal approach. In: Baeten, J.C.M., Mauw, S. (eds.) CONCUR 1999. LNCS, vol. 1664, pp. 46–65. Springer, Heidelberg (1999)

Generating Reduced Tests for FSMs with Extra States

Adenilso Simão[1,2], Alexandre Petrenko[2], and Nina Yevtushenko[3]

[1] São Paulo University, São Carlos, São Paulo, Brazil
[2] Centre de recherche informatique de Montreal (CRIM)
Montreal, Quebec, Canada
[3] Tomsk State University, Tomsk, Russia
adenilso@icmc.usp.br, petrenko@crim.ca,
ninayevtushenko@yahoo.com

Abstract. We address the problem of generating tests from a deterministic Finite State Machine to provide full fault coverage even if the faults may introduce extra states in the implementations. It is well-known that such tests should include the sequences in the so-called traversal set, which contains all sequences of length defined by the number of extra states. Therefore, the only apparent opportunity to produce shorter tests is to find within a test suite a suitable arrangement of the sequences in the inescapable traversal set. We observe that the direct concatenation of the traversal set to a given state cover, suggested by all existing generation methods with full fault coverage, results in extensive test branching, when a test has to be repeatedly executed to apply all the sequences of the traversal set. In this paper, we state conditions which allow distributing these sequences over several tests. We then utilize these conditions to elaborate a method, called SPY-method, which shortens tests by avoiding test branching as much as possible. We present the results of the experimental comparison of the proposed method with an existing method which indicate that the resulting save can be up to 40%.

1 Introduction

Finite State Machines (FSMs) have been used to model systems in many areas, such as hardware design, formal language recognition, conformance testing of protocols [1] and object-oriented software testing [2]. Regarding test generation, one of the main advantages of using FSMs is the existence of generation methods which guarantee full fault coverage: given a specification FSM with n states and any black-box implementation which can be modelled as an FSM with at most m states, $m \geq n$, the methods generate a test suite, often called m-complete test suite, which has the ability to detect all faults in any such implementations. In the particular case of $m = n$, there are many efficient methods which generate complete test suites [7] [3] [5] [10] [4].

However, on the other hand, in spite of the fact that the problem of generating m-complete test suites for $m > n$ is a longstanding one which can be traced back to the work of Moore [11] and Hennie [9], it has received much less attention compared to the problem of constructing n-complete test suites. One of the main reasons might be the fact that test generation becomes more challenging in the case of extra states. It is known that an m-complete test suite should include each sequence in the so-called

M. Núñez et al. (Eds.): TESTCOM/FATES 2009, LNCS 5826, pp. 129–145, 2009.

traversal set, which contains all input sequences with $m - n + 1$ inputs [13]. Moreover, the traversal set should be applied to each state of the specification. Not surprisingly, all, not numerous, existing methods for generating m-complete test suites [13] [3] [5] [14] [4] [8] [12] do exactly this and differ only in a type of state identification sequences they add to traversal sequences.

Driven by this observation and the obvious absence of significant progress in solving the longstanding problem of generating m-complete test suite, we revisit it in this paper and aim at answering the question whether m-complete test suite is irreducible due to the inevitability of the traversal set.

We observe that a considerable part of an m-complete test suite is not related to the traversal set itself, but to the test branching when a test has to be repeatedly executed to apply all the sequences of the traversal set. Apparently, the test length reduction can only be achieved by reducing the test branching, which in turn can be obtained by distributing the traversal set over several tests. The caveat is that an arbitrary distribution of the traversal set may break the m-completeness of a resulting test suite. Thus, we need first to establish conditions for a distribution of the traversal set such that the m-completeness of a test suite is preserved. The main idea developed in this paper is to distribute it among those tests in a test suite which are convergent, i.e., transfer to the same state, in all FSMs of the fault domain which pass the test suite. The approach we elaborate is based on properties of FSM tests, namely their convergence and divergence. We investigate when the convergence and divergence of tests in the specification (which can be easily checked) can be safely assumed to also hold in the implementation under test. The divergence of two tests can be witnessed by different outputs produced by the tests. On the other hand, although convergence of two tests cannot be directly ascertained by considering only the two tests, we show that the knowledge of the maximum number of states of FSMs in the fault domain can be used to formulate conditions for the convergence of tests. We then use the notion of convergence and divergence to state necessary and sufficient conditions for a test suite to be m-complete.

Based on these conditions, we elaborate a method, called SPY-method, for m-complete test suite generation. The method distributes the sequences of the traversal set over several tests in order to reduce test branching and generate shorter test suites. To assess the potential saving which can be obtained with the approach proposed in this paper, we experimentally compare it with the HSI method [14]. The results suggest that SPY-method can generate test suites up to 40% shorter, on average.

The rest of the paper is organized as follows. In Section 2, we provide the necessary basic definitions. In Section 3, we formally state the problem of generating m-complete test suites and discuss existing methods. In Section 4, we investigate test properties and formulate conditions for guaranteeing the m-completeness of test suites. In Section 5, we develop a generation method based on the proposed conditions. In Section 6, the method is illustrated on an example. Experimental results are reported in Section 7 and Section 8 concludes the paper.

2   Definitions

A Finite State Machine is a (complete) deterministic Mealy machine, which can be defined as follows.

Definition 1. *A* Finite State Machine (FSM) *S is a 6-tuple* $(S, s_0, X, Y, \delta_S, \lambda_S)$, *where*

- *S is a finite set of states with the initial state* s_0,
- *X is a finite set of inputs,*
- *Y is a finite set of outputs,*
- $\delta_S : S \times X \to S$ *is a transition function, and*
- $\lambda_S : S \times X \to Y$ *is an output function.*

A tuple $(s, x) \in S \times X$ is a *transition* of S. We extend the transition and output functions from input symbols to input sequences, including the empty sequence ε, as usual: for $s \in S$, $\delta_S(s, \varepsilon) = s$ and $\lambda_S(s, \varepsilon) = \varepsilon$; and for input sequence α and input x, $\delta_S(s, \alpha x) = \delta_S(\delta_S(s, \alpha), x)$ and $\lambda_S(s, \alpha x) = \lambda_S(s, \alpha)\lambda_S(\delta_S(s, \alpha), x)$. An FSM S is said to be *initially connected*, if for each state $s \in S$, there exists an input sequence $\alpha \in X^*$, called a *transfer* sequence for state s, such that $\delta_S(s_0, \alpha) = s$. In this paper, only initially connected machines are considered. Input sequences *converge* if they are transfer sequences for the same state. Similarly, input sequences *diverge* if they are transfer sequences for different states of the same FSM. A set $K \subseteq X^*$ is a *state cover* for S if it contains at least one transfer sequence for each state of S. A state cover is *minimal* if it contains exactly one transfer sequence for each state. A set $A \subseteq X^*$ *covers* a transition (s, x) if there exist $\alpha, \alpha x \in A$, where α is a transfer sequence for s. The set A is a *transition cover* for S if it covers every transition of S. A set of sequences is *initialized*, if it contains the empty sequence.

Given sequences $\alpha, \beta, \gamma \in X^*$, if $\beta = \alpha\gamma$, then α is a *prefix* of β, and γ is a *suffix* of β; if γ is not the empty sequence, then α is a *proper* prefix of β. We also say that a prefix of γ *extends* α (*in* β) and that β is an *extension* of α. We denote by *pref*(β) the set of all prefixes of β. For a set of sequences A, *pref*(A) is the union of *pref*(β), for all $\beta \in A$. If $A = pref(A)$, then we say that A is *prefix closed*. Given two sets of sequences A and B, we denote by $A.B$ the set of sequences $A.B = \{\alpha\beta \mid \alpha \in A \text{ and } \beta \in B\}$. We will slightly abuse the notation by writing $\alpha.B$ instead of $\{\alpha\}.B$ and $A.\beta$ instead of $A.\{\beta\}$. For a natural number k, we denote by $X^{\leq k}$ the set of all input sequences of length at most k.

Given a set $A \subseteq X^*$, states s and s' are *A-equivalent*, if $\lambda_S(s, \gamma) = \lambda_S(s', \gamma)$ for all $\gamma \in A$. Otherwise, s and s' are *A-distinguishable*. We say that γ distinguishes s and s', if s and s' are $\{\gamma\}$-distinguishable. States s, s' are *equivalent*, if they are X^*-equivalent. Similarly, they are *distinguishable* if they are X^*-distinguishable. We define distinguishability and equivalence of machines as a corresponding relation between their initial states. An FSM is *minimal*, if all states are pairwise distinguishable. In this paper, all the FSMs are assumed to be minimal. A *characterization set* is a set of sequences W such that every two states are W-distinguishable. The set $W_s \subseteq W$ is a *state identifier* for state s if any other state is W_s-distinguishable from s. A *family of harmonized state identifiers* is a collection of sets $\{H_s \mid s \in S\}$, such that states s and s' are $(pref(H_s) \cap pref(H_{s'}))$-distinguishable.

3 Problem Statement and Existing Methods

In this section, we discuss the problem of generating test suites with full fault coverage along with the existing methods and present the main idea of the approach elaborated in this paper.

Henceforth, we assume that $S = (S, s_0, X, Y, \delta_S, \lambda_S)$ and $Q = (Q, q_0, X, Y', \delta_Q, \lambda_Q)$ are a specification FSM and an implementation FSM, respectively. Moreover, n is the number of states of S. We denote by $\Im$ the set of all minimal implementation FSMs with the same input alphabet as S. The set $\Im$ is called a *fault domain* for S. For $m \geq n$, let $\Im_m$ be the FSMs of $\Im$ with at most m states, i.e., the set $\Im_m$ represents all faults that can occur in an implementation of S with at most m states. We denote the maximum number of extra states that an implementation may have by $\Delta = m - n$. Faults can be detected by tests, which are input sequences of the specification FSM S.

Definition 2. *An input sequence of FSM S is called a* test case *(or simply a* test*) of S. A* test suite *of S is a finite prefix closed set of tests of S. A test suite T of FSM S is m-complete, if for each FSM $Q \in \Im_m$, distinguishable from S, there exists a test in T that distinguishes them.*

An FSM *passes* a test suite T if it is T-equivalent to the specification. Thus, a test suite is m-complete if the FSMs in $\Im_m$ which pass it are equivalent to the specification. Two tests α and β in a given test suite T are T-*separable*, if there exist $\alpha\gamma, \beta\gamma \in T$, such that states $\delta_S(s_0, \alpha)$ and $\delta_S(s_0, \beta)$ are $\{\gamma\}$-distinguishable. Clearly, if T-separable tests α and β are convergent in some implementation FSM, it can be distinguished from S by either $\alpha\gamma$ or $\beta\gamma$.

Since the distinguishability of FSMs is defined as the corresponding relation of their initial states, tests are assumed to be applied in the initial state. For accounting to the reset operation required to bring the FSMs to the initial state, we define the length of a test α as $|\alpha| + 1$, where $|\alpha|$ is the number of input symbols in α. As the application of a test results in the application of all its prefixes, the length of a test suite T, denoted by $len(T)$, is the sum of the lengths of all tests in T which are not proper prefixes of other tests in T.

In this paper, we address the problem of generating an m-complete test suite, when implementation FSMs can have more that n states, i.e., $m \geq n$. This problem has received much less attention compared to the (classical) problem of constructing n-complete test suites, often called checking experiments. One of the main reasons might be the fact that test generation becomes more challenging. To illustrate this, let us consider the FSMs in Figures 1 and 2, where S_0 is the specification machine and S_1 is an implementation machine, which has two extra states. Notice that states 1 and 2 in S_1 are similar to states 1 and 2 in S_0, except that S_1 has two extra states 1' and 2', and the transition $(2, b)$ leads to an "erroneous" state 2'.

The shortest test able to distinguish S_0 and S_1 should be formed by the input sequence a, which is a transfer sequence for state 2, and the input sequence baa. Indeed, for any other input sequence of length three, it is possible to construct a distinguishable FSM with two extra states for which only that particular sequence applied to a proper state distinguishes it from S_0. As those FSMs are in the fault

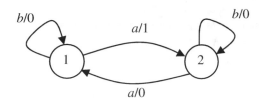

Fig. 1. FSM S_0

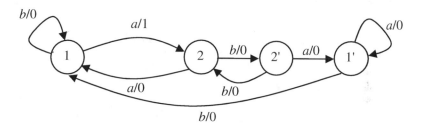

Fig. 2. FSM S_1

domain $\mathfrak{I}_4$, any 4-complete test suite for S_0 should include all input sequences of length three, applied to all states of S_0. In the general case, an m-complete test suite for an FSM with n states should include all input sequences of length $\Delta + 1$, applied to each state. An early work of Moore [11] uses such sequences to establish a lower bound for sequences identifying "combination lock" machines. In fact, the lower bound for the length of an m-complete test suite for an FSM with n states and p inputs is $O(n^3 p^{\Delta+1})$, i.e., it is exponential on the number of extra states [13].

Existing methods, such as W [13] [3], Wp [5], HSI [14] and H [4], which generate an m-complete test suite T for a given minimal deterministic FSM S can be summarized as follows.

Step 1: Determine a minimal initialized state cover K for S.
Step 2: Extend the sequences in K by the (traversal) set $X^{\leq \Delta+1}$.
Step 3: Extend the sequences in $K.X^{\leq \Delta+1}$ in such a way that any two divergent sequences, i.e., reaching distinct states in S, are T-separable.

Existing methods differ mainly in the sequences they use to ensure T-separability in Step 3. In the W method, all sequences in $K.X^{\leq \Delta+1}$ are extended by a characterization set. The Wp method uses a characterization set for sequences in K. $X^{\leq \Delta}$ and state identifiers for the other sequences. The HSI method uses the harmonized state identifiers for all sequences in $K.X^{\leq \Delta+1}$. The H method determines on-the-fly a distinguishing sequence for states reached by each pair of divergent sequences in K. $X^{\leq \Delta+1}$.

We illustrate the generation of a 3-complete test suite for the 2-state FSM in Figure 1 following the strategy used by the existing methods. For this machine, the characterization set corresponds to a family of harmonized state identifiers $W = H_1 = H_2$ = $\{a\}$. A minimal state cover for this FSM is $K = \{\varepsilon, a\}$. Then, in the W, Wp, HSI, H methods the sequences in $K.X^{\leq\Delta+1} = pref(\{aaa, aab, aba, abb, ba, bb\})$ are extended by the sequence a. The resulting test suite is $T_1 = pref(\{aaaa, aaba, abaa, abba, baa, bba\})$ of length 28; Figure 3 shows its tree representation, where nodes are labelled with states of the specification FSM and edges are labelled with inputs. Each test corresponds to the sequence of inputs along a path from the root to a node.

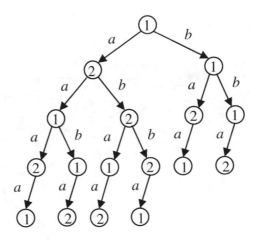

Fig. 3. Tree representation of a 3-complete test suite for S_0

If, in Step 1, shortest transfer sequences are included into a state cover and, in Step 3, shortest distinguishing sequences are used, tests in a resulting m-complete test suite cannot be shortened and if we want to reduce the total length of a test suite we need to find a way of reducing test branching. Indeed, once a test of length l branches into k tests, the test prefix of l inputs contributes kl inputs to the total length of a test suite. For instance, each of tests aa, ab and b branches into two tests in $T1$, thus contributing twice to its total length. In the existing methods, test branching occurs mainly in Step 2, where each test in a minimal state cover is extended by the sequences in the traversal set $X^{\leq\Delta+1}$. As a result of this, such a test branches into at least $|X|^{\Delta+1}$ tests. Apparently, the test length reduction could be achieved by reducing the test branching, which in turn can be performed by distributing the traversal set $X^{\leq\Delta+1}$ over several tests. As soon as one of these tests is a proper prefix of another the overall test branching and thus the test length are reduced. This key observation is illustrated in Figure 4. Assume that test α should be extended by the sequences aa and ba. In Figure 4(a) both sequences extend α, branching the test. Consequently, α contributes twice to the length of the test suite. Suppose that tests α and αb are convergent, and, instead of α, the test αb is extended by aa, as shown in Figure 4(b). We note that this results in a test suite which is, all things being equal, $|\alpha| - 1$ inputs shorter than before. The problem is that an arbitrary distribution of the traversal set may break the m-completeness of a resulting test suite. Thus, we need first to establish conditions for a distribution of the traversal set $X^{\leq\Delta+1}$ such that the m-completeness of a test suite is

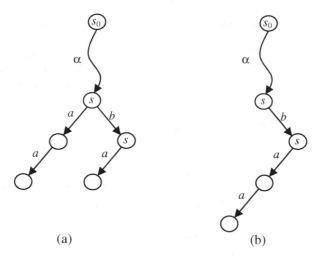

Fig. 4. Test branching (a) *versus* test extension (b)

preserved. The main idea developed in this paper is to distribute it among those tests in a test suite which are convergent, i.e., transfer to the same state, in all FSMs of the fault domain which pass the test suite, reducing test branching.

4 Test Properties

The approach elaborated in this paper is based on properties of FSM tests, namely their convergence and divergence. Recall that two defined input sequences of an FSM converge or diverge if they are transfer sequences for the same state or for different ones, respectively. We generalize these notions to sets of FSMs. Given a non-empty set of FSMs $\Sigma \subseteq \Im$ and two tests $\alpha, \beta \in X^*$, we say that α and β are Σ-*convergent*, if they converge in each FSM of the set Σ. Similarly, we say that α and β are Σ-*divergent*, if they diverge in each FSM of Σ. Two tests are S-convergent (S-divergent) if they are $\{S\}$-convergent ($\{S\}$-divergent). Moreover, when it is clear from the context, we will drop the set in which tests are convergent or divergent.

Test convergence and divergence with respect to a single FSM are complementary, i.e., any two tests are either convergent or divergent. However, when a set of FSMs Σ is considered, some tests are neither Σ-convergent nor Σ-divergent. Notice that the Σ-convergence relation is reflexive, symmetric, and transitive, i.e., it is an equivalence relation over the set of tests. Given a test α, let $[\alpha]$ be the corresponding equivalence class in a non-empty set Σ of FSMs with the same input alphabet. The test convergence and divergence possess the following properties.

Lemma 1. *Given tests α, β, such that $[\alpha] = [\beta]$, the following properties hold:*

    (i) $[\alpha\gamma] = [\beta\gamma]$, *for any input sequence γ.*

    (ii)   *For any test φ, if $[\alpha] \neq [\varphi]$, then $[\beta] \neq [\varphi]$.*

An important property of T-separable tests is that they are divergent in all FSMs which are T-equivalent to S. Given a test suite T, let $\Im(T)$ be the set of all $Q \in \Im$, such that Q and S are T-equivalent, i.e., $\Im(T)$ is the set of all FSMs in $\Im$ which pass the test suite T.

Lemma 2. *Given a test suite T of an FSM S, T-separable tests are $\Im(T)$-divergent.*
Proof. Let tests α and β be T-separable. Thus, there exist a sequence γ such that $\alpha\gamma$, $\beta\gamma \in T$ and $\lambda_s(\delta_s(s_0, \alpha), \gamma) \neq \lambda_s(\delta_s(s_0, \beta), \gamma)$. Let Q be an FSM T-equivalent to S; thus, we have that $\lambda_s(\delta_s(s_0, \alpha), \gamma) = \lambda_Q(\delta_Q(q_0, \alpha), \gamma)$ and $\lambda_s(\delta_s(s_0, \beta), \gamma) = \lambda_Q(\delta_Q(q_0, \beta), \gamma)$. It follows that $\lambda_Q(\delta_Q(q_0, \alpha), \gamma) \neq \lambda_Q(\delta_Q(q_0, \beta), \gamma)$. Thus, $\delta_Q(q_0, \alpha) \neq \delta_Q(q_0, \beta)$.   ◆

Existing methods for test generation ensure that two tests are divergent by extending them with an appropriate distinguishing sequence. However, Lemmas 1 and 2 indicate that the convergence and divergence of tests also applies to their equivalence classes. It is thus important to identify under which conditions tests are guaranteed to be convergent, i.e., belong to the same equivalence class.

Ensuring convergence is more involved than ensuring divergence; divergence of two tests can be witnessed by different outputs produced in response to a common suffix sequence. The two tests are thus divergent in any FSM T-equivalent to S. However, convergence of two tests cannot be directly ascertained by considering only the two tests. It turns out that the knowledge of the maximum number of states of FSMs in the fault domain allows us to formulate conditions for the convergence of tests. Given a test suite T and a natural number $m \geq n$, let $\Im_m(T) = \Im_m \cap \Im(T)$, i.e., the set of FSMs in $\Im$ which are T-equivalent to S and have at most m states.

As S is in the fault domain $\Im_m(T)$, tests which are $\Im_m(T)$-convergent are also S-convergent. Thus, two tests can be $\Im_m(T)$-convergent only if they are S-convergent.

Definition 3. *A set of tests is $\Im_m(T)$-convergence-preserving if all its S-convergent tests are $\Im_m(T)$-convergent. Similarly, a set of tests is $\Im_m(T)$-divergence-preserving if all its S-divergent tests are $\Im_m(T)$-divergent.*

In other words, a set of tests is $\Im_m(T)$-convergence-preserving if the convergence in the specification FSM is "preserved" in each FSM which passes the test suite T. Similarly, a set of tests is $\Im_m(T)$-divergence-preserving if the divergence in the specification FSM is preserved in each FSM which passes the test suite T.

In the following lemma, the $\Im_m(T)$-convergence relation is considered; thus, $[\alpha]$ is the subset of tests of T which are $\Im_m(T)$-convergent with test α.

Lemma 3. *Given a test suite T for an FSM S and $\Delta = m - n \geq 0$, let π and φ be S-convergent tests in T, such that, for any sequence υ of length Δ, there exist tests $\alpha \in [\pi]$, $\beta \in [\varphi]$, and an $\Im_m(T)$-divergence-preserving state cover for S in T containing $\{\alpha, \beta\}.pref(\upsilon)$. Then, π and φ are $\Im_m(T)$-convergent.*

Proof. Suppose that π and φ are not $\Im_m(T)$-convergent. Thus, there exists $Q \in \Im_m(T)$, such that π and φ are Q-divergent. As π and φ are S-convergent, the FSM Q is not equivalent to S and there must exist an input sequence γ such that S and Q are $\{\pi\gamma, \varphi\gamma\}$-distinguishable. Assume that γ is a shortest input sequence with this property. Thus,

$$S \text{ and } Q \text{ are } (([\pi] \cup [\varphi]).\gamma')\text{-equivalent, for all } \gamma', \text{ such that } |\gamma'| < |\gamma|. \tag{1}$$

We have that $|\gamma| > \Delta$, since otherwise there would exist $\alpha' \in [\pi]$ and $\beta' \in [\varphi]$ such that $\{\alpha'\gamma, \beta'\gamma\} \subseteq T$, implying that S and Q are T-distinguishable.

Let $\alpha \in [\pi]$ and $\beta \in [\varphi]$ be such that there exists an $\mathfrak{I}_m(T)$-divergence-preserving state cover for S in T containing the set $\{\alpha, \beta\}.pref(\gamma_\Delta)$, where γ_i is the prefix of γ of length i. Without loss of generality, we assume that S and Q are $\{\alpha\gamma\}$-distinguishable, i.e., $\lambda_Q(q_0, \alpha\gamma) \neq \lambda_S(s_0, \alpha\gamma)$. Let $A_i = \{\alpha, \beta\}.pref(\gamma_i)$, $0 \leq i \leq \Delta$. The tests $\alpha\gamma_i$ and $\beta\gamma_i$ are Q-divergent and, moreover, A_i is $\mathfrak{I}_m(T)$-divergence-preserving. We show by induction that, for all $0 \leq i \leq \Delta$, $|\delta_Q(q_0, A_i)| \geq i + |\delta_S(s_0, A_i)| + 1$.

Base case: For $i = 0$, we have that $A_0 = \{\alpha, \beta\}$. As α and β are S-convergent and Q-divergent, the result follows, since $|\delta_Q(q_0, A_0)| = 2$ and $|\delta_S(s_0, A_0)| = 1$.

Inductive Step: Suppose that the result holds i, $0 \leq i < \Delta$, i.e.,

$$|\delta_Q(q_0, A_i)| \geq i + |\delta_S(s_0, A_i)| + 1. \tag{2}$$

We show that the result holds for $i + 1$. Let $j \leq i$. Suppose that $\alpha\gamma_{i+1}$ and $\alpha\gamma_j$ are S-divergent; then $\alpha\gamma_{i+1}$ is Q-divergent with $\alpha\gamma_j$ and $\beta\gamma_j$, since A_{i+1} is $\mathfrak{I}_m(T)$-divergence-preserving. Suppose now that $\alpha\gamma_{i+1}$ and $\alpha\gamma_j$ are S-convergent. Let χ be the suffix which extends γ_{i+1} in γ, i.e., $\gamma = \gamma_{i+1}\chi$. If $\alpha\gamma_{i+1}$ is Q-convergent with $\alpha\gamma_j$, then $\alpha\gamma_j\chi$ distinguishes S and Q, since $\lambda_Q(q_0, \alpha\gamma_j\chi) = \lambda_Q(q_0, \alpha\gamma_{i+1}\chi) = \lambda_Q(q_0, \alpha\gamma) \neq \lambda_S(s_0, \alpha\gamma) = \lambda_S(s_0, \alpha\gamma_{i+1}\chi) = \lambda_S(s_0, \alpha\gamma_j\chi)$. As $|\gamma_j\chi| < |\gamma_{i+1}\chi| = |\gamma|$, it follows that $\alpha\gamma_{i+1}$ should be Q-divergent with $\alpha\gamma_j$ and $\beta\gamma_j$, since otherwise we have a contradiction to (1). By the same token, the test $\alpha\gamma_{i+1}$ is Q-divergent with $\beta\gamma_j$. Thus, $\alpha\gamma_{i+1}$ is Q-divergent with $\alpha\gamma_j$, $j \leq i$, i.e., with all tests in A_i and reaches a state in Q which is not reached by the tests in A_i. Hence,

$$|\delta_Q(q_0, A_{i+1})| \geq |\delta_Q(q_0, A_i)| + |\delta_Q(q_0, \alpha\gamma_{i+1})| \geq |\delta_Q(q_0, A_i)| + 1. \tag{3}$$

If $\alpha\gamma_{i+1}$ is S-convergent with some test in A_i, then

$$|\delta_S(s_0, A_{i+1})| = |\delta_S(s_0, A_i)|. \tag{4}$$

The induction thus applies, since

$|\delta_Q(q_0, A_i)| \geq i + |\delta_S(s_0, A_i)| + 1$ \quad (inductive hypothesis (2))
$|\delta_Q(q_0, A_i)| + 1 \geq (i + 1) + |\delta_S(s_0, A_i)| + 1$
$|\delta_Q(q_0, A_{i+1})| \geq (i + 1) + |\delta_S(s_0, A_{i+1})| + 1$ \quad (due to (3) and (4))

On the other hand, if $\alpha\gamma_{i+1}$ is S-divergent with all tests in A_i, then

$$|\delta_S(s_0, A_{i+1})| = |\delta_S(s_0, A_i)| + 1 \tag{5}$$

In this case, $\beta\gamma_{i+1}$ is also Q-divergent with all tests in A_i, since A_{i+1} is $\mathfrak{I}_m(T)$-divergence-preserving. Moreover, $\beta\gamma_{i+1}$ is Q-divergent with $\alpha\gamma_{i+1}$. Thus, we have that

$$|\delta_Q(q_0, A_{i+1})| = |\delta_Q(q_0, A_i)| + |\delta_Q(q_0, \{\alpha\gamma_j, \beta\gamma_j\})| \geq |\delta_Q(q_0, A_i)| + 2 \tag{6}$$

The induction also applies, since

$|\delta_Q(q_0, A_i)| \geq i + |\delta_S(s_0, A_i)| + 1$ \quad (inductive hypothesis (2))
$|\delta_Q(q_0, A_i)| + 2 \geq (i + 1) + (|\delta_S(s_0, A_i)| + 1) + 1$
$|\delta_Q(q_0, A_{i+1})| \geq (i + 1) + |\delta_S(s_0, A_{i+1})| + 1$ \quad (due to (5) and (6))

This concludes the induction proof. Then, for all $0 \leq i \leq \Delta$, it holds that $|\delta_Q(q_0, A_i)| \geq i$ $+ |\delta_S(s_0, A_i)| + 1$. In particular, the set of tests A_Δ reaches at least $\Delta + |\delta_S(s_0, A_\Delta)| + 1$ states in Q.

Consider now a smallest set K, such that $K \cup A_\Delta$ is an $\Im_m(T)$-divergence-preserving state cover for S in T; thus, $|K| = n - |\delta_S(s_0, A_\Delta)|$, since α and β are S-convergent. As $K \cup A_\Delta$ is $\Im_m(T)$-divergence-preserving, the tests of the set K reach exactly $n - |\delta_S(s_0, A_\Delta)|$ states in Q, and each of them is distinct from all states reached by A_Δ. Thus, the tests in $K \cup A_\Delta$ reach at least $n - |\delta_S(s_0, A_\Delta)| + \Delta + |\delta_S(s_0, A_\Delta)| + 1 = n + m - n + 1 = m$ $+ 1$ states in Q, contradicting the fact that Q has at most m states.   ◆

The importance of Lemma 3 for test generation is that it shows how to ensure the $\Im_m(T)$-convergence of two S-convergent tests. This in turn, allows including these tests into the same equivalence class. Then, Lemma 1 can be applied, which indicates that if a test should be extended by given sequences, e.g., from the traversal set, any tests of its equivalence class can be chosen, distributing these sequences over several tests. Lemma 3 also leads to the necessary and sufficient conditions for test completeness with respect to the fault domain $\Im_m$, where each FSM has at most m states, $m \geq n$.

Theorem 1. *Let T be a test suite for an FSM S with n states and $m \geq n$. Then, the following statements are equivalent:*

(i) T is an m-complete test suite for S

(ii) T contains an $\Im_m(T)$-convergence-preserving initialized transition cover for S.

Proof

(ii) $\Rightarrow$ (i) Let T contain an $\Im_m(T)$-convergence-preserving initialized transition cover A for S, and $Q \in \Im_m(T)$. Define the relation $h \subseteq S \times Q$ as follows:

$(s, q) \in h \Leftrightarrow$ there exists $\alpha \in A$, such that $\delta_S(s_0, \alpha) = s$ and $\delta_Q(q_0, \alpha) = q$.

As A is a transition cover for S, for each $s \in S$ there exists $q \in Q$ such that $(s, q) \in h$. Moreover, as A is $\Im_m(T)$-convergence-preserving, for each $s \in S$, there exists only one $q \in Q$ such that $(s, q) \in h$; thus, h is a mapping. As $\varepsilon \in A$,

$$h(s_0) = q_0.$$

Let $s \in S$ and $x \in X$. As A is a transition cover for S,

there exists $\alpha x \in A$ such that $\delta_S(s_0, \alpha) = s$.

Correspondingly,

$$h(\delta_S(s_0, \alpha), x) = h(\delta_S(s_0, \alpha x)) = \delta_Q(q_0, \alpha x) = \delta_Q(\delta_Q(q_0, \alpha), x) = \delta_Q(h(\delta_S(s_0, \alpha)), x)$$

and

$$\lambda_S(\delta_S(s_0, \alpha), x) = \lambda_Q(\delta_Q(q_0, \alpha), x) = \lambda_Q(h(\delta_S(s_0, \alpha)), x),$$

as $Q \in \Im_m(T)$.

Thus, h is an isomorphism and, as $h(s_0) = q_0$, it follows that Q is equivalent to S.

(i) $\Rightarrow$ (ii) Let T be an m-complete test suite. First, notice that any m-complete test suite is a transition cover for the FSM S. Otherwise, there exists a transition of S which is not traversed by the test suite; an FSM that is T-equivalent to, but distinguishable from, $\bar{S}$ can be obtained from S by mutating the output in this transition. By definition, T is prefix closed, thus, it is an initialized transition cover.

As T is an m-complete test suite, each FSM $Q \in \mathfrak{I}_m(T)$ is equivalent to S, i.e., there exists a mapping $h: S \rightarrow Q$ such that $h(s_0) = q_0$ and for each transition (s, x) it holds that

$$h(\delta_s(s, x)) = \delta_Q(h(q), x)$$

and thus, since $h(s_0) = q_0$, for each input sequence α it holds that

$$h(\delta_s(s_0, \alpha)) = \delta_Q(h(s_0), \alpha) = \delta_Q(q_0, \alpha).$$

Let α and β be S-convergent, i.e., $\delta_s(s_0, \alpha) = \delta_s(s_0, \beta)$. It follows that

$$\delta_Q(q_0, \alpha) = h(\delta_s(s_0, \alpha)) = h(\delta_s(s_0, \beta)) = \delta_Q(q_0, \beta).$$

Thus, α and β are also Q-convergent and, consequently, the set is $\mathfrak{I}_m(T)$-convergence-preserving. ◆

Considering the generation methods discussed in Section 3, we note that the conditions of Lemma 3 are satisfied for all pairs of S-convergent tests in $K \cup K.X$, which turns out to be a transition cover for S. Thus, the test suites generated by these methods satisfy the conditions of Theorem 1, since $K \cup K.X$ is an initialized transition cover. At the same time, Theorem 1 suggests that rather than considering the whole set of tests in $K.X^{\leq \Delta+1}$ at once, as the existing methods do, it is sufficient to ensure convergence of tests covering all transitions, using Lemma 3. Moreover, Lemmas 1, 2, and 3 indicate that this can be achieved in an iterative way, namely, the convergence for tests covering a current transition can be ensured based on the convergence established for other transitions. In the next section we elaborate this idea in a method for complete test suite generation.

5   Test Generation Method

In this section, we present a method, called SPY-method, which generates an m-complete test suite by building an $\mathfrak{I}_m(T)$-convergence-preserving transition cover. In the method, the knowledge about test convergence and divergence obtained during the execution helps identify the possibility of extending tests already in the test suite. Such an extension avoids branching of tests and thus contributes to test suite shortening. During the execution of the method, the $\mathfrak{I}_m(T)$-convergence of tests is determined. Notice that any two $\mathfrak{I}_m(T)$-convergent tests are also $\mathfrak{I}_m(T')$-convergent, for each $T' \supseteq T$. Thus, the inclusion of new tests in T does not invalidate this property.

As the $\mathfrak{I}_m(T)$-convergence relation is an equivalence relation, it can be represented by the partition it induces. In a given stage of the method execution only a subset of the $\mathfrak{I}_m(T)$-convergence relation might be known. We denote by Π the partition induced by the pairs of tests which are known to be $\mathfrak{I}_m(T)$-convergent. Given a test $\alpha \in T$, we denote by $[\alpha]_\Pi$ the block of the partition Π which contains α.

We assume that a family H of harmonized state identifiers is provided. Given a test α, let $H(\alpha) \in H$ be the state identifier for state $\delta_s(s_0, \alpha)$. The method starts by determining a minimal initialized state cover K, as in Step 1 of existing methods.

Then, the tests in K are extended by the appropriate state identifiers. Each block in the initial partition Π is a singleton, since no convergence is initially known. The method iterates until the set of tests which are $\mathfrak{I}_m(T)$-convergent with the tests in K becomes a transition cover for S.

During the execution of the method, it is necessary to extend two tests in T to ensure their divergence. As the divergence of tests also applies to other tests in their blocks, when more than one test is available in a given block, the one which will result in a shorter test suite is selected. This is achieved as follows. Suppose that test $\alpha \notin T$ should be added to T. Let β be the longest prefix of α which is in T. If β is not a proper prefix of another test in T, we have that $len(T \cup \{\alpha\}) = len(T) + |\alpha| - |\beta|$, i.e., adding α to T results only in extending the test β by $|\alpha| - |\beta|$ input symbols. On the other hand, if β is a proper prefix of some other test in T, it holds that $len(T \cup \{\alpha\}) = len(T) + |\alpha| + 1$, as it results in an additional testing branching. Thus, selection of a test which has to be extended by some input sequence, e.g., a state distinguishing sequence, should result, whenever possible, in extending some test in T that is not a proper prefix of another test.

After adding new tests two blocks containing tests that are $\mathfrak{I}_m(T)$-convergent, are merged, i.e., replaced by their union, iteratively. The merge of blocks can result in a new partition for which the $\mathfrak{I}_m(T)$-convergence of other tests can be concluded, due to the application of Lemma 1(i) and thus, the procedure of merging should be repeated. We denote by $closure(\Pi)$ the partition obtained after merging the blocks of Π as much as possible, by applying subset merging and Lemma 1(i).

We now present SPY-method.

Input: An FSM S with n states, a family of harmonized state identifiers H and a natural number $m \geq n$.
Output: An m-complete test suite.
Determine a minimal initialized state cover K.
$T := pref(\{\alpha.H(\alpha) \mid \alpha \in K\})$
$\Pi := \{\{\alpha\} \mid \alpha \in T\}$
While there exists a transition (s, x) not covered by the set of tests in T which are $\mathfrak{I}_m(T)$-convergent with some test in K

    Let $\alpha, \beta \in K$ be such that $\delta_s(s_0, \alpha) = s$ and $\delta_s(s_0, \beta) = \delta_s(s, x)$

    For each $\gamma \in X^{\leq \Delta}$, each $\sigma \in H(\beta\gamma)$

        Select $\alpha' \in [\alpha]_\Pi$, such that $len(T \cup \{\alpha'x\gamma\sigma\})$ is minimal

        $T := T \cup pref(\alpha'x\gamma\sigma)$

        Select $\beta' \in [\beta]_\Pi$, such that $len(T \cup \{\beta'\gamma\sigma\})$ is minimal

        $T := T \cup pref(\beta'\gamma\sigma)$

        $\Pi := closure(\Pi \cup \{\{\chi\} \mid \chi \in \{\alpha'x, \beta'\}.pref(\gamma\sigma)\})$

    End for

    $\Pi := closure(\Pi \cup \{[\alpha x]_\Pi \cup [\beta]_\Pi\})$

End while
Return T

Theorem 2. *SPY-method generates an m-complete test suite T for S.*

Proof. Let $C = \{\beta \in [\alpha]_\Pi \mid \alpha \in K\}$, i.e., C is the set of tests which are $\Im_m(T)$-convergent with some test in K. Notice that C is $\Im_m(T)$-convergence-preserving, since by its definition, any two tests in C which are S-convergent are also $\Im_m(T)$-convergent. We first show that in each iteration of the method, C is extended to cover a transition (s, x) which was not yet covered. Let $\alpha, \beta \in K$ be such that $\delta_s(s_0, \alpha) = s$ and $\delta_s(s_0, \beta) = \delta_s(s, x)$. The method then uses the state identifiers required to ensure that tests αx and β are $\Im_m(T)$-convergent. Indeed, for all $\gamma \in X^{\leq \Delta}$, tests α' and β', which are $\Im_m(T)$-convergent with α and β, respectively, are selected and the tests $\alpha' x \gamma$ and $\beta' \gamma$ are extended with the corresponding state identifiers. As the state cover K is also extended by the state identifiers, we have that for each sequence γ of length Δ, the set $K \cup \{\alpha x, \beta\}.pref(\gamma)$ is $\Im_m(T)$-divergence-preserving; thus, the conditions of Lemma 3 are satisfied and tests αx and β are $\Im_m(T)$-convergent. The the blocks containing αx and β are merged. As a result, the transition (s, x) is covered by C. When the method terminates, C is a transition cover for S. As K is initialized and $K \subseteq C$, C is also initialized. Hence, by Theorem 1, T is m-complete, since $C \subseteq T$ is an $\Im_m(T)$-convergence-preserving initialized transition cover. ◆

In each iteration the proposed method deals with the set $X^{\leq \Delta}$, while the theoretical results indicate that an m-complete test suite should include all sequences in the traversal set $X^{\leq \Delta+1}$ [11] [8]. Notice, however, that to obtain a transition cover as required by Theorem 1, the tests of a state cover has to be extended by X, which is in its turn extended by $X^{\leq \Delta}$. Therefore, all sequences in the traversal set $X^{\leq \Delta+1}$ are indeed present in the resulting test suite. Nevertheless, the distribution of the traversal set over several tests usually results in shorter test suites, as demonstrated by the example and the experimental results on the next sections.

Compared with the existing methods for m-complete test suite generation, SPY-method requires the additional operations of handling the partitions of tests and selecting the tests in a partition which lead to a minimal length increase. We discuss the overhead imposed by these operations. The partitions used in the method can be efficiently handled using a *union-find* structure [6]. The operation of merging blocks and determining to which block a test belongs can be performed in $O(Ack^{-1}(l, l))$, where $Ack^{-1}(l, l)$ is the inverse of the extremely quickly-growing Ackermann function [6]. For any reasonable value of l, $Ack^{-1}(l, l)$ is less than five, i.e., the running time of these operations is effectively a small constant. In order to efficiently calculate a length increase caused by new tests, test suites can be represented by trees. Then it is possible to identify when a test will create a new test (branching at a non-leaf node) or extend an existing one (extending a leaf node) by retrieving the information about nodes in the tree. As the size of the tree is proportional to the length of the test suite, the overhead imposed by the additional operations required by the method, i.e., maintaining the partitions and determining the length increase, is polynomial in the length of the test suite.

6 Example

In this section, we illustrate the execution of the method. Consider the FSM in Figure 1. We generate a 3-complete test suite, using the family of harmonized state identifiers as in Section 3, $H_1 = H_2 = \{a\}$. Note that as before, $n = 2$ and $m = 3$.

The method determines a minimal initialized state cover $K = \{\varepsilon, a\}$. The test suite is initialized with $T := \{\alpha.H(\alpha) \mid \alpha \in K\} = pref(aa)$ and the partition $\Pi := \{\{\varepsilon\}, \{a\}, \{aa\}\}$. Notice that the tests in K already cover the transition $(1, a)$. Then, the method iterates until all the other transitions are also covered by the tests which are $\Im_m(T)$-convergent with either ε or a. Notice that in this example, both H_1 and H_2 contain only the sequence a. Therefore, each state identifier used in the method is always equal to $\{a\}$, i.e., $\sigma = a$ throughout this example.

The method selects the transition $(s, x) = (1, b)$; thus $\alpha = \beta = \varepsilon$. At this stage each block is a singleton; thus, selecting the empty sequence ε is the only option in the first iteration. For each $\gamma \in X^{\leq\Delta} = \{\varepsilon, a, b\}$, the test ε is extended by $x\gamma\sigma$ and $\gamma\sigma$; namely, the empty sequence is extended by the sequences ba, a, baa, aa, bba, and ba. The test suite becomes $T = pref(\{aa, baa, bba\})$ and the partition Π is updated to include the new tests (each of them also becomes a singleton block in the partition). According to Lemma 3, ε and b are now $\Im_m(T)$-convergent, thus, blocks $\{\varepsilon\}$ and $\{b\}$ should be merged. After updating the partition and determining its closure, the partition $\Pi = \{\{\varepsilon, b, bb\}, \{a, ba, bba\}, \{aa, baa\}\}$ is obtained. The resulting test suite is represented in Figure 4. The nodes with the same color are in the same block of the partition Π.

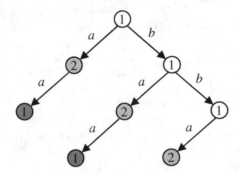

Fig. 4. Tree representation of $pref(\{aa, baa, bba\})$

The methods selects the transition $(s, x) = (2, a)$. Then $\alpha = a$ and $\beta = \varepsilon$. In this iteration, the blocks of the partition contain several tests; thus, there are choices when selecting the test which is extended by the state identifier. For each $\gamma \in X^{\leq\Delta} = \{\varepsilon, a, b\}$, some test in $[\alpha]_\Pi = [a]_\Pi$ should be extended by $x\gamma\sigma$ and some test in $[\beta]_\Pi = [\varepsilon]_\Pi$ should be extended by $\gamma\sigma$. For $\gamma = \varepsilon$ some test in $[a]_\Pi = \{a, ba, bba\}$ has to be extended by $x\gamma\sigma = aa$; the test suites resulting from extending a, ba and bba by aa have lengths 12, 12 and 13, respectively. Thus, the test a is selected and aaa is added to T. Then, some test in $[\varepsilon]_\Pi = \{\varepsilon, b, bb\}$ should be extended by a. As $a \in T$, no additional test is included. For $\gamma = a$, some test in $[a]_\Pi$ has to be extended by $x\gamma\sigma = aaa$ and some test in $[\varepsilon]_\Pi$ by $\gamma\sigma = aa$. A test suite of shorter length can be obtained by extending either a or ba. The test a is selected and $aaaa$ is added to T. There is no need to extend any sequence in $[\varepsilon]_\Pi$ by $\gamma\sigma = aa$, since $aa \in T$. For $\gamma = b$, $\sigma = a$, some test in $[a]_\Pi$ should be extended by $x\gamma\sigma = aba$ and some test in $[\varepsilon]_\Pi$ by $\gamma\sigma = ba$.

Extending tests a, ba and bba by aba results in test suites of lengths 17, 15 and 16, respectively. The test ba is, then, selected and $baaba$ is added to T. Again, there is no need to extend any sequence in $[\varepsilon]_\Pi$ by $\gamma\sigma = ba$. The test suite becomes $T = pref(\{aaaa, baaba, bba\})$. The tests ε and aa are now $\mathfrak{I}_m(T)$-convergent and thus, blocks $\{\varepsilon, b, bb\}$ and $\{aa, baa\}$ should be merged. After merging these blocks and deriving the closure, the partition $\Pi = \{\{\varepsilon, aa, aaaa, b, baa, baab, bb\}, \{a, aaa, ba, baaba, bba\}\}$ is obtained. Figure 5 represents the resulting test suite.

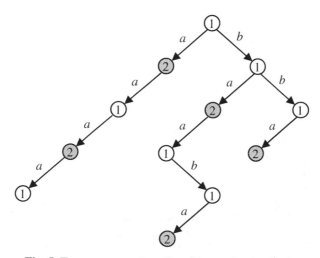

Fig. 5. Tree representation of $pref(\{aaaa, baaba, bba\})$

It remains to cover the transition $(s, x) = (2, b)$; thus $\alpha = \beta = a$. For $\gamma = \varepsilon$, some test in $[a]_\Pi = \{a, aaa, ba, baaba, bba\}$ should be extended by $x\gamma\sigma = ba$ and $\gamma\sigma = a$. The test suites obtained by extending either test $baaba$ or bba by ba have the same length; the test bba is then selected and $bbaba$ is added to T. Some test in $[a]_\Pi$ has to be extended by $\gamma\sigma = a$, which does not need any additional test, since $aa \in T$. For $\gamma = a$, some test in $[a]_\Pi$ should be extended by $x\gamma\sigma = baa$ and $\gamma\sigma = aa$. The test suite of a shorter length is obtained by extending bba by baa and the test $bbabaa$ is added to T. There is no need to extend any test in $[a]_\Pi$ by aa, since $aaa \in T$. For $\gamma = b$, some test in $[a]_\Pi$ should be extended by $x\gamma\sigma = bba$ and $\gamma\sigma = ba$. The test suite of a shorter length is obtained by extending $baaba$ by bba and the test $baababba$ is added to T. To extend some test in $[a]_\Pi$ by $\gamma\sigma = ba$, no additional test is required, since $baaba \in T$ and $baa \in [a]_\Pi$. The resulting test suite is $T = pref(\{aaaa, baababba, bbabaa\})$ of length 21. Recall that the test suite T_1 obtained by the existing methods for the machine in Figure 1 has length 28.

7 Experimental Results

In this section, we present the results of an experiment with the HSI method and the proposed method, comparing the length of the test suites they generate. We randomly generate minimal FSMs with five inputs, five outputs and the number of states n ranging from five to 50. We executed both the HSI method and the proposed method

for generating m-complete test suites, for $n \leq m \leq n + 3$ and calculated the ratio of
reduction, i.e., the average ratio of the length of the test suite generated by SPY-
method and the length of the test suite generated by the HSI method. For each setting
(values of n and m), we generated 30 FSMs and the respective test suites, totalling
5520 FSMs. In Figure 6, we plot the variation of the average ratio with respect to the
number of states. We notice that the test suites generated by our method are on
average up to 40% shorter than the test suites obtained by the HSI method; moreover,
the larger the number of states in the specification FSM and the number of extra states
in implementations, the bigger the reduction.

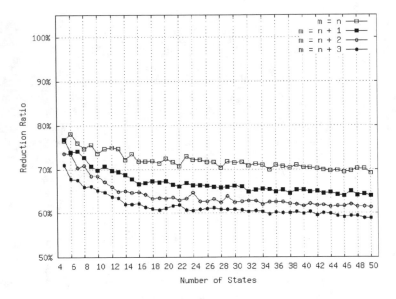

Fig. 6. Average reduction ratio

8   Conclusions

In this paper we investigated the problem of generating m-complete test suites for an
FSM with n states, when implementation FSMs may have extra states.

The main contributions of this paper are as follows. Firstly, although we have not
refuted the inevitability of including the sequences of a traversal set in an m-complete
test suite, we showed that these sequences can be arranged in such a way that test
branching is significantly reduced. Secondly, we stated conditions which guarantee
that the resulting test suite is indeed m-complete and elaborated a test generation
method based on these conditions. Differently from all existing methods, the proposed
method distributes the sequences in the traversal set over several tests avoiding as
much as possible test branching and thus leading to shortening of the resulting test
suite. Finally, we experimentally compared the proposed method with the HSI-
method. The experimental results indicate that obtained tests are on average up to
40% shorter.

As future work, it is possible to combine the on-the-fly determination of distinguishing sequences used in the H method with the possibility of distributing them. Another possible extension is the further investigation of properties of test convergence and divergence.

Acknowledgements

The authors acknowledge financial supports of NSERC (Grant OGP0194381), Brazilian Funding Agency CNPq (Grant 200032/2008-9), and FCP Russian program (contract 02.514.12.4002).

References

1. Bochmann, G.v., Petrenko, A.: Protocol testing: review of methods and relevance for software testing. In: ACM International Symposium on Software Testing and Analysis (ISSTA 1994), pp. 109–124. ACM Press, New York (1994)
2. Binder, R.: Testing Object-Oriented Systems. Addison-Wesley, Inc., Reading (2000)
3. Chow, T.S.: Testing software design modeled by finite-state machines. IEEE Trans. Softw. Eng. 4(3), 178–187 (1978)
4. Dorofeeva, R., El-Fakih, K., Yevtushenko, N.: An improved conformance testing method. In: Wang, F. (ed.) FORTE 2005. LNCS, vol. 3731, pp. 204–218. Springer, Heidelberg (2005)
5. Fujiwara, S., von Bochmann, G., Khendek, F., Amalou, M., Ghedamsi, A.: Test selection based on finite state models. IEEE Trans. Softw. Eng. 17(6), 591–603 (1991)
6. Galil, Z., Italiano, G.F.: Data structures and algorithms for disjoint set union problems. ACM Comput. Surv. 23(3), 319–344 (1991)
7. Gonenc, G.: A method for the design of fault detection experiments. IEEE Trans. on Comput. 19(6), 551–558 (1970)
8. Lee, D., Yannakakis, M.: Principles and methods of testing finite state machines - a survey. Proceedings of the IEEE. 84(8), 1090–1123 (1996)
9. Hennie, F.C.: Fault-detecting experiments for sequential circuits. In: Proceedings of Fifth Annual Symposium on Circuit Theory and Logical Design, Princeton, New Jersey, pp. 95–110 (1965)
10. Hierons, R.M., Ural, H.: Optimizing the length of checking sequences. IEEE Trans. on Comput. 55(5), 618–629 (2006)
11. Moore, E.F.: Gedanken-experiments on sequential machines. Automata Studies, Annals of Mathematical Studies (34), 129–153 (1956)
12. Petrenko, A., Higashino, T., Kaji, T.: Handling redundant and additional states in protocol testing. In: IFIP 8th Inter. Workshop on Protocol Test Systems, pp. 307–322. Chapman & Hall, Boca Raton (1995)
13. Vasilevskii, M.P.: Failure diagnosis of automata. Cybernetics 4, 653–665 (1973)
14. Yevtushenko, N., Petrenko, A.: Synthesis of test experiments in some classes of automata. Automatic Control and Computer Sciences 24(4), 50–55 (1990)

An Approach for Test Selection for EFSMs Using a Theorem Prover

Mahadevan Subramaniam[1], Ling Xiao[1], Bo Guo[1], and Zoltan Pap[2]

[1] Computer Science Department
University of Nebraska at Omaha
Omaha, NE 68182, USA
msubramaniam@mail.unomaha.edu
[2] Ericsson, Hungary
pap@tmit.bme.hu

Abstract. This paper describes an automatic approach for selecting tests from a test suite to validate the changes made to an extended finite state machine (EFSM). EFSMs supporting variables over commonly used data types including booleans, numbers, arrays, queues, and records, and communicating with the environment using parameterized messages are considered. Changes to the EFSM add/delete/replace one or more transitions. Tests are described using a sequence of input and output messages with parameter values. We introduce a class of *fully-observable* tests. The description of a fully-observable test contains all the information to accurately determine the transitions executed by the test. Interaction among the EFSM transitions captured in terms of a *compatibility* relation is used along with a given test description to automatically identify fully-observable tests. A procedure is described for selecting a test for a given change based on accurately predicting if the test executes the change transition. We then describe how several tests can be simultaneously selected by grouping them based on overlap of their descriptions. The proposed approach has been implemented using a theorem prover and applied to several examples including protocols and web services with encouraging results.

1 Introduction

Evolution and maintenance of communication systems is a challenging problem. Comprehensive testing of the changes in each evolution step is essential to gain confidence that the modifications behave as intended without any adverse consequences. Test suites used to validate these systems are usually very large, comprised of both hand-crafted and generated tests. Re-running the entire test suite at each evolution step is impractical [8].

Regression test selection addresses this problem by identifying tests in a given test suite that are relevant to validate the changes performed in an evolution step. This is an active area of research with earlier works involving the evolution and maintenance of software programs (see [9] for an excellent survey) as well as state-based communication system models [2,5,6].

M. Núñez et al. (Eds.): TESTCOM/FATES 2009, LNCS 5826, pp. 146–162, 2009.

In this paper, we describe a novel and automatic approach for test selection for extended finite state machines(EFSMs) supporting a rich set of commonly used data types including booleans, numbers, arrays, queues, and records. Changes to the EFSM in each evolution step are performed at the transition level. Changes can add/delete/replace one or more transitions. Test descriptions contain a sequence of input and output messages with parameter values over the supported data types. EFSMs have been extensively used to model communication systems and also serve as formal models underlying several state-based concurrent specification languages. More recently, there has been a lot of interest in EFSMs supporting various data types to model web services[1].

Given a change and a test description, the proposed approach automatically analyzes the test description to determine whether the test will exercise the change in which case the test is selected. A class of tests called **fully-observable tests** is identified. The description of a fully-observable test contains adequate information to accurately determine if the test exercises a given change without actually executing the test. Interaction among the transitions, captured in terms of compatibility of transitions, is used to identify fully-observable tests. A procedure for identifying fully-observable tests that uses a theorem prover in a push-button manner to reason about data types is described. A given change is **matched** with a test description and it is shown that it suffices for a test to be fully-observable up to the point of the match to accurately predict whether a change will be exercised. A procedure to select tests is described. We also describe how several tests can be simultaneously selected by grouping them based on overlap of their descriptions.

The proposed approach has been implemented using the theorem prover *Simplify* extended with an in-house rewrite engine and has been applied to several EFSMs. Our initial results from preliminary experiments on seven examples including protocols and web services from the literature are highly promising. They show that the time for test selection together with the running of the selected tests is always lesser than re-running the entire test suite [8].

An overview of the approach using an example follows next. Section 2 describes related work. Section 3 defines a compatibility relation among transitions. Section 4 introduces fully-observable tests and a procedure for identifying these tests. Section 5 discusses how tests are selected for a given change and extends this approach to handle multiple tests in a test suite. Section 6 describes experiments and Section 7 concludes the paper.

1.1   A Simple Example

Consider a simple bank web service EFSM depicted in Figure 1. Users start by opening an account with a cash amount greater than or equal to a minimum balance amount (min) and are given a unique account id (a positive integer). They can then perform deposits and withdrawals using the id until closing the account. Withdrawals exceeding the current account balance represented by the

---

[1] Please see Testcom2006, Testcom2007, Testcom 2008 for relevant papers.

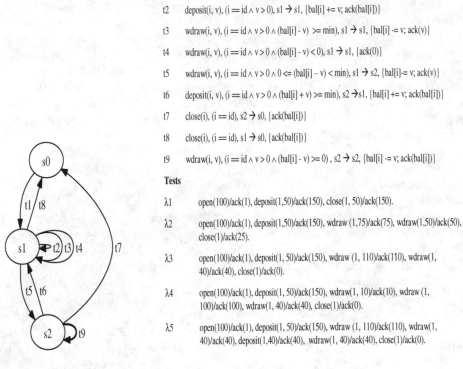

t1   open(v), (v >= min), s0 → s1, {id += 1; bal[id] = v; ack(id)}

t2   deposit(i, v), (i == id ∧ v > 0), s1 → s1, {bal[i] += v; ack(bal[i])}

t3   wdraw(i, v), (i == id ∧ v > 0 ∧ (bal[i] - v) >= min), s1 → s1, {bal[i] -= v; ack(v)}

t4   wdraw(i, v), (i == id ∧ v > 0 ∧ (bal[i] - v) < 0), s1 → s1, {ack(0)}

t5   wdraw(i, v), (i == id ∧ v > 0 ∧ 0 <= (bal[i] – v) < min), s1 → s2, {bal[i]-:= v; ack(v)}

t6   deposit(i, v), (i == id ∧ v > 0 ∧ (bal[i] + v) >= min), s2 →s1, {bal[i] += v; ack(bal[i])}

t7   close(i), (i == id), s2 → s0, {ack(bal[i])}

t8   close(i), (i == id), s1 → s0, {ack(bal[i])}

t9   wdraw(i, v), (i == id ∧ v > 0 ∧ (bal[i] - v) >= 0) , s2 → s2, {bal[i] -= v; ack(bal[i])}

Tests

λ1   open(100)/ack(1), deposit(1,50)/ack(150), close(1, 50)/ack(150).

λ2   open(100)/ack(1), deposit(1,50)/ack(150), wdraw (1,75)/ack(75), wdraw(1,50)/ack(50), close(1)/ack(25).

λ3   open(100)/ack(1), deposit(1, 50)/ack(150), wdraw (1, 110)/ack(110), wdraw(1, 40)/ack(40), close(1)/ack(0).

λ4   open(100)/ack(1), deposit(1, 50)/ack(150), wdraw(1, 10)/ack(10), wdraw (1, 100)/ack(100), wdraw(1, 40)/ack(40), close(1)/ack(0).

λ5   open(100)/ack(1), deposit(1, 50)/ack(150), wdraw (1, 110)/ack(110), wdraw(1, 40)/ack(40), deposit(1,40)/ack(40), wdraw(1, 40)/ack(40), close(1)/ack(0).

Fig. 1. Bank web service with Overdraft Update

Fig. 2. Transitions and tests

array $bal[]$ are returned and a withdrawal resulting in balance falling below the min amount suspends future withdrawals until the balance becomes at least the min amount.

The EFSM has 8 transitions t_1-t_8, depicted in Figure 2. Suppose we modify this EFSM by adding a transition t_9 to allow withdrawals not exceeding the balance even when the balance falls below min^2.

Consider the test suite in Figure 2, with tests λ_1-λ_5 for validating this new EFSM. Each test in this suite starts the EFSM with global variables $min = 50$; (account id) $id = 0$; $bal[] = initarray$ (array with all accounts having an undefined value) and serially applies the test inputs and compares the generated outputs with the corresponding outputs in the test to assign pass/fail verdict. Each test input is processed after executing all the transitions enabled by the previous test input. Such a test suite may include tests used for original EFSM and new tests generated using approaches like constrained path selection [5].

---

[2] Note that unspecified inputs received in an EFSM state are simply ignored. For e.g., withdrawals exceeding balance in state s_1 return 0 whereas they are ignored in state s_2 without affecting the balance.

We want to find which tests from the test suite in Figure 2, if any, are to be re-run to check the newly added transition t_9. Usually, tests which execute t_9, are the candidates[3].

First, considering each test one by one, the input conditions (and the output message) of t_9 are matched with those in the test description[4]. Transition t_9 is likely to be executed by a test to process its matching test input(s).

Test λ_1 where there is no match need not be re-run.

The next test λ_2 is matched by transition t_9 at its third and fourth inputs and is further analyzed to determine if t_9 is guaranteed to be executed by this test. A sequence of sets of transitions, $\phi = [\{t_1\}, \{t_2,t_6\}, \{t_3,t_4,t_5,t_9\}, \{t_3,t_4,t_5,t_9\}, \{t_7,t_8\}]$, point-wise matching the inputs of λ_2 is obtained. Note that, if any of the sets in ϕ are empty then the test has unspecified inputs and is discarded. Pairs of transitions from consecutive sets of ϕ are analyzed to see if ϕ has all the information about the transitions that the test λ_2 will execute. If so, we form an executable path up to (and including) the processing of the test input(s) matched by t_9 and choose the test as a candidate to be re-run if this path includes t_9.

The first test input of λ_2 must be processed by the transition t_1 in the first set in ϕ. Hence the description of λ_2 has all the information about the transitions that λ_2 will execute to process the first test input.

Now, we check if the second input of λ_2 can be processed by t_2 or t_6 from the second set in ϕ, immediately following t_1. Transition t_6 cannot immediately follow t_1 since the input state of t_6 differs from the output state of t_1. However, transition t_2 can process the second test input immediately following t_1[5].

Note that it may be possible to execute a transition such as t_6 after executing some other transition following transition t_1. Since we cannot find this intermediate transition based on the test description, we rule out t_6. If all the transitions in some set in ϕ of a test are ruled out then we can stop since this means that the test description does not contain all the information about the transitions that the test will execute. Such tests are not re-run and may either involve unspecified inputs or may execute transitions not appearing in ϕ.

For the third input of λ_2, we consider each transition in the corresponding set of ϕ with t_2. Transition t_9 cannot immediately follow t_2. Nor can t_4 immediately follow t_2 since t_4's input guard instantiated with the test input: $id == 1 \wedge 75 > 0 \wedge (bal[1] - 75) < 0$, requires that the formula: $(bal[1] - 75 + 50) < 0$ to be true after executing t_2 which requires: $(bal[1] - 75 + 50) < 0 \wedge (bal[1] == 100)$ to be true after executing t_1, which is not possible. Similarly, we can rule out transition t_5. The only remaining transition t_3 can immediately follow t_2 and can process the third input and hence we go to the next input of λ_2.

---

[3] These tests are called modification-traversing tests [9].

[4] Input conditions match if the messages in the description are instances of those in the transition and the transition guard is satisfied by the test input values. More details are in Section 3.

[5] Interaction among transitions is analyzed using post-images and pre-images computed from the transitions. For more details see Section 4.

Transition t_9 cannot immediately follow t_3. However, t_5 can immediately follow and process the fourth test input. Since the description of λ_2 contains all the information about the transitions executed up to (and including) the processing of the last test input matched by t_9, we can guarantee that t_9 will not be executed by λ_2. Therefore, test λ_2 need not be re-run to test t_9.

Test λ_3 has the same sequence of matching transitions as λ_2, except that the parameters in its third and fourth inputs are different. Analysis of λ_3 as described above, shows that t_1 and t_2 will process the first two test inputs. The third input will be processed by t_5 since its instantiated guard: $id == 1 \wedge 110 > 0 \wedge (0 <= bal[1]$ - $110 < min)$ can be satisfied after executing t_1 and t_2. Similarly, it can be shown that the next test input will be processed by t_9, which guarantees that t_9 will appear in its test run. Hence test λ_3 will be re-run and is a candidate to test t_9. It can be similarly verified that t_9 will be executed by the last two tests λ_4 and λ_5 to process their fifth and sixth inputs respectively making them candidates to test t_9 as well. Changes that delete and replace transitions can also be handled by the proposed approach and are discussed in Section 4.

The reader would have noticed the repetitive analysis of tests λ_3-λ_5 due to the sharing of test inputs in their descriptions. Tests can be grouped together based on the overlapping inputs in their descriptions to reduce selective re-testing costs. Section 5 gives more details.

2   Related Work

There is a lot of earlier work on regression test selection (see [9] for an excellent survey). Regression test selection for EFSMs has been studied earlier [2,5,6] for model-based regression test selection and test prioritization. In [5], Korel et. al, discuss a method for model-based test selection of EFSMs involving addition and deletion of transitions. Using control and data dependencies between the change transition and the rest of the model they identify equivalent tests to reduce the test suite. Since a test may cover multiple changes, tests are included only if their changes are not covered by others. In [2], Chen et. al, extend the work in [5] to consider new type of replacements called change transitions and refine control and data dependencies proposed in [5]. The work in [6] focusses on test prioritization and proposes several heuristics for the same.

The proposed approach extends these earlier works in several ways. First, we support more expressive, executable EFSMs with a rich set of data types including booleans, numbers, arrays, queues, and records. In this sense, this work bridges the gap between the code-based [9] and the model-based [2, 5, 6] approaches. Second, unlike model-based approaches, we do not consider tests to be explicit sequence of transitions. Our tests are a sequence of input assignments to the data variables (much like programs), with expected outputs and a verdict of pass/fail. We use a theorem prover to analyze a test to determine if it executes a given modified transition and select such tests. In this sense our notion of affected tests is similar to that of modification-traversing tests of [9]. Finally, we use a theorem prover to support richer set of data types than that have been traditionally considered by model-based approaches. Most importantly, this allows us to be more precise in comparison to the conservative data flow techniques used by model-based approaches.

3   Preliminaries

Extended Finite State Machines: An extended finite state machine (EFSM) [1,7,10] is a finite state machine extended with variables and communicates with the environment by exchanging parameterized messages using (possibly infinite) FIFO queues. An EFSM $E = (I, O, S, V, T)$, is a 5-tuple where I, O, S, V, and T are finite sets of parameterized input and output messages, states, variables, and transitions respectively. Message m has typed, distinct, parameters $p_1, \cdots,$ p_k, written as $\overrightarrow{p}$; types can be one of – boolean, number, array, queue, and record. The set $V = X \cup \{IQ, OQ\}$, is the union of the global variables X and the queue variables IQ and OQ denoting the input and output queues from (to) the environment respectively. A transition t in T is of the form: $m_k(\overrightarrow{p})$, P_t, $s_t \mapsto q_t$, $m_l(\overrightarrow{e})$, A_t where the predicate P_t, action list A_t, and $\overrightarrow{e} = (e_1, \cdots,$ $e_w)$ respectively are, a conjunction of atomic predicates, an ordered sequence of assignments, and a series of expressions over the data and queue variables and parameters $p_1, \cdots p_k$. The input(output) messages are optional in a transition.

Transitions having both input and output messages are **explicit**[6] transitions.

Semantics of EFSM: A **global state**, $g = (\langle s \rangle, pred)$ is a pair whose first element $s \in S$; second element $pred$ is a conjunction of atomic predicates over V including a (possibly empty) set of equalities representing the actions executed by the transitions to reach the global state g[7]. An atomic predicate is formed by using relational operators $(and, or, not, ==, \neq, <, \leq, >, \geq)$ over expressions over the different data types (booleans, numbers, arrays, queues, and records). An **initial global state** of E is a global state g in which state s belongs to the initial state of S, the second element $pred$ is the **initial predicate**, a conjunction of atomic predicates over queue variables stating that the output queue has the initial value $initq$, the input queue has environment messages, and the data variables have their initial values. Transition is **enabled** in a global state if its input message matches the head of IQ in the state and its input condition is satisfied at that state. An **execution step**, $g \rightarrow_t g'$, executes the transition t enabled in g resulting in the global state g'. A **run** $r = g_0 t_0 g_1 \cdots t_{n-1} g_0$ is a sequence of consecutive execution steps starting and ending in the initial global state.

Simplify Prover. Theorem prover Simplify [3] extended with rewrite rules is used to analyze tests in a push-button manner. Quantified formulas called verification conditions are generated by automatically translating the EFSM predicates and assignments [10] and input to the prover. The prover returns *valid* if input formula F is true under all the assignments to the variables in F

---

[6] Analogous to explicit transitions in SDL.

[7] Equalities in *pred* are represented as rewrite rules to aid equality simplification. More details are in [10].

and returns *invalid*, otherwise. To check if F is satisfiable, its negation is input to the prover. Simplify contains decision procedures for numbers, booleans, equality, partial-orders, and the theory of maps [3]. The theory of maps is used to reason about data types such as arrays, records including message queues.

A global state whose variables are fully instantiated (with constant values) is a **concrete global state**. Each global state represents a (possibly infinite) set of concrete global states obtained using satisfying assignments to the predicates (including message queues). Tests and test runs deal with executability and hence use concrete global states.

EFSMs are deterministic, i.e., in each concrete global state (that includes message queues) at most one transition is enabled.

3.1   Tests, Changes, and Affected Tests

An EFSM **test** (description) $\lambda = \langle g_0, [i_1/o_1, \cdots, i_n/o_n] \rangle$ is a concrete global state g_0 along with a finite sequence of input/output elements where each element is a sequence of assignments to the data and the message queue variables. Test λ is **applied** by starting the machine in the concrete global state g_0 and repeatedly executing the enabled EFSM transitions and serially processing the test inputs. The **test run** $r_\lambda = g_0 t_0, \cdots t_m g_m \cdots g_0$, is an EFSM run produced by applying λ to the EFSM in state g_0; all the global states in r_λ are concrete global states. Each test λ has a unique run r_λ since the EFSM is deterministic, i.e., at most one transition is enabled in any concrete global state.

In this paper, we focus on tests that are designed to execute specified behaviors. Tests that check the EFSM behavior by providing unspecified or inappropriate inputs are not considered. However, the approach applies equally to these as well. Please see [11] for identifying such failing tests.

Changes to the EFSM are done at the transition level. A change $\delta = \langle sign, t \rangle$, $sign \in \{+,-\}$ either adds or deletes the transition t respectively. Change can add explicit transitions having the same input and output messages with different input states and/or input conditions. Newly added transitions can also refer to new messages and/or new states. In such cases, we will assume that the test suite from which tests are to be selected already contains tests with these new messages [5]. Replacement of transitions can be modeled using addition and deletion of transitions. Change $\delta = \langle t_d, t_a \rangle$ denotes a replacement deleting t_d and adding t_a. More complex updates are specified by using a set of order-independent [11] transition changes.

Test λ is *affected* by a change δ if the test run executes the transition t in δ. Then, λ is a candidate to be re-run for testing the change δ.

4   Analyzing Interaction among Transitions

Pre-image of t, $Pre(t) = \langle s_t, (nP_t \wedge IQ.\text{hd} == m_j(\overrightarrow{p}) \wedge OQ \neq full^8) \rangle$, is a symbolic global state that includes every global state g (possibly none) where the

---

[8] For brevity, we assume output queues to be unbounded, henceforth.

transition is enabled. It is generated using transition t; nP_t is got from predicate P_t of t by renaming variables to refer to their latest instances [10].

Example: Transition t_5 in Figure 2, $Pre(t_5) = \langle s_1, (i == id \land v > 0 \land 0 <= (bal_0[i] - v) \land (bal_0[i] - v) < min_0 \land IQ_0.\text{hd} = wdraw(i, v)) \rangle$ where bal_0, min_0, and IQ_0 refer to the latest instances of these variables. $\square$

The **post-image** of t, $Pos(t) = \langle q_t, (nP_t \land IQ_1 == deq(IQ_0) \land IQ_0.\text{hd} == m_j(\vec{p}) \land OQ_1 == \langle OQ_0, m_l(\vec{ne}) \rangle \land nA_t) \rangle$, is a symbolic global state that includes every global state g' (possibly none) that can be obtained after executing t. It is automatically generated using t; $I(O)Q_0$ and $I(O)Q_1$ stand for the queues before and after executing t; $\vec{ne}$ denotes the parameter expressions in the output message using the latest instances of variables; nA_t is similarly obtained from the action statements A_t after translating them into equalities [10].

Example: $Pos(t_5) = \langle s_2, (i == id \land v > 0 \land 0 <= (bal_0[i] - v) \land (bal_0[i] - v) < min_0 \land IQ_1 == deq(IQ_0) \land IQ_0.\text{hd} == wdraw(i, v) \land OQ_1 == \langle OQ_0, ack(v) \rangle \land bal_1[i] == bal_0[i] - v) \rangle$. $\square$

Below, we view $Pre(t)$ and $Pos(t)$ as formulas with the EFSM state being an equality predicate over a predefined state variable st.

Compatibility of Transitions. Compatibility relation among transitions determines if a transition can immediately follow another in the EFSM runs. Given transitions t_i and t_j with input messages m_i and m_j respectively, let $\psi = (IQ_0 == \langle m_i(\vec{p_i}), m_j(\vec{p_j}) \rangle)$. Formula ψ provides the context with the input queue having the two input messages and the output queue capacity being set so that both transitions can enqueue their outputs.

Transition t_j is **incompatible** with t_i if t_j cannot immediately follow t_i in any EFSM run. Transition t_j is found to be incompatible with t_i by checking that $\psi \land Pos(t_i) \land Pre(t_j)$ is an unsatisfiable formula.

Example: In Figure 2, transition t_9 is incompatible with transition t_6. Context $\psi = (IQ_0 == \langle deposit(i_1, v_1), wdraw(i_2, v_2) \rangle)$.
$Pos(t_6) = \langle s_1, (i_1 == id \land v_1 > 0 \land (bal_0[i_1] + v_1) >= min_0 \land IQ_1 == deq(IQ_0) \land IQ_0.\text{hd} == deposit(i_1, v_1) \land OQ_1 == \langle OQ_0, ack(bal_1[i_1]) \rangle \land bal_1[i_1] == bal_0[i_1] + v_1) \rangle$.
$Pre(t_9) = \langle s_2, (i_2 == id \land v_2 > 0 \land (bal_0[i_2] - v_2) >= 0 \land IQ_1.\text{hd} = wdraw(i_2, v_2)) \rangle$. It is verified using the prover that $\psi \land Pos(t_6) \land Pre(t_9)$ is an unsatisfiable formula. $\square$

Note that t_j being incompatible with t_i is independent of the input parameters in t_i and t_j since they are renamed and are disjoint.

Transition t_j is **strongly compatible** with t_i if t_j can immediately follow t_i in all EFSM runs. Transition t_j is found to be strongly compatible with t_i if ($\psi \land Pos(t_i)$) $\implies PreElim(t_j)$ is a valid formula. $PreElim(t_j)$ is obtained from $Pre(t_j)$ by eliminating conjuncts that involve only the input parameters of t_j. This ensures that t_j immediately follows t_j regardless of the values of the input parameters.

Example: Transition t_8 is strongly compatible with transition t_6 in Figure 2. Context $\psi = (IQ_0 == \langle\ wdraw(i_1, v_1),\ close(i_2)\ \rangle);\ Pre(t_8) = PreElim(t_8) = \langle s_1,\ IQ_1.hd = close(i_2)\rangle;\ Pos(t_6)$ is given above. It is verified using the prover that $(\psi \wedge Pos(t_6)) \implies PreElim(t_8)$ is a valid formula.

Note also that t_6 is also strongly compatible with the t_2 in Figure 2 since $(\psi \wedge Pos(t_6)) \implies PreElim(t_2)$ is a valid formula. However, it is evident $(\psi \wedge Pos(t_6) \implies Pre(t_2)$ is not a valid formula since the conjunct in $Pre(t_2)$ derived from the condition $v > 0$ of t_2 is not valid.   □

More than one transition can be strongly compatible with a transition provided these transitions have mutually exclusive predicates over the input parameters. Consider a deterministic EFSM[9] with transitions, $t_1: m_1,\ true,\ s_0 \mapsto s_1,\ ack;\ t_2$ $m_2(v),\ v > 0,\ s_1 \mapsto s_1,\ ack;\ t_3: m_3(v),\ v < 0,\ s_1 \mapsto s_1,\ ack$. It is easily verified that both t_2 and t_3 are strongly compatible with t_1. Note however, that only one of t_2 or t_3 can immediately follow t_1 in any concrete global state.

Transition t_j is **compatible** with t_i if t_j can immediately follow t_i in some EFSM runs but not in others. Transition t_j is found to be compatible with t_i if t_j is neither incompatible nor strongly compatible with t_i.

Example: Transition t_3 is compatible with t_1 in Figure 2, since $Pos(t_1) \wedge Pre(t_3)$ is not unsatisfiable and $Pos(t_1) \implies PreElim(t_3)$ is not a valid formula.   □

Many transitions can be compatible with a given transition. It is also possible to have transitions t_j and t_k where t_j is strongly compatible and t_k is compatible with a given transition t_i. Consider a deterministic EFSM whose transitions include, $t_1: m_1(),\ s_0 \mapsto s_1,\ ack,\ \{x = 1;\};\ t_2: m_2(),\ x > 0,\ s_1 \mapsto s_1,\ ack,\ \{\};\ t_3: m_3(),\ y > 0,\ s_1 \mapsto s_1,\ ack,\ \{\}$. Transition t_2 is strongly compatible with t_1 since it can always immediately follow t_1. However, since the value of y is unknown after executing t_1, t_3 can immediately follow t_1 in some runs but not in others. In this case, for deterministic behavior, the EFSM must ensure that t_1 is only executed in a concrete state in which the value of y is not positive.

The pre-image and post-image of EFSM transitions and the compatibility of transitions can be pre-computed using a theorem prover before test selection and used to identify fully-observable tests as described next.

5 Selecting Fully-Observable Tests

Test λ is **fully-observable** if every transition in the test run r_λ is an explicit transition. Recall from Section 2, that transitions having both input and output messages are explicit transitions. We can identify these tests by using their descriptions as described below.

Consider test (description) $\lambda = \langle g_0, [i_1/o_1, \cdots, i_n/o_n]\rangle$. Transition t_k **matches** i_k/o_k in λ if input i_k (output o_k) is an instance of the input (output) message of t_k and the input condition of t_k instantiated with parameter values from i_k is a satisfiable formula. As an example, the transition t_5 in Figure 2, matches

---

[9] Please see Section 3.

the input $wdraw(1, 110)/ack(110)$ of λ_3 since the input and output messages $wdraw(i, v)$ and $ack(v)$ are instances of the test input and test output respectively and the condition of t_5 instantiated with the parameters: $(1 == id) \land (110 > 0) \land (bal[1] - 110) >= 0 \land (bal[1] - 110) < min$ is a satisfiable formula.

Let $T(i_k/o_k)$ denote the set of transitions matching i_k/o_k and $\phi=[T(i_1/o_1),\cdots, T(i_n/o_n)]$ denote the sequence of sets of transitions that point-wise match the sequence $[i_1/o_1, \cdots, i_n/o_n]$. As an example, $\phi = [\{t_1\}, \{t_2,t_6\}, \{t_3,t_4,t_5,t_9\}, \{t_3,t_4,t_5,t_9\}, \{t_7,t_8\}]$ for the test λ_2 in Figure 2.

Note that if transitions t_k and t'_k both belong to some set $T(i_k/o_k)$ then they cannot both be strongly compatible with a transition t_i. If this were to happen then both of them can immediately follow t_i in every EFSM run. Since this is not possible in a deterministic EFSM they must have mutually exclusive predicates involving their input parameters in which case they both cannot both match the input i_k and hence cannot both belong to $T(i_k/o_k)$. However, if transition t_k is strongly compatible with t_i whereas t'_k is only compatible with t_i then we can conclude that t_k must immediately follow t_i.

Transition Compatibility Graph. Compatibility information among the transitions in the sequence ϕ for a test λ is represented by a directed acyclic graph TCG. In addition to $start$ node, TCG has one node for each occurrence of each transition in the sequence ϕ. Transitions in the set $T(i_k/o_k)$ in ϕ appear at level k; $start$ is at level 0. There are labeled directed edges between nodes in consecutive levels. Edge with label s from t_k to t_{k+1} is present if t_{k+1} is strongly compatible with t_k; edge with label c from t_k to t_{k+1} is present if t_{k+1} is compatible with t_k. Edge from $start$ to a node t_1 with label s is added if $pred \implies Pre(t_1)$ is a valid formula where $pred$ is the predicate in the concrete initial global state g_0 of the test λ.

Note that there can be at most one outgoing edge with label s from any node since a node can be strongly compatible with at most one element from a set of transitions matching a test input as discussed above. Further, since all the variables are fully instantiated in g_0 there is exactly one outgoing edge from $start$ to a node in level 1 and this has the label s.

As an example, the TCG for the test λ_3 is given in Figure 3.

5.1   Identifying Fully-Observable Tests

Test λ is **initial** if every transition in $T(i_1/o_1)$ is incompatible with every non-explicit transition i.e., no transition can precede any transition from $T(i_1/o_1)$. Similarly, test λ is **final** if every non-explicit transition is incompatible with every transition in $T(i_n/o_n)$ i.e., no non-explicit transition can follow any transition in $T(i_n/o_n)$.

A test must be both initial and final for the test to be fully-observable. Then, the TCG is used to check if the test is fully-observable as described below.

1. Terminate with success if there is path from $start$ to some node in the last level labeled by s.

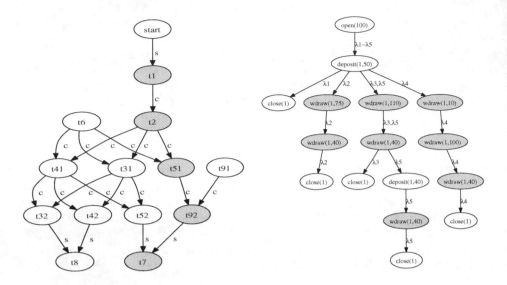

Fig. 3. TCG for Test λ_3 **Fig. 4.** Test Suite Tree for Bank Example

2. Remove nodes (and corresponding edges) that do not either have any predecessors (except *start*) or do not have any successors (except those at the last
level) until no more such nodes exist.

3. Remove all outgoing edges from node t_k with a label c if there is an outgoing edge from t_k with label s. Repeat previous step to remove the resulting
unconnected nodes.

4. The resulting graph is then processed iteratively level by level in an attempt
to construct an executable path from *start* to some node in the last level. At
each step, a formula labeling a node in the previous level is propagated to all
the successors. A new formula is generated at each successor. If it is a valid
formula then it is assigned to be the label of that node and the process moves
to the next level until reaching the last level, in which case, an executable path
from *start* to a node in the last level has been found and the test is declared
fully-observable; the path comprises of nodes that have been assigned a label.
If none of the formulas generated at the successors at a level are valid formulas
then the process terminates declaring test to be not fully-observable. At level 1,
the label assigned to the node t_1, $L(t_1) = pred \implies Pre(\sigma(t_1))$[10] where *pred*
is the predicate of state g_0 and $\sigma(t_1)$ is an instance of t_1 obtained by uniformly
replacing all occurrences of the input parameters by the corresponding values
from the test input i_1. At the kth step, given $L(t_k)$, the formula generated at
successor t_{k+1} is: $L(t_k) \wedge Pos(\sigma_k(t_k)) \implies Pre(\sigma_{k+1}(t_{k+1}))$, which if valid is
assigned as $L(t_{k+1})$. Note that the process can be terminated with success at a
level k if all the subsequent levels are connected by s label edges.

---

[10] σ is a substitution from input parameters of t_1 to the input values in the corresponding test input generated by matching.

Example: Test λ_3 is both initial and final. The TCG in Figure 3 is constructed and analyzed level by level since there is no path from *start* to either t_7 or t_8 labeled s. Unconnected nodes t_6 and t_{91} and the associated edges are removed. The formula generated at node t_1 is:$\langle s_0, (min == 50) \wedge IQ_0 == \langle open(100),$ $deposit(1, 50), wdraw(1, 110), wdraw(1,40), close(1))\rangle \implies \langle s_0, IQ_0.hd ==$ $open(100) \wedge 100 > 0\rangle$ is a valid formula and hence is assigned to be $L(t_1)$. The formula generated at node t_2 using $L(t_1)$ is again found to be valid and assigned to be $L(t_2)$.

At the third level, t_2 has three successors t_{31}, t_{41} and t_{51}. The formula generated at level t_{31} is of the form $(L(t_2) \wedge Pos(\sigma_2(t_2))) \implies Pre(\sigma_3(t_{31}))$ where σ_2 uniformly substitutes i by 1 and v by 50 in t_2 and σ_3 uniformly substitutes i by 1 and v by 110 in t_3. Since a conjunct in the consequent: $((bal_1[1] - 110) >= 50)$ cannot be established from the conjuncts: $(bal_1[1] == bal_0[1] + 50)$ and $bal_0[1]$ $== 100$ in the antecedent, the formula is not valid and the node t_{31} is skipped. Similarly, node t_{41} is also skipped. The relevant conjunct in the formula generated for t_{51} : $(bal_1[1] - 110 < 50)$, follows from those in the antecedent, resulting in a valid formula. Hence t_{51} is labeled with this formula as its label $L(t_{51})$. The next two levels have a single successor, nodes t_{92} and t_7 respectively. The formula generated at t_{92} using $L(t_{51})$ is a valid formula and is assigned to $L(t_{92})$. The formula generated at t_7 is also valid and is assigned to $L(t_7)$, resulting in the executable path that is highlighted in Figure 3. Therefore, the test λ_3 is declared to be fully-observable.

5.2   Selecting Tests

Given a fully-observable test λ and a change $\delta = (sign, t)$, the above procedure can be used in a straightforward way to accurately determine whether λ is affected.

Addition Change. Consider a change $\delta = (+, t_a)$ that adds a single transition t_a to the EFSM.

To determine if δ affects a test λ, the sequence ϕ of matching transitions is extracted from the description of λ. If t_a is an explicit transition and does not appear in ϕ then the test λ is unaffected. Suppose that the new transition t_a appears exactly once at the kth set in ϕ. Using the compatibility information of the original transitions, we construct TCG and determine whether λ is fully-observable up to (and including) level k of the graph. Then, λ can be declared unaffected without even analyzing the compatibility of transition t_a with other transitions since λ will execute a transition other than t_a at the kth level, the only level where t_a can appear.

Suppose that λ is fully-observable only up to level k - 1 with node t_{k-1} being labeled with formula $L(t_{k-1})$. Now, compatibility of t_a with t_{k-1} is determined. If t_a is strongly compatible then the test is declared affected. If t_a is compatible then we generate: $(L(t_{k-1}) \wedge Pos(\sigma_{k-1}(t_{k-1}))) \implies Pre(\sigma_k(t_a))$, and check if it is a valid formula. If so, λ is declared affected. If t_a is incompatible with

t_{k-1} or if λ is not fully-observable up to level k - 1 then the approach fails and cannot accurately determine whether the test is affected. In such cases, λ may be conservatively selected as being affected since t_a matches some element in λ.

Suppose that transition t_a matches λ at multiple positions covered by an interval $[i, k]$ then if λ is fully-observable up to a level m that is greater than or equal to k then λ can be unaffected regardless of compatibility t_a. If m equals a level that immediately precedes a matching level, say, level k - 1, which contains node t_{k-1} such that $L(t_{k-1})$ is a valid formula then we compute compatibility of t_a with t_{k-1} and determine whether λ is affected as described above. In all other cases, λ may be conservatively selected to test t_a.

Deletion and Replacement Changes. To determine if a change $\delta = (-, t_d)$ affects a test λ the above procedure is slightly modified to handle unspecified behaviors that may arise due to missing transitions. To do this, we allow test suite to have tests with unexpected inputs to indicate adverse impact of deletion.

Suppose that transition t_d matches the description of test λ at a level k and the node t_d is assigned a label as described above. If test λ ignores its kth input due to absence of t_d (and the following inputs) and belongs to the test suite of the original EFSM then λ is not selected since it results in an expected unspecified behavior caused by deletion of t_d. However, if λ is newly generated then it is selected to indicate the adverse impact of deleting t_d.

We also select tests which indicate that deleting t_d does not cause any adverse effects. Effects of t_d are first nullified by removing its output actions and making output state identical to its input state. A test λ is selected to indicate that no adverse effect happens due to deleting transition t_d that matches λ provided t_d is assigned label and the test is found to be fully-observable. Even if t_d does not match a test λ, we can check if the conditions enabling t_d can occur while executing λ by adding the modified t_d to each kth set of transitions of ϕ whenever t_d is compatible or strongly compatible with at least one of the transitions in previous set. Then the analysis is repeated and test λ is selected as done for addition with multiple matches as described above.

In situations where the updates contain many changes the above approach for deletion may miss certain tests because their runs cannot reach a concrete global state where the deleted transition t_d is enabled without the new transitions. In such cases, an interim EFSM [11] can be created by applying all the changes in the update except for δ and the analysis performed using the transitions available in this EFSM.

To determine if a replacement change $\delta = (t_d, t_a)$ affects a test λ, we view it as a deletion change involving t_d followed by addition of t_a. A test λ is affected by δ if it is either affected by the deletion of t_d or the addition of t_a. The effect of deleting t_d is computed using both the original system and the intermediate system obtained by adding t_a. The effect of addition of t_a is similarly computed using both the original system as well as the intermediate system obtained after deleting t_d.

5.3   Handling Multiple Tests

Consider a test suite $TS = \{\lambda_1, \cdots, \lambda_n\}$ comprised of fully-observable tests. To determine the tests in TS that are affected by an addition or deletion change $\delta = (sign, t)$, TS is modeled as a forest with each tree (TST) comprised of all tests starting with the same state g_0 and having same starting test input(outputs are not used to determine affected tests and are ignored). Nodes in each TST are test inputs. Edges are labeled by sets of tests. Node u is a parent of node v if the input of u is applied before that of v at some test λ_i of TS. Then, the test λ_i is added to the set of tests labeling the edge between nodes u and v.If inputs i_1 and i_2 can appear in any order then we break the cycle by creating separate trees. In each TST, the set of tests labeling the edge to each parent is a union of the sets of tests labeling the edges to its children. So, the set of tests in TST are refined as we go down the tree. For example, the bank example from Section 1, has a single test suite tree depicted in Figure 4.

Given a change transition t, and a test suite tree TST, we first find the nodes u matching t_d and annotate the paths to each u with matching sets of transitions. Each node has a single matching set of transitions. Let $T(u)$ stand for the matching set corresponding to a node u. A left-right traversal of the tree picks the first matching node u in each TST path $p = v_1 v_2 \cdots v_n u$ and checks if the sequence $\phi = [T(v_1), \cdots, T(v_n), T(u)]$ is fully-observable and t_d is the labeled transition in the set $T(u)$. If so, all the tests on the edge incident on node u are marked affected, the node and its descendants are removed and we analyze the remaining TST paths. Otherwise, we update transition sets $T(v_1) = \{t_1\}, \cdots,$ $T(v_n) = \{t_n\}$, and $T(u) = \{t_u\}$ where t_i are the labeled transitions found while checking full-observability of p and continue analyzing the extensions of the path p reaching another matching node u. The process terminates once every path reaching a matching node is analyzed and all the unmarked tests at the end of the process are declared unaffected. Note that if node u appears at level k of p which is fully-observable only up to a level $m < k$ then we can ignore all siblings of u whose common ancestor is at level l, $m < l < k$.

The matching nodes u for the bank example are highlighted in Figure 4. A left-to-right traversal of this tree detects affected tests λ_3-λ_5 at level 4 after which the matching node at level 6 can be removed.

6   Preliminary Experiments

We have implemented the proposed approach in Perl using a package supporting graph subroutines. Given an EFSM, modified EFSMs are generated by instrumenting the transitions as added(+), deleted(-) and replaced(r)[11]. Addition and deletion of every transition in the original EFSM is covered. Then, by using the instrumentations in the modified EFSM files, changes are extracted, test description templates with uninstantiated parameter values are generated for each

---

[11] Conference protocol also includes more specific changes as discussed below.

Example	Ntsc	Stsc	C_1(secs)	C_2(secs)	C_3(secs)
Atm (9)	9	3	35	8	17
Bnk (9)	46	26	1108	285	621
Cmp (7)	9	1	15	2	4
Cnf (19)	40	11	390	63	134
Tcp (14)	9	3	41	7	8
Thp (15)	16	8	134	28	76
Ven (8)	10	4	41	11	27

Fig. 5. Regression Test Selection Costs

change by using transition coverage of the modified (as well as the original EF-SMs). Test descriptions are produced from these templates by randomly assigning constant values to the parameters and included in the test suite. Non-executable test descriptions are removed by performing symbolic execution. We also added hand-crafted tests. We then analyzed each test in the test suite for each change using the proposed approach. During analysis, EFSM expressions are automatically translated into the language of the prover, and the prover is invoked in a push-button manner to check satisfiability of the generated formulas.

We have studied seven simple examples from the literature: completion, two-phase commit, and conference protocols (*Cmp*, *Tcp*, *Cnf*)[12], third-party call (*Thp*), automatic teller machine (*Atm*) [2,5], bank example (*Bnk*) web services, and a vending machine (*Ven*). The main goal was to compare the effectiveness of the proposed approach with the retest-all approach based on the cost model of [8]. According to this model test selection is more economical than using the entire suite if the cost of selection(C_3) is less than the cost of running tests that the selection lets us omit (C_1 - C_2); C_1 is the cost of running the full test suite; C_2 is the cost of running the selected tests.

Our results are summarized in the table in Figure 5. For each example, first column gives the total number of transitions without instrumentation; second column Ntsc is the number of test cases in the test suite; third column Stsc is the average number (rounded) selected tests *per change*; and the next three columns give the costs C_1, C_2 and C_3 in terms of the running times. These times were averaged (rounded) by considering a set of changes that cover every transition.

Conference protocol *Cnf* above, is a chatbox-like protocol and has been used earlier by formal testing approaches. We used the EFSM description (c) available from the web site and changed to the description (d) in the same web site. The four changes specified there to do this are additions that allow members to send data before joining the conference. Our use of the more expressive parameterized EFSMs allowed us to specify conference id as a parameter because of which two additions suffice to evolve EFSM (c) to EFSM (d).

---

[12] http://schemas.xmlsoap.org/ws/2004/10/wsat/Completion;
http://schemas.xmlsoap.org/ws/2004/10/wsat/Volatile2PC(Durable2PC);
http://fmt.cs.utwente.nl/ConfCase/

As evident from the table, in each case, we were able to select a non-empty set of tests for the chosen change. The average number of tests selected per change results in a smaller test suite in all cases. Further, our results show that the cost of regression selection is economical $C_3 < (C_1 - C_2)$ in all of our examples. For the examples, *Atm* and *Ven*, the reduction in test suite size does not reflect on the economy of regression test selection. Even though a lot of tests are eliminated, the cost of regression test selection is high in these examples since the tests removed do not take much time to execute. However, the proposed approach has the potential to perform highly economical regression test selection since it can eliminate long running tests by only partially analyzing them. But our initial experiments did not reflect that since our test descriptions were restricted to be sequences of no more than size 20 and we averaged over all changes.

7   Conclusion and Future Work

A novel approach for regression test selection for EFSMs supporting a rich set of commonly used data types including booleans, numbers, arrays, queues, and records is proposed. Changes to the EFSM are performed at the transition level by adding/deleting/replacing one or more transitions. Test descriptions supporting input and output values from these data types are automatically analyzed using a theorem prover to identify tests that exercise a given change. A class of fully-observable tests is identified. It is shown that the description of a fully-observable test contains adequate information to accurately predict whether the test will exercise a given change. Procedures to identify fully-observable tests and select tests to exercise changes that add/delete/replace transitions are described. We also extend the proposed approach to simultaneously analyze several tests in a test suite to reduce analysis costs. Initial results of our experiments on 3 web services and 4 protocols based on a well-known cost model for regression testing [8] are promising. They show that the cost to select tests is smaller than the difference in execution times between running all vs. running only the selected tests.

Acknowledgements. The first author would like to thank Gregg Rothermal, for fruitful discussions and help on earlier works on regression test selection.

References

1. Brand, D., Zafiropulo, P.: On Communicating Finite State Machines. JACM 30(2) (1983)
2. Chen, Y., Probert, R., Ural, H.: Regression test suite reduction using extended dependence analysis. In: SOQUA 2007, September 3-4 (2007)
3. Detlefs, D., Nelson, G., Saxe, J.B.: Simplify: A Theorem Prover for Program Checking. Journal of the ACM 52(3) (2005)
4. Kapur, D., Zhang, H.: An Overview of Rewrite Rule Laboratory (RRL). In: Dershowitz, N. (ed.) RTA 1989. LNCS, vol. 355, pp. 559–563. Springer, Heidelberg (1989)

5. Korel, B., Tahat, L., Vaysburg, B.: Model Based Regression Test Reduction Using Dependency Analysis. In: Proceedings of the International Conference on Software Maintenance (ICSM 2002), October 03-06, p. 214 (2002)
6. Korel, B., Koutsogiannakis, G., Tahat, L.H.: Application of system models in regression test suite prioritization. In: IEEE International Conference Software Maintenance, ICSM 2008, September 28-October 4, vol. (2008)
7. Lee, D., Yiannakakis, M.: Principles and Methods of Testing Finite State Machines – A Survey. Proceedings of the IEEE 84(8) (1996)
8. Leung, H.K.N., White, L.: A Cost Model to Compare Regression Test Strategies. IEEE Conf. on Software Maintenance, ICSM (1991)
9. Rothermel, G., Harrold, M.J.: Analyzing Regression Test Selection Techniques. IEEE Transactions on Software Engineering (1996)
10. Subramaniam, M., Guo, B.: A Rewrite-based Approach for Change Impact Analysis of Communicating Systems Using a Theorem Prover, CS Dept. University of Nebraska-Omaha (cst-2008-3) Technical Report (Work in progress paper in Testcom 2008) (2008)
11. Subramaniam, M., Pap, Z.: Updating Tests Across Protocol Changes. In: Proc. of IFIP Conference on Testing of Communicating Systems (2006)

TTCN-3 Based Conformance Testing of Mobile Broadcast Business Management System in 3G Networks

Zhiliang Wang[1,3], Xia Yin[2,3], Yang Xiang[2,3], Ruiping Zhu[4], Shirui Gao[2,3], Xin Wu[2,3], Shijian Liu[2,3], Song Gao[5], Li Zhou[2,3], and Peng Li[2,3]

[1] Network Research Center, Tsinghua University
[2] Department of Computer Science and Technology, Tsinghua University
[3] Tsinghua National Laboratory for Information Science and Technology (TNList)
[4] China Mobile Research Institute
[5] School of Software and Microelectronics, Peking University
Beijing, P.R. China
{wzl,yxia,xiangy08,gaoshirui,wuxin,lsj,
gaosong,zhouli,lipeng}@csnet1.cs.tsinghua.edu.cn,
zhuruiping@chinamobile.com

Abstract. Mobile broadcast service is one of the emerging most important new services in 3G networks. To better operate and manage mobile broadcast services, mobile broadcast business management system (MBBMS) should be designed and developed. Such a system, with its distributed nature, complicated XML data and security mechanism, faces many challenges in testing technology. In this paper, we study the conformance testing methodology of MBBMS, and design and implement a MBBMS protocol conformance testing tool based on TTCN-3, a standardized test description language that can be used in black-box testing of reactive and distributed system. In this methodology and testing tool, we present a semi-automatic XML test data generation method of TTCN-3 test suite and use HMSC model to help the design of test suite. In addition, we also propose an integrated testing method for hierarchical MBBMS security architecture. This testing tool has been used in industrial level's testing.

1 Introduction

Mobile broadcast service, e.g. mobile TV, is one of the emerging most important new services in 3G networks. 3GPP (3rd Generation Partnership Project) has defined a new transport technology, called MBMS (Multimedia Broadcast/Multicast Services)[1,2]. MBMS, using 3G mobile networks as its bearer network, is a point-to-multipoint service in which data is transmitted from a single source entity to multiple recipients[2]. MBMS focuses on the transport aspects of mobile broadcast and multicast services[3], while for service layer technologies, OMA (Open Mobile Alliance) has standardized the Mobile Broadcast Services 1.0 (BCAST 1.0) specification[4,5]. BCAST 1.0 defines some functions such as Service Provisioning, Service Guide, Service and Content protection, File and Stream distribution, etc[5], and can be used over several different broadcast distribution systems, including 3GPP MBMS.

M. Núñez et al. (Eds.): TESTCOM/FATES 2009, LNCS 5826, pp. 163–178, 2009.
© IFIP International Federation for Information Processing 2009

With the rapid development of bearer technologies of mobile broadcast services and the deployment of real services, operation and management of these services are also becoming very important. To better operate and manage mobile broadcast services, Mobile Broadcast Business Management System (MBBMS) has been designed and developed[6]. Referring to the related specifications of 3GPP and OMA, MBBMS uses both mobile communication network and broadcast network to make use of advantages of both kinds of network. Via mobile communication network, mobile terminals interact with MBBMS to implement the following functions: authentication and authorization, service subscription and unsubscription, service guide delivery and service key delivery, etc. Via broadcast network, demanded traffic data can be delivered from content sources to mobile terminals.

MBBMS is a very complicated system so that many challenges are faced in its design, development and testing. This paper focuses on the testing technology of MBBMS. Software testing and protocol testing techniques are widely used in order to ensure the quality of network protocol and communication system implementations. Conformance testing is a basic method of protocol testing, which can be used to test whether an implementation conforms to its protocol specification. In the field of conformance testing, many literatures have been published, such as international standard ISO/IEC 9646[7]. TTCN-3 (Testing and Test Control Notation)[8,9] is a new test specification language standardized by ETSI (European Telecommunications Standards Institute) and can be used in black-box testing of reactive and distributed system. TTCN-3 has been widely applied in many fields of testing, especially the testing of communication systems.

In this paper, we study the conformance testing methodology of MBBMS, and design and implement a MBBMS protocol conformance testing tool based on TTCN-3. In this methodology and testing tool, we present a semi-automatic XML test data generation method of TTCN-3 test suite and use HMSC (High-Level Message Sequence Charts)[24,25] model to help the design of test suite. In addition, we also propose an integrated testing method for hierarchical security architecture of MBBMS. This testing tool has been used in industrial level's testing.

The rest of the paper is structured as follows. Section 2 introduces related work. Section 3 gives an overview of MBBMS architecture. Section 4 gives test architecture for MBBMS. In Section 5, we present a framework of designing MBBMS TTCN-3 test suite. Section 6 proposes the testing method of MBBMS security mechanism. Conclusion and future work are given in Section 7.

2 Related Work

TTCN-3 has been applied in many areas. For example, in conformance testing, [10,11] applied TTCN-3 in RIPng and Mobile IPv6 respectively. In performance testing, [12] studied the performance testing of a mobile management protocol BCMP, and [13] applied TTCN-3 into distributed load testing. In our previous work [14], we designed and implemented a TTCN-3 based protocol integrated test system called PITSv3, and applied it in BGPv4+ (Border Gateway Protocol) conformance testing and OSPFv2 (Open Shortest Path First routing protocol) robustness testing.

Especially, [15,16] used TTCN-3 in web service and web application testing respectively. [17,18] developed the TTCN-3-based conformance testing tools for OMA MMS (Multimedia Messaging Service) and Push-to-talk service over Cellular in 3G or 4G networks respectively.

In the field of MSC-based testing, [19] introduced a tool developed by UK Systems and Software Engineering Research group of Motorola Labs to automatically generate test cases from a combination of MSCs and PDUs, especially, this tool can generate TTCN-2 test cases from MSCs. [20] studied TTCN-3 Test Case Generation from MSCs, and gave translation rules of MSC into TTCN-3. [11] presented an approach of TTCN-3 test cases generation from SDL (Specification and Description Language) and MSC specifications and applied the approach in testing Mobile IPv6 protocol.

In MBBMS, XML messages are used in protocol interactions, thus the mappings from XML to TTCN-3 is important for TTCN-3 based MBBMS testing. [21] has standardized the mapping from XML schemas to TTCN-3 standard data types and provided a method of using XML in TTCN-3. However, as shown in [22], this method has many limitations: for example, it will increase the complexity of the implementation of TTCN-3 encoder and decoder. So this method is difficult to be used in practical testing. Different from the method of [21], this paper presents a simple XML TTCN-3 representation and a semi-automatic XML test data generation method of TTCN-3 test suite.

In this paper, we present a TTCN-3 based MBBMS protocol conformance testing methodology, and integrate various techniques (e.g., HMSC, XML) into the testing tool.

3 An Overview of MBBMS Architecture

Figure 1 shows the architecture of MBBMS network. MBBMS uses both mobile communication network and broadcast network to make use of advantages of both kinds of network.

Via mobile communication network, mobile terminals interact with mobile broadcast service platform (for short, platform), which is the core network element in MBBMS. The main functional modules of mobile broadcast service platform are as follows:

(1) Service Guide (SG) Server: its function is service guide generation and delivery.

(2) Bootstrapping Service Function (BSF) Server: this module interacts with mobile terminals and HLR (Home Location Register) to execute GBA (Generic Bootstrapping Architecture) procedure[23] in order to support user authentication and authorization.

(3) Network Application Function (NAF) Server: the main functions of this module are service/user management (e.g., service subscription and unsubscription) and service key management (e.g., service key generation and delivery).

Via broadcast network, demanded traffic data can be delivered from content sources to mobile terminals.

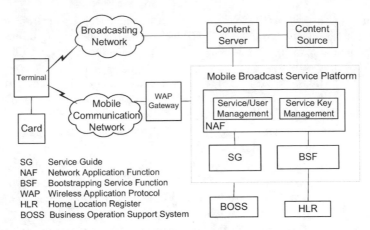

Fig. 1. MBBMS Architecture[6]

4 Test Architecture

In MBBMS, two important network elements, mobile terminal and mobile broadcast service platform, are required to be tested. Figure 2 shows the test environment for MBBMS in a test lab. In the test environment, terminals under test can be attached to the lab mobile communication network; mobile broadcast service platform under test is attached to the lab wired network; WAP (Wireless Application Protocol) gateway is used to connect the lab mobile communication network and wired network and translate and forward the messages between terminals and the platform. The test tool is located in the lab wired network. When testing terminals under test, the test tool should act as simulated platform; while when testing platform under test, the test tool should act as simulated terminal.

Figure 3 shows the test architecture to test terminal (Figure 3(a)) and platform (Figure 3(b)). In TTCN-3 test tool, when testing a new protocol or system, TTCN-3 test suite should be designed and developed. In addition to test suite, two modules related to specific protocol under test, Test Adapter and Encoding/Decoding, should be developed in order to execute test suite. In Figure 3(a), one test system interface

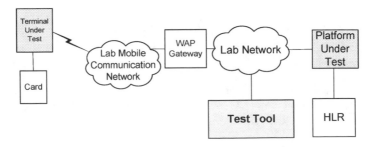

Fig. 2. Test Environment for MBBMS

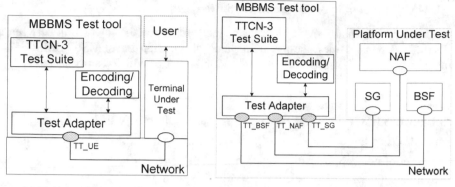

(a) Test Architecture to Terminal   (b) Test Architecture to Platform

Fig. 3. Test Architecture

TT_UE is defined to interact with terminal under test; and in Figure 3(b), three test system interfaces TT_SG, TT_NAF, TT_BSF are defined to interact with SG, NAF, BSF servers respectively.

5 Design of TTCN-3 Test Suite

TTCN-3 test suite is the core in TTCN-3 based conformance testing. Figure 4 shows the design framework of MBBMS conformance test suite. The starting point of test suite design is the MBBMS protocol specification, from which we can get XML schemas of protocol messages and the HMSC model of protocol control flow. In this paper, we use HMSC (High-Level Message Sequence Charts)[24,25] model to help the design of test suite (see Section 5.1) and present a semi-automatic XML test data generation method in TTCN-3 test suite (see Section 5.2).

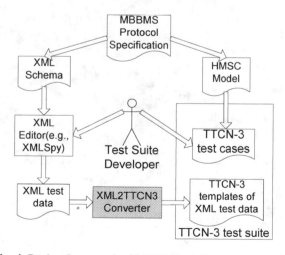

Fig. 4. Design framework of MBBMS conformance test suite

5.1   HMSC Model of MBBMS and Test Suite Organization

Message Sequence Charts (MSC) is a language to describe the interaction between a number of independent message-passing instances[24]. High-Level MSC (HMSC) [24] is an extended model of MSC. In HMSC model, a set of MSCs can be combined to form a directed graph, in which nodes can be represented as MSCs and edges indicate the execution flows of MSCs. We give the formal definition of HMSC as Definition 1.

Definition 1. *HMSC (High-Level Message Sequence Charts)[26,27]*

An HMSC is a tuple $H = (S, \rightarrow, s^0, s^f, \lambda)$, where $(S, \rightarrow, s^0, s^f)$ is a transition system with set of nodes S, transition relation $\rightarrow \subseteq S \times S$, initial nodes s^0 and set of final nodes s^f. Each node $s \in S$ is labeled by an MSC, denoted by $\lambda(s)$.

An *execution* of H is the labeling $\lambda(s_0) \lambda(s_1)...\lambda(s_k)$ for some path s_0, s_1, ..., s_k in H, where, $s_0 = s^0$, $s_k = s^f$, $(s_i, s_{i+1}) \in \rightarrow$ $(i=0,1,2,...,k-1)$.   □

According to its protocol specification, we can get the HMSC model of MBBMS. Figure 5 shows the simplified HMSC model, in which $\triangledown$ is the start symbol and $\triangle$ is the end symbol. This model contains the following 8 MSC nodes: GBA (Generic Bootstrapping Architecture) procedure; Service Activation, meaning to activate the mobile broadcast service; SG (Service Guide) Retrieval; Service Subscription; Subscription Information Update; Account Inquiry, meaning to inquire the specific services; Service Unsubscription and SK (Service Key) Retrieval, meaning to unsubscribe a service and retrieve the service key respectively after a service has been subscribed. Figure 5 also gives the MSC of Service Subscription, in which two instances Terminal and NAF are contained. The terminal firstly sends a Service Request message to the NAF server to subscribe a specific service, and then the NAF server sends a Service Response back to the terminal to reply the subscription result.

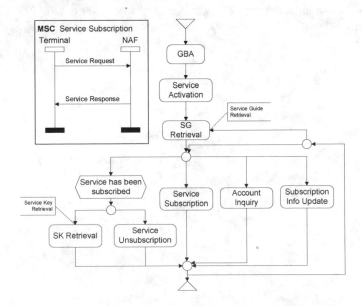

Fig. 5. The simplified HMSC model of MBBMS

With the help of MBBMS HMSC model, we give the strategy of test suite design. We implement one test group (i.e., a TTCN-3 module) for each MSC node. Some normal (i.e., to test the normal behaviors of the system) and abnormal (e.g., to test how to handle invalid inputs) test cases are contained in each test group. The method proposed in [20] can be used to map a MSC to a TTCN-3 test case. The organization of test suite we design is shown as table 1.

Table 1. Test suite organization

No	Test Groups	Test cases for terminal under test			Test cases for platform under test		
		# of Normal Test Cases	# of Abnormal Test Cases	# of Total Test Cases	# of Normal Test Cases	# of Abnormal Test Cases	# of Total Test Cases
1	GBA	1	5	6	2	3	5
2	Service Guide Retrieval	5	2	7	9	10	19
3	Subscribe Info Update	3	5	8	2	3	5
4	Service Activation	4	2	6	5	6	11
5	Service Subscription	2	3	5	2	4	6
6	Service Unsubscription	2	3	5	2	3	5
7	Account Inquiry	3	2	5	3	3	6
8	Service Key Retrieval	3	1	4	4	2	6
	Total Number	23	23	46	29	34	63

To test a complete flow of MBBMS, a test path (i.e., an execution of HMSC) should be firstly extracted from HMSC model. For example, in Figure 5, a test path covering all 8 MSC nodes is as shown in Figure 6.

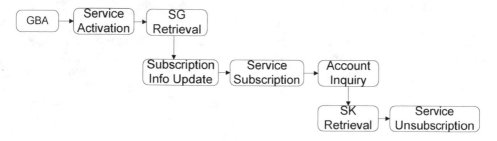

Fig. 6. A test path of HMSC covering all 8 MSC nodes

Such a test path can be implemented by the control part of a TTCN-3 module (see Figure 7). The statement **execute**, defined in TTCN-3 [9], is used to execute test cases in the TTCN-3 module control. In the TTCN-3 code of Figure 7, line 9 executes the test case Subscribe_1Service() and gets its verdict. In line 10, if the verdict of test case Subscribe_1Service() is **pass**, i.e., the service has been subscribed successfully, the following three test cases will be executed, else the three test cases will not be executed.

5.2 XML Test Data Representation and Generation

In the MBBMS protocol, HTTP+XML is used as protocol message format. How to describe the XML test data in TTCN-3 is a difficult problem. In this paper, we present a semi-automatic XML test data generation method in TTCN-3 test suite to simplify the development process of test suite. The framework of this method is shown in Figure 4. Firstly, XML schemas of protocol messages can be extracted from protocol specification; and then an XML editor, such as XMLSpy[28], can be used to generate the XML test data from XML schemas; we present a method of TTCN-3 XML test data definition and also implement a XML2TTCN3 converter tool to convert the XML test data to TTCN-3 templates automatically.

```
01 module MBBMS{
02     ......
03     control{
04         execute(GBA_Basic() );          //execute basic GBA procedure
05         execute(Activation_Open() ); //activate service
06         execute(SGRetrieval_all() ); //retrieve all SG info
07         execute(SubscriptionUpdate_NoSub() );
                   //subscription info update (when no subscribed service)
08         verdicttype sub_verdict;
09         sub_verdict := execute(Subscribe_1Service() );
                                             //subscribe one service
10         if(sub_verdict == pass) {
               //service subscription should be successful
11             execute(AccountInquiry_1Service() ); //account inquiry
12             execute(SKRetrieve_Normal() );
                       //retrieve service key of the subscribed service
13             execute(Unsubscribe_1Service() );
                           //unsubscribe the subscribed service
14         }
15     }
16 }
```

Fig. 7. The control part of a TTCN-3 module corresponding to Figure 6

According to the characteristic of XML data, we define a generic recursive TTCN-3 type of XML messages as shown in Figure 8.

We take the Service Request message[1] in MBBMS for example. From XML schema of this message and with the help of XML editor tool, we can get a XML test data as shown in Figure 9. We divide a XML data into three parts: begin, content and end part. In the example of Figure 9, the begin part is "<ServiceRequest requestID="1">" and the

---
[1] Service Request message structure can be found in section 5.1.5.2.1 of [5].

```
01 type record NameValueType {
02   universal charstring name optional,
03   universal charstring val optional
04 }    //Name-Value pair in XML
05 type record of NameValueType NameValueTypeArray;   //can be an array
06 type record XMLBeginType{
07   universal charstring prefix optional,
08   NameValueTypeArray attributes optional,
09   universal charstring suffix optional
10 }
11 type record XMLContentType {
12   XMLBeginType begin optional,
13   XMLContentTypeArray content optional,
14   universal charstring end optional
15 }
16 type record of XMLContentType XMLContentTypeArray; //can be an
array
```

Fig. 8. Generic recursive TTCN-3 type definition of XML messages

end part is "</ServiceRequest>", and the content part is just located between the begin and end parts, which is a nested XML message (e.g., the example of Figure 9) or an array of several nested XML messages. Thus we define a generic record type of "XMLContentType" (see Figure 8). The begin part can be further defined as a record type of "XMLBeginType", which is comprised of the prefix, attribute and suffix part. In the example of Figure 9, the prefix of the begin part is a universal charstring "<ServiceRequest "; the suffix part is a universal charstring ">"; the attribute part is an array of Name-Value pairs, which is defined as a record type "NameValueType".

```
<ServiceRequest requestID="1">
  <PurchaseItem gloalIDRef="10"></PurchaseItem>
</ServiceRequest>
```

Fig. 9. An example of Service Request XML test data

In TTCN-3, templates are the test data definitions, which are used to either transmit a set of values or to test whether a set of received values matches the template specification[9]. The TTCN-3 template definition of ServiceRequestPayload, corresponding to the XML test data in Figure 9, is shown in Figure 10. This template is a parameterized one with two formal parameters, requestid and globalid, thus the XML test data in Figure 9 can be represented as ServiceRequestPayload("1", "10"), in which two formal parameters are replaced by actual parameters "1" and "10" respectively. In addition, we also implement a TTCN-3 function "findInXML", by which we can easily extract the data value of the field we are interested in.

Compared with the method in [21], using this method of TTCN-3 XML test data definition and semi-automatic XML test data generation is beneficial for test developers in the following aspects:

(1) This method of TTCN-3 XML test data representation is simple and easy to understand. The recursive XML data type definition is generic, which simplifies the test data definitions when developing TTCN-3 test suite manually.

```
01 template XMLContentType ServiceRequestPayload(
02    universal charstring requestid, universal charstring globalid):={
03    begin := {
04       prefix := "ServiceRequest",
05       attribute := {
06          [0] := { name := "requestID", val := int2unichar(34) & reques-
tid & int2unichar(34) }//Name-Value pair: requestID="requestid"
07       },
08       suffix := omit
09    }, //begin = <ServiceRequest requestID="1">
10    content := {
11       [0] := {
12          begin := {
13             prefix := "PurchaseItem",
14             attribute := {
15                [0] := { name := "globalIDRef", val := int2unichar(34) &
globalid & int2unichar(34) } //Name-Value pair: gloalIDRef="globalid"
16             },
17             suffix := omit
18          },
19          content := omit,
20          end := omit
21       }
22    }, //content = <PurchaseItem gloalIDRef="globalid "></PurchaseItem>
23    end := omit
24 }
```

Fig. 10. TTCN-3 template definition of XML test data in Figure 9

(2) This method can simplify the development of encoding/decoding module. When encoding, some symbols, such as ">", "<" and "=", should be added; and when decoding, these symbols should be taken off. Though this requires the additional operations of encoding/decoding module, the complexity of the encoder/decoder is much smaller than the method in [21].

(3) The method of semi-automatic XML test data generation can lighten test developers' workload of defining large numbers of TTCN-3 templates. Especially, in MBBMS, some XML messages, e.g., Service Guide related messages[29], have complex structures. Using automatic XML2TTCN-3 converter simplifies the development of the TTCN-3 test data largely.

6   Testing MBBMS Security Mechanism

Security in mobile broadcast service is important to transmit data from server to a set of users. 3GPP MBMS security architecture has been proposed to provide the mechanism of authentication, key distribution and data protection for a MBMS User Service[30]. MBBMS system makes use of 3GPP MBMS security architecture in service/ user management, key management and content delivery. This security architecture, for its complexity, faces many challenges in testing technology. In this section, we propose an integrated testing method to hierarchical MBBMS security architecture.

6.1   MBBMS Security Architecture

Hierarchical MBBMS security architecture is shown in Figure 11.

Firstly, by using HTTP Digest AKA (Authentication and Key Agreement) protocol[31], terminal and BSF server in platform execute GBA[23] procedure to establish share keys (Ks) in order to protect the point-to-point communication between terminal and platform. From Ks, two kinds of keys, MRK (MBMS Request Key) and MUK (MBMS User Key)[30], can be derived both in terminal and platform according to the same algorithm.

Secondly, the interactions of service/user management process between terminal and NAF server should be protected by HTTP digest authentication as defined in RFC 2617 [32]. In HTTP digest authentication, MRK will be used as password.

Thirdly, in the process of key management, MSK (MBMS Service Key) [30] is generated in platform and delivered to terminals. In this delivery, MIKEY (Multimedia Internet KEYing) [33] protocol message is transmitted to carry encrypted MSK and MUK is used to encrypt MSK to protect it.

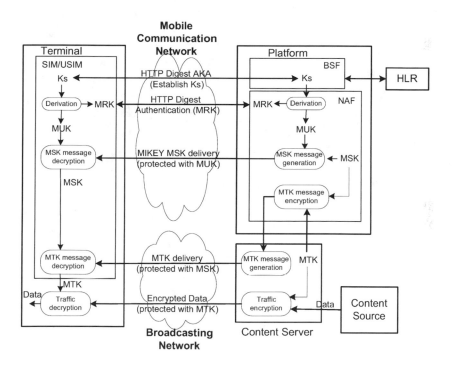

Fig. 11. MBBMS Security Architecture[30,6]

Fourthly, MTK (MBMS Traffic Key) [30] is generated in the content server, and the encrypted MTK with MSK is delivered to terminal in the broadcast network. At last, the data from content source can be encrypted with MTK and transmitted in the broadcasting network securely.

In this security architecture, mobile communication network will be used in GBA procedure, HTTP digest authentication and MSK delivery. Since the test tool focuses on the interactions between terminal and platform in the mobile communication network, we only consider these three mechanisms in this paper.

6.2 Testing Method of MBBMS Security Mechanism

Since various MBBMS security mechanisms are related to each others very closely as shown in Figure 11, we present an integrated testing method in this paper. The framework of testing method is shown in Figure 12. We use the specific test cases to test the three levels of MBBMS security mechanisms and the three kinds of test cases can be generated from the MBBMS HMSC models. In this framework, two configuration files are used: static config file contains some static configurable parameters such as IP-Port information and the parameters of GBA algorithms, and dynamic config file contains the dynamically generated parameters in GBA procedure such as the share key Ks. TTCN-3 external function mechanism[9] is used to implement complex GBA related algorithms and HTTP Digest Authentication algorithms in the test adapter module. In this way, complex calculations in TTCN-3 test suite can be avoided.

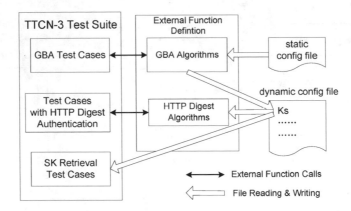

Fig. 12. The framework of testing methods to MBBMS security architecture

To test HTTP Digest Authentication mechanism, we use EFSM (Extended Finite State Machine) to model the protocol behaviors of both terminal and platform. Figure 13 (a) and (b) show the EFSM models of terminal and platform respectively. The INIT state is the initial state of both the two EFSMs. The OK state means the successful ending of HTTP Digest Authentication. From EFSM models, test sequences can be generated by using existing EFSM based test generation method. For example, Figure 13(c) shows an example of test sequence generated from Figure 13(a), which corresponds to the heavy lines of Figure 13(a). This test sequence is easy to be mapped to a TTCN-3 test case, which we have implemented in the test tool.

We integrate the security testing supports into the test adapter and encoding/decoding modules as follows in Figure 14. The test adapter module contains two threads, the main thread and the receiving thread, which are responsible for sending and receiving test data respectively. In encoding/decoding module, gzip function is integrated to support gzip compression and decompression, which will be used in service guide delivery[29]. Calculating center is also implemented to provide some external function definitions, mainly about HLR/AuC (GBA) related algorithms and HTTP Digest Authentication algorithms.

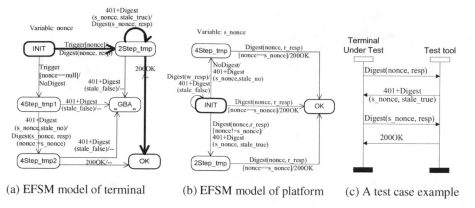

(a) EFSM model of terminal　　(b) EFSM model of platform　　(c) A test case example

Fig. 13. EFSM models of HTTP Digest Authentication

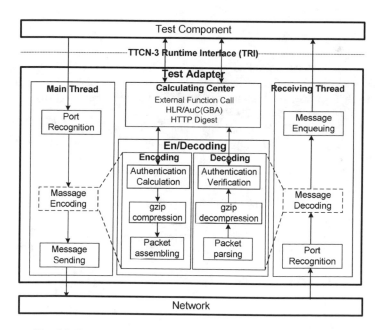

Fig. 14. Test adapter and Encoding/Decoding modules structure

7 Conclusions

In this paper, we study the conformance testing methodology of MBBMS. Many challenges are faced in MBBMS testing, for its distributed nature, complicated XML data and security mechanism. We integrate various techniques in the testing methodology. For the design framework of MBBMS conformance test suite, we present a semi-automatic XML test data generation method of TTCN-3 test suite and use HMSC model to help the design of test suite. In addition, we also propose an integrated testing method for hierarchical security architecture of MBBMS. We have implemented the testing tool based on a commercial TTCN-3 tool telelogic tester [34] and this testing tool has been used in industrial level's testing.

Currently, only one test component, i.e., MTC (Main Test Component), is used in test cases. In the future work, distributed test architecture with multiple test components can be used to enhance the testing capability. Remote testing for terminals can be another possible future direction.

Acknowledgments. This work is partially supported by the National Natural Science Foundation of China under Grant (No. 60572082), Young Faculty Research Funding of Ministry of Education of China (No. 200800031063) and National Key Technology R&D Program of China (No. 2008BAH37B04). The authors thank Yong Li, Wei Zhang, Jing Wang, Hui Wang, etc., for their discussions and helps.

References

1. 3GPP TS 23.246 (v9.0.0): Multimedia Broadcast/Multicast Service (MBMS); Architecture and Functional Description (Release 9) (March 2009)
2. 3GPP TS 26.346 (v8.2.0): Multimedia Broadcast/Multicast Service (MBMS); Protocols and Codecs (Release 8) (March 2009)
3. Hartung, F., Horn, U., Huschke, J., Kampmann, M., Lohmar, T., Lundevall, M.: Delivery of Broadcast Services in 3G Networks. IEEE Transactions on Broadcasting 53(1), 188–199 (2007)
4. Open Mobile Alliance: Mobile Broadcast Services Architecture (OMA-AD-BCAST-V1_0-20090212-A) (February 2009)
5. Open Mobile Alliance: Mobile Broadcast Services (OMA-TS-BCAST_Services-V1_0-20090212-A) (February 2009)
6. Zhang, H., Chang, J., Tang, J., Yang, Z.: Analysis and Design of Mobile Broadcast Business Management System. Telecom Engineering Techniques and Standardization 2, 1–4 (2008) (In Chinese)
7. ISO/IEC: ISO/IEC 9646: Information technology, open systems interconnection, conformance testing methodology and framework. Geneva, Switzerland (1991)
8. Grabowski, J., Hogrefe, D., Rethy, G., et al.: An introduction to the testing and test control notation (TTCN-3). Computer Networks 42(3), 375–403 (2003)
9. ETSI: ETSI standard ES 201 873-1 V3.4.1: The Testing and Test Control Notation version 3; Part 1: TTCN-3 Core Language. European Telecommunications Standards Institute (ETSI), Sophia-Antipolis, France (September 2008)
10. Floch, A., Roudaut, F., Sabiguero, A., et al.: Some lessons from an experiment using TTCN-3 for the RIPng testing. In: Khendek, F., Dssouli, R. (eds.) TestCom 2005. LNCS, vol. 3502, pp. 318–332. Springer, Heidelberg (2005)
11. Noudem, F., Viho, C.: Modeling, verifying and testing mobility protocol from SDL language. In: Prinz, A., Reed, R., Reed, J. (eds.) SDL 2005. LNCS, vol. 3530, pp. 198–209. Springer, Heidelberg (2005)
12. Dibuz, S., Szabo, T., Torpis, Z.: BCMP performance test with TTCN-3 mobile node emulator. In: Groz, R., Hierons, R.M. (eds.) TestCom 2004. LNCS, vol. 2978, pp. 50–59. Springer, Heidelberg (2004)

13. Din, G., Tolea, S., Schieferdecker, I.: Distributed load tests with TTCN-3. In: Uyar, M.Ü., Duale, A.Y., Fecko, M.A. (eds.) TestCom 2006. LNCS, vol. 3964, pp. 177–196. Springer, Heidelberg (2006)
14. Yin, X., Wang, Z., Jing, C., Shi, X.: A TTCN-3-based protocol testing system and its extension. Science in China Series F: Information Sciences 51(11), 1703–1722 (2008)
15. Werner, E., Grabowski, J., Troschutz, S., Zeiss, B.: A TTCN-3-based Web Service Test Framework. In: Software Engineering 2008 Workshops, pp. 375–382 (2008)
16. Stepien, B., Peyton, L., Xiong, P.: Framework testing of web applications using TTCN-3. International Journal on Software Tools for Technology Transfer. 10(4), 371–381 (2008)
17. Lin, Y.-B., Liang, C.-F., Chen, K.-H., Liao, H.-Y.: NTP-SIOT: a test tool for advanced mobile services. IEEE Network 21(1), 21–26 (2007)
18. Lin, Y.-B., Wang, C.-C., Lu, C.-H., Hsu, M.-R.: NTP-PoCT: a conformance test tool for push-to-talk over cellular network. Wireless Communications and Mobile Computing 8, 673–686 (2007)
19. Baker, P., Bristow, P., Jervis, C., King, D.J., Mitchell, B.: Automatic Generation of Conformance Tests from Message Sequence Charts. In: Sherratt, E. (ed.) SAM 2002. LNCS, vol. 2599, pp. 170–198. Springer, Heidelberg (2003)
20. Ebner, M.: TTCN-3 Test Case Generation from Message Sequence Charts. In: IEEE International Symposium on Software Reliability Engineering (ISSRE 2004) Workshop on Integrated-reliability with Telecommunications and UML Languages (ISSRE 2004: WITUL 2004) (2004)
21. ETSI: ETSI standard ES 201 873-9 V3.3.1: The Testing and Test Control Notation version 3; Part 9: Using XML schema with TTCN-3. European Telecommunications Standards Institute (ETSI), Sophia-Antipolis, France (July 2008)
22. Using XML Schema with TTCN-3,
    http://wiki.openttcn.com/media/index.php/OpenTTCN/
    Working_documents/Reviews/Using_XML_Schema_with_TTCN-3
23. 3GPP TS 33.220 (v8.6.0): Generic Authentication Architecture (GAA); Generic bootstrapping architecture (Release 8) (March 2009)
24. ITU-TS Recommendation Z.120: Message Sequence Chart (MSC). ITU-TS, Geneva (2004)
25. Mauw, S., Reniers, M.A.: High-level message sequence charts. In: Cavalli, A.R., Sarma, A. (eds.) Proc. of the 8th International SDL Forum (SDL 1997), pp. 291–306. Elsevier, Amsterdam (1997)
26. Genest, B., Hélouët, L., Muscholl, A.: High-Level Message Sequence Charts and Projections. In: Amadio, R.M., Lugiez, D. (eds.) CONCUR 2003. LNCS, vol. 2761, pp. 311–326. Springer, Heidelberg (2003)
27. Genest, B., Muscholl, A., Seidl, H., Zeitoun, M.: Infinite-state high-level MSCs: Model-checking and realizability. Journal of Computer and System Sciences 72(4), 617–647 (2006)
28. XMLSpy, http://www.altova.com/products/xmlspy/xmlspy.html
29. Open Mobile Alliance: Service Guide for Mobile Broadcast Services(OMA-TS-BCAST_Service_Guide-V1_0-20090212-A) (February 2009)
30. 3GPP TS 33.246 (v8.3.0): 3G Security; Security of Multimedia Broadcast/Multicast Service (MBMS) (Release 8) (March 2009)
31. Niemi, A., Arkko, J., Torvinen, V.: Hypertext Transfer Protocol (HTTP) Digest Authentication Using Authentication and Key Agreement (AKA). IETF RFC 3310 (September 2002)

32. Franks, J., Hallam-Baker, P., Hostetler, J., et al.: HTTP Authentication: Basic and Digest Access Authentication. IETF RFC 2617 (June 1999)
33. Arkko, J., Carrara, E., Lindholm, F., et al.: MIKEY: Multimedia Internet KEYing. IETF RFC 3830 (August 2004)
34. Telelogic tester,
    `http://www.telelogic.com/Products/tester/index.cfm`

Applying Model Checking to Generate Model-Based Integration Tests from Choreography Models

Sebastian Wieczorek[1], Vitaly Kozyura[1], Andreas Roth[1], Michael Leuschel[2],
Jens Bendisposto[2], Daniel Plagge[2], and Ina Schieferdecker[3]

[1] SAP Research, CEC Darmstadt,
Bleichstr. 8, 64283 Darmstadt, Germany
firstname.lastname@sap.com
[2] University of Düsseldorf,
Universitätsstrasse 1, 40225 Düsseldorf, Germany
lastname@cs.uni-duesseldorf.de
[3] Fraunhofer Institute for Open Communication Systems (FOKUS),
Kaiserin-Augusta-Allee 31, 10589 Berlin, Germany
ina.schieferdecker@fokus.fraunhofer.de

Abstract. Choreography models describe the communication protocols between services. Testing of service choreographies is an important task for the quality assurance of service-based systems as used e.g. in the context of service-oriented architectures (SOA). The formal modeling of service choreographies enables a model-based integration testing (MBIT) approach. We present MBIT methods for our service choreography modeling approach called Message Choreography Models (MCM). For the model-based testing of service choreographies, MCMs are translated into Event-B models and used as input for our test generator which uses the model checker ProB.

Keywords: Model Checking, Model-based Testing, Formal Methods, Integration Testing, Service Choreography Models.

1 Introduction

Service choreography models play an important role in SOA development and can provide a basis for ensuring quality at several levels, e.g., through verification and testing. In previous work [25], we defined precise requirements on choreography modeling languages that would allow supporting three software quality related development methods: design, verification, and testing. However, we observed that state of the art choreography languages such as WS-CDL [15] or BPMN [1] do not fulfill all these requirements simultaneously, mainly due to high abstraction level, imprecise semantics, assumption of ideal channels, lack of termination symbols, etc. Therefore SAP Research developed a language for modeling service choreographies called Message Choreography Modeling (MCM) and an Eclipse-based editor for it. In [26], we introduced MCM and provided an overview of the implemented editor and of its verification and testing plugins. In this paper, we present the model based testing (MBT) approach for service integration testing utilizing MCMs in detail.

M. Núñez et al. (Eds.): TESTCOM/FATES 2009, LNCS 5826, pp. 179–194, 2009.

As MCMs are based on communicating extended finite state machine (EFSM) semantics, constraint solving techniques have to be applied for the automatic test generation. Therefore, we translate the models to Event-B [4] which can be processed by the model checker ProB [17]. Using ProB, we are able to generate test suites for service integration that are not only covering all transitions of the communication protocols described in the MCMs, but also optimize the test generation towards minimizing the effort of test concretization (e.g. test data provisioning) and execution. We use CSP [12] process algebra expressions, synchronized with the Event-B models, to encode concurrent aspects of the test case generation algorithm. In this paper we aim to show that MBT and formal methods can be applied in an industrial context and explain the practical considerations that have to be made (e.g. model coverage, test suite optimization criteria).

The remainder of this paper is structured as follows. Section 2 briefly introduces the running example for this paper and explains the necessary steps of our MBIT approach. In Section 3, the formal MCM syntax is given as a basis for the translation of MCM to Event-B in Section 4. Section 5 describes the implementation details of the test generation algorithm and Section 6 discusses related test generation approaches. Section 7 concludes the paper and gives future work directions.

2 Overview

Our approach to model-based integration testing (MBIT) comprises the modeling of the conversation between SOA components, the translation of the obtained models and the subsequent generation of test suites. In order to illustrate the approach, we first introduce the following running example, which will be referred to throughout the paper.

Two service components, a buyer and a seller, negotiate a sales order. The buyer starts the communication by sending a *Request* message that will be answered with a *Confirm* by the seller. The buyer afterwards has the choice either to send a *Cancel* that rolls back the previous communication and allows to restart the negotiation or to send an *Order* that successfully concludes the ordering process. Because we assume a (reliable) communication channel that is not necessarily preserving the message order, it might be observed that a *Cancel* is delivered after a new negotiation process already started.

2.1 MCM Modeling

The service choreography modeling language MCM complements the structural information of the communicating components (e.g. service interface descriptions and message types) with information on the message exchange between them. A detailed discussion of the underlying concepts of MCM and how they support service development can be found in [26]. MCM consists of different model types each defining different aspects of service choreographies.

- **Global Choreography Model.** The global choreography model (GCM) is a labeled transition system which specifies a high-level view of the conversation between service components. Its purpose is to define every allowed sequence of observed messages.

- **Local Partner Model.** The local partner models (LPMs) specify the communication-relevant behavior for exactly one participating service component. Due to the design process of MCM, each LPM is a structural copy of the GCM with extra constraints on some of the local transitions, usually leading to the affected sending actions being deactivated.
- **Channel Model.** The channel model (CM) describes the characteristics of the communication channel on which messages are exchanged between the service components. These characteristics determine for example whether messages sent by one component preserve their order during transmission and are formalized by the WS-RM standard [23].

Figure 1 shows how the example described above can be described using the MCM artifacts. In the GCM at the top of Figure 1, the arrows labeled with an envelope depict the interactions *Request, Confirm, Cancel, Order,* and *Cancel(deprecated[1])* which are ordered with the help of the states *Start, Request, Reserved,* and *Ordered.* The states *Ordered* and *Start* are so-called target states (thus connected with the filled circle). Only in these states, the communication between the partners is allowed to terminate.

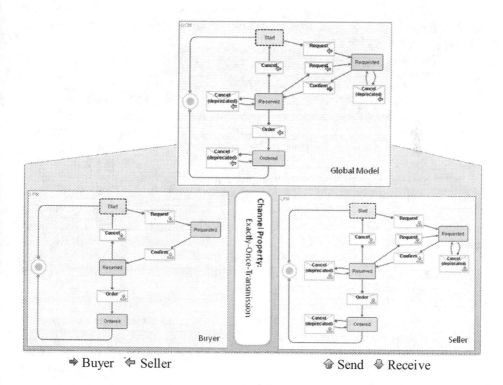

Fig. 1. GCM (top) of the choreography and LPMs of the buyer (left) and the seller (right)

---

[1] Deprecated here means that the message is out-dated and no-longer relevant as the negotiation has been restarted.

To keep the model deterministic, a set variable called *ID_SET* is declared and initialized with Ø. It stores the transaction ids from the header of *Request* messages that have not yet been addressed by *Cancel, Cancel (deprecated)* or *Order* messages (the headers of these messages also store the ids). Whenever a *Request* interaction takes place, an assignment *ID_SET := ID_SET ∪ {msg.Header.ID}* is executed referring to the *ID* stored in the header of the *Request* message. This assignment is needed to distinguish between a deprecated and an actual *Cancel* in state *Reserved*. Thus for the interaction *Cancel* an additional necessary precondition *ID_SET \ {msg.Header.ID})* = Ø ∧ *msg.Header.ID* ∈ *ID_SET* can be modeled in MCM while for *Cancel(deprecated)* we add the precondition *(ID_SET \ {msg.Header.ID}) ≠ Ø ∧ msg.Header.ID∈ ID_SET*. In Section 3 the formal syntax and the complete set of preconditions and assignments for our example is described.

The LPM of the buyer partner of our example is depicted in the lower left part of Figure 1. It is a structural copy of the GCM, but the interaction symbols now represent send or receive events of the buyer. Moreover some send-events are "inhibited" by special *local constraints*. It is for example inhibited that a *Cancel(deprecated)* is ever sent (thus these send-events have been erased) and that a *Request* is sent in the *Reserved* state. However, due to possible message overtaking on a channel that does not guarantee to enforce the message order during transmission, receiving a deprecated *Cancel* is possible on the seller side (for details see Section 3 and 4). The LPM of the seller is depicted in the lower right part of Figure 1.

2.2 Transformation

Our goal is to generate test cases automatically from MCMs. FSM-based approaches [5,6,11] would be applicable for the test generation if the annotated constraints of the model have no impact on the communication behavior. In our example however this is not the case (e.g. the message *Cancel(deprecated)* is active only if at least two IDs have been stored in the variable *ID_SET*). As the example incorporates a quite common pattern of the enterprise software domain, approaches that are able to compute constraint-compliant paths have to be used for MCM based test generation.

An analysis showed that implementing a tool for the test generation that directly runs on MCM models from scratch would be inefficient and hence infeasible. Therefore, we decided to transform our models to the formal modeling language Event-B. Event-B [4] is an evolution of the B-Method [1] that puts emphasis on a lean design. In particular, the core language of Event-B is (with a few exceptions) a subset of the language used in its predecessor.

Event-B fits quite naturally to MCM: interactions can be seamlessly expressed as events and the relationship between GCM and LPMs can be formulated as Event-B refinement (although we use this technique in our transformation, it is not substantial to understand the test generation and therefore left out of scope for this paper). Also other formalisms, such as UML [20] have also been successfully translated into Event-B, so that we were able to utilize past experiences and practices.

Another distinguishing aspect is the tool support in form of the Eclipse-based Rodin tool [3]. Due to the extensible architecture, various plugins for Rodin exist. The tool can be integrated with other Eclipse-based tools such as the MCM editor. With ProB, a flexible model checker for Event-B models exists that can be utilized for the test generation and enables us to build on the previous experiences with B and model checking in the area of MBT.

Apart from deriving tests, a transformation into Event-B opens a variety of possibilities to analyze the model: e.g. checking the refinement relation ensures the local enforceability of the service choreography. Though being an important part of the overall MCM approach, also formal model analysis is not in the scope of this paper.

2.3 Test Generation

After having obtained a formal representation of the MCM model, we can employ a model checker to derive a test suite for integration testing. Similar to [24], we define integration testing as testing of an assembly of individually already tested components. Because of the confidence about the correctness of the participating components (which results from quality ensuring techniques on the component level, e.g. unit tests), our testing approach focuses on showing that each sent message is interpreted in the correct way by the receiver. This can be determined by checking for each interaction, that the intended message effect has been caused. Consequently, a test suite should cover all receive events modeled in the LPMs.

For automatic test generation, a local model that incorporates information from both LPMs and the CM (to connect the send and receive events) can be used. Because various cases studies (e.g. [10]) show that state space explosion is the major stumbling point when applying automatic test generation to industrial settings, we decided to use the GCM to drive the test generation instead of the much more complex local model. While transition coverage of the GCM is equivalent to receive event coverage of the LPMs in most cases, the state space that needs to be explored is significantly lower.

In [27], we discussed possible coverage criteria that can be used to drive service integration testing and how to choose them accordingly depending on effort and fault assumptions. For this approach, we decided to use transition coverage, i.c. that all interactions are contained in the test suite, because it already uncovers a significant amount of integration faults with relatively small efforts [22]. For example in the MBIT approach of [6], transition coverage of a global communication model was able to detect about 90% of integration related faults.

Important from an industrial perspective is, that our approach further aims to be optimal regarding the minimization of the effort in the subsequent test concretization (e.g. provisioning of test data), test execution and test analysis phases. Based on practical experience of the testing process at SAP [28], we concluded that optimal corresponds to the following list of objectives which is sorted from highest to lowest priority:

1. *Each path should start in the initial state and end in a target state:* As described in [28] setting system states in test preambles is complicated and time consuming. Stopping a test while the system is not in a target state leads to problems with inconsistent data that might hamper consequent test executions.
2. *The length of the longest generated path should be minimal:* The longer a test case gets, the harder it is to maintain. Therefore especially for generated tests a top priority is to carefully control path lengths.

3. *Message racing should be minimal:* Testing the effects that message racing has
    on the interaction is an important part of each test suite. Tests are mostly carried
    out in rather idealistic environments where messages are received in the same or-
    der they have been sent. Therefore, during test execution, message racing has to
    be emulated on the channel in a controlled way, usually leading to much higher
    effort.
4. *The number of test steps should be minimal:* As the effort increases with the
    overall length of all test cases, the sum of test steps should be minimized.

Section 5 describes the resulting steps of the test generation and their implementation,
namely the generation of global test cases, the mapping to local test cases and the test
suite optimization.

3 MCM Syntax

In this section, we present the abstract syntax of MCM, which is the basis for the
translation into Event-B and the subsequent test generation.

For a simplified presentation, we assume that all choreographies consist of exactly
two participating components. Then, a message choreography model $MCM=(GCM,$
$LPM_1, LPM_2, CM)$ consists of a global choreography model (GCM), two local partner
models (LPM_1 and LPM_2) and a channel model CM.

Global Choreography Model. The GCM is based on a finite state machine $L=(S, I,$
$\Rightarrow)$, where S is a finite set of states, I is a finite set of interactions and $\Rightarrow \subseteq \mathbb{P}(S) \times I \times S$.
The system has an initial state $init \in S$ and target states $\{e_1,...,e_n\}$, where $e_i \in S$.

Below we define the language used for additional guards and actions of the GCM.
Since the additional guards and actions refer to entries in the exchanged (XML)
messages, we define record types representing the schemas the messages comply
with. A finite set ET of elementary types (e.g. including the natural numbers) and a
finite set of labels F are given. For these, the set T of record *types* is inductively defined to be the smallest superset of the *elementary types ET*, the set CT of *complex
types* $\{(f, t) \mid t \in T, f \in F\} \subseteq CT$, and the set of *set types* $Set(t)$ with $t \in T$. Further each t
$\in T$ has a unique assigned name $name(t)$ from a set of data type names.

Each interaction $i \in I$ is then assigned to a type $itype(i) \in T$. Further we assume a set
V_t of variables of type $t \in T$. For each interaction $i \in I$ there is a special variable $msg_i \in$
$V_{itype(i)}$ referring to the message exchanged during an interaction. Furthermore we
define a set C_t of constants (including e.g. $0,1,2,...,$ or $\emptyset$) of type $t \in T$.

The set $Term_t$ of terms for $t \in T$ is defined as the smallest set with

* $V_t \cup C_t \subseteq Term_t$ and
* $s.f \in Term_t$ with $(f, t) \in ct$ for some complex data type $ct \in CT$ and $s \in Term_{ct}$
* $s_1 + s_2 \in Term_t$ with $t=\mathbb{N}$, $s_1,s_2 \in Term_\mathbb{N}$ (analogous for other arithmetic oper-
    ations)
* $s_1 \cup s_2 \in Term_t$ with $t=Set(T)$, $s_1,s_2 \in Term_{Set(T)}$ (analogous for other set opera-
    tions)

The set *Term* consists of the union of *Term_t* over all $t \in T$. The set *Form* of formulae is the set of first order formulae over *Term*, the predicates $\{=, <, >, \in, \setminus, \cup\}$ and the variables V (respecting typing in an obvious manner).

A global choreography model for a set of data types T is a tuple $GCM = (L, V, C, itype, pre, act)$ with preconditions *pre: I→ Form* and actions *act: I → (V↦Term)*, where *V↦Term* is a partial function with $act(i)(v) \in Term_t$ and $v \in V_t$. The formulae of a precondition and the terms of actions of an interaction i must not contain variables $msg_{i'}$ with $i \neq i'$. If clear from the context we thus just write *msg* instead of msg_i.

Example. As explained in Section 2, the GCM of our example has the following variables, preconditions, and actions:

$V = \{ID\_SET\}$

$pre(Request) = msg.Header.ID \notin ID\_SET$

$act(Request)\ (ID\_SET) = ID\_SET \cup \{msg.Header.ID\}$

$pre(Order) = msg.Header.ID \in ID\_SET$

$act(Order)\ (ID\_SET) = ID\_SET \setminus \{msg.Header.ID\};$

$pre(Cancel) = ID\_SET \setminus \{msg.Header.ID\}) = \emptyset$
$\quad \wedge msg.Header.ID \in ID\_SET$

$act(Cancel)\ (ID\_SET) = \emptyset;$

$pre(Cancel(deprecated))$
$\quad = (ID\_SET \setminus \{msg.Header.ID\}) \neq \emptyset \ \wedge$
$\quad\quad msg.Header.ID \in ID\_SET$

$act(Cancel(deprecated))\ (ID\_SET)$
$\quad = (ID\_SET \setminus \{msg.Header.ID\})$

Local Partner Model. LPM_1 and LPM_2 are obtained from the *GCM* by duplicating, for each of them, the states and the global variables. Moreover each interaction $i \in I$ is transformed into the corresponding element from $PI = \{send\_i, receive\_i \mid for\ all\ i \in I\}$. The elements from *PI* inherit types, states, preconditions and actions from elements from *I*. LPMs can be further extended with an additional inhibitor function *inhib: I→P(S)* which describes that the partner must not *send* a message associated with *I* if it is in one of the states *inhib(i)*.

Example. From the interaction *Request* in GCM, we obtain *send_Request* in LPM$_1$ and *receive_Request* in LPM$_2$. LPM$_1$ contains a set $V_1 = \{ID\_SET_1\}$ and *pre* and *act* of the LPMs are adapted accordingly (w.r.t. GCM), e.g.:

$pre(send\_Request) = msg\_1.Header.ID \notin ID\_SET_1$
$act(send\_Request)\ (ID\_SET_1) = ID\_SET_1 \cup \{msg.Header.ID\}$

In order to disallow for *send_Request* in the state *Reserved*, we set *inhib(send_Request)={Reserved}*.

Channel Model. Let us consider a set of message types $MT \subseteq ET$, which are root elements of *itype(I)*. The channel model *CM* is a total function from a sequence of messages (of types *MT*) to a sequence of messages (of types *MT*). With $MT' \subseteq MT$ and a message sequence s, $\pi_{IT'}(s)$ denotes the projection of s to sequences of messages of types *MT''*. Let $\pi_{IT'}$ be canonically extended on the channel model. The channel model CM is then based on assignments of disjoint subsets *MT'* of *MT* to channel reliability guarantees[2] which enforce that $\pi_{IT'}(CM)$ satisfies certain properties. Reliability guarantees such as those from WS-RM standard [16] can be modeled:

---

[2] In the context of SAP applications, it is common to assign reliability guarantees per message type for the communication between two components.

- exactly once in order (EOIO) where $\pi_{IT'}(CM)$ is the identity function on interaction sequences and
- exactly once (EO) where $\pi_{IT'}(CM)$ is a permutation on an interaction sequence.

4 Translating MCM to Event-B

We chose Event-B for the purpose of obtaining a formally analyzable representation of MCM, which serves as basis for test derivation. In the following, we give a brief overview on Event-B, and sketch our translation from MCM.

Event-B is, as mentioned in Section 2.2, an evolution of the B-Method. It distinguishes between static and dynamic properties of a system; while static properties are specified in a context, the dynamic properties are specified in a so-called machine. A context contains definitions of carrier sets, constants as well as a number of axioms. A machine basically consists of a finite set of variables and events. The variables form the state of the machine and can be restricted by invariants. The events describe transitions from one state into another state. An event has the form EVENT $\triangleq$ **ANY** t **WHERE** G(t,x) **THEN** S(x,t) **END**. It consists of a set of local variables t, a predicate G, called the guard and a substitution S(x,t). The guard restricts possible values for t and x. If the guard of an event is false, the event cannot occur and is called disabled. The substitution S modifies the variables x. It can use the old values of x and the local variables t. E.g., an event that takes two natural number a, b and adds the product ab to the state variable x could be written as EVENT $\triangleq$ **ANY** a,b **WHERE** a$\in\mathbb{N}$ $\wedge$ b$\in\mathbb{N}$ **THEN** x:=x+a*b **END**. For events that do not require local variables, the abbreviated form EVENT $\triangleq$ **WHEN** G(x) **THEN** S(x) **END** can be used. The primary way to structure a development in Event-B is through incremental refinement preserving the system's safety and termination properties.

Design Considerations of Translation. We are interested in a formal representation of both, the GCM for a global test generation and the two local LPMs with a connecting channel model. The latter is necessary to map the generated global test cases to local test cases that can be executed on the implemented components. Therefore the subsequently described translation generates two Event-B machines which use a common context: the Global Model describing the *GCM* and the Local Model, describing the composition (defined as in [8]) of the two *LPMs* and the *CM*. Both machines describe the exchange of messages – the first in terms of observing a message, and the latter in terms of sending and receiving messages.

As messages with the same type and content may occur more than once, to each message a unique natural number is assigned, which is incremented when a new message is sent. Further to each message a type is assigned while it is possible to specify the content of the message as functions on the message.

Because we aim at the use of a model checking technique the translation result is designed to be as deterministic as possible. We experimented with an assignment of types to messages which is non-deterministically initialized upfront; however this resulted in an indigestible state space for the model checker.

Translation Description. By defining a translation from the global and from the local MCM models into the two Event-B machines we obtain a precise semantics of MCM, which we present in the following. The translation is implemented and can thus be applied completely automatically.

Global Model. For each transition in the GCM we generate exactly one event. For representing the states we define a global variable `status` with elements from a set type $\{s_1, \ldots, s_k\}$, with constants $s_1, \ldots, s_k$. It is initialized with *init* $\in S$. The basic translation of an Interaction $i \in I$ with $(\{s_1, \ldots, s_k\}, I, s_m) \in \Rightarrow$ is as follows:

```
i  ≙
WHEN
guard1: status=s1 V … V status=sk
THEN
act1: status := sm
END
```

This basic translation must be augmented with preconditions and actions associated with that interaction. Therefore we have to represent data types, constants, variables, terms and formulae used in *MCM* in terms of Event-B. This is done as follows. For each data type $t \in T$ we define a set in the Event-B context without explicit characterization of elements. These sets are named in Event-B according to their type name *name(t)*. For each complex data type $t = \{(f, t')\}$ we define a partial function `f`: *name(t)* ↦ *name(t')*. `f` is initialized with `f` := ∅.

The constants and global variables are defined in a standard way. For each constant $c \in C_t$ an element is added to the set *name(t)*. For the interactions $I = \{i_1, \ldots i_n\}$ we additionally define a set `MESSAGES` = $\{name(itype(i_1,)), \ldots, name(itype(i_n))\}$.

Example. Consider the interaction *Request* with *pre(Request)* = *msg.Header.ID* ∉ *ID_SET* and *act(Request)* (*ID_SET*) = *ID_SET* ∪ *{msg.Header.ID}* of our running example. For it, we define the functions `Header`: ℕ ↦ `MessageHeader` and `ID`: `MessageHeader` ↦ `InstanceID` (*MessageHeader* and *InstanceID* here are the corresponding names from *name(T)*), and the local variables `t1` and `t2` in order to choose appropriate values to be assigned in the functions. Because *ID_SET* $\in T_{Set(InstanceId)}$ we define an Event-B variable `ID_SET` of type ℙ(`InstanceID`).

```
Request    ≙                        THEN
ANY t1 t2                           act1: status := Requested
WHERE                               act2: Header (msg):=t1
grd1: status=Reserved V status=Start   act3: ID(t1):=t2
grd2: t1 ∈ MessageHeader            act4: type(msg) := Request
grd3: t2 ∈ InstanceID               act5: ID_SET:=ID_SET U {t3}
grd4: t3 ∉ ID_SET                   act6: msg := msg + 1
grd5: t1∈dom(ID)⇒ID(t1)=t2          END
```

The guard `grd5` describes a consistency property: if the function is already defined on an element, then the value must be the corresponding term.

For the target state $e_i \subseteq S$ we define a special event `terminate` with a guard `status=c₁` V ... V `status=c₁` (*for all* $c_i \in e_i$) and an action `targetstate:=true`, where `targetstate` is a global variable. In each event from the translation of *GCM* we additionally add an action `targetstate:=false`. As a result, `targetstate` equals *true* iff the system state is a target state.

Local Model. In the local model we generate events representing sending and receiving of messages. Depending on the viewpoint either the send or the receive event can be defined to be a refinement of the corresponding interaction in GCM.

By definition of *LPMs*, the variables from V and the status variable are duplicated (one for each partner). The variable *msg* is translated as for the GCM in order to keep the unique message enumeration. It is only used by send events, where it is set in the same way as in the GCM. In receive events, local variables (parameters) are used in order to obtain some message from a channel.

A channel is defined as a global variable of type $\mathbb{P}(\mathbb{N})$ denoting the set of messages on the being exchanged. It is initialized with $\emptyset$. Typically, we have two partners P_1 and P_2 and two sequencing contexts (EO and EOIO). In that case we obtain four possible channels in the model (two in each direction).

Example. Below we show a translation of the interaction *Request* from the *LPMs* for the partners *buyer (B)* and *seller (S)* of the example. The duplicated variables can be distinguished by the corresponding prefixes. The channel from *buyer* to *seller* having the sequencing EO is denoted by `channel_BS_EO`.

```
send_Request     ≙
ANY t1 t2
WHERE
grd1: B_status=Reserved V
      B_status=Startgrd2: t1 ∈
MessageHeader
grd3: t2 ∈ InstanceID
grd4: t3 ∉ B_ID_SET
grd5: t1∈dom(ID)⇒ID(t1)=t2
THEN
act1: B_status:=Requested
act2: Header(msg):=t1
act3: ID(t1):=t2
act4: type(msg):=Request
act5: B_ID_SET:=B_ID_SET ∪ {t3}
act6: channel_BS_EO:=channel_BS_EOU{msg}
act7: msg := msg + 1
END
```

```
receive_Request    ≙
ANY m
WHERE
grd1: S_status=Reserved V
      S_status=Start
grd2: m ∈ channel_BS_EO
grd3: type(m) = Request
grd4: m ∈ dom(Header)
grd5: Header(m)∈dom(ID)grd6:
ID(Header(m))∉S_ID_SET
THEN
act1: S_status := Requested
act2: S_ID_SET := S_ID_SET ∪
      {ID(Header(m))}
act3: channel_BS_EO :=
      channel_BS_EO \ {m}
END
```

The translation of a send event is very similar to the translation of the corresponding event in *GCM*. In receive events all function values are already set so the purpose is to find a suiting message *m* in the channel and "receive" it (delete from the channel). If a sequencing context is EOIO then we need an additional guard that checks, that the message m has a smallest number in the channel.

For inhibitor conditions $inhib(i)=C$ *(with $i \in I$)* we add a guard `status∉C` to the event `send_i`. In our example, we add the guard `grd6: B_status∉{Reserved}` to `send_Request`. It remains future work to optimize the translation by simplifying this and `grd1` to `B_status=Initial`.

Target states are treated similar to the translation of *GCM* except that we additionally demand `channel=∅` for all of them. Only if all channels are empty the system can enter into a target state. For all other events of the translation from the *LPM* we add an action `targetstate:=false`.

5 Test Generation

In this section we describe how we utilize ProB to obtain an optimized test suite (regarding the objectives explained in Section 2.3) from the translated MCM models.

ProB [15] is a validation toolset originally written for the B method. Its automated animation facilities allow users to animate and model-check their specifications which are valuable capabilities in the development of formal specifications. While consistency can be proven within tools such as Rodin or AtelierB, they are not capable of validating whether the model matches the specification that the modeler intended. Using the ProB animator, confidence in the models can be gained while using the model checker allows (at least for a part of the model's state space) to verify that a certain property holds. ProB has been adapted to support a number of formalisms such as Z, CSP, and CSP‖B [9]. Recently a ProB plug-in for the Rodin Platform has been developed, that can be used to animate and model check an Event-B specification within Rodin and to export Event-B models for using it in the ProB application. In the MCM editor the animation of the generated models is used but a detailed description in this paper is out of scope.

The test generation algorithm we developed for the MBIT approach based on MCM is separated into three steps. In the following we describe each step, give details about the implementation and show the computed results when applying it to the example from Section 2.

Step 1: Generation of the Initial Global Test Suite. As explained, our aim is to cover each transition of the global communication model, i.e. each interaction of the GCM. As each interaction is translated into a separate Event-B event, we have to ensure that every event is covered by at least one concrete transition in the state space of the global Event-B model, from which a valid end state can be reached. Note that the same event is typically covered by many different transitions, as its parameters can be valued in many different ways. In our particular example, the full state space is actually infinite, due to the use of integers as message identifiers. In order to reduce the state space, we have to configure ProB to compute only a few possible ways to enable any event.[3]

To satisfy the first and second objective given in Section 2.3, we have extended ProB to detect when full transition coverage is obtained[4]. This is gained by exploring the state space of the model breadth first, stopping when full coverage is achieved. Note that we also need to secure that for every operation we can reach a valid end state.

---

[3] This approach has proven to be sufficient so far, but in future, we will consider using ProB's symmetry reduction instead.

[4] Note that this is a property that cannot be expressed as an LTL formula, as it is not a property of individual paths but of the entire state space explored so far.

This has been ensured by refining the Event-B translation described in Section 4, by adding a `history` variable, storing the set of executed events, and adding a corresponding end-event for every original event `e` which can be triggered if we are in a valid end state and if e∈history. Afterwards all traces that end in a target state are extracted from the explored state space to form the initial test suite. From the example in this paper, we obtain the following initial test suite:

```
[Request, Confirm, Order], [Request, Confirm, Cancel],
[Request, Confirm, Cancel, Request, Confirm, Order],
[Request, Confirm, Cancel, Request, Confirm, Cancel],
[Request, Confirm, Request, Confirm, Order],
[Request, Confirm, Request, Confirm, Order, Cancel(depr.)],
[Request, Confirm, Request, Confirm, Cancel],
[Request, Confirm, Request, Confirm, Cancel(depr.), Order],
[Request, Confirm, Request, Confirm, Cancel(depr.), Cancel],
[Request, Confirm, Request, Cancel(depr.), Confirm, Order],
[Request, Confirm, Request, Cancel(depr.), Confirm, Cancel]
```

The computation takes 0.32 seconds on a 2.33 GHz Core2 Duo laptop and should scale up to much larger examples.

Step 2: Mapping of Global to Local Paths. In order to obtain executable test cases the global sequence of message observations for each path has to be mapped to the corresponding send and receive events of partners. As the GCM uses receive semantics, the global observe sequences can be directly translated to sequences of receive events. In the case of the path

```
[Request, Confirm, Request, Confirm, Cancel(depr.), Cancel]
```

the resulting sequence is (? reads "receives"):

```
[ Seller?Request, Buyer?Confirm, Seller?Request, Buyer?Confirm,
  Seller?Cancel(depr.), Seller?Cancel]
```

Afterwards for each receive event a corresponding send event is generated and added to the path in such a way that the local behavior descriptions are not violated. In the mentioned sequence the send event for *Cancel(deprecated)* has to be added before the second *Request* as the Buyer is not able to send these messages in the same order as they have to be received for the test. The resulting local sequence from our example therefore is (! reads "sends"):

```
[ Buyer!Request, Seller?Request, Seller!Confirm, Buyer?Confirm,
  Buyer!Cancel, Buyer!Request, Seller?Request, Seller!Confirm,
  Buyer?Confirm, Seller?Cancel(depr.), Buyer!Cancel, Seller?Cancel]
```

The message racing in the illustrated local path is underlined. While the *Cancel* message is sent by the buyer before the *Request* message, the seller receives the *Request* message first.

Similar to Step 1, it is again infeasible to exhaustively explore the full state space (as the state space of the local model is actually even considerably bigger) to find a suitable mapping from global to local traces. One could encode the problem as an LTL formula, but this formula will be very big with ensuing consequences for the complexity of model checking. The solution we have come up with, is to encode the desired LCM scenarios into a CSP [12] process. This process is synchronized with the Event-B model, using the technology of [9], suitably guiding the model checker. The CSP Process is divided into two components.

The first process encodes the desired trace of receive events, followed by an event on the goal channel, indicating to the model checker that this is a goal state we are looking for. For the trace given above it looks as follows:

```
RECEIVER =  Seller?Request -> Buyer?Confirm -> Seller?Request ->
            Buyer?Confirm -> Seller?Cancel(depr.) ->
            Seller?Cancel -> goal -> STOP
```

The second process encodes the sender events. We know how many send events of each type must occur, but the order of these is unknown.

```
SENDER(n1,n2,n3,n4) =
            n1>0 & Buyer!Request -> SENDER(n1-1,n2,n3,n4) []
            n2>0 & Seller!Confirm -> SENDER(n1,n2-1,n3,n4) []
            n3>0 & Buyer!Cancel -> SENDER(n1,n2,n3-1,n4) []
            n4>0 & Buyer!Order -> SENDER(n1,n2,n3,n4-1)
```

The sender process is now simply interleaved with the receiver process.[5]

```
MAIN = SENDER(2,2,2,0) ||| RECEIVER
```

Now, ProB will ensure that every event of the Event-B model synchronizes with an event of the CSP process (MAIN) guiding it and stopping when the CSP process can perform an event on the goal channel. For the initial test suite from Step 1, we compute a described mapping for each global trace in 0.064 seconds.

Step 3: Test Suite Reduction. The resulting test suite incorporating the local traces is now ready to be optimized according to the third and fourth objective from Section 2.3. The optimization of the test suite and the test suite reduction has been implemented in Java. In the first prototypical version we use a brute force algorithm that computes every possible combination of test cases and selects the optimal one according to the given objectives. The computed optimal test suite incorporates the local equivalents of the following global paths:

```
[Request, Confirm, Request, Cancel(depr.), Confirm, Order],
[Request, Confirm, Request, Confirm, Cancel(depr.), Cancel],
[Request, Confirm, Request, Confirm, Order, Cancel(depr.)]
```

For the given example the test suite is produced in less than a millisecond, implying that it is applicable in practice. However as the algorithms computational complexity is exponential in the number of test cases of the extended suite, we are planning to apply the following more sophisticated approach that reduces the number of computations: First it is analyzed which of the global interactions can only be covered by paths incorporating message racing. In our example these are the three interactions called *Cancel (deprecated)*. For these a minimal set of covering paths is determined

---

[5] Note that we could have additionally encoded that every receive event must be preceded by a corresponding send event in the CSP process, but this will be automatically checked by the Event-B model anyway.

using a greedy algorithm. If more than one possibility exists, the one that has the highest overall interaction coverage is chosen. The resulting test suite is filled with the minimum set of paths (not incorporating message racing) that covers the remaining interactions.

6 Related Work

The academic test generators TorX [21] and TGV [14] utilize model checkers to generate test cases from labeled transition systems (e.g. EFSM). However, problems with scalability have been identified as the major weakness of their approaches in case studies of the AGEDIS project [10]. Our work is based on a different abstraction level and formalism, which we hope will overcome those issues. For example, symmetry can be detected and exploited very easily in B. Also, the use of a higher-level formalism can significantly reduce the blowup of the associated state space [16].

There are various MBT approaches that generate test cases from classical B models, upon which we build. One is the commercial LEIROS tool [13], based on the former BZ-testing tool [7], which is rooted in constraint logic programming to find boundary values. The other approach [18,19] uses ProB [17] – itself also rooted in constraint logic programming – and is based on adding tautologies (e.g., $x=\emptyset$ or $x\neq\emptyset$) to guards and the invariant and then uses the disjunctive normal form (DNF) to partition the executed operations according to the particular disjuncts covered. Traces are generated which try to cover every operation in every reachable partition. An expensive part of [18,19] is the generation of the DNF, which is effectively used to compute boundary cases. In our approach we overcome the need for the DNF and the need to find boundary cases by using Event-B, where events are more fine-grained than in classical B (e.g., due to the absence of complicated substitutions such as CASE or IF-THEN-ELSE). As such, events are already "partitioned" into individual cases by construction. Also, the above approaches do not address the problem of optimizing the test suite or test generation for decomposed systems, which are both a major consideration in our article.

7 Conclusion

In this paper we presented an approach to generate test suites for service choreographies, modeled in MCM, by using model checking. We described how choreography models are translated to Event-B models, which are a suitable input format for ProB, the model checker we used for the test generation. We have extended ProB to detect transition coverage, and have made use of the possibility to guide an Event-B model by a CSP process in order to translate high-level traces into low-level ones. The flexibility of ProB was crucial in addressing the various aspects of choreography models. We further explained the overall integration testing approach including the test goals and introduced the according test generation algorithm as well as its implementation. The test suite for the running example of this paper, has been computed automatically by our implementation. As MCM explicitly considers asynchronous communication, the generation of test suites incorporating message racing is a direct contribution to the research community, as is the utilization of a higher level of abstraction (the global model) to compute an integration test suite, thus avoiding the well known problem of state explosion.

As explained our test generation approach was designed such that the resulting test suite causes a minimal effort during later test concretization and execution. However we see some potential optimizations that could be applied to the test generation steps without sacrificing our goal of minimal test effort. We will also evaluate the fault uncovering capabilities of transition coverage compared to other applicable criteria and therefore will continue to work on suitable test generation algorithms. In order to assess our approach we are currently conducting additional experiments using typical case studies at SAP.

Acknowledgments. This work was partially supported by the EC-funded projects Modelplex[6] and Deploy[7] (grants no. 034081 and 214158).

References

1. Business Process Modeling Notation (BPMN) Specification 2.0, Submitted Draft Proposal V0.9, http://www.omg.org/cgi-bin/doc?bmi/08-11-01
2. Abrial, J.-R.: The B–Book: Assigning Programs to Meanings. Cambridge University Press, Cambridge (1996)
3. Abrial, J.-R., Butler, M., Hallerstede, S., Voisin, L.: A roadmap for the Rodin toolset. In: Abstract State Machines, B and Z (2008)
4. Abrial, J.-R., Hallerstede, S.: Refinement, Decomposition, and Instantiation of Discrete Models: Application to Event-B. Fundam. Inform. 77(1-2), 1–28 (2007)
5. Aho, A.V., Dahbura, A.T., Lee, D., Uyar, M.Ü.: An Optimization Technique for Protocol Conformance Test Generation Based on UIO Sequences and Rural Chinese Postman Tours. IEEE Trans. Commun. 39, 1604–1615 (1991)
6. Ali, S., Briand, L., Jaffar-Ur Rehman, M., Asghar, H., Iqbal, M.Z., Nadeem, A.: A State-Based Approach to Integration Testing Based on UML Models. Information & Software Technology 49(11–12), 1087–1106 (2007)
7. Ambert, F., Bouquet, F., Chemin, S., Guenaud, S., Legeard, B., Peureux, F., Utting, M., Vacelet, N.: BZ-Testing-Tools: A Tool-Set for Test Generation from Z and Busing Constraint Logic Programming. In: Proc. of FATES 2002, pp. 105–120 (2002)
8. Butler, M.: Decomposition Structures for Event-B. In: Integrated Formal Methods (2009)
9. Butler, M., Leuschel, M.: Combining CSP and B for specification and property verification. In: Fitzgerald, J.S., Hayes, I.J., Tarlecki, A. (eds.) FM 2005. LNCS, vol. 3582, pp. 221–236. Springer, Heidelberg (2005)
10. Craggs, I., Sardis, M., Heuillard, T.: AGEDIS Case Studies: Model-Based Testing in Industry. In: Proc. of ECMDA 2003, pp. 129–132 (2003)
11. Gallagher, L., Offutt, A.J., Cincotta, A.: Integration Testing of Object-oriented Components using Finite State Machines. J. Software Testing, Verification, and Reliability (2006)
12. Hoare, C.: Communicating Sequential Processes. Prentice Hall, Englewood Cliffs (1985)
13. Jaffuel, E., Legeard, B.: LEIRIOS Test Generator: Automated Test Generation from B Models. B 2007, 277–280 (2007)

---

[6] http://www.modelplex-ist.org
[7] http://www.deploy-project.eu

14. Jard, C., Jeron, T.: TGV: theory, principles and algorithms. J. Software Tools for Technology Transfer 7(4), 297–315 (2005)
15. Kavantzas, N., Burdett, D., Ritzinger, G., Lafon, Y.: Web services choreography description language. W3C candidate recomm (2005), http://www.w3.org/TR/ws-cdl-10
16. Leuschel, M.: The High Road to Formal Validation. In: Börger, E., Butler, M., Bowen, J.P., Boca, P. (eds.) ABZ 2008. LNCS, vol. 5238, pp. 4–23. Springer, Heidelberg (2008)
17. Leuschel, M., Butler, M.: ProB: A Model Checker for B. In: Araki, K., Gnesi, S., Mandrioli, D. (eds.) FME 2003. LNCS, vol. 2805, pp. 855–874. Springer, Heidelberg (2003)
18. Satpathy, M., Leuschel, M., Butler, M.: ProTest: An Automatic Test Environment for B Specifications. In: Proc. ENTCS 111, pp. 113–136 (2005)
19. Satpathy, M., Butler, M., Leuschel, M., Ramesh, S.: Automatic Testing from Formal Specifications. In: Gurevich, Y., Meyer, B. (eds.) TAP 2007. LNCS, vol. 4454, pp. 95–113. Springer, Heidelberg (2007)
20. Snook, F., Butler, M.: UML-B: Formal modeling and design aided by UML. ACM Trans. Softw. Eng. Methodol. 15(1), 92–122 (2006)
21. Tretmans, J., Brinksma, E.: TorX: Automated Model Based Testing. In: EMSOFT (2002)
22. Utting, U., Legeard, B.: Practical Model-Based Testing – A Tools Approach. Morgan Kaufmann Publ., San Francisco (2007)
23. Web Services Reliable Messaging (WS-ReliableMessaging), Version 1.1. OASIS Consortiom, http://docs.oasis-open.org/ws-rx/wsrm/v1.1/wsrm.pdf
24. Weyuker, E.: Testing component-based software – a cautionary tale. IEEE Software 15(5), 54–59 (1998)
25. Wieczorek, S., Roth, A., Stefanescu, A., Charfi, A.: Precise Steps for Choreography Modeling for SOA Validation and Verification. In: SOSE, pp. 148–153. IEEE, Los Alamitos (2008)
26. Wieczorek, S., Roth, A., Stefanescu, A., Kozyura, V., Charfi, A., Kraft, F.M., Schieferdecker, I.: Viewpoints for Modeling Choreographies in Service-Oriented Architectures. In: Proc. of WICSA 2009. IEEE Computer Society, Los Alamitos (to appear, 2009)
27. Wieczorek, S., Stefanescu, A., Großmann, J.: Enabling Model-Based Testing for SOA Integration Testing. In: MOTIP, pp. 77–82. Fraunhofer IRB Verlag (2008)
28. Wieczorek, S., Stefanescu, A., Schieferdecker, I.: Model-based Integration Testing of Enterprise Services. In: Proc. TAICPART. IEEE Computer Society, Los Alamitos (2009)
29. Wieczorek, S., Stefanescu, A., Schieferdecker, I.: Test Data Provision for ERP Systems. In: Proc. of ICST, pp. 396–403. IEEE Computer Society, Los Alamitos (2008)

Analyzing Response Inconsistencies in Test Suites

Benjamin Zeiss and Jens Grabowski

Institute for Computer Science, University of Göttingen, Germany
{zeiss,grabowski}@cs.uni-goettingen.de

Abstract. Extensive testing of modern communicating systems often involve large and complex test suites that need to be maintained throughout the life cycle of the tested system. For this purpose, quality assurance of test suites is an inevitable task that eventually has an impact on the quality of the system under test as well. In this work, we present a means to analyze response inconsistencies in test suites. We define a response consistency relation and describe a method that identifies candidates for the analysis. Using these candidates, we find response inconsistent states. The applicability of this method is discussed for local test cases, local test cases with different response orders, and distributed test cases with concurrent behavior.

1   Introduction

Current industrial test suites for modern communicating systems are often huge in size and complex in their behavior. The tested devices are becoming increasingly sophisticated and at the same time, such devices have to become more reliable than ever before. Extensive testing nowadays involves not only the specification, the selection, and the execution of test cases, but also includes the maintenance of test suites throughout the life cycle of the tested system. For this purpose, quality assurance of test suites is an inevitable task that eventually has an impact on the quality of the *System Under Test* (SUT) as well. There is always a reciprocal effect between the quality of the test suite and the quality of the tested system. In addition, just like normal software, manually written test suites suffer from software aging [1] and it is thus sensible to find quality issues in tests as early as possible.

In our previous work, we introduced a quality engineering approach for test specifications. For the quality assessment, a quality model is given and metrics are used to quantify quality characteristics of the test specification. The quality improvement is based on refactoring and smell detection for issue discovery [2,3]. We prototyped this approach with our *TTCN-3 Refactoring and Metrics Tool* (TRex) [4] for the *Testing and Test Control Notation* (TTCN-3) [5]. An extension of the proposed quality engineering approach includes the reverse-engineering of test case models and a subsequent analysis of property patterns that should never occur in these models [6]. However, all these analyses were based on the test case as an entity and never regarded the test suite as a whole, i.e., the analyses disregarded how test cases relate to each other. In this paper, we present first results describing such inconsistencies in test suites that may indicate quality problems for the test suite.

Test suites are composed of multiple test cases. In this work, we contribute a method to analyze response inconsistencies. Response inconsistencies are situations that arise

M. Núñez et al. (Eds.): TESTCOM/FATES 2009, LNCS 5826, pp. 195–210, 2009.

when multiple test cases in a test suite have the same stimuli sequences, but expect different responses after the stimuli have been sent. Using this response inconsistency criterion, we identify test cases that are contained in each other or that expect completely different messages despite their equivalent stimuli sequences. We discuss response inconsistencies for sequential test cases with a strict stimuli–response order and then for responses that may arrive in different orders as well as concurrent test behavior.

In general, the work on quality assurance of test cases or test suites is rare. Besides our own work mentioned above, Vega, Din, and Schieferdecker have worked on guideline checking of TTCN-3 test suites in order to improve the maintainability of test suites [7]. Besides guideline checking, they have worked on quality measures for test data [8,9]. Together with Zeiss, Neukirchen and Grabowski, they participated in the definition of a quality model for test specifications [10].

The test suite consistency description by Boroday, Petrenko, and Ulrich [11] is related to our work. The paper describes mutual consistency criteria on test cases. In their description, two test cases are inconsistent when the expected SUT outputs for one state of their product are different. In our work, we deal with cases that they call *strongly inconsistent* and define a consistency relation that is based on the idea of weakening the bisimulation relation. In addition, we describe the analysis based on linear extensions of partially ordered models.

Numerous works on test case selection deal with similarity measures between test cases. For example, Cartaxo et al. [12] describe a similarity function based on the observed number of identical transitions. Similarly, Alilovic-Curgus and Vuong [13] have proposed a distance metric that penalizes mismatching symbols in execution sequences. The overall number of different proposals to measure test case similarity for test case selection are too high to list. Books such as [14] by Utting and Legeard provide a general overview on the typical criteria involved and the corresponding literature. To our knowledge, there is no work that bases a similarity measure on equivalent stimuli sequences though. Equivalent stimuli sequences are primarily interesting for analyzing inconsistencies in a test suite rather than being a generic similarity measure.

The paper is structured as follows: in Section 2, we provide a basic definition for the model in which we represent our test cases. Sections 3 and 4 comprise the main contributions of this paper. Section 3 presents how we define response consistency and correspondingly response inconsistency between two test cases. Section 4 describes a method on how to analyze response inconsistencies by finding candidate pairs and then analyzing the candidates. Section 5 describes how the presented relations are applicable to test cases with different response orders. Section 6 discusses concurrent test cases. Finally, we conclude with a summary and an outlook in Section 7.

2   Test Suite Model

We first introduce a basic transition system that we use to describe our test cases $T_1, T_2, \ldots, T_n$ in a test suite TS. Our base model is the *Labeled Transition System* (LTS) with actions partitioned into inputs and outputs as described, for example, by Tretmans [15]. In addition, we describe unobservable actions by their own partition.

Definition 1 (Labeled Transition System (LTS) with Inputs and Outputs). *An LTS T is defined by the tuple (S, A, λ, s_0) where*

- *S is a finite and non-empty set of states,*
- *A is a set of actions that is partitioned into the sets of input actions A_I, the set of output actions A_O, and a set unobservable actions A_U with $A = A_O \cup A_I \cup A_U$, $A_I \cap A_O \cap A_U = \emptyset$.*
- *λ is a transition relation with $\lambda \subseteq S \times A \times S$,*
- *s_0 is the initial state.*

A transition from the set λ is written as triple (s, a, s') or $s \xrightarrow{a} s'$.

We also refer to the elements of the four-tuple by using them as index of T, e.g., T_S refers to the set of states in T. The elements of each set may have an upper index to refer to the model they belong to, for example, $s_i^{T_S}$ refers to a state $s_i \in T_S$. To ease the distinction between input actions and output actions, we also use the notation $?a$ if $a \in A_I$ and $!a$ if $a \in A_O$. We use the notation $p!a$ or $p?a$ if a message a sent through a channel p or received through a channel p respectively. Since channels are not explicitly a part of our model, the channels can be interpreted as a label prefix. We continue by providing various further definitions that extend the formal framework. Note: in this paper, we discuss properties of test cases as subject rather than properties of the tested system. Therefore, we switch the meaning of inputs and outputs and take the view of the test case to have a more intuitive understanding from its perspective. This means that inputs in our models are inputs to the test case, i.e., responses from the system whereas outputs are outputs to the system, i.e., the stimuli.

Definition 2 (Path). *A path $s_i \xrightarrow{\sigma} s_n$ of an LTS T is a finite and non-empty sequence $\langle s_i, a_i, s_{i+1}, a_{i+1}, ..., a_{n-1}, s_n \rangle$ with $i, n \in \mathbb{N}$ such that the transitions $s_j \xrightarrow{a_j} s_{j+1}, j \in \mathbb{N}, i \le j < n$ exist in λ.*

Definition 3 (Traces). *A trace σ in an LTS T is a finite sequence $\langle a_i, a_{i+1}, ..., a_{n-1} \rangle$ such that the sequence $\langle s_i, a_i, s_{i+1}, a_{i+1}, ..., a_{n-1}, s_n \rangle$ is a path in T. We denote the set of all traces over a set of actions A with A^*. We concatenate actions to denote action sequences using the $\cdot$ sign, e.g., $?a \cdot !b \cdot ?c \cdot !d$ would denote a sequence of actions that is read from left to right.*

The notation $s \xrightarrow{a_1 \cdot a_2 \cdot ... \cdot a_n} t$ means that transitions $s \xrightarrow{a_1} s' \xrightarrow{a_2} ... \xrightarrow{a_n} t$ exist. We write $s \xrightarrow{a_1 \cdot a_2 ... a_n}$ if there exists a state t with $s \xrightarrow{a_1 \cdot a_2 ... a_n} t$.

With the double arrow, we denote paths that skip unobservable actions in A_U, i.e., if we have a path $s \xrightarrow{a_1 \cdot a_2 \cdot a_3 \cdot a_4} s'$ where $a_1, a_4 \in A_I \cup A_O$ and $a_2, a_3 \in A_U$, we may write $s \xRightarrow{a_1 \cdot a_4} s'$ for the abstracted sequence of observable actions. To be more concrete: $s \xRightarrow{\varepsilon} s' \Leftrightarrow s = s'$ or $s \xrightarrow{a_1 \cdot a_2 \cdot ... \cdot a_n} s', a_i \in A_U$ and $s \xRightarrow{a} s' \Leftrightarrow (s \xRightarrow{\varepsilon} t \xrightarrow{a} t' \xRightarrow{\varepsilon} s', a \in A_I \cup A_O \cup A_U) \vee (s = s' \text{ and } a \in A_U)$. Analogously, we use the notations $s \xRightarrow{a_1 \cdot a_2 \cdot ... \cdot a_n} t \Leftrightarrow s \xRightarrow{a_1} s' \xRightarrow{a_2} ... \xRightarrow{a_n} t$ and $s \xRightarrow{\sigma}$ iff there exists a state t with $s \xRightarrow{\sigma} t$.

Furthermore, with $traces(T)$ we denote the set of of all traces that can be produced in model T from the start state s_0, i.e., $traces(T) := \{\sigma \in A^* | T \xRightarrow{\sigma}\}$. Here, the LTS T refers to the initial state s_0 of T.

Definition 4 (Determinism). *An LTS is deterministic if $t = t'$ for paths $s \overset{\sigma}{\Rightarrow} t$ and $s \overset{\sigma}{\Rightarrow} t'$, for every $s, t \in S$.*

Definition 5 (Parallel Composition Operator). *Given two LTSs T_1 and T_2, the synchronous parallel composition $P = T_1 \| T_2$ is defined as follows:*

- $P_S = T_{1_S} \times T_{2_S}$.
- $P_A = T_{1_A} \cup T_{2_A}$.
- P_λ *is defined by the following inference rules:*
  - $(s,t) \overset{a}{\to} (s',t) \in P_\lambda$ $\quad$ *if* $s \overset{a}{\to} s' \in T_{1_\lambda}$ *and* $a \in T_{1_A} \setminus T_{2_A}$,
  - $(s,t) \overset{a}{\to} (s,t') \in P_\lambda$ $\quad$ *if* $t \overset{a}{\to} t' \in T_{2_\lambda}$ *and* $a \in T_{2_A} \setminus T_{1_A}$,
  - $(s,t) \overset{a}{\to} (s',t') \in P_\lambda, a \in A_U$ $\quad$ *if* $s \overset{a}{\to} s' \in T_{1_\lambda}$ *and* $t \overset{a}{\to} t' \in T_{2_\lambda}$ *and* $(a \in T_{1_{A_I}} \wedge a \in T_{2_{A_O}}) \vee (a \in T_{1_{A_O}} \wedge a \in T_{2_{A_I}})$.
- $P_{s_0} = (T_{1_{s_0}}, T_{2_{s_0}})$.

The third rule connects corresponding input actions with output actions of the same label where the action becomes an unobservable action in A_U. If we used a channel as label prefix for the synchronized input and output actions, we will indicate them in the synchronized action by separating channel and label with a ".", e.g., $p!a$ and $p?a$ becomes $p.a$. Note that due to our partitioning in inputs A_I, outputs A_O, and internal actions A_U, we are not in need of a special τ symbol that avoids multiway synchronization as actions in A_U are never synchronized. With the proposed composition operator and no queues in between, the send operations are blocking until a corresponding receive operation takes place.

3 Response Inconsistencies

The inconsistencies presented in this paper are based on the fact that the behavior of two different test cases T_1 and T_2 coincides up to a certain state s^{T_1} and respectively s'^{T_2}. Here, coinciding behavior intuitively means that there is a common action sequence σ such that the transitions $s_0 \overset{\sigma}{\Rightarrow} s$ can be found in T_{1_S} and $s_0 \overset{\sigma}{\Rightarrow} s'$ can be found in T_{2_S}. When s and s' respectively are states that expect only responses, they should expect the same responses — after all, the preceding action sequence between T_1 and T_2 matched and thus the responses should be the same.

Imagine the test case models illustrated in Figure 1a and 1b. Both models start with a stimulus $!a$ and thus have the same observable prefix. However, in test case T_1, the test case expects messages $?b, ?c,$ or $?d$ while test case T_2 only expects messages $?b$ or $?c$. T_2 expects a subset of the messages that T_1 expects and is essentially contained in T_1. In this situation, it is unclear why T_1 does not handle a possible incoming message d — it simply may be an inconsistency due to a human mistake or a redundancy. Three general cases can be distinguished how such test cases differ in a receiving state with the same preceding stimuli sequence:

- the test cases expect the same messages,
- one test case handles a subset of the expected messages of another test case,
- one test case expects completely different messages than another test case. The receive sets are disjoint.

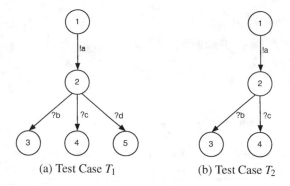

(a) Test Case T_1 (b) Test Case T_2

Fig. 1. Different Responses

The example in Figure 1 illustrates case 2. The general underlying assumption, in this local scenario is that a test case is initiated by stimuli, responses follow in answer to the stimuli, and then again possibly a new stimuli–response sequence is initiated or the test case ends. In other words, we are assuming that we deal with test cases that have a repeating stimuli–response pattern. Within these patterns, we want to find contradictions in the responses when comparing test case pairs. Of course, the scenario of the presented Figure 1 is essentially the simplest possible case. In practice, we also deal with test cases that may possibly have varying response orders or concurrent behavior altogether.

For this purpose, we will define a binary relation that describes what a response consistent test case pair is. The relation is very general and is applicable for local test cases, test cases with varying response orders, and test cases with concurrent behavior. Informally, there are three distinct cases when we consider a test case pair response consistent:

- the test cases are observationally equivalent in their behavior,
- the test cases have entirely different stimuli sequences,
- the test cases have coinciding stimuli sequence prefixes and the stimuli responses within this prefix are consistent.

The first two cases can be considered as borderline cases for the last case. Obviously, if two test cases are observationally equivalent, there are no contradictions in the responses. The traditional relation that describes systems whose observable moves cannot be distinguished from each other is weak bisimulation [16]. We provide a definition of weak bisimulation defined for two separate transition systems (whereas the usual definition is given over a single transition system). Weak bisimulation, as opposed to strong bisimulation, abstracts from internal transitions in the behavior and thus only regards observable behavior for its notion of equivalence.

Definition 6 (Weak Bisimulation). *Given two LTSs T_1 and T_2, a binary relation $R \subseteq T_{1_S} \times T_{2_S}$ is a weak bisimulation iff the following conditions hold for every $(s,t) \in R$ and an action $a \in (T_{1_A} \cup T_{2_A})$:*

- $s \xrightarrow{a} s' \in T_{1_\lambda}$ implies that there is a t' in T_{2_S} such that $t \xrightarrow{a} t' \in T_{2_\lambda}$ and $(s', t') \in R$
- Symmetrically: $t \xrightarrow{a} t' \in T_{2_\lambda}$ implies that there is a s' in T_{1_S} such that $s \xrightarrow{a} s' \in T_{1_\lambda}$ and $(s', t') \in R$

We call two states s and t weakly bisimilar or $s \approx t$ iff $(s,t) \in R$. Similarily, we call two LTSs T_1 and T_2 weakly bisimilar, or $T_1 \approx T_2$, iff for every $s \in T_{1_S}$, there exists a $t \in T_{2_S}$ such that $s \approx t$ and for every $t \in T_{2_s}$, there exists an $s \in T_{1_S}$ such that $s \approx t$.

We assume that response contradictions can only occur when the stimuli sequences coincide. By stimuli sequences, we formally mean rewritten traces where only those actions are concatenated that are outputs from the test case. For this purpose, we define the *stimuliseq* operator that essentially slices all actions from a trace except the stimuli.

$$stimuliseq(a_1 \cdot a_2 \cdot \ldots \cdot a_n) := \forall a_i, a_j \in A_O, i < j : a_i \cdot a_j$$

Due to our assumption that we have a repeating stimuli–responses pattern, deviating stimuli sequences from the first stimulus indicate that the test case is intended to test something different. However, if the stimuli sequences coincide in both test cases having a common stimuli sequence prefix and then diverge into different stimuli suffixes, the responses to the coinciding stimuli still have to be consistent.

Definition 7 (Response Consistency (reco)). Let T_1, T_2 be two LTSs. Then T_1 and T_2 are response consistent, or T_1 **reco** T_2 iff one of the following conditions hold:

- $\nexists \sigma \in traces(T_1), \varsigma \in traces(T_2) : stimuliseq(\sigma) = stimuliseq(\varsigma)$,
- $\exists s_0 \xrightarrow{\sigma} s, \sigma \in traces(T_1), t_0 \xrightarrow{\varsigma} t \in T_{2_\lambda}, \varsigma \in traces(T_2) : stimuliseq(\sigma) = stimuliseq(\varsigma)$, where for all $s \xrightarrow{a} s'$ with $a \in A_I^{T_1}$, there exists a $t \xrightarrow{a} t'$ with $a \in A_I^{T_2}$ and vice versa: for all $t \xrightarrow{a'} t'$ with $a' \in A_I^{T_2}$, there exists an $s \xrightarrow{a} s'$ with $a \in A_I^{T_1}$.

In comparison to the weak bisimulation relation, the **reco** relation is weak in its condition. It essentially demands that for all states in a test case T_1 reachable by a common stimuli sequence and with an outgoing response transition, there must be corresponding response transition in T_2 in a state that is reachable by the same stimuli sequence and vice versa. In addition, the matching stimuli sequence condition also implies that test cases can be response consistent that drift apart in their stimuli at some point. The consistency criterion is only concerned with those states that are reachable by coinciding stimuli sequences.

As mentioned above, weak bisimulation and entirely different stimuli sequences are essentially borderline cases of the **reco** relation. In the following, we demonstrate that two response consistent test cases are weakly bisimilar when the stimuli sequences for all traces symmetrically match and the response orders are the same. It helps to differentiate **reco** and weak bisimulation and illustrates where the two relations meet.

Proposition 1. *If two test cases T_1 and T_2 with inputs and outputs fulfil the following conditions*

- T_1 **reco** T_2,
- $\forall s_0 \overset{\sigma}{\Rightarrow} s$ with $\sigma \in traces(T_1) \exists \varsigma \in traces(T_2) : stimuliseq(\sigma) = stimuliseq(\varsigma)$ and vice versa: $\forall t_0 \overset{\varsigma}{\Rightarrow} t$ with $\varsigma \in traces(T_2) \exists \sigma \in traces(T_1) :$ $stimuliseq(\varsigma) = stimuliseq(\sigma)$,
- there is a relation $R \subseteq S^{T_1} \times S^{T_2}$, where for all pairs (s,t) reachable by the the same stimuli sequences and all $(s,t) \in R$, $s \overset{a}{\rightarrow} s'$ with $a \in A_I^{T_1}$, there exists a $t \overset{a}{\Rightarrow} t'$ with $a \in A_I^{T_2}$ with $(s,t) \in R$ and vice versa: for all $t \overset{a'}{\rightarrow} t'$ with $a' \in A_I^{T_2}$, there exists an $s \overset{a}{\Rightarrow} s'$ with $a \in A_I^{T_1}$ and $(s,t) \in R$,

then T_1 and T_2 are weakly bisimilar.

Proof. Imagine two test cases T_1 and T_2 that are not weakly bisimilar. This means there is a state pair in the bisimulation relation $(s,t) \in R$ where there is a $s \overset{a}{\rightarrow} s' \in T_{1_\lambda}$ for which there is no $t \overset{a}{\Rightarrow} t' \in T_{2_\lambda}$ or there is a $t \overset{a}{\rightarrow} t' \in T_{2_\lambda}$ for which there is no $s \overset{a}{\Rightarrow} s' \in T_{1_\lambda}$. The fact that (s,t) is in the bisimulation relation implies that either $s = s_0$ and $t = t_0$ or that there are transitions $s_0 \overset{\sigma}{\Rightarrow} s$ and $t_0 \overset{\sigma}{\Rightarrow} t$ where for every observable transition, there is a bisimilar state pair that leads to (s,t). The hypothesis must hence be false for transitions following (s,t).

In the case that $a \in A_U$, then there is always a transition $s \overset{a}{\rightarrow} s'$ with a corresponding $t \overset{a}{\Rightarrow} t'$ and vice-versa as $s \overset{a}{\Rightarrow} s$ and $t \overset{a}{\Rightarrow} t$ always exist for internal actions (See Definition 3).

In the case that $a \in A_I$, then we know that for all $s \overset{a}{\rightarrow} s'$ with $a \in A_I^{T_1}$, there exists a $t \overset{a}{\Rightarrow} t'$ with $a \in A_I^{T_2}$ and vice versa: for all $t \overset{a'}{\rightarrow} t'$ with $a' \in A_I^{T_2}$, there exists an $s \overset{a}{\Rightarrow} s'$ with $a \in A_I^{T_1}$ if states s and t respectively are reachable by a common stimulus sequence. In addition, the relation R in the hypothesis ensures structural equivalence. Furthermore, according to the hypothesis, the stimuli sequences mutually exist for all traces in T_1 and T_2. Thus, there are always sequences $s_0 \overset{\sigma}{\Rightarrow} s$ and $t_0 \overset{\varsigma}{\Rightarrow} t$ where $stimuliseq(\sigma) = stimuliseq(\varsigma)$.

Finally, let $a \in A_O$ be an output action. If $s \overset{a}{\rightarrow} s' \in T_{1_\lambda}$, then there must be a $t \overset{a}{\Rightarrow} t' \in T_{2_\lambda}$. Otherwise, we must have traces σ and ς with $s_0 \overset{\sigma}{\Rightarrow} s'$ and $t_0 \overset{\varsigma}{\Rightarrow} t'$ where $stimuliseq(\sigma) \neq stimuliseq(\varsigma)$ which contradicts the hypothesis. The symmetric case can be shown analogously.

For input and output transitions, the hypothesis must be false in order to violate the bisimulation criteria for the pair (s,t). Hence, its contrapositive, i.e., the original statement, must be true.

If we once again take a look at the example in Figure 1, we notice that T_1 **reco** T_2 is false. The test cases do not differ in their stimuli sequences as both test cases start with a $!a$ transition. Therefore, we know that the third condition must hold. But it fails. There are no traces with the same stimulus sequence where the responses between the stimuli match completely. The traces where the stimuli sequence matches reach state 2,3,4, or 5 in T_1. However, a corresponding transition in T_2 for $?d$ is missing. For T_2, however, there are corresponding response transitions in state 2. Therefore, the condition fails.

4   Response Inconsistency Analysis

Given a a test suite TS which is a set of of test case models $T_1, T_2, \ldots, T_n$, we suggest a response inconsistency analysis involving the following steps:

- Finding candidate test case pairs for the analysis,
- For each candidate test case pair, we find states responding to stimuli that contradict each other in their responses.

In the following, we describe each of the two analysis steps in more detail.

4.1   Partial Stimuli Equivalent Test Case Pairs

The first step in finding response inconsistent test case pairs is to identify candidates for the analysis. To identify such candidates, we classify all test cases by the stimuli sequences that they can produce. The reasoning behind this is the stimulus–response pattern. We assume that responses happen as reaction to the stimuli sent to the system and thus stimuli sequences are independent from possible response contradictions while they still identify the gist of a test case, namely those behaviors of the test case that control the behaviors and reactions of the SUT. However, since there may be causal relationships between responses and subsequent stimuli, we define a partial order that is used to preserve these relationships.

Definition 8 (Linear Extension of a *Partially Ordered Set* (poset)). *Given a poset $(S_P, \leq)$, i.e., a binary relation "$\leq$" over a set S_P that is reflexive, antisymmetric, and transitive, a linear extension of $(S_P, \leq)$ is a total order S_T for which, whenever $x \leq y$ in P, $x \leq y$ also holds in S_T. We define $\mathcal{L}(S_P)$ to be the set of all possible linear extensions of S_P.*

We use posets for each unique stimuli sequence that essentially match all traces with the same stimuli sequences. These posets for each stimuli sequence order the stimuli among each other and responses to their corresponding stimuli, but not the responses themselves. Using these posets, we can require that there exists at least one common linear extension in the test case pair that leads to the next stimulus.

Definition 9 (Partial Stimuli Equivalence (psteq)). *Let T_1, T_2 be two LTSs and let $PO_{\sigma_0} := (A^{T_1}, \leq)$ and $PO_{\varsigma_0}(A^{T_2}, \leq)$ be partially ordered sets for each unique stimulus sequence σ_0 and ς_0 defined over the actions of T_1 and T_2 respectively. We then say that T_1 is partially stimuli equivalent to T_2, i.e., T_1 psteq T_2 if and only if all of the following conditions hold:*

- *$\exists \sigma \in traces(T_1) \cap A^*$ with a corresponding $\varsigma \in traces(T_2) \cap A^*$ such that $stimuliseq(\sigma) = stimuliseq(\varsigma)$,*
- *$\forall a_i, a_j \in \sigma$ with $i < j : a_i, a_j \in PO_{stimuliseq(\sigma)}$ and $a_i \leq a_j$ iff $a_i, a_j \in stimuliseq(\sigma)$ or $a_i \leq a_j$ iff $a_i \in A_I^{T_1} \wedge a_j \in stimuliseq(\sigma)$,*
- *vice-versa: $\exists \varsigma \in traces(T_2) \cap A^*$ with a corresponding $\sigma \in traces(T_1) \cap A^*$ such that $stimuliseq(\varsigma) = stimuliseq(\sigma)$.,*

- $\forall a_i, a_j \in \varsigma$ with $i < j : a_i, a_j \in PO_{stimuliseq(\varsigma)}$ and $a_i \leq a_j$ iff $a_i, a_j \in stimuliseq(\varsigma)$ or $a_i \leq a_j$ iff $a_i \in A_I^{T_2} \wedge a_j \in stimuliseq(\varsigma)$,
- $\exists \sigma \in traces(T_1) \cap A^*, \varsigma \in traces(T_2) \cap A^*$ such that $stimuliseq(\sigma) = stimuliseq(\varsigma)$ such that the intersection of the linear extensions of the corresponding posets is non-empty, i.e, $\mathcal{L}(PO_{stimuliseq(\sigma)}) \cap \mathcal{L}(PO_{stimuliseq(\varsigma)}) \neq \emptyset \vee (stimuliseq(\sigma) = \sigma \wedge stimuliseq(\varsigma) = \varsigma)$.

While the stimuli sequences are required to be equal in any case, the requirement that there is a linear extension in both T_1 and T_2 for each stimuli sequence that also includes responses that are ordered to their stimuli makes sure that causal relationships between responses and subsequent stimuli are preserved (see Section 5).

Using this partial stimuli equivalence criterion, we can partition the test cases in TS, i.e., $T_1, T_2, \ldots, T_n$ into partially output equivalent pairs $TS_C := \{(T_i, T_j) | \forall T_i, T_j \in TS : T_i \text{ psteq } T_j\}$.

4.2   Finding Response Inconsistent States

Given the set of candidates that have coinciding stimuli prefixes TS_C, we can now analyze test case pairs (T_i, T_j) for possible response inconsistencies. For this purpose, we define the set of inconsistent states $IS_i \subseteq S^{T_i}$ that contains those states of T_i that are inconsistent with T_j.

$$IS_i := \{s | s \in S^{T_i} : \tag{4.1}$$
$$\exists \sigma, \varsigma \text{ with } stimuliseq(\sigma) = stimuliseq(\varsigma), s_0^{T_i} \xRightarrow{\sigma} s^{T_i}, t_0^{T_j} \xRightarrow{\varsigma} t^{T_j} \wedge$$
$$\exists t := (s^{T_i} \xrightarrow{a} s'^{T_i}), a \in A_I^{T_i} \text{ for which there exists no } (t^{T_j} \xrightarrow{a} t'^{T_j}), a \in A_I^{T_j}\}$$

Informally, the conditions describe that there is a trace σ in T_i and ς in T_j that reach corrsponding states s_{T_i} and S_{T_j} by applying the same stimulus sequence. The state s_{T_i} reached is a state where only responses take place and there is a response transition with an input action a that does not exist in T_j.

Analogously, IS_j defines those states $IS_j \subseteq S^{T_j}$ that contains the states of T_j that are inconsistent with T_i, i.e., i and j are swapped. We then say that T_i and T_j are response inconsistent if $IS_i \cup IS_j \neq \emptyset$.

5   Response Inconsistency Analysis with Different Response Orders

The provided examples so far always assumed that the response events of the compared test cases are ordered in the same way. Similarly, we have only discussed local test cases without concurrent behavior so far. In general, we need to distinguish the following cases when we compare test cases for response inconsistencies:

- we compare a local test case to another local test case where both have the same response orders,

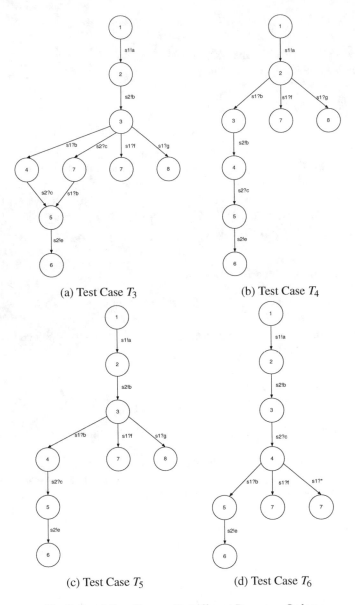

(a) Test Case T_3

(b) Test Case T_4

(c) Test Case T_5

(d) Test Case T_6

Fig. 2. Local Test Cases with Different Response Orders

- we compare a local test case to another local test case where both have different response orders,
- we compare a concurrent test case to a local test case,
- we compare two concurrent test cases.

The differentiation already indicates that there is a high degree of variety how test cases can be designed. Also, different test case designs can be used to model essentially the same behavior. For example, test cases with concurrent behavior can produce the same behavior as a local test case when they are synchronized properly. Similarly, deterministic local test cases, can systematically regard different message receival orders. We explicitly want to state that we do not find every kind of test design mentioned above and in the following reasonable for real-world testing. However, they may occur and therefore we need to discuss them.

We continue the discussion by comparing test cases T_3 and T_4 regarding inconsistent responses (Figure 2). Both are local test cases which have the same stimuli sequences ($s1!a, s1!a \cdot s2!b$, and $s1!a \cdot s2!b \cdot s2!e$), but with a different response order. At first glance, it seems that these are valid candidates for the response inconsistency comparison, but in actuality, they are not. T_4 requires that $s1?b$ is received before the $s2!b$ stimulus is sent whereas T_3 sends both stimuli subsequently. T_3 suggests that the $s1!a$ and $s2!b$ stimuli are either independent or that the responses following $s2!b$ depend on both stimuli whereas in T_4, the stimulus $s2!b$ is follow-up behavior to the response $s1?b$, i.e., there is a causal relationship between them. The example illustrates the necessity for the additional partial order condition in the definition of the partial stimuli equivalence relation (Section 4). While the stimuli sequences match, there is no linear extension that matches for the stimuli sequence $s1!a \cdot s2!b \cdot s2!e$. The only linear extension of $PO_{stimuliseq(s1!a \cdot s2!b \cdot s2!e)}$ in T_4 is

– $s1!a \cdot s1?b \cdot s2!b \cdot s2?c \cdot s2!e$.

The two linear extensions of $PO_{stimuliseq(s1!a \cdot s2!b \cdot s2!e)}$ in T_3 are

– $s1!a \cdot s2!b \cdot s2?c \cdot s1?b \cdot s2!e$, and
– $s1!a \cdot s2!b \cdot s1?b \cdot s2?c \cdot s2!e$.

By regarding linear extensions of the responses in between the stimuli, we notice that in T_3 the $s!b$ transition would not happen without a preceding $s1?b$ transition. Since the linearization sets for the examined stimuli sequence are disjoint, T_3 and T_4 are not regarded as partially stimuli equivalent. The **reco** relation also fails for these two test cases as the possible responses after the $s1!a$ stimulus in T_4 cannot be consumed in T_3 after the same stimulus.

The situation is different for test cases T_5 and T_6. They have again the same stimulus sequences $s1!a$, $s1!a \cdot s2!b$, and $s1!a \cdot s2!b \cdot s2!e$. For $s1!a$, there are no responses and thus the stimuli sequence equals its trace with responses. The same is the case for $s1!a \cdot s2!b$. However, for the stimuli sequence $s1!a \cdot s2!b \cdot s2!e$, we have the following linear extensions for T_5:

– $s1!a \cdot s2!b \cdot s1?b \cdot s2?c \cdot s2!e$, and
– $s1!a \cdot s2!b \cdot s2?c \cdot s1?b \cdot s2!e$.

For T_6, the linear extensions are

– $s1!a \cdot s2!b \cdot s1?c \cdot s1?b \cdot s2!e$, and
– $s1!a \cdot s2!b \cdot s1?b \cdot s1?c \cdot s2!e$

The responses for $s2!b$ are ordered before the $s2!e$ action and have no order among each other. Therefore, T_4 and T_5 are in fact not only partially stimuli equivalent, but stimuli equivalent. The actual determination of the inconsistent states is working independent from any orderings. In T_5, the states expecting responses reachable through the stimuli sequence $s1!a \cdot s2!b$ are state 3 and 4. For each transition in state 3 and 4, there are corresponding transitions in T_6 that are reachable by the same stimuli sequence (in T_6, those states are states 3 and 4). Hence, there are no response inconsistencies in T_5 and T_6. Taking a look at the **reco** relation also exhibits that T_5 and T_6 are response consistent. After the $s1!a$ stimulus, both test cases do not expect any responses. Once the $s1!a \cdot s2!b$ sequence has been sent, there are states in both test cases that expect the $s1?b, s1?f, s1?g$, and $s2?c$ responses. Finally, both test cases again do not expect any responses after $s1!a \cdot s2!b \cdot s2!e$.

The latter example illustrates that the **reco** relation is a weak criterion in comparison to weak bisimulation due to its disregardment of structural properties within the response receival orders. This is intended as on the one hand, we cannot be sure that the test developer did not confuse orders by accident — this always needs to be validated by hand. On the other hand, this kind of freedom within the response orders is necessary to analyze test cases with concurrent behavior.

6   Response Inconsistency Analysis in Concurrent Test Cases

Nowadays test cases are often written with *Parallel Test Components* (PTCs) that are executed concurrently, they have queued messages, and ports. Here, the determination of inconsistent responses is not as intuitive since the behavior is defined by composite models where non-determinisms can happen easily due to their interleaving structure.

Figure 3 illustrates an example for a concurrent test case. Figure 3a shows the *Main Test Component* (MTC) and Figure 3b shows the PTC of a test case. In this test case, there are three channels involved: $s1$ and $s2$ are channels connected to the SUT while channel p is a connection between the MTC and the PTC. A common paradigm is that a PTC is placed at each channel of the SUT and hence, the MTC communicates with the SUT via channel $s1$ and the PTC communicates with the SUT via channel $s2$. The PTC can only send the message $s2!e$ when its behavior is synchronized with the MTC through $p?d$ and $p!d$, i.e., the message must only be sent if $s1?b$ was received in the MTC. The composite model $T_7 = T_{7_a} \| T_{7_b}$ according to Definition 5 is presented in Figure 3c. To reduce the size of this model, we omitted all states and transitions that are unreachable from the start state. The order of the events depends on which events are independent from each other and on which events are dependant. For example, $s1!a$ must take place before $s1?b$ or $s1?g$, but $s2!b$ may take place any time in between. Furthermore, in the composite model, we have non-determinisms between inputs and outputs (e.g., in state $(2,1)$) and also between multiple outputs (e.g., in state $(1,1)$).

Based on the observations discussed in Section 5, we can compare such test cases against test case designs that are local, local with different response orders, and test cases that have concurrent behavior as well. There is no limitation how the response consistency and partial stimuli equivalence relations are applicable to interleaved models. We demonstrate this by example. We compare test cases T_3 and T_7. Both contain the stimuli sequences $s1!a$, $s1!a \cdot s2!b$, and $s1!a \cdot s2!b \cdot s2!e$. T_7 contains the additional stimuli sequences $s2!b$, $s2!b \cdot s1!a$, $s2!b \cdot s1!a \cdot s2!e$ that are not contained in T_3 and hence

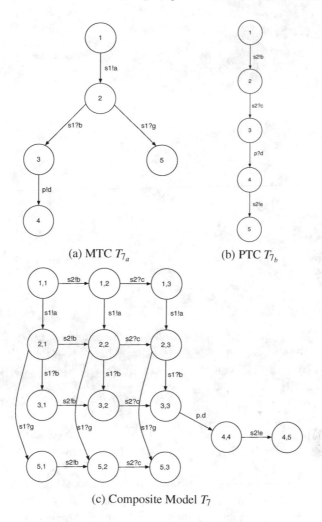

(a) MTC T_{7_a} (b) PTC T_{7_b}

(c) Composite Model T_7

Fig. 3. Test Case T_7 (Concurrent Test Case)

are left unregarded as the **reco** relation only regards traces that exhibit equal stimuli sequences. In every observable $s1!a$ trace in T_3, there are not corresponding responses. After the $s1!a \cdot s2!b$ stimuli sequence in T_3, there are states where every response can be consumed, i.e., $s1?b, s1?f, s1?g$, and $s2?c$. Finally, after the $s1?a \cdot s2!b \cdot s2!e$ stimuli sequence, there are again no states in which responses are consumable. In T_7, the consumable responses are quite different. After $s1!a$, there are states in which $s1?b$ and $s1?g$ are expected. The stimuli sequence $s1!a \cdot s2!b$ leads to states that can consume $s1?b, s1?g$, and $s2?c$. Finally, after $s1!a \cdot s2!b \cdot s2!e$, there may be no more responses in T_7. When evaluating the possible responses after traces with the same stimuli, we notice that the $s1!a$ sequence delivers a response mismatch where the response sets contradict each other, i.e., the response set for T_3 is empty while it is non-empty for T_7. Therefore, T_3 is not response consistent with T_7. However, T_3 and T_7 are partially stimuli

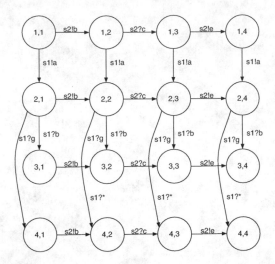

Fig. 4. Test Case T_8: Composite Test Case T_7 Without Synchronization

equivalent. They have both common stimuli sequences and for every common stimuli sequence, they have a common linear extension. Therefore, T_3 and T_7 are considered to be partially stimuli equivalent and thus classified as candidates for the response inconsistency analysis. However, due to missing responses after $s1!a$ in T_3, state $(2,1)$ is declared a response inconsistent state in IS_7 while $IS_3 = \emptyset$. Since $IS_7 \cup IS_3 \neq \emptyset$, T_3 and T_7 are response inconsistent.

The comparison between T_3 and T_7 indicates that the comparison between local and concurrent test cases will often exhibit inconsistencies when they are not necessarily considered a possible anomaly from the point of view of the test developer. Testers who write test cases with concurrent test behavior accept or even disregard the fact that the traces in subsequent executions of the same test may vary. For T_3, a possible interpretation is that the stimuli are independent from each other and the responses on $s1$ and $s2$ are independent from each other as well. However, the test case design is to send both stimuli $s1!a$ and $s2!b$ before expecting the responses for both stimuli rather than sending $s1!a$, then handling the responses for $s1!a$, and then sending $s2!b$ before handling the responses for $s2!b$. While the responses between T_3 and T_7 are strictly different (as the violated response consistency criteria suggests), it may be useful to find an even weaker criterion that declares such test cases as response consistent – after all, the local test case handles the all responses as well, just not in as many states as in the concurrent case.

We conclude the discussion with a comparison between two concurrent test cases. T_8 is essentially the composition of test cases T_{7_a} and T_{7_b} without the $p!d$ and $p?d$ transitions that synchronize the behavior. The purpose of this synchronization is to wait with the $s2!e$ transition in T_{7_b} until $s1?b$ or $p!d$ respectively took place in T_{7_a}. Removing this synchronization essentially means that $s2!e$ can take place anytime after $s2?c$ was received in T_{7_b}. As a result the $s1?b$ and $s1?g$ responses may still take place after the $s2!e$ transition happened in T_8 and thus the response set of the $s1!a \cdot s2!b \cdot s2!e$ stimuli sequence is not empty for T_8, but there exist states which consume the responses $s1?b$ and $s1?g$ after the stimuli sequence took place. In T_7, such states do not exist after the same stimuli sequence and thus, T_7 and T_8 are not response consistent. However, there exist common linear extensions for all stimuli sequences and thus, they are stimuli equivalent and candidates for the analysis. Here, states $(1,4)$, and $(2,4)$ are considered inconsistent states in T_8.

7   Conclusion

We have presented what response consistency and inconsistency between test cases in a test suite means. For that purpose, we have defined a response consistency relation and described how to analyze test suites for response inconsistent test case pairs. For the analysis, we have discussed different test case designs (i.e., local behavior, different response orders, and concurrent test cases) and how the relations are applicable in these different scenarios.

Additional test suite based inconsistencies exist and may be subject of further studies. For example, we could analyze follow-up transitions after coinciding traces and check whether upcoming transitions are consistently responses or stimuli. Another interesting subject of analysis would be to include test case verdicts into the analysis, i.e., checking whether verdicts are consistent when the observable traces match. To handle different (or equal) message parameter values more carefully, it would be interesting to modify this approach for symbolic LTSs with constraints.

In addition, we are currently evaluating response inconsistencies on industrial-size test suites, such as the *European Telecommunications Standards Institute* (ETSI) test suite for the *Session Initiation Protocol* (SIP) protocol [17]. For this purpose, we reuse a refined version of our reverse engineering algorithm that was presented in [6] and intend to measure how often the described inconsistencies occur in practice. The reverse engineering algorithm constructs simplified models from TTCN-3 test specifications and therefore, there is the possibility for false positives when a response inconsistency is detected. This is a generic problem as the reverse engineering of semantically complete and correct transition systems from complex languages (like TTCN-3) is arguably not practically achievable with an acceptable effort. The practical impact of this problem remains to be evaluated. Furthermore, the analyses presented in this paper obviously suffer from the state explosion problem when we deal with parallel behavior. However, in comparison to system specifications, the complexity of test case behavior is (in most cases) rather low in our experience. Therefore, we suspect that there is a chance that the computation of the described comparisons is possible with todays machines without the necessity to define new heuristics or optimizations that may lower the precision of the approach.

Finally, we believe that the partial stimuli equivalence relation can also be adapted and used for test case selection, i.e., finding a smaller number of test cases by eliminating test cases with equivalent stimuli.

Acknowledgements. This work is supported by Siemens AG Corporate Technology. We would like to thank Andreas Ulrich for feedback and inspiring discussions.

References

1. Parnas, D.: Software Aging. In: Proceedings of the 16th International Conference on Software Engineering (ICSE), Sorrento, Italy, May 16–21, pp. 279–287. IEEE Computer Society/ACM Press (1994)
2. Neukirchen, H., Zeiss, B., Grabowski, J., Baker, P., Evans, D.: Quality Assurance for TTCN-3 Test Specifications. Software Testing, Verification and Reliability (STVR) 18(2) (2008)
3. Neukirchen, H., Zeiss, B., Grabowski, J.: An Approach to Quality Engineering of TTCN-3 Test Specifications. International Journal on Software Tools for Technology Transfer (STTT) 10(4), 309–326 (2008)
4. TRex Website, http://www.trex.informatik.uni-goettingen.de (Last Checked May 15, 2009)
5. European Telecommunications Standards Institute (ETSI): ETSI ES 201 873 V3.4.1 (2008-2009): The Testing and Test Control Notation version 3; Parts 1–10 (2008)
6. Zeiss, B., Grabowski, J.: Reverse-Engineering Test Behavior Models for the Analysis of Structural Anomalies. In: Suzuki, K., Higashino, T., Ulrich, A., Hasegawa, T. (eds.) TestCom/FATES 2008. LNCS, vol. 5047. Springer, Heidelberg (2008)
7. Din, G., Vega, D., Schieferdecker, I.: Automated Maintainability of TTCN-3 Test Suites Based on Guideline Checking. In: Brinkschulte, U., Givargis, T., Russo, S. (eds.) SEUS 2008. LNCS, vol. 5287, pp. 417–430. Springer, Heidelberg (2008)
8. Vega, D., Din, G., Taranu, S., Schieferdecker, I.: Application of Clustering Methods for Analysing of TTCN-3 Test Data Quality. In: Proceedings of the 2008 The Third International Conference on Software Engineering Advances, ICSEA 2008 (2008)
9. Vega, D., Schieferdecker, I., Din, G.: Test Data Variance as a Test Quality Measure: Exemplified for TTCN-3. In: Petrenko, A., Veanes, M., Tretmans, J., Grieskamp, W. (eds.) TestCom/FATES 2007. LNCS, vol. 4581, pp. 351–364. Springer, Heidelberg (2007)
10. Zeiss, B., Vega, D., Schieferdecker, I., Neukirchen, H., Grabowski, J.: Applying the ISO 9126 Quality Model to Test Specifications – Exemplified for TTCN-3 Test Specifications. In: Proceedings of Software Engineering 2007 (SE 2007). Lecture Notes in Informatics (LNI), vol. 105. Köllen Verlag (2007)
11. Boroday, S., Petrenko, A., Ulrich, A.: Test Suite Consistency Verification. In: Proceedings of the 6th IEEE East-West Design & Test Symposium (EWDTS 2008), Ukraine (2008)
12. Cartaxo, E.G., Neto, F.G.O., Machado, P.D.L.: Automated Test Case Selection Based on a Similarity Function. In: Proceedings of the 2nd Workshop on Model-Based Testing (MOTES 2007) (2007)
13. Alilovic-Curgus, J., Vuong, S.T.: A Metric Based Theory of Test Selection and Coverage. In: Proceedings of the IFIP TC6/WG6.1 Thirteenth International Symposium on Protocol Specification, Testing and Verification XIII, North-Holland, pp. 289–304 (1993)
14. Utting, M., Legeard, B.: Practical Model-Based Testing – A Tools Approach. Morgan Kaufmann Publishers, San Francisco (2007)
15. Tretmans, J.: Test Generation with Inputs, Outputs, and Quiescence. In: Margaria, T., Steffen, B. (eds.) TACAS 1996. LNCS, vol. 1055. Springer, Heidelberg (1996)
16. Milner, R.: A Calculus of Communication Systems. LNCS, vol. 92. Springer, Heidelberg (1980)
17. ETSI: TS 102 027-3: SIP ATS & PIXIT; Part 3: Abstract Test Suite (ATS) and partial Protocol Implementation eXtra Information for Testing (PIXIT). European Telecommunications Standards Institute (ETSI), Sophia-Antipolis, France (2005)

Model-Based Testing of Web Applications Using NModel

Juhan Ernits[1], Rivo Roo[2], Jonathan Jacky[3], and Margus Veanes[4]

[1] University of Birmingham, UK
j.ernits@cs.bham.ac.uk
[2] Reach-U Ltd,Tartu, Estonia
rivo.roo@reach-u.com
[3] University of Washington, Seattle, WA, USA
jon@u.washington.edu
[4] Microsoft Research, Redmond, WA, USA
margus@microsoft.com

Abstract. We show how model-based on-the-fly testing can be applied in the context of web applications using the NModel toolkit. The concrete case study is a commercial web-based positioning system called WorkForce Management (WFM) which interacts with a number of other services, such as billing and positioning, through a mobile operator. We describe the application and the testing, and discuss the test results.

1 Introduction

In model-based testing, test cases are generated automatically from a model that describes the intended behavior of the system under test [1,4,2]. This contrasts with conventional unit testing, where the test engineer must code each test case. Therefore model-based testing is recommended where so many test cases are needed to achieve adequate coverage that it would be infeasible to code them all by hand.

Model-based testing is especially indicated where an implementation must support ongoing data- and history- dependent behaviors that exhibit nondeterminism, so that many variations (different data values, interleavings etc.) should be tested for each scenario (or use case). Web applications are examples. A web application is a program that communicates with a client using the HTTP protocol, and possibly other web protocols such as SOAP, WebDAV etc. Here nondeterminism arises from the multiple valid orderings of observable messages that may be returned by the system under test (SUT) in response to some set of stimuli sent by the tester. Such orderings depend on many factors such as for example load of certain components in the system or utilisation of the network links.

We present a nontrivial case study of applying on-the-fly model-based testing on a component of a distributed web application - a web-based positioning system developed by Reach-U Ltd called WorkForce Management (WFM). The purpose of the system is to allow subscribers to track the geographical position of their employees by mobile phones for the purpose of, for example, improving the practice of a courier service. In addition to the web interface, the system interfaces with a number of software components of the mobile operator, for example billing and positioning systems.

M. Núñez et al. (Eds.): TESTCOM/FATES 2009, LNCS 5826, pp. 211–216, 2009.

There are many model-based testing tools, see [4] for an overview. For this study we chose the open-source NModel testing framework, where the models are expressed in C# and web services are accessed with .NET libraries [2]. NModel supports on-the-fly testing (section 5) and uses composition of models for both structuring and scenario control (section 2).

2   Model Programs

In model-based testing the model acts as the test case generator and oracle. In the NModel framework, the model is a program called a *model program*. Test engineers must write a model program for each different implementation they wish to test.

Model programs represent behavior (ongoing activities). A *trace* (or run) is a sample of behavior consisting of a sequence of *actions*. An *action* is a unit of behavior viewed at some level of abstraction. Actions have names and arguments. The names of all of a system's actions are its *vocabulary*. For example some of the actions in the system we tested are `Initialize`, `WebLogin_Start` and `WebLogin_Finish`.

Traces are central; the purpose of a model program is to generate traces. In order to do this, a model program usually must contain some stored information called its *state*. The model program state is the source of values for the action arguments, and also determines which actions are enabled at any time.

There are two kinds of model programs in NModel:

Contract model program is a complete specification (the "contract") of the system it models. It can generate every trace (at the level of abstraction of the model) that the system might execute including known faults and appropriate responses to those.

In the NModel framework, contract model programs are usually written in C#, augmented by a library of modeling data types and attributes. The valuations of variables of the model program are its state. The actions of the model program are the methods labeled with the `[Action]` attribute (in C#, an *attribute* is an annotation that is available at runtime). For each action method, there is an *enabling condition*: a boolean method that returns true in states where the action is enabled (the enabling condition also depends on the action arguments).

Scenario model program constrains all possible runs to some interesting collection of runs (subset of all allowed behaviours) that are related in some way. Scenario model programs can be thought of as abstract test cases as it is possible to specify certain states and the sequence in which the states need to be traversed while leaving the intermediate states to be decided by the contract model program.

To enhance maintainability and keep a close match between the textual specification and the formalized model, we make heavy use of the composition facilities provided by NModel [6]. *Composition* of model programs enables one to build up larger models from smaller ones, and to restrict larger models to specific scenarios. Composition combines two or more model programs into a new model program called the product. Composition synchronizes shared actions (that appear in more than one of the composed programs) and interleaves unshared actions (that appear in only one). The composition facilities allow us to split separate actions but also separate functionality performed by the same actions into separate classes annotated with the `[Feature]` attribute. We distinguish contract features and scenario features, where the former define specified behaviour and the latter constrain it in some interesting way determined by the test designer.

The specification was grouped into features which represent logically tightly related functionality. We modeled *Login, LogOff, Positioning, BillingAndHistory* and *Restart* as separate *features* in NModel [6] that when composed specify the *contract model program* of the positioning functionality of WFM.

To focus the test on some particular part of the system we used different compositions of components. For example for focusing the test just at the login functionality we instantiated a model by composing *Login* ⊕ *Logoff*. For the purpose of testing the positioning functionality, we restricted the logging in and logging off by scenario features. The *OneLogin* feature restricts new login attempts by a user when already logged in. This enabled us to keep the tests focused on the positioning functionality while letting the developers investigate a potential issue with the login functionality that the tests revealed. The *CorrectPassword* feature is used to further constrain the login to try only correct passwords.

3   Test Setup

To automatically test a web application, replace the usual client (for example, a user with a web browser) with a test tool. The tool generates test cases that correspond to client behaviors, including sending requests to the server, and checks the server's responses to determine whether it passes or fails each test.

The test setup that is used throughout the current paper is given in Fig. 1. The model resides in the component called the "Model of the web application".

The `IAsyncStepper` interface, which stands for "asynchronous stepper", supports mapping synchronous actions from the model to the actual implementation and vice versa and mapping asynchronous actions to action terms in the appropriate observer

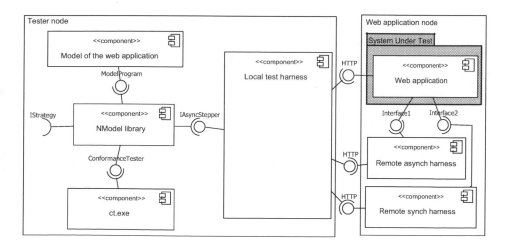

Fig. 1. A SysML component diagram of the setup of model-based testing of a web application

queue (see figure). Synchronous actions correspond to the behavior where the action blocks until the response is received. In the web application setting this corresponds to sending a GET or POST query to the web application from the client and waiting for the response that is received as the result.

Such actions can also be split into a pair of split actions defining action start and action finish separately. This enables to split the controllable part of invoking the action and the observable part of receiving a response to be split and allow other actions to take place during the time in between. This requires registering observers for asynchronous observable actions which are invoked by the web application. A concrete example of such an action is the event where the record of a completed transaction reaches the log database. It should not occur when no transaction has completed but can occur with a certain delay depending on the performance of the subsystems involved in completing the transaction. The implementation of the IAsyncStepper interface provides means for passing such messages on to the model after they have been converted to the abstraction level of the model in the harness.

The division of the components into tester node and web application node in Fig. 1 is based on how the test system is deployed. The tester can perform tests of the web application over the network, but it may be required to have some remote components of the test harness reside in the same node as the web application, as explained later.

4   Test Harness

The connection of the model programs to the actual web application requires building a *test harness* (sometimes also called an *adapter*). The test harness defines parameterized HTTP-queries and expected answers to the queries, and sets them into accordance with transitions in the model using the IAsyncStepper interface. The intuition is that the test harness makes the model and the system work in lock step.

A concrete test harness is generally application specific. We were able to use the .NET libraries for producing HTTP queries. Thus building support of cookies, GET and POST queries into the test harness required only a modest amount of work. We used packet capturing methods for acquiring queries that were added to the harness in an appropriately parameterized form.

Some observations, which are important from the point of view of determining the verdict of test runs made on some internal ports of the system, are intercepted by a custom script which triggers callbacks to our test harness.

5   Running the Tests

The tests were run with different compositions of features. For example, we used the following compositions for testing (*OneLogin* and *CorrectPassword* are abbreviated as OL and CP respectively):

1. $Login \oplus Logoff$
2. $Login \oplus Positioning \oplus OL \oplus CP$
3. $Login \oplus Positioning \oplus BillingAndHistory \oplus OL \oplus CP$
4. $Login \oplus Positioning \oplus BillingAndHistory \oplus Restart \oplus OL \oplus CP$

We carried the tests out in two main phases according to the progress of the development of the test harness. In the first phase we ran the tests using the web interface of the system and in the second phase we incorporated server side test adapter components to communicate additionally via the Billing and History ports of the system.

We used *on-the-fly* testing in this study. This contrasts with offline test generation, where test cases are generated in advance and stored until test execution. In that case, the generated test suites can be quite large, because they can include many similar sequences that are allowed by nondeterminism, but are never executed (because the system under test does not choose them at test execution time). On-the-fly testing dispenses with computing test cases in advance, and instead generates the test case from the model as the test executes, considering only the sequences that are actually executed. When testing in this way, conformance is based on establishing the alternating refinement relationship between the application and the model program, as discussed in [5].

6 Results

Table 1 contains a summary of the proportion of time and effort spent on building the model-based test system of WFM. Lines of code include comments. It shows that about 40% of time was spent on modeling and 60% on building various components of the test harness.

Several of the components developed in this case study are generic, independent of WFM, and can be reused for similar applications.

Table 1. Time and effort spent on model based testing the WFM system

Part of the test system	Lines of code	Time (%)
Model	1000	40
Asynchronous test harness local to the tester	850	38
Web server in the test harness	200	15
Restart module	125	4
Modifications in WFM code	125	3
Total	2300	100

These test failures occurred:

1. While running $Login \oplus Logoff$ tests an "Internal Server Error" message sometimes occurred after entering the correct user name and password.
2. Running $Login \oplus Positioning \oplus OL \oplus CP$ revealed a situation where the after receiving a positioning request the server kept replying that there are no new positioning results.
3. Running $Login \oplus Positioning \oplus OL \oplus CP$ causes the system sometimes to return an "Internal Server Error" message.
4. Running $Login \oplus Positioning \oplus BillingAndHistory \oplus Restart \oplus OL \oplus CP$ re-confirmed that all positioning requests that had not completed by the time of restart

were lost. After the system came back up, the positioning requests remained unanswered. Deployed WFM systems work in a cluster and if one server goes offline the work is carried on by another server. Our test setup did not include the cluster.

The functionality of the WFM system had previously been tested by a 3rd party using JMeter [3]. Model-based testing found errors in that were not discovered using that tool. It also provided more flexibility for automated testing.

As the model based testing toolkit is also a piece of software, our experiment revealed two errors in NModel. Both were fixed in the toolkit.

7 Conclusions

The WFM case study showed that model-based tests exposed errors in the web application that were not exposed by conventional methods.

It is possible to build a domain-specific web service testing application with a modest effort, roughly a few man-months.

The main drawbacks were related to complexities in building the test harness and a relatively steep learning curve. The functionality that was tested is a fairly small fraction of the overall functionality of the WFM system.

References

1. Broy, M., Jonsson, B., Katoen, J.-P., Leucker, M., Pretschner, A. (eds.): Model-Based Testing of Reactive Systems, Advanced Lectures. LNCS, vol. 3472. Springer, Heidelberg (2005)
2. Jacky, J., Veanes, M., Campbell, C., Schulte, W.: Model-based Software Testing and Analysis with C#. Cambridge University Press, Cambridge (2008)
3. JMeter: http://jakarta.apache.org/jmeter/ (accessed May 2009)
4. Utting, M., Legeard, B.: Practical Model-Based Testing: A Tools Approach. Morgan-Kaufmann, San Francisco (2006)
5. Veanes, M., Campbell, C., Schulte, W., Tillmann, N.: Online testing with model programs. SIGSOFT Softw. Eng. Notes 30(5), 273–282 (2005)
6. Veanes, M., Schulte, W.: Protocol modeling with model program composition. In: Suzuki, K., Higashino, T., Yasumoto, K., El-Fakih, K. (eds.) FORTE 2008. LNCS, vol. 5048, pp. 324–339. Springer, Heidelberg (2008)

Observability and Controllability Issues in Conformance Testing of Web Service Compositions

Jose Pablo Escobedo[1], Christophe Gaston[2], Pascale Le Gall[3], and Ana Cavalli[1]

[1] TELECOM & Management SudParis (ex INT) - CNRS SAMOVAR
9 rue Charles Fourier, 91011 Évry, France
{jose.escobedo,ana.cavalli}@it-sudparis.eu
[2] CEA LIST, Point Courrier 94, 91191, Gif-sur-Yvette, France
christophe.gaston@cea.fr
[3] Programme d'Épigénomique Université d'Évry-Val d'Essonne, 91000 Évry, France
Laboratoire MAS, Grande Voie des Vignes, 92195 Châtenay-Malabry, France
pascale.legall@ecp.fr

Abstract. We propose a model-based black-box testing approach to test conformance of Web Service Compositions (WSC). When a WSC under test makes use of implementations of Web Services, two situations may occur: either communications between the WSC and the Web Services are observable or hidden internal actions. We show by means of an example how to generate test cases whose verdicts are provided with explanations taking into account the status of the Web Services.

Keywords: Conformance testing, Web Service composition, observability and controllability, verdict testing report.

1 Introduction

Web Services (WS) are available through the network to be accessed by any computer that wants to communicate with them. *Web Services Compositions* (WSC) are mechanisms to produce new services by making use of already existing WSs. In this paper we address the problem of testing such kind of WSC following a model-based approach like in [4], using Input/Output Symbolic Transition System (IOSTS) to represent WSC specifications. Contrarily to systems considered in [4], the system under test may include not only the WSC system, but also some Web Services interacting with it. As the approach described in [1], the most natural solution to overcome that problem is to reduce it to the case of unit testing case by isolating WSCs from their Web Services so that the tester may directly interact with WSCs. Communication channels with Web Services are then qualified as **controllable**. However, it may occur that channels used to communicate with Web Services may technically be uncontrollable by the tester. In such cases, two situations may occur: either channels are **observable**, which means that the tester may observe exchanges of values through them, or

M. Núñez et al. (Eds.): TESTCOM/FATES 2009, LNCS 5826, pp. 217–222, 2009.

they are **hidden**, and in that case, exchanges of messages through them can only be considered as internal actions. The paper presents a model-based testing approach for testing WSC implementations in the context of a system also containing some Web Services.

The paper is structured as follows. The test architecture and a running example are presented in Section 2. In Section 3, we present the key ideas of our approach by illustrating it on the example.

2   The Context: Test Architecture

WS-BPEL stands for Web Services Business Process Execution Language [3], and is a standard for specifying Web Services Compositions in the form of orchestrations (or choreographies), where a central entity guides the composition. Basically, it defines how the interaction between Web Services is coordinated in order to achieve a business goal.

Let us introduce the Loan Request example depicted in Fig. 1. Three partners interact in the process: the user (bank's client), the WS-BPEL process (LR-WSC) and the Loan Service (LS, the Web Service). The behavior of the Loan Request WS-BPEL is as follows. The client initiates the process by sending his ID, the amount of money he wants to borrow and the maximal reimbursement duration. The LR-WSC sends this information to the LS, which first decides whether the loan is approved or not. If approved, it returns the minimum duration and the monthly fee and then, the LR-WSC sends the monthly fee to the user. Otherwise, the process ends and the user gets a Good bye reply message. If the duration computed by the bank and the one proposed by the client are the same, the loan is approved by sending a Good bye message to the user. Otherwise, if the duration proposed by the client is greater than the duration computed by the LS, the client can try again by proposing a new value for the duration until the loan is approved or until he decides to finish the process.

Following the classification given in the Introduction, a communication channel between the WSC and a WS is said to be (see Figure 2 for an illustration):

Controllable, if communications over the channel are controllable by the tester through control points **CP**. The tester has a complete control over the channel, both for stimulating the System Under Test (SUT) implementing the WSC with inputs and for observing its outputs. If all communication channels

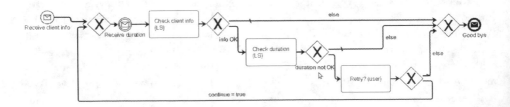

Fig. 1. Diagram of the Loan Request (LR) example

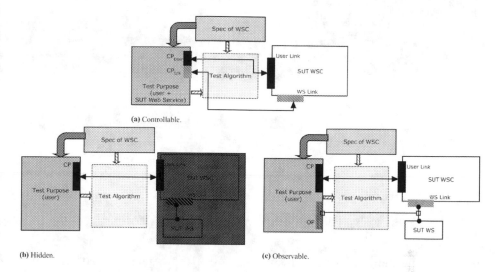

(a) Controllable.

(b) Hidden.

(c) Observable.

Fig. 2. Testing scenarios according to the accessibility to the communication channels

are controlled, the WSC becomes an independent component which can be tested according to a classical unit testing framework.

Hidden, if the tester cannot access the communication channel. This is the usual case when using the implementations of Web Services. The SUT is not just the WSC in isolation but a system composed of the WSC providing an interface to the user and of some encapsulated Web Services.

Observable, if the tester can only observe the communication channel through observation points **OP**.

Figure 3 shows the Loan Request example written as an IOSTS [4]. The user is represented by the letter u. IOSTS contain attribute variables useful to store data values. In the case of the LR-WSC, attribute variables are: d, for the (maximal) duration proposed by the client to pay the loan; a, for the amount of money the user wants to borrow; id, for the client's ID; b, for the boolean variable indicating if the user wants to try (if possible) to get another loan proposition with a smaller duration; min, for the minimal duration computed by the LS for the reimbursement period allowed; $approve$, for the boolean variable used by LS to indicate if the duration proposed by the client is satisfactory or not; and mf, for the monthly fee computed by the LS. Channels are represented, for readability reasons, as $EntityName\_ChannelName\_OperationName$. The initial state is q_0 and the final state is q_9.

Transitions of IOSTS are defined by a guard, an action (reception, emission or internal action) and assignments of attribute variables. Transition $q_0 \rightarrow q_1$ represents the initialization of the WS-BPEL process (LR-WSC). Transitions $q_1 \rightarrow q_2$, $q_2 \rightarrow q_3$ represent the first communication between the LR-WSC and the LS to check if the information given by the client is correct. Transition $q_4 \rightarrow q_5$ represents a positive answer from LS, and transition $q_5 \rightarrow q_6$ represents the corresponding following information sent by the LR-WSC to the user informing

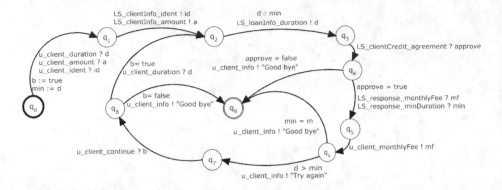

Fig. 3. The Loan Request example expressed as an IOSTS

him about the monthly fees. Transition $q_4 \rightarrow q_9$ represents a negative answer from LS and the corresponding Good bye message sent to the user. Transition $q_6 \rightarrow q_9$ represents the approval of the loan request and the corresponding Good bye message notifying the user. Transitions $q_6 \rightarrow q_7$, $q_7 \rightarrow q_8$ $q_8 \rightarrow q_2 \cdots$, $q_8 \rightarrow q_9$ represent respectively, the case where, if $min \neq m$, the user is asked to propose a new value for the duration of the reimbursement and start the process again or to finish the loan request process.

3   Our Approach of Conformance Testing for WSC

The first step consists in symbolically executing the IOSTS representing the WSC under test. The technique uses symbols instead of concrete data and allows us to represent all behaviors in a symbolic execution tree. The tree is then modified to take into account observable and hidden communication channels. The symbolic tree is first enriched by transitions carrying on the quiescence action δ and indicating that the WSC is waiting for a request either from the user or from a WS on an hidden or observable channel. Then, WS requests on observable channels are transformed into special observations (denoted as outputs). Finally, all transitions on hidden channels are translated into internal actions and the resulting symbolic tree is reduced by removing all internal actions which are useless from a testing point of view. Fig. 4 shows the dedicated symbolic execution tree of the LR example with the assumption that the LS's communication channels are all *hidden.*

With the dedicated symbolic execution tree, we adapt the rule-based algorithm of test case generation presented in [4] and defined for the classical ioco conformance relation. In few words, the algorithm consists in a simultaneous traversal of the modified execution tree and a test purpose defined as selected finite paths of the tree, in order to stimulate and observe the SUT in such a way that, as long as possible, the sequence of stimulations and observations corresponds to a trace of the test purpose. In practice, each path of the tree beginning in the initial state and ending in the final one can be used as a test purpose. Each

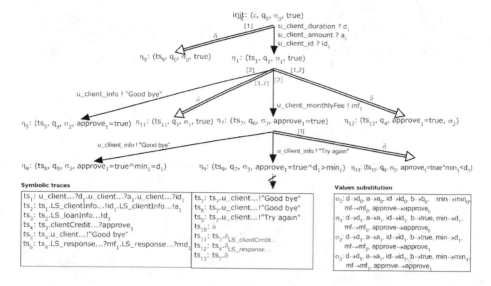

Fig. 4. Observable behaviors of LR-WSC, assuming that LS is hidden. Transitions labeled by [1] (resp. [2]) are introduced by applying *enrichment by quiescence* (resp. by *hiding transitions on hidden channels* and *internal actions reduction*).

(a)

Action	Values
stim	u_client_duration→12 u_client_amount→1000 u_client_id→42
obs	δ
Verdict	INCONC, {(u_client...?d$_1$.u_client...?a$_1$.u_client...?id$_1$.LS_clientInfo...!id$_1$.LS_clientInfo...!a$_1$. LS_loanInfo...!d$_1$.LS_clientCredit...?approve$_1$.δ, d=12^a=1000^id=12^b=true^min=12^mf=mf$_0$^approve=true), (u_client...?d$_1$.u_client...?a$_1$.u_client...?id$_1$.LS_clientInfo...!id$_1$.LS_clientInfo...!a$_1$. LS_loanInfo...!d$_1$.δ,d=12^a=1000^id=12^b=true^min=12 ^mf=0^approve=approve$_0$)}

(b)

Action	Values
stim	u_client_duration→12 u_client_amount→1000 u_client_id→42
obs	u_client_monthlyFee→100
obs	u_client_info→"Good bye"
Verdict	PASS, {(u_client...?d$_1$.u_client...?a$_1$.u_client...?id$_1$.LS_clientInfo...!id$_1$.LS_clientInfo...!a$_1$. LS_loanInfo...!d$_1$.LS_clientCredit...?approve$_1$. LS_response...?mf$_1$.LS_response...?min$_1$. u_client...!mf$_1$.u_client...!"Good bye".,d=12^a=1000^id=12^b=true^min=12^mf=100 ^approve=true)}

Fig. 5. Verdicts for hidden channels

algorithm step involves the computation of constraints issued from the values of messages exchanged in the beginning of the test sequence and the constraints stored in the symbolic states of the tree and of the test purpose. This process is repeated until a verdict is emitted together with a testing report illustrating the trace (exchange of values) and explaining which conditions lead to that verdict.

Fig. 5 shows results when the algorihm is performed with the test purpose characterised as the restriction of the tree in Fig. 4 with η_8 as the (accept) state. In case *(a)*, the tester sends the stimulation *u_client_duration* $\rightarrow$ 12,

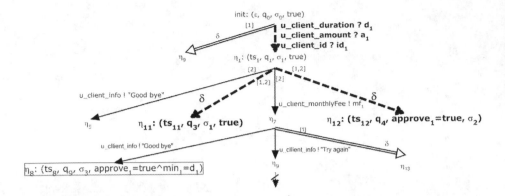

Fig. 6. Two possible scenarios when observing δ after sending the client information

$u\_client\_amount \rightarrow 1000$, $u\_client\_id \rightarrow 42$ and observes δ. The observation belongs to a trace of the execution tree but not of the test purpose. So, we obtain the *inconclusive* verdict. The report produces the two scenarios as shown in Fig. 6: (1) the LS does not send the *approve* answer or, (2) the LS sends the approve answer, but does not send the monthly fee and minimum duration. In case *(b)*, the tester stimulates the SUT with the sequence $u\_client\_duration \rightarrow 12$, $u\_client\_amount \rightarrow 1000$, $u\_client\_id \rightarrow 42$ and observes the monthly fee proposed by the LR-WSC, followed by the message *Good bye*. The algorithm produces the verdict *pass* with its corresponding scenario report (Fig. 5). In [2], more examples are available.

In this article, we have shown an example of how to test a WSC (orchestration) from its specification taking into account that WSs are connected to it during the testing phase. This corresponds to a situation of *test in context* or *embedded testing* for which no knowledge is available of the rest of the system (made of WSs invoked by the WSC). The complete formal description can be found in [2].

References

1. Bentakouk, L., Poizat, P., Zaïdi, F.: A Formal Framework for Service Orchestration Testing based on Symbolic Transition Systems. In: Núñez, M., et al. (eds.) TEST-COM/FATES 2009. LNCS, vol. 5826, pp. 16–32. Springer, Heidelberg (2009); Long version as technical report of LRI, University of Paris-Sud
2. Escobedo, J., Le Gall, P., Gaston, C., Cavalli, A.: Examples of testing scenarios for web service composition. Technical Report 09003_LOR, TELECOM & Management SudParis, 22 pages (2009), http://www.it-sudparis.eu/
3. Alves, A., et al.: Web Services Business Process Execution Language Version 2.0 (April 2007),
   http://docs.oasis-open.org/wsbpel/2.0/OS/wsbpel-v2.0-OS.html
4. Gaston, C., Le Gall, P., Rapin, N., Touil, A.: Symbolic Execution Techniques for Test Purpose Definition. In: Uyar, M.Ü., Duale, A.Y., Fecko, M.A. (eds.) TestCom 2006. LNCS, vol. 3964, pp. 1–18. Springer, Heidelberg (2006)

Towards Automatic Generation of a Coherent TTCN-3 Template Framework

Roland Gecse

Ericsson Hungary Ltd., P.O.Box 107, H-1300 Budapest 3, Hungary
roland.gecse@ericsson.com

Abstract. The template framework is a subset of TTCN-3 template declarations, which determines the entire template hierarchy within an abstract test suite. This paper introduces a deterministic method for generating such a template framework from type definitions.

1 Introduction

Test data and particularly TTCN-3 [1] templates account for significant part of test suite design both in terms of size and development time. The template framework expresses the relationship between the individual templates. It consists of template declarations, which describe the messages required for implementing dynamic test behaviour. TTCN-3 offers dedicated language constructions for organizing the template framework such as template parameterization or modification. A well-designed template framework is a precondition to concise templates, which are compact, well-organized and easy to maintain.

The template framework should be designed before test suite development with several requirements in mind. Excessively short or long as well as similar template declarations should be avoided. The template parameterization and modification shall also be used moderately. The perfect arrangement is hard to find because the requirements are often contradictory. It is thus desirable to have an automated template framework generation method even when the obtained result is not optimal.

The present article intends to facilitate test design by introducing the means and methods for generating an initial template framework from given type definitions with the ambition of assisting testers especially in the early phase of test suite design.

2 Type Structure Graph (TSG)

The TSG represents the encapsulation of structured types in order to reason about the hierarchy of the generated template framework. It captures the essential structural information but neglects some otherwise important properties such as the number and ordering of elements within a type. The simple and enumeration types are not container types so these are excluded from the model. The sub-type constraints of input type definitions are also ignored in TSG.

M. Núñez et al. (Eds.): TESTCOM/FATES 2009, LNCS 5826, pp. 223–228, 2009.

Formally, the $TSG = (V, E)$ is a directed graph whose V vertices model structured type definitions and $E \subseteq V^2$ directed edges express containment. An $uv \triangleq (u, v) \in E$ edge means that u includes v. The vertices of TSG are subdivided depending on the modeled structured type into pairwise disjoint sets $V_R = \{\text{record} \vee \text{set } types\}$, $V_C = \{\text{union } types\}$ and $V_L = \{\text{record of} \vee \text{set of } types\}$, such that $V_R \cup V_C \cup V_L = V$. The sets V_R, V_C and V_L are called record, choice and list nodes, respectively. The vertices of the graph are labeled with the structured type identifiers. The TSG edges are categorized, similarly to vertices, into pairwise disjoint sets $E_R = \{uv : u \in V_R\}$, $E_C = \{uv : u \in V_C\}$ and $E_L = \{uv : u \in V_L\}$, such that $E_R \cup E_C \cup E_L = E$. The sets E_R, E_C and E_L are named record, choice and list edges, in the order of definition.

The TSG may include self-loops and cycles as TTCN-3 supports recursive types. Multiple edges can also appear because a structured type definition may contain many identical type elements. The TSG is disconnected when the modeled type hierarchy includes independent messages. The sinks of TSG represent those structured types, which consist of simple type elements only. The sources of TSG do not necessarily correspond to the Protocol Data Units (PDUs). Hence, the $V_D \subseteq V$ set is used to mark those distinguished types for which the templates are declared. The PDU types, which represent the initial content of V_D, are obtained from the TTCN-3 port type definitions.

Certain TSG properties reveal interesting features of type hierarchy. The graph diameter, for instance, corresponds to the maximal depth of type hierarchy, which is a measure of encapsulation. The out-degree and the all-pairs shortest path length distribution of nodes express the size and complexity of type hierarchy.

The presence of Strongly Connected Components (SCCs) in TSG indicates recursion. The introduced method, however, does not intend to generate templates for recursive structures. However, the vertices of SCCs are saved into the set V_S as these require special attention during template framework generation.

3   Preliminaries of Template Generation

The template framework is constructed using an incremental method without backtracking. The **join** procedure merges templates in order to reduce the small ones while the **makepar** adds formal parameters to templates to avoid the large ones. The algorithm in Section 4 performs a careful analysis of arguments to determine the procedure to be invoked during the generation.

3.1   Template Join

The **join**$(t(u), t(v))$ procedure creates some new templates for type u by attaching the $t(v)$ templates to the $t(u)$ templates at each reference to v. The resulting templates replace the original content of $t(u)$ but $t(v)$ is not modified. The formal parameter lists of argument templates are also merged when necessary. The templates of u and v can be joined if TSG has at least one $u \cdots v$ path. If there exists only an uv edge then $t(v)$ is joined to $t(u)$ directly at u. Otherwise, the $t(u)$ and $t(v)$ templates are joined recursively, in reverse topological order of edges along the set of all possible $u \cdots v$ paths.

The exact method of joining the templates of some neighbouring u, v nodes along the uv edge depends on the type of u, the $|t(u)|, |t(v)|$ number of templates for the involved nodes and the $|uv|$ number of connecting edges. If $u \in V_R$ then the $|t(v)|$ pieces of templates are attached to all $|uv|$ places in every $|t(u)|$ templates. Since each template can appear in many positions at the same time, the number of resulting templates can increase drastically. If $u \in V_C$ then u gets a new template declared for each $t(v)$ attached to all $|uv|$ places. The number of obtained templates is less than in case of records because the choice templates consist of a single field only. The $u \in V_L$ nodes are never joined with their elements. The number of templates after joining along the uv edge can be calculated with Equation 1.

$$|t(u)| \leftarrow \begin{cases} |t(u)| \cdot |t(v)|^{|uv|} & \text{if } u \in V_R \\ |t(u)| + |t(v)| \cdot |uv| & \text{if } u \in V_C \end{cases} \tag{1}$$

3.2   Template Parameterization

The **makepar**$(t(u), v)$ procedure creates formal parameters from all type v fields of $t(u)$ templates. The newly created parameters are appended to the existing formal parameter list of templates. The number of templates in $t(u)$ does not change during the execution. Similarly to the join procedure, performing the parameterization is only possible if v is reachable from u. The parameter references are inserted at those u' nodes for which $u \cdots u'v$ path exists. If there are many $u \cdots v$ paths then more type v parameters are appended. The original content of $t(u)$ is overwritten at u' elements by a reference to the new type v parameter. If v becomes a formal parameter then it must also be added to V_D so that its $t(v)$ templates are preserved during the generation.

4   Algorithm

The introduced direct method produces a template framework from the type definitions. The created templates together cover the entire TSG except the SCCs. The coverage of a template is defined as the set of TSG nodes, whose fields appear in the template declaration. The resulting templates may partially overlap and can also be parameterized but template modification is avoided. The algorithm comprises of three steps. Initially, a set of default templates is declared for each node. Next, the TSG is partitioned into subgraphs along the choice and list edges. The obtained subgraphs are rather small and include all record edges of TSG. The default templates of subgraph nodes are merged into subgraph templates using the **join** and **makepar** procedures. The subgraph templates cover all nodes and record edges of TSG. The final step assembles the template framework by joining the subgraph templates along the remaining choice and list edges either statically or dynamically using parameterization.

4.1   Default Template Generation

The default templates are declared for the $V \setminus V_S$ nodes of TSG such that the nested assignment of structured type fields is avoided.

The present approach assigns predefined values to all simple type fields, which remain unmodified during the template generation. Hence, the value used at initialization represents the final value of that field in all templates of the framework. The content of structured type fields of default templates can be set arbitrarily (e.g. to any value matching) as these get overwritten during generation.

The number of default templates varies by type. The records get only a single default template declared. The choices, however, get a separate default template generated for each field. The list nodes get a single parameterized template assigned, in which the formal parameter list comprises of the list type itself. The obtained default templates serve as input for the subgraph template generation.

4.2   Subgraph Template Generation

The generation of the template framework begins with splitting the TSG into $TSG[S_i]$ vertex induced subgraphs. The S_i nodes correspond to the (S_i, E_i) subgraphs obtained by excluding the $E_C \cup E_L$ edges from TSG. The induced subgraphs have pairwise disjoint vertex sets such that $\forall i, j : S_i \cap S_j = \emptyset$ and $\bigcup_i S_i = V$. The adjacent subgraphs are connected with the $E_B = E \setminus (\bigcup_i E_i)$ edges whose terminating vertices are called entry nodes. The SCCs are always considered independent subgraphs regardless of their internal structure.

The goal of subgraph template generation is to declare a minimal number of templates covering the maximal number of subgraph nodes. The default templates of adjacent nodes are joined recursively in bottom up order along the E_i edges until all entry nodes have their subgraph templates ready (Figure 1). According to Equation 1, the **join** procedure may create a huge number of templates even when the parameters (i.e. $|t(u)|, |t(v)|$ and $|uv|$) are small. Therefore, **join** is performed only if the join condition (Equation 2) is satisfied.

$$\begin{cases} |t(u)| = |t(v)| = 1 \vee |t(v)| = |uv| = 1 \vee |t(u)| = |uv| = 1 & \text{if } u \in V_R \\ |t(v)| = 1 \vee |uv| = 1 & \text{if } u \in V_C \end{cases} \quad (2)$$

The join condition constrains the template generation to permit only an additive increase in the number of resulting templates. It allows at most one of the three parameters to exceed one for V_R nodes. The join condition for V_C nodes is less restrictive as it does not include $t(u)$. When Equation 2 is not satisfied then the **makepar** procedure is invoked instead of **join**. It adds type v fields to formal parameters of all templates in $t(u)$ and promotes them to the V_D distinguished types.

The default templates, which could not be joined with any other templates become subgraph templates. The original default templates in $t(v)$ can be discarded after processing the templates of all predecessors if $v \notin V_D$.

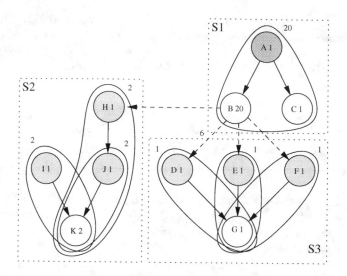

Fig. 1. An extract from an imaginary TSG: All entry nodes are shaded; vertex A is a distinguished node. The number of default templates appears next to the name inside the nodes. The S1, S2, S3 subgraphs and the generated subgraph templates are marked distinctively. S1 is covered by 20 overlapping subgraph templates while S2 has 2, and S3 contains 1 subgraph template for each entry node. The template framework generation algorithm joins the $t(H), t(D), t(E), t(F)$ templates with $t(B)$ and produces 21 templates for A (not shown in the Figure). The $2 + 2$ subgraph templates of I, J nodes are also preserved.

4.3   Template Framework Generation

The template framework is assembled from the templates generated for the TSG$[S_i]$ subgraphs (Figure 1). The S_p, S_c adjacent subgraphs are processed in reverse topological order such that S_p must not be a subgraph of an SCC (S_c can be any subgraph of TSG). The algorithm iterates through the entry nodes of the S_c subgraph and processes the $xy \in E_B : x \in S_p, y \in S_c$ edges one by one. It locates those $T \subseteq t(S_p)$ subgraph templates, which cover the xy edge (i.e. include a reference to node x containing y). The types of T templates are collected into set $W \subseteq S_p$. Clearly, W consists of those nodes of S_p subgraph, which have a path including the xy edge. The node x may not even appear in W because its default templates may have been joined with some of its predecessors' templates or became parameters during the subgraph template generation. If $y \in V_S$ then **makepar**(T, y) is invoked to make all references to the SCC node formal parameters in all referencing templates. Otherwise, the algorithm examines the $w \in W$ types of T templates.

If the processed w type is a record then all of its $t \in t(w) \cap T$ templates are joined with the $t(y)$ templates of the given entry node provided the join condition is satisfied. The join condition for records in Equation 2 normally checks $|t(x)|, |t(y)|$ and $|xy|$ properties of the edge. This time, it can happen that $w \neq x$ meaning that the $t(w) \cap T$ and $t(y)$ arguments of the join are not adjacent templates. If the w and y nodes are not adjacent then the join needs to be performed along all the $w \cdots xy$ paths as described in Section 3. Consequently, the join condition for records needs to be interpreted differently. The selected templates of w are processed one by one, thus $|t| = 1$ needs to appear in the join condition instead of $|t(x)|$. Furthermore, the $|xy|$ has to be replaced with the number of references to xy in t, which is denoted by N. The join condition depends thus on N and $|t(y)|$ only. Therefore, the $\mathbf{join}(\{t\}, t(y))$ is only performed if $N = 1 \vee |t(y)| = 1$. If the join condition does not hold then $\mathbf{makepar}(\{t\}, y)$ is executed in order to replace all references to type y with parameters in template t.

If the processed w type is a choice then the $\mathbf{join}(t(w) \cap T, t(y))$ is executed once the join condition in Equation 2 is satisfied. When joining the subgraph templates is not feasible then the references to y become formal parameters by invoking $\mathbf{makepar}(t(w) \cap T, y)$.

Finally, at the end of generation all unnecessary templates, which are not declared for distinguished types, are removed.

5   Conclusion

The introduced deterministic algorithm creates some subgraph templates covering the adjacent record nodes of TSG and constructs the template framework by joining or parameterizing the obtained templates. The join is performed only if the number of resulting templates increases moderately. The parameterization is used to rule out a multiplicative increase of template declarations. The final values of simple type fields are set to dummy values by default because the protocol type definitions alone are insufficient for assigning template elements with semantically correct data. A more advanced method of value assignment exists but its discussion exceeds the limits of this article.

The template framework generation algorithm has been implemented as a prototype plugin of TITAN TTCN-3 Test Executor. It has been evaluated on some protocols with satisfactory results, which proved that it is possible to create a proper template framework exclusively from the type hierarchy. Nevertheless, the framework generation can be further optimized using the methods and infrastructure presented in [2]. The algorithm could be improved to take the statistical properties of abstract protocol syntaxes into account. The generated framework could be refined interactively during test suite development. A comparison with heuristic algorithms would also be meaningful.

References

1. Methods for Testing and Specification; The Testing and Test Control Notation version 3; Part 1: TTCN-3 Core Language, ETSI ES 201 873-1 Edition 3.4.1 (2008)
2. Wu-Hen-Chang, A., Le Viet, D., Bátori, G., Gecse, R.: High-level restructuring of TTCN-3 test data. In: Grabowski, J., Nielsen, B. (eds.) FATES 2004. LNCS, vol. 3395, pp. 180–194. Springer, Heidelberg (2005)

OConGraX – Automatically Generating Data-Flow Test Cases for Fault-Tolerant Systems

Paulo R.F. Nunes, Simone Hanazumi, and Ana C.V. de Melo

Department of Computer Science,
University of São Paulo, São Paulo, Brazil
prnunes@ime.usp.br, hanazumi@ime.usp.br, acvm@ime.usp.br

Abstract. The more complex to develop and manage systems the more software design faults increase, making fault-tolerant systems highly required. To ensure their quality, the normal and exceptional behaviors must be tested and/or verified. Software testing is still a difficult and costly software development task and a reasonable amount of effort has been employed to develop techniques for testing programs' normal behaviors. For the exceptional behavior, however, there is a lack of techniques and tools to effectively test it. To help in testing and analyzing fault-tolerant systems, we present in this paper a tool that provides an automatic generation of data-flow test cases for objects and exception-handling mechanisms of Java programs and data/control-flow graphs for program analysis.

1 Introduction

The more complex to develop and manage systems the more software design faults increase[1] and, today, a significant amount of code is dedicated to error detection and recovery[2]. Exception-handling mechanisms provide a clear separation of codes for error recovery and normal behavior, helping in decreasing code complexity and software design faults. Due to these benefits, exception-handling is recognized as a good approach to provide fault-tolerant software[1].

To ensure the quality of fault-tolerant systems, normal and exceptional behaviors must be tested. One promising approach is the data-flow testing, which focuses on data status[3], analyzing the life cycle of data to find out unexpected or anomalous behaviors. However, testing programs is still an expensive software development activity because it is aimed at dynamically analyzing the product. One of the main problems is related to the number of test cases necessary to cover the whole program, and test criteria [4,5,6,7,8,9] have been created with this aim. These criteria establish how much a program must be tested to achieve certain quality requirements. Although they reduce the test space, there is still a large set of test cases, making in practice the test activity neglected if a tool support is not provided to support automating test cases and suites.

To help in reducing the test activity cost and enhancing program analysis, this paper presents *OConGraX* (*O*bject *Con*trol-Flow *Gra*ph with e*X*ceptions), a tool that generates the data-flow testing requirements for objects and exceptions

M. Núñez et al. (Eds.): TESTCOM/FATES 2009, LNCS 5826, pp. 229–234, 2009.

of Java programs. Using *OConGraX*, testers can concentrate on generating test suites for the corresponding data-flow test cases, instead of manually creating graphs and test coverage requirements, reducing software development cost.

In this paper, some concepts of data-flow techniques will be presented in Sect. 2. Section 3 presents the tool and its use for testing the normal and exceptional behaviors. Finally, Sect. 4 concludes presenting practical uses of the tool, its limitations and future works.

2   Data-Flow Testing and Fault-Tolerant Programs

Fault-tolerant programs must comprise the *normal behavior* code, in which errors are detected and the corresponding exceptions are raised; and the *exception handler* code[10], in which the exceptional behavior is treated resulting in the error recovery. To test them, a set of techniques that explore object-flow information was developed to guide test cases selection in the object-oriented paradigm[6,8,9]. The tool presented here is based on two coverage criteria: for normal the behavior, the criteria proposed by Chen and Kao[6]; and for the exceptional behavior, the criteria proposed by Sinha and Harrold[9,8]. Some concepts related to both criteria are briefly discussed here:

Object-definition: when the constructor of the object is invoked; the value of an attribute is explicitly assigned; or a method that initiates or update attributes of the object is invoked.

Object-usage: an object is used when one of its attributes is used in a predicate or a computation; one method that uses an attribute value is invoked; or an object is passed as parameter in a method invocation.

DU Pairs: all **du** (definition and use) pairs relating a definition and further use (without redefinition) of an object in the program control-flow.

Exception: *Object*: an exception class instance denoted as $eobj_i$, where i corresponds to the code-line in which it is instantiated. *Variable*: a variable of type exception. *Temporary Variable*: an exception related to a *throw* command – represented by $evar_i$, where i corresponds to the *throw* code-line. *Object activation/deactivation*: an exception object is activated when it is raised with a *throw* command and deactivated when it is treated or a *null* value is given (an active object is represented by $evar_{active}$, and it is unique at each execution instant).

Exception-definition: a value is assigned to an exception variable or to an exception variable in *catch*; or a temporary variable is used in *throw*.

Exception-usage: an exception variable value is used; a variable value is used in *catch*; or a temporary exception variable is used in *throw*.

E-DU Pairs: a value is assigned to an exception variable that is further used in a *throw*; a parameter has its value accessed in a *catch* block; an exception variable is activated and deactivated (treated).

Object coverage criterion: *all-du-pairs*: all **du** pairs are tested.

Exception coverage criteria: *all-throw*: all *throw* commands are tested; *all-catch*: all *catch* commands are tested; *all-e-defs*: all exception definitions, associated to at least one use, is tested; *all-e-use*: all **e-du** pairs are tested; *all-e-act*: all activated exception, related to at least one deactivation, is tested; *all-e-deact*: all pairs of exception activation-deactivation (e-ad) pairs are tested.

To satisfy those criteria[6,9,8], test cases must be created to cover all object and exception **du** and act-deact-pairs. To identify the actual **du** pairs, one must first identify all **du** of objects and exceptions and create the object and exception control-flow graphs (OCFG). Building the OCFG for objects and exceptions is very error-prone and cannot be left to users. The forthcoming section presents a tool to automate these steps.

3 *OConGraX* – Test Cases for the Normal and Exceptional Behaviors

OConGraX has been created to help in testing (data-flow) and analyzing Java programs. The tool reads a Java Project and provides the following basic services:

- Definitions, uses and def-use pairs of objects: the set of test cases based on the criterion of **all definition-use** (**du**) pairs of objects are generated;
- Definitions, uses and def-use pairs of exceptions: the set of test cases based on the criterion of **all definition-use** (**e-du**) pairs of exceptions are generated;
- OCFG with the additional information on exception-handling;
- Graphs and test cases exported as images or XML files.

OConGraX can be used to automatically generate test cases for normal and exceptional behaviors of Java systems. This section shows the use of the tool to this purpose. First, an example is presented (Fig. 1) followed by the data-flow

```
 1: public class DataBaseManipulation {
 2:    DatabaseConnection dbConn =
                  new DatabaseConnection();
 3:    String sqlCmd = "";
 4:    Array row;
 5:
 6:    void dbUpdateOperation () {
 7:      dbConn.open();
 8:      try{
 9:        row = dbConn.select(sqlCmd);
10:        sqlCmd = updateFields(row);
11:        dbConn.update(sqlCmd);
12:      }
13:      catch(UpdateException ue) {
14:        showMessage(ue);
15:      }
16:      finally {
17:          dbConn.close();
18:      }
19:    }
20: }
21: public class DatabaseConnection {
22:    void update(String cmd) throws
                        UpdateException {
23:      int status;
24:      if ((status = executeCmd(cmd))==0) {
25:        UpdateException u = new
                        UpdateException();
26:        throw u;
27:      }
28:    }
29:    void open() {//open DB connection}
30:    void close() {//close DB connection}
31: }
```

Fig. 1. Example code

test cases generated for the normal and exceptional behaviors. The example was adapted from the one showed in [9] and illustrates a simple database connection and update operations. The operations are invoked in `DataBaseManipulation` class and they are implemented in `DataBaseConnection` class.

In *OConGraX*, once an input is chosen, a tree with all information about the selected project can be accessed as shown in Fig. 2(a). To obtain the definitions and uses of objects (and exceptions), one can select from the "View" menu the option "Def-Use". A tab will come along on the right panel in which the Package, Class and Method can be selected and the code lines where a definition or a use occur will be presented. Figure 2(b) shows this for the example when **package: default package**, **class:** `DatabaseConnection` and **method: update** are selected. To view only the definitions and uses of exceptions, one can select the option "Def-Use Exc" – Fig. 2(c). The **du** (or **e-du**) pairs are obtained by selecting the "Def-Use Pairs" option together with the class and object (or exception) – they are shown as (`<def`.

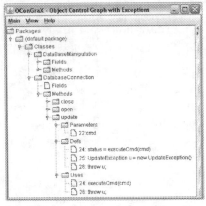

(a) Software source information tree

(b) Definitions and uses view

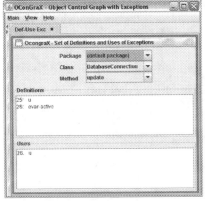

(c) Exception definitions and uses view

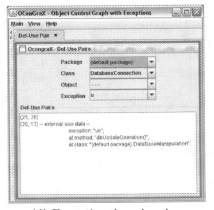

(d) Exception du pairs view

Fig. 2. Tool features related to definitions and uses view

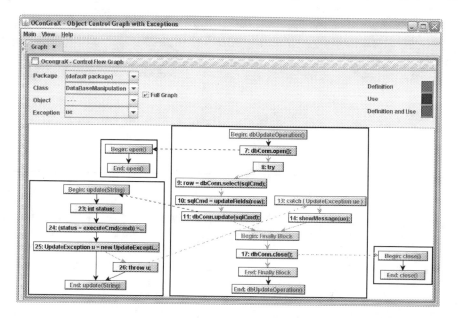

Fig. 3. Graph View

code-line>, <use code-line>). Figure 2(d) shows the **e-du** pairs for the example when **class:** DataBaseManipulation and **exception:** ue are selected. The OCFG with exceptions can also be obtained by selecting the "Graph" option and then the Package, Class and Object/Exception. The option "Full Graph" shows the whole graph, otherwise only parts of the graph related to the selected object will appear. Figure 3 shows the graph obtained when we select **package:** default package, **class:** DataBaseManipulation and **exception:** ue with the "Full Graph" option selected.

4   Concluding Remarks

Despite being widely used, the exception-handling mechanisms are mainly defined at program level, instead of at the design level. As a result, assuring fault-tolerant systems functionalities relies on testing and verification at program level. Testing a program depends very much on tools support; otherwise this activity could be neglected in the development process to reduce costs.

The data-flow testing criteria are based on code coverage and can be defined with static analysis. To automate the test cases generation, this paper presented *OConGraX*, a tool that can detect definition and use of objects and exceptions; generate du-pairs of objects and exceptions; generate the OCFG (for objects and exceptions); and export information about **du** and **e-du** pairs as XML files and graphs as images files. To actually test programs, the test suites still need to be created. This feature is not yet provided by the tool and we are now investigating the viability of integrating it with tools to generate test data. *OConGraX* has been developed to automate test cases for objects and exceptions under data-flow testing techniques, but can be used to help in understanding programs and be integrated with verification tools to take advantages of the V&V approach. In [11], we suggested an approach, and a corresponding tool support, to integrate and automate testing and verification activities for fault-tolerant systems.

Although *OConGraX* presents useful features, many other features remain to be developed: extracting code measures automatically, such as number of object usages; introducing other code coverage criteria, such as the ones based on decisions; and generating data test. Besides theses, developing new parsers for other Object-Oriented programming languages can make all the *OConGraX* features available for other languages – more widely applied.

Acknowledgments. This project has been co-funded by the National Council for Scientific and Technological Development (CNPq - Brazil), the State of São Paulo Research Foundation (FAPESP) and the Ministry of Education Research Agency (CAPES - Brazil). The author Ana C. V. de Melo also thanks the Oxford University Computing Laboratory for providing research facilities during her stay on sabbatical leave at the University of Oxford.

References

1. Lee, P.A., Anderson, T.: Fault Tolerance: Principles and Practice. Springer, Secaucus (1990)
2. Randell, B.: The evolution of the recovery block concept. In: Lyu (ed.) Software Fault Tolerance, pp. 1–21 (1995)
3. Badlaney, J., Ghatol, R., Jadhwani, R.: An introduction to data-flow testing. Technical Report (2006) 22, http://www.csc.ncsu.edu/research/tech/reports.php (Last access Feburary 2009)
4. Weyuker, E.J.: The evaluation of program-based software test data adequacy criteria. Commun. ACM 31(6), 668–675 (1988)
5. McGregor, J.D., Korson, T.D.: Integrated object-oriented testing and development processes. Commun. ACM 37(9), 59–77 (1994)
6. Chen, M.H., Kao, H.M.: Testing object-oriented programs – an integrated approach. In: Proceedings of ISSRE 1999, p. 73. IEEE Computer Society, Los Alamitos (1999)
7. Kung, D., Suchak, N., Hsia, P., Toyoshima, Y., Chen, C.: Object state testing for object-oriented programs. In: Proceedings of COMPSAC 1995, p. 232. IEEE Computer Society, Los Alamitos (1995)
8. Sinha, S., Harrold, M.J.: Criteria for testing exception-handling constructs in Java programs. In: Proceedings of ICSM 1999, p. 265. IEEE Computer Society, Los Alamitos (1999)
9. Sinha, S., Harrold, M.J.: Analysis of programs with exception-handling constructs. In: Proceedings of ICSM 1998, p. 348. IEEE Computer Society, Los Alamitos (1998)
10. Cristian, F.: Exception handling and software fault tolerance. In: FTCS-25: Highlights from Twenty-Five Years, p. 120. IEEE Computer Society, Los Alamitos (1995)
11. Xavier, K.S., Hanazumi, S., de Melo, A.C.V.: Using formal verification to reduce test space of fault-tolerant programs. In: Proceedings of SEFM 2008, pp. 181–190. IEEE Computer Society, Los Alamitos (2008)

Debugging into Examples

Leveraging Tests for Program Comprehension

Bastian Steinert, Michael Perscheid, Martin Beck,
Jens Lincke, and Robert Hirschfeld

Software Architecture Group
Hasso Plattner Institute, University of Potsdam, Germany
`firstname.lastname@hpi.uni-potsdam.de`

Abstract. Enhancing and maintaining a complex software system requires detailed understanding of the underlying source code. Gaining this understanding by reading source code is difficult. Since software systems are inherently dynamic, it is complex and time consuming to imagine, for example, the effects of a method's source code at run-time. The inspection of software systems during execution, as encouraged by debugging tools, contributes to source code comprehension. Leveraged by test cases as entry points, we want to make it easy for developers to experience selected execution paths in their code by debugging into examples. We show how links between test cases and application code can be established by means of dynamic analysis while executing regular tests.

Keywords: Program comprehension, dynamic analysis, test coverage.

1 Introduction

Developers of object-oriented software systems spend a significant amount of time reading code. Using, extending, or modifying parts of a system's source code requires an in-depth understanding, ranging from the intended use of interfaces to the interplay of multiple, interdependent system parts. Comprehending source code is an essential and important part of software development. It is, however, difficult for several reasons:

Abstraction: Source code describes the general behavior desired for a class of scenarios by abstracting from several concrete execution paths. When reading source code, developers have to imagine the effects on concrete execution paths.

Context: Every single class or method of a complex program can contribute to a large-scale collaboration of object teams. Knowing related classes and their contributions is important for efficient and exact source code comprehension. This context information, however, is not apparent in standard development environments.

Object-oriented Language Concepts: Object-oriented language concepts such as inheritance, sub-typing, and polymorphism are well-suited to describe system behavior, but late binding makes understanding the effects of

M. Núñez et al. (Eds.): TESTCOM/FATES 2009, LNCS 5826, pp. 235–240, 2009.

a method and following a message flow more difficult [4,16]. For instance, behavioral properties, such as message exchange in object-oriented programs, can only be determined precisely at run-time [1].

We argue that comprehending source code, imagining its effects, and understanding usage contexts can be supported by enabling developers to experience source code by examples of concrete execution paths from which the source code abstracts.

Related research results have already emphasized the usefulness of examples and extensions to Integrated Development Environments (IDEs) for source code comprehension [5,6,12,14]. In [5], for example, the author argues that unit tests can often be considered as usage examples for the units under test. He suggests using coding conventions to make the link between tests and the corresponding units explicit. To our knowledge, an approach that allows to experience execution examples directly while browsing source code has not been reported. Debugging tools also support familiarization with source code. They offer the opportunity to understand source code by means of stack trace inspection. Still, being able to debug requires an appropriate entry point.

In this paper, we suggest to regard test cases as natural entry points to source code, provided they are linked to the application code. We present an efficient approach to run-time analysis for establishing these links during the execution of tests.

In Section 2, we describe our approach to debugging into concrete execution paths by leveraging test cases. Section 3 explains how the required run-time information can be collected efficiently during the execution of tests. Section 4 discusses related work and Section 5 summarizes our results.

2   Using Test Cases as Entry Points

We suggest the use of debugging tools to support source code comprehension by leveraging test cases as entry points. This requires each method of interest to be covered by at least one test case. Looking at this from another perspective, every test case covers a set of methods of interest during execution. Consequently, the set of test cases covering a particular method describes prospective entry points for debugging this method. So, this set needs to be determined upfront by making the implicit relationship between test cases and covered methods explicit.

To discover relationships between source code entities, static as well as dynamic analysis [2] can be used. Static source code analysis, however, has limited applicability due to programming language concepts such as inheritance and polymorphism. In contrast to static analysis, dynamic analysis allows to collect run-time information such as method bindings [13] during the execution of a particular path. As this is essential for making coverage links explicit, our approach is based on dynamic analysis.

Application code is analyzed during test execution. When a test case is executed, all covered methods are recorded. Having obtained these run-time data,

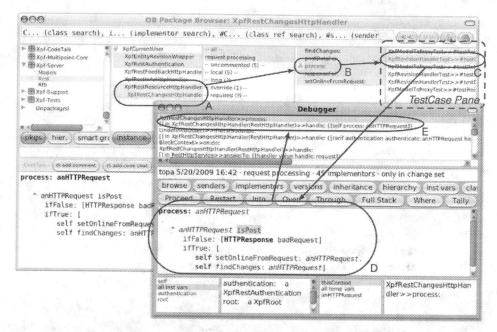

Fig. 1. An extended code browser and a debugger window in Squeak. The code browser has an additional pane on the right (C) that shows a list of test cases covering the selected method named *process:*. Classes (A) and methods (B) covered by tests are highlighted with a background color.

we can mark the set of test cases that cover a certain method during execution, so that we can provide developers with the required entry points.

The list of entry points, the test cases, can be leveraged by IDE extensions enabling developers to experience a run-time view of a method directly while browsing it. We extended the source code browsing tools of Squeak Smalltalk [9]. Figure 1 depicts an extended Squeak code browser. In its base version, it consists of four panes containing lists of available packages, classes, method categories, and methods respectively (from left to right). We added a fifth pane showing the list of all test cases covering the selected method.

Selecting a test case opens a debugger (Figure 1 D), allowing the user to analyze the covered method of interest during execution (Figure 1 E). The selected test case is executed, the execution halts at the selected method, and the debugger is opened. Developers may now explore collaborating objects and examine their state. They can further step down in the stack and inspect the execution of the calling method, or they can step into a called method.

3   Efficient Tracing during Test Execution

In this section, we discuss selected implementation details of our tracing approach. Traditional tracing approaches are typically inefficient and produce large amounts of data [3]. As we analyze the execution of test cases, the overhead caused by tracing has to be minimal. If running tests is time-consuming, developers will either not run them very often or reject our approach.

Most tracing approaches are designed for general analysis purposes and thus have to record lots of data such as the state of all objects for each step in the execution [12]. However, creating and persisting deep copies of many objects is time consuming. We could significantly reduce the overhead by collecting only required run-time information, i.e., references to methods being covered during test execution. Test execution performance is thus only decreased by a factor of two on average, which is usually not perceivable when single tests are executed.

To record the relevant run-time data, we apply aspect-oriented programming techniques [8,10]. We developed a tracing aspect that intercepts all calls of selected application methods [7]—developers are usually not interested in tracing all libraries of the system. The tracing aspect is deployed dynamically during test execution. For each test case, the aspect code collects for each test case the set of application methods covered during test execution.

This coverage information is stored in the Squeak system so that tools such as our browser extension can access it easily and efficiently. In a Squeak system, source code entities such as classes and methods are managed as objects. We enriched the interfaces to method objects to manage and persist coverage information. This information is managed as a bidirectional relationship between test case method objects and application method objects. With that, our browser extension can easily retrieve all test cases that cover a selected method of interest.

4   Related Work

To the best of our knowledge, there are only a few approaches that integrate results of dynamic analysis into development environments.

The feature driven browser [14] is based on the ideas of feature location [6] and combines an interactive visual representation of features with its related source code entities within the Squeak IDE. The feature driven browser summarizes dynamic behavior from the features' points of view. A case study has shown that developers using this browser are faster in fixing defects when they know corresponding solution artifacts. In contrast to this approach, we offer concrete sample traces that can be further inspected with a debugging tool.

The Squeak IDE extension Hermion [15] enriches source code views with run-time data. It provides additional type information and offers dynamic reference information for locating classes actually used. Hermion further supports a new navigation technique based on executed methods. In contrast to Hermion, our approach allows developers to explore concrete execution paths at run-time and to examine how objects behave and change step by step.

WhyLine [11] is a debugger rather than an IDE but offers sophisticated means for inspecting the system at run-time. During the execution, developers can ask a set of "why did" and "why didn't" questions derived from the program's code and behavior. Based on static and dynamic slicing, call graph analysis, and several other techniques, WhyLine can answer questions such as why a line of code was not reached. However, the WhyLine approach can currently not meet our performance needs. Recording the huge amount of required run-time data and their analysis is too time-consuming.

5   Summary and Outlook

In this paper, we describe the need for additional views on software systems that allow developers to explore concrete examples from which source code usually abstracts. Contemporary debugging tools enable developers to inspect concrete execution paths, but do not suggest appropriate entry points for application exploration. In our approach, we propose test cases as candidates for such entry points.

We present an efficient tracing technique for collecting coverage data during the execution of test cases; and we show that these data can be used in IDEs to give developers the opportunity to debug into a method of interest and experience concrete sample executions of this method. With that, our paper reveals another benefit of developing and maintaining tests cases; they may be leveraged to provide a run-time view on source code and thus ease its comprehension.

The benefit of having these links is the ability to re-execute corresponding tests after source code modifications automatically. The debugging facilities should be integrated into standard code browsing tools, enabling a seamless transition between static and dynamic views. Furthermore, research results described in [5] might be useful to filter and order the list of possible entry points according to relevance.

Acknowledgments. We gratefully acknowledge the financial support of the Hasso Plattner Design Thinking Research Program for our project "Agile Software Development in Virtual Collaboration Environments". We thank Michael Haupt for valuable feedback on earlier versions of this paper.

References

1. Arisholm, E.: Dynamic Coupling Measures for Object-Oriented Software. In: IEEE International Symposium on Software Metrics (2002)
2. Ball, T.: The Concept of Dynamic Analysis. In: ESEC/FSE-7: Proceedings of the 7th European Software Engineering Conference held jointly with the 7th ACM SIG-SOFT International Symposium on Foundations of Software Engineering, London, UK, pp. 216–234. Springer, Heidelberg (1999)
3. Denker, M., Greevy, O., Lanza, M.: Higher Abstractions for Dynamic Analysis. In: 2nd International Workshop on Program Comprehension through DynamicAnalysis (PCODA 2006), pp. 32–38 (2006)
4. Dunsmore, A., Roper, M., Wood, M.: Object-oriented Inspection in the Face of Delocalisation. In: ICSE 2000: Proceedings of the 22nd International Conference on Software Engineering, pp. 467–476. ACM, New York (2000)

5. Gaelli, M.: Modeling Examples to Test and Understand Software. PhD thesis, University of Berne (2006)
6. Greevy, O.: Enriching Reverse Engineering with Feature Analysis. PhD thesis, University of Berne (May 2007)
7. Gschwind, T., Oberleitner, J.: Improving Dynamic Data Analysis with Aspect-Oriented Programming. In: CSMR 2003: Proceedings of the Seventh European Conference on Software Maintenance and Reengineering, Washington, DC, USA, pp. 259–268. IEEE Computer Society, Los Alamitos (2003)
8. Hirschfeld, R.: AspectS – Aspect-Oriented Programming with Squeak. In: Aksit, M., Mezini, M., Unland, R. (eds.) NODe 2002. LNCS, vol. 2591, pp. 216–232. Springer, Heidelberg (2003)
9. Ingalls, D., Kaehler, T., Maloney, J., Wallace, S., Kay, A.: Back to the Future: The Story of Squeak, a Practical Smalltalk Written in Itself. In: OOPSLA 1997: Proceedings of the 12th ACM SIGPLAN conference on Object-oriented programming, systems, languages, and applications, pp. 318–326. ACM, New York (1997)
10. Kiczales, G., Lamping, J., Mendhekar, A., Maeda, C., Lopes, C.V., Loingtier, J.-M., Irwin, J.: Aspect-oriented Programming. In: Aksit, M., Matsuoka, S. (eds.) ECOOP 1997. LNCS, vol. 1241, pp. 220–242. Springer, Heidelberg (1997)
11. Ko, A.J., Myers, B.A.: Debugging Reinvented: Asking and Answering Why and Why Not Questions about Program Behavior. In: ICSE 2008: Proceedings of the 30th International Conference on Software Engineering, pp. 301–310. ACM Press, New York (2008)
12. Pauw, W.D., Lorenz, D., Vlissides, J., Wegman, M.: Execution Patterns in Object-Oriented Visualization. In: COOTS 1998: Proceedings of the 4th Conference on Object-Oriented Technologies and Systems, Berkeley, CA, USA, pp. 16–16. USENIX Association (1998)
13. Richner, T., Ducasse, S.: Recovering High-Level Views of Object-Oriented Applications from Static and Dynamic Information. In: ICSM 1999: Proceedings of the IEEE International Conference on Software Maintenance, Washington, DC, USA, pp. 13–22. IEEE Computer Society, Los Alamitos (1999)
14. Röthlisberger, D., Greevy, O., Nierstrasz, O.: Feature Driven Browsing. In: ICDL 2007: Proceedings of the 2007 International Conference on Dynamic Languages, Lugano, Switzerland, pp. 79–100. ACM Press, New York (2007)
15. Röthlisberger, D., Greevy, O., Nierstrasz, O.: Exploiting Runtime Information in the IDE. In: ICPC 2008: Proceedings of the 16th IEEE International Conference on Program Comprehension, Washington, DC, USA, pp. 63–72. IEEE Computer Society, Los Alamitos (2008)
16. Wilde, N., Huitt, R.: Maintenance Support for Object-oriented Programs. IEEE Transactions on Software Engineering 18(12), 1038–1044 (1992)

Structural Analysis of Large TTCN-3 Projects

Kristóf Szabados

Ericsson Hungary

Abstract. Experience has shown that the Testing and Test Control Notation version 3 (TTCN-3) language provides very good concepts for adequate test specification, but it was not presented yet how large test systems written in TTCN-3 are structured. This paper presents my efforts to analyze the structure of TTCN-3 projects, to see if such problems manifest, and if possible to provide methods that can detect these problems.

1 Introduction

The Testing and Test Control Notation version 3 (TTCN-3) is a high level programming language standardized by the European Telecommunications Standards Institute (ETSI) for automated black box and reactive tests. It was designed mainly for testing of telecommunication protocols and Internet protocols, but nowadays it is also used for testing aerospace, automotive or service oriented architectures. Although it was not able to get a wide community yet, several companies interested in network protocols are already using it for testing their systems.

Inside Ericsson there are projects whose amount of source code has almost reached 1 million lines. As we realized the amount of code in existence, it became a major area of interest to study its structure. When the code structure of a project becomes too complex, the maintenance costs are expected to grow as several problems start to surface.

At this point it is important to note, that in TTCN-3 the highest code structuring construct is the module of which every project is built up. TTCN-3 modules are like classes in C++ or Java (however TTCN-3 is actually closer in its philosophy to C). But unlike C++, which has namespaces and Java, which has packages to structure their classes, TTCN-3 does not provide any higher level primitives that the user could use to group their modules.

2 Motivation

The main interest is to analyze the structure of the large source code bases, to find a way to provide guidelines for projects to follow, or to compare against their measured data. Up to now such huge projects were evolving on their own without any tool to monitor them. So as a first step what was need most was some kind of visualization of their structure.

M. Núñez et al. (Eds.): TESTCOM/FATES 2009, LNCS 5826, pp. 241–246, 2009.

3   Experimental Setup

The module structure of 9 projects was analyzed by measuring the incoming and outgoing connections of each module, and creating graphs on the collaborations between them.

A tool was written to process the semantic graph of the projects and collect statistics regarding the collaboration graphs of modules. The base for all the measurements and charts produced was the number of graph nodes and for each node the number of its incoming and outgoing connections.

Out of these 9 projects 6 are completely different, developed by standalone organizations inside Ericsson. IMSM_SIP and Simple hello are built on the load test framework of Ericsson Hungary. ETSI IPv6 is a standardized testsuite.

4   Results

I measured for each module how many others it imports (I(project)), and how many times it is imported (O(project)) by other modules. Table 1 shows for all projects the $I_{max}(project)$ (the biggest number of modules imported by the same module) and $O_{max}(project)$ (the biggest number of modules importing the same module). It is easy to see that projects having more modules are more likely to have a higher $I_{max}(project)$ and $I_{max}(project)$ values.

In almost all of the projects we can see that $O_{max}(project)$ is roughly between 40%-50% of the number of modules (with only CAI3G standing out considerably).

Table 1. Importation data

Project vs test	Number of modules	$I_{max}(project)$	$O_{max}(project)$	Linecount
TGC_traffic	20	10	6	127.470
ADC_OMA	42	23	8	21.174
CAI3G	65	51	57	53.583
ETSI IPv6	68	29	46	67.505
Test automation Wireline	71	15	34	97.672
Simple Hello (TitanSim)	124	38	49	71.751
IMSM_SIP (TitanSim)	171	49	71	79.613
W_MOCN	205	36	85	442.784
MTAS	331	78	181	794.829

4.1   Importation Data Analyzed by Projects

Figure 1(a) shows the distribution of $I(module)$ and $O(module)$ values for all of the modules in CAI3G. There are only a few modules that import many others, or are imported many times, most of the modules import only a few others, often < 5 others.

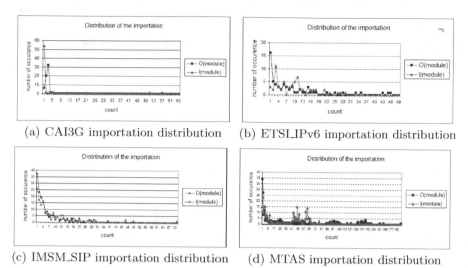

(a) CAI3G importation distribution   (b) ETSI_IPv6 importation distribution

(c) IMSM_SIP importation distribution   (d) MTAS importation distribution

Fig. 1. Distributions of importation

Figures 1(b) and 1(c) show that the distributions of $O(module)$ and $I(module)$ become smoother as the number of modules increases. In fact the distribution charts of both $O(module)$ and $I(module)$ values visibly converges to the shape of an exponential function with a long tail.

Figure 1(d) does not fit this schema as for both distributions, there are values which appear far more often than expected. Possibly indicating serious code organizational issues, parts of the library section of this project seems to be highly coupled.

Figure 2, that where $I(module)$ is high, $O(module)$ is usually very low, and vice versa. This implicitly indicates, that the load of the functionality seems to be distributed better among the modules, more than in any other project we have seen so far.

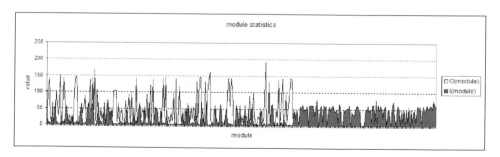

Fig. 2. $|I(module) - O(module)|$ values on MTAS, colored by the larger one

While checking MTAS deeply I have found that in fact the testcases (top level entry points in TTCN-3) are not concentrated in a few files, but are distributed among many. About 1/4 or 1/5 of the modules did mostly only contain testcases.

4.2   Project Diameter

Figure 3 shows one of the most surprising findings of my research. In case of TTCN-3 the diameter of the module importation graph (the longest path from the set of the shortest paths between any two nodes in the graph) does not seem to depend on the number of modules present in the project.

In TTCN-3 this means that the testers working on MTAS does not actually have to know how every little part works. They only need to understand and check the modules they are working with, and the ones depending on these. In this structure the amount of such modules is very limited.

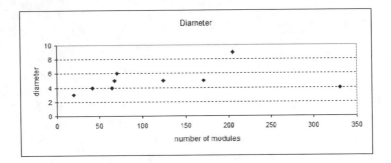

Fig. 3. Diameter of the graphs

5   Is It Scale-Free?

As the diameter of projects was very small, we checked whether the projects were scale-free ([2] showed, that scale-free graphs have a very small diameter).

Scale-free graphs include the physical connection forming the Internet, networks of personal contacts [6], and even the connectivity graph of neurons in the human brain [4] [5]. It was also shown, that the class, method and package collaboration graphs of the Java language [1], and the object graph (the objects instances created at runtime) of most of the Object Oriented programming languages in general [7], [3] also show scale-free properties.

Figure 4 shows that both Simple Hello and IMSM_SIP displays the expected power law distribution (as a straight line with a slope), but MTAS deviates far from what we expected to see. This has to be checked with the developers of MTAS as if this is not natural in the language it might show serious structural problems.

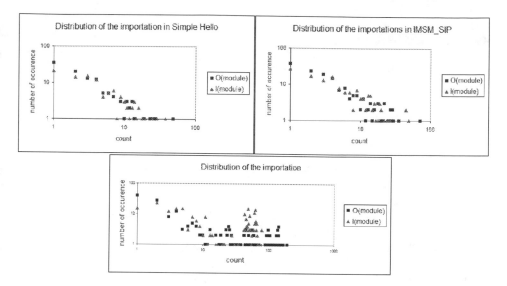

Fig. 4. Simple Hello, IMSM_SIP and MTAS on log-log scale

From these data the most we can say is that TTCN-3 is, or seemingly converges to being scale-free as the language has not yet gained wide audience, leaving the number of lines of code written so far is rather small.

Being scale-free is very important as it was proven [8] that such networks have good resistance against random failures, but at the same time have an Achilles' Heel against direct attacks. The more vulnerable nodes can be detected with $I_{max}(project)$ and $O_{max}(project)$.

6   Conclusions

The measured data revealed some interesting information that had to be checked in more detail to validate that the measured data is in fact showing something of importance.

TTCN-3 projects tend to have a few modules that are imported much more often than others. These were identified to be the modules containing the type definitions, for the protocols being tested. As the language does not support transitive importation, developers either have to import the types they wish to work with directly, or have to create wrapper functions for almost all possible values that the given types can have.

In one of the projects I have found that the $O_{max}(project)$ was way below the expected numbers. Looking into the code I have found that the developers were trying to create a layer between the data types and the actual testcases. As the messages being sent on the network were rather large, and variant, some of the functions at the time of my investigation had over 50 formal parameters.

These metrics, both the highest values and their distribution for all modules turned out to be useful:

1. A low diameter indicates very low complexity for the testers to work with
2. Values and distribution of $I(module)$ being more than expected, indicates too many direct interactions with the data, which could be improved by following better code reuse principles(like extracting very often used common parts into functions).
3. Values and distribution of $I(module)$ being much lower than expected, indicates to many layers in the software, leading to huge hierarchies of functions.
4. For modules not imported ($O(module) = 0$), their whole subgraph might not be needed in the given project, or to a given task. Tools can be provided to allow for more people to work in parallel (as random side effects will not corrupt the whole graph), and with lower build times (by filtering out un-needed code parts).
5. Having only a few modules in a project where $I(module)$ is high indicates that the functionality was not distributed evenly in the code.

References

1. Hyland-Wood, D., Carrington, D., Kaplan, S.: Scale-Free Nature of Java Software Package, Class and Method Collaboration Graphs. Submitted to the 5th International Symposium on Empirical Software Engineering, Rio de Janeiro, Brazil, September 21-22 (2005)
2. Cohen, R., Hevlin, D.: Scale-Free Networks are Ultrasmall. Physical Review Letters 90, 58701 (2003)
3. de Muora, A.P., Lai, Y.C., Motter, A.E.: Signatures of small-world and scale-free properties in large computer programs. Physical review E 68, 17102 (2003)
4. Jeong, H., Tombor, B., Albert, R., Oltvai, Z.N., Barabási, A.-L.: The large-scale organization of metabolic networks. Nature 407, 651–654 (2000)
5. Barabási, A.-L.: Linked: The New Science of Networks. Perseus Press, New York (2002)
6. Zipf, G.: Psycho-Biology of Languages. Houghtton-Mifflin, Boston (1935)
7. Potanin, A., Noble, J., Frean, M., Biddle, R.: Scale-free geometry in OO programs. Communications of the ACM 48(5), 99–103 (2005)
8. Albert, R., Jeong, H., Barabasi, A.-L.: Error and attack tolerance of complex networks. Nature 406(6794), 378–382 (2000)

Author Index